Advice, Social Learning, and the Evolution of Conventions

As societies progress, old generations of social agents die and are replaced by new ones. This book explores what happens in this transition as the old guard instructs the new arrivals about the wisdom of their ways. Do new entrants listen and follow the advice of their elders or dismiss it? Is intergenerational advice welfare-improving or can it be destructive? Does such advice enhance the stability of social conventions or disrupt it? Using the concept of an intergenerational game and the tools of game theory and experimental economics, this study delves into the process of social learning created by intergenerational advice passed from generation to generation. This book presents a unique theoretical and empirical study of the dynamics of social conventions not offered elsewhere.

ANDREW SCHOTTER is professor of economics and Director of the Center for Experimental Social Science at New York University.

Advice, Social Learning, and the Evolution of Conventions

ANDREW SCHOTTER
New York University

CAMBRIDGE
UNIVERSITY PRESS

CAMBRIDGE
UNIVERSITY PRESS

Shaftesbury Road, Cambridge CB2 8EA, United Kingdom

One Liberty Plaza, 20th Floor, New York, NY 10006, USA

477 Williamstown Road, Port Melbourne, VIC 3207, Australia

314–321, 3rd Floor, Plot 3, Splendor Forum, Jasola District Centre,
New Delhi – 110025, India

103 Penang Road, #05–06/07, Visioncrest Commercial, Singapore 238467

Cambridge University Press is part of Cambridge University Press & Assessment,
a department of the University of Cambridge.

We share the University's mission to contribute to society through the pursuit of
education, learning and research at the highest international levels of excellence.

www.cambridge.org
Information on this title: www.cambridge.org/9781316518076

DOI: 10.1017/9781009049092

© Andrew Schotter 2023

First published 2023

A catalogue record for this publication is available from the British Library.

Library of Congress Cataloging-in-Publication data
Names: Schotter, A., author.
Title: Advice, social learning and the evolution of conventions / Andrew Schotter.
Description: Cambridge, United Kingdom ; New York, NY :
    Cambridge University Press, [2023] | Includes bibliographical references
    and index.
Identifiers: LCCN 2022040466 (print) | LCCN 2022040467 (ebook) |
    ISBN 9781316518076 (hardback) | ISBN 9781009048880 (paperback) |
    ISBN 9781009049092 (epub)
Subjects: LCSH: Socialization. | Social learning. | Intergenerational
    communication. | Intergenerational relations. | Game theory. |
    Experimental economics.
Classification: LCC HM686 .S35 2023 (print) | LCC HM686 (ebook) |
    DDC 303.3/2–dc23/eng/20220922
LC record available at https://lccn.loc.gov/2022040466 LC ebook record available
at https://lccn.loc.gov/2022040467

ISBN 978-1-316-51807-6   Hardback
ISBN 978-1-009-04888-0   Paperback

To Marcy and Ross for being good people

Brief Contents

Contents

Figures

Tables

Preface

I have always admired scholars with research agendas. I am frequently in awe of scientists running labs whose web pages spell out their research agenda and describe what research they have done in the past and what they will be doing in the foreseeable future. It all seems so logical and well thought out.

I have been too insecure as a scholar to put all my scholarly eggs in one agenda basket and hence I never thought of myself as a person with an agenda. I wrote across many different topics. However, one day I looked back at a set of papers I wrote over the years and, lo and behold, I did have an agenda, I just did not realize it.

This agenda started when, not heeding the advice of the profession that young economists don't write books, I published *The Economic Theory of Social Institutions* (Cambridge University Press, 1981). In an article-driven profession, writing a book before one has tenure is a risky (suicidal?) endeavor, and I was told just that.

That book is a book about the emergence of economic institutions defined as conventions of behavior developed to solve a set of societal problems (more about this in the Introduction in Chapter 1). In some sense one might consider this book a sequel in that it asks not how conventions emerge but rather how they evolve over time and get transmogrified or transformed by a process of social learning via intergenerational advice. In between these two books is a set of about twelve papers investigating this theme and its consequences. So in retrospect this is the agenda I have engaged in, but I assure you that it was not a conscious choice. It just happened and was camouflaged by a set of other papers on topics that were very different.

I was fortunate in this endeavor in having a set of co-authors who took parts of this journey with me, starting with my papers with Barry Sopher. Barry was foolish enough to think that our intergenerational setup was potentially interesting and we wrote a number of papers together. Then came collaborations with Ananish Chaudhuri, Raghuram Iyengar, Tingting Ding, Shachar Kariv, Yaw Nyarko, Bogachan Çelen, Elizabeth Potamites, and Andrew McClellan, many of whom incorporated the intergenerational-game approach into topics of their interest. These co-authors all made this work enjoyable and productive. I am in their debt.

I'd also like to thank the National Science Foundation (NSF) for a number of grants that allowed me to conduct this research. In this connection, I especially want to thank Catherine Eckel, who helped me get my first NSF grant on this topic (with Barry Sopher) in 1997 when she was serving as Program Director. Without those funds I suspect I never would have started on this path. I was also lucky to receive two later grants from the NSF to pursue this research further. In addition, I owe a great deal to the support of the Center for Experimental Social Science (CESS) at New York University (NYU) which has provided logistical support for a lot of this research and to Anwar Ruff for his programming assistance and support. Let me also thank Phillip Good, who shepherded this book through the editorial process at Cambridge University Press and always offered good and supportive advice, and Geoff Amor, who painstakingly copy-edited the entire manuscript and rid it of many of the inconsistencies I had introduced into it over the months of writing.

Finally, in addition to my co-authors, I owe a great debt to three talented graduate students at NYU, Alexander (Sasha) Dorofeev, Mauricio Almeida Couri Ribeiro, and Sam Kapon, who painstakingly read every chapter of the book and gave me comments and advice. It's rare that writing a book makes one feel younger, but my experience with Sasha, Mauricio, and Sam did just that, because when I read their comments on my chapters and discussed those with them, I was immediately transported back to my graduate student days getting feedback from experienced scholars. Their comments were mature way beyond their years and picked out many of the faults in my earlier drafts. It was a role reversal that was both embarrassing and refreshing. I enjoyed it but was glad to have a number of years of accomplishments under my belt in order to absorb their pointed criticisms. Finally, let me thank Pujita Sunder, who carefully read many chapters and whose eye caught and corrected many stylistic mistakes, my colleague Guillaume Fréchette, who commented on some of the chapters and whose wise counsel I seek for whatever I attempt to do, and Georg Weizsäcker, who was willing to spend some of his sabbatical leave at NYU looking over some of what I have written here.

I   Introduction

This is a book on advice, its importance for decision making, and its influence on the evolution of conventions of behavior. The idea is simple. As societies progress, old generations of social agents die and are replaced by new ones. We are interested in what happens in this transition as the old guard instructs the new arrivals about the wisdom of their ways. Do new entrants listen and follow the advice of their elders or dismiss it? Is intergenerational advice welfare-improving or can it be destructive? Many times wise advice is rejected only to have new generations repeat the mistakes of their parents instead of learning from them.

But advice also exists outside of this intergenerational context. In our everyday lives we are constantly asking for advice from friends, family, and experts. The question here is how does advice alter our thinking about the problems we face and the decisions we make? If advice is influential and ubiquitous, then it needs to be incorporated into economic theory, yet it hardly is. If advice is influential, then experiments performed without it may be missing some external validity. Also, if advice is beneficial, then there should exist a market for it and people should strive to be the type of people from whom others seek advice since such a person is likely to gain influence, power, and wealth.

Advisors need not be experts. There is also something beneficial in seeking advice from someone who is as naive as you are about the decision you are about to make because simply discussing things and hearing a different opinion is valuable. As we will see later, in some situations people do not seem very capable of learning lessons from the past, and simply presenting them with historical data is not enough to allow them to behave properly. That data must be interpreted and that is where advice plays a role. As the saying goes, if we can't learn from the past "we are condemned to repeat it", but we are more likely to repeat past mistakes if we misinterpret the past, and good advice helps us avoid that mistake.

The types of questions we want to ask here are rarely asked by economists and social scientists in general but they are natural ones to think about if we are interested in learning why we behave the way we do and, as a result, have the set of conventions we have governing our daily lives.

In the pages below we will demonstrate that the impact of advice is varied and complicated. Most often, having advisors makes things better, but sometimes they make things worse. Sometimes people follow the recommendations of their predecessors or advisors and sometimes they reject them. Sometimes the conventions of behavior determined by our forefathers are adhered to and sometimes they are ignored. This makes life difficult but it also makes it interesting.

Our analysis here will be primarily experimental. In other words, we will investigate the impact of advice by conducting a set of laboratory experiments whose aim is to isolate the impact of such advice on strategic decision making. While our experiments will all be theory driven, in the sense that we will rely on theory to guide us in our investigations, our focus is empirical and our aim is to use experimental methods to tell a story about a phenomenon that is a feature of our daily lives – decision making (strategic and non-strategic) under the influence of advice and the conventions of behavior created in such environments.

On a methodological note, the use of advice in experiments has numerous benefits. In a profession that celebrates revealed preference, allowing an investigator to read the advice one decision maker offers another provides an insight into that subject's thinking that cannot be obtained by viewing actions or choices alone. For example, offering a 50–50 split of a $100 pie in an ultimatum game may appear to be a sign of a preference for equity, but that interpretation may have to be modified when one reads advice that suggests that equity is a constraint and not a goal. To illustrate, consider one piece of advice offered by one of our subjects to her generational successor in an ultimatum game discussed in Chapter 5:

> The guy before me thought I should send 50. Although that would be fair, it's not going to maximize your payoff. I was greedy and offered 10, thinking that the other guy would accept anything he got, BUT that wasn't the case. They rejected. So my advice is to be a little more generous, so about 30 should do it. Good luck.

From this quote we see how complex a subject's thinking can be before she makes a decision. Seemingly generous actions are many times not that at all but simply strategic ploys. Having insights into the minds of subjects via advice is invaluable. It allows us to avoid inference when direct evidence exists. It answers the question often heard in seminars: "Why don't you just ask the subjects why they did what they did?" With incentivized advice, advice where the advisor has an incentive to provide her best guess as to what the right action is for the advisee to take, we get a direct pipeline into the mind of the decision maker and her explanation of what is the best choice to make. There is little need to fall back on fancy inference to estimate subject preferences. We can just listen to them verbalize their thinking. Finally, the comments made as advice may lead to insights that can be explored in future experiments and therefore be used to generate new avenues of exploration.

In the remainder of this chapter we aim to introduce the types of problems that motivate our discussion (societal and man-made problems or mechanisms) and the need they create for societies to establish conventions of behavior to solve them and then pass these conventions down from generation to generation via intergenerational advice. We will also discuss the influence of advice on decision making outside of this intergenerational-game context.

I.I   THE SOCIETAL PROBLEM

All societies, as they develop, must solve a set of problems in order to function properly. For example, they have to choose a religion (Judaism, Christianity, Islam, Hinduism, etc.), a legal system (common or civil),[1] a banking system, a political system (monarchy, parliamentary democracy, etc.), a set of inheritance laws (primogeniture or ultimogeniture), a system of property rights (common or private), a constitution, a family structure (liberal or authoritarian),[2] what commodity to use as a medium of exchange (Kiyotaki and Wright, 1989; Li, 1995), and even what side of the road to drive on. Those societies that solve these problems efficiently and create the proper set of conventions or institutions to deal with them flourish while those who fail to do so stagnate.[3]

However, as Kloosterman and Schotter (2016) point out, finding the proper set of solutions to these societal problems is not easy since these problems are interconnected. Solving one problem early in the history of a society may preclude or constrain the proper solution to a different problem later on or create externalities not envisioned.

For example, consider the problem of choosing a religion. If early in its development a society chooses Islam as their religion, it will find itself constrained later on when it has to decide on the rules of a banking system and lending, since lenders will be constrained not to charge interest. Islamic banking (see Kuran, 2012) looks different from Western banking because of the different religious paths selected. Also there is evidence that Protestant societies developed differently

---

[1] See, La Porta et al. (1998) and Glaeser and Shleifer (2002).

[2] See Todd (1989, 1990) (strong or weak) and Alesina and Giuliano (2010, 2015).

[3] See the classic study by Acemoglu and Robinson (2012) for an exhaustive study of the importance of institutions for economic development, as well as North (1990).

than Catholic societies (until the ban on usury was lifted), again because of their stricture on the use of interest.

In addition, the way inheritance is determined may have large unintended or unanticipated consequences for the institution of marriage. For example, primogeniture, an inheritance system where estates are passed on to the first-born male child, was created in order to consolidate family wealth and prevent it from being diluted by splitting it across many heirs. Of course this meant that all children in the family except the first-born male were excluded. As any reader of Jane Austen knows, this rule had a great impact on the institution of marriage and the marriage market for the daughters of the wealthy where such women spent inordinate amounts of time searching for wealthy mates and consciously forcing a type of assortative mating that might not have occurred otherwise. It also impacted the disinherited male offspring who took up careers in the military or the church or careers trying to snag a wealthy wife and spare themselves from a career in trade which they disdained.

Such questions, about the emergence of conventions, was the focus of *The Economic Theory of Social Institutions* (Schotter (1981)). That book asked how social institutions (defined as conventions) emerged to solve societal problems. This book takes the next step and asks how such conventions, once established, evolve over time through a process of intergenerational advice.[4]

Our answer to this question is intimately related to social learning and advice giving. Basically these formative societal problems do not disappear once a convention is established to "solve" them. Rather they form a set of recurrent problems or games that are played by sets of generational agents who pass on advice to their successors about adhering to the established convention or not as they arrive

---

[4] One could think of the questions we ask here as starting after a convention has been established and asking what happens from that point on, i.e., how stable is the convention, if there are multiple equilibrium conventions, will one emerge or will life fluctuate between them.

to take their place in society.[5] The idea is that, while such games have infinite lives, the people playing them have finite lives and when they die or retire they pass on advice to the next generation of players. In some sense the conventions created in the past need to be maintained.[6]

To illustrate, consider the CEOs of major corporations (Ford and GM) who play a Cournot pricing game against each other for which certain (possibly collusive) conventions exist. When they retire and are replaced by new blood, they take their successors aside and pass on advice about the industry norms, corporate culture (conventions), and how to interpret the actions of their opponents.

Presidents and prime ministers of countries pass on advice about the way international affairs are conducted when they leave office as possibly exemplified by the famous letters that exiting U.S. presidents leave for their successors in a drawer in the desk of the Oval Office (in addition to the extensive briefings that their staffs exchange).

In game-theoretic terms, while the games people play may have infinite lives, the people who play them have only finite lives and when they retire or die they are replaced by new agents who take their place. These generations are connected by a sense of generational caring in that each generation cares about the welfare of its successor and hence passes on advice that takes their welfare into account. For example, parents care about their children and as a result pass on advice that they feel is in their best interest (Bisin and Verdier, 1998, 2000). CEOs of corporations may have retirement packages tied to the performance of the firm after they retire and hence have an incentive to offer profit-maximizing advice above and beyond the pride they may have in the firm they devoted their life to doing

---

[5] Of course, as the world changes over time, conventions may find themselves outdated and as a result may need to be abandoned. That may require coordination and advice.

[6] These agreed-to conventions form the culture of a society since societies differ culturally when they create different sets of conventions to help them solve the same set of societal problems they all face.

well. As a result, generational agents learn how to behave by being socialized by their predecessors and passing on their wisdom to future generations. This is the social learning process we will investigate in this book.

This framework defines what we will call an "intergenerational game" where sets of generational agents play an infinitely repeated game for a finite amount of time and when they leave pass on advice to their successors. Because of intergenerational caring, the advice offered is potentially beneficial and should be considered seriously by successors.

Note that such a setup differs considerably from the way economists typically view infinitely repeated games and social learning. In the conventional theory of repeated games, sets of players live forever and discount their future payoffs.[7] The fact that they have an infinite future together leads them to contemplate how their actions today will influence the shape of their relationship in the future. The opportunity to punish bad behavior today with punishments in the future keeps players under control and encourages cooperation. However, as I said above, while games may last forever, e.g., there may always be a GM and a Ford playing an oligopoly game,[8] their CEOs do not and hence it seems natural to look at infinitely repeated games through an intergenerational lens. This takes the focus off of the relationship built between two infinitely lived agents and the punishments that might occur when equilibria are deviated from, and places it on the kind of advice offered between generational agents and their willingness to follow the advice of their elders or predecessors.

Our view of social learning also differs from the standard theory. In the conventional social learning problem (see Gale (1996),

---

[7] There are models of reputation building where there is an infinitely lived player playing against a sequence of finitely lived opponents. Such models may be considered hybrids but they do not involve any intergenerational advice.

[8] The 2008 financial crisis did cast this assumption in doubt since the auto industry needed to be bailed out.

Bikhchandani et al. (1992), and Chamley (2004) for theoretical approaches and Anderson and Holt (1997) and Çelen and Kariv (2004, 2005) for experimental evidence) a set of decision makers make a choice sequentially one after the other. There is an unknown payoff-relevant state of the world and each agent, before they make their decision, is able to observe a signal about the state and also observe the choices that his or her predecessor(s) have made. What can not be observed is the signals observed by predecessors, that is private information. Based on their signal and the decision(s) of previous agents, the decision makers have to guess what the true state of the world is and, if they do this correctly, they receive a significant payoff. So in the standard social learning problem the object of learning is the discovery of the true state of the world, an objective truth. Learning is social because people can observe the actions of predecessors and update their priors accordingly.

The type of social learning we study here is very different. Here (with the exception of Chapter 10) there is no objective payoff-relevant state of the world that has to be discovered. What each generation has to do is decide on how to behave in the game defined by the societal problem they are facing. This means that they have to learn the convention governing the problem and assess what the likelihood is that their opponents also know it and are likely to follow it given the fact that each decision maker receives advice from his or her predecessor, knows that his or her opponent (or opponents) received advice but not what that advice is, and possibly knows the entire history of choices before him. What people want to learn here is how to behave in the situation they are thrust into and not what is the true objective state of the world. The convention established for the game they face is what they need to know and whether they can rely on others knowing and adhering to it. If they can, then one might expect it to persist but, as we will see often, the fact that a convention of behavior is firmly established today means little for the expectation that it will be adhered to tomorrow. The process of learning via intergenerational advice is typically stochastic.

I.2 ADVICE AND MECHANISM DESIGN

When we investigate the properties of economic mechanisms in the lab, we have a choice. We can study them in the environment defined by the theorist (using the game form defined by the mechanism) or the way they are actually played in the real world. To illustrate, let us look at school matching mechanisms, which we study in Chapters 12 and 13.

School matching mechanisms are typically installed in cities to manage the matching of students and schools. The theory for these mechanisms is, by and large, static and deals with a one-shot matching problem. In reality, however, the school matching problem is a recurrent problem faced by new parents every year. These parents engage in the match, and then exit only to be replaced by a new generation of parents in the following year. So the problem is a recurrent problem but one played intergenerationally with new generations of parents replacing old ones and receiving advice from them as to how to act strategically in the match.

For example, they may suggest applying to their second or third ranked school first in an effort to secure a slot out of fear of being closed out of all good schools by acting too greedily. They are advised to "play it safe" and not rank their first choice first. Such advice may come "horizontally" from parents in the same cohort as them, or "vertically" from previous generations as in our intergenerational setup. The question here is whether such intergenerational advice makes things better or worse? Do the parents establish a convention of behavior that is suboptimal and pass it along from generation to generation or does intergenerational advice lead to convergence to a stable matching (or perhaps an efficient one if the two are not synonymous)?

Questions about conventions are typically outside the purview of matching theory since, as mentioned above, these mechanisms are typically static one-shot games. We will investigate what happens to these mechanisms when they are played in an intergenerational manner for real.

Economic mechanisms present us with a different type of inter-generational problem than many of those we deal with earlier in our book. Basically a mechanism is a "man-made" game designed for us to play in order to achieve a given purpose, like matching students and schools in a stable manner or helping us contribute efficiently to a public good. These are different from what we might call "naturally occurring" problems which no one designs but just naturally occur. However, such mechanisms are typically employed to help us solve naturally occurring problems that we have failed to successfully cope with on our own. Such problems are similar to coordination problems like the problem of deciding which side of the road to drive on or naturally occurring externality problems like social dilemmas. There is no mechanism designer lurking behind the scenes here, only naturally occurring human dilemmas. The conventions established by society to deal with these naturally occurring problems substitute for the mechanisms imposed in other situations.

The interesting aspect of looking at mechanisms played inter-generationally is that they may lead to unintended modes of behavior that the designer never anticipated. The consequence of this is the lesson that once, a mechanism designer puts a mechanism in place, she cannot just walk away and think that everything will be OK. Inefficient conventions of behavior can be established which, if not monitored, can lead to bad societal outcomes.

1.3   CHOICE UNDER THE INFLUENCE OF ADVICE

As we mentioned above, advice also exists outside of our intergener-ational setting, and in several chapters, we investigate the influence of advice on decision making in static one-person decision problems. One issue here is that advice competes with other types of informa-tion that decision makers seek before making a choice. For example, someone may say "keep your advice, just give me data and I can make up my own mind". Here the decision maker might feel she is better at processing data than her advisor is and would rather rely on data than the filtering of such data through the mind of the advisor. One might also prefer to have information about the beliefs held by an advisor over random variables (states of the world) rather than the advice they offer based on those beliefs because one might doubt the ability of an advisor to best respond to the beliefs they hold. Finally, there is the simple technical problem of how does one incorporate advice into decision making – a process that might involve inverting the advice to infer the information encoded in it. Hence, in addition to our focus on intergenerational games and intergenerational advice, we will offer a number of chapters that deal with decision problems under the influence of advice. In these chapters we also look at the market for advice mentioned above.

I.4   OUTLINE OF THE BOOK

This book is divided into parts, with each part addressing a different set of issues. All of the chapters starting with Part III are based on articles I have published in the past with various co-authors. For each chapter I cite the article it is based on and I urge you to refer to those articles for a fuller or more detailed analysis than I offer here. As stated in the Preface, I owe a great deal to all of my co-authors who shared this work with me.

In Part I (consisting of Chapters 2 and 3) I will present some background material we will need to do our analysis. Here, in Chapter 2 we focus on advice, since it is so central to all of what we do. We hope to understand what advice is, what are the different types of advice out there, and how different academic disciplines (namely economics and psychology) investigate the impact of advice on decision making.

Chapter 3 looks at conventions, social learning, and intergenerational games. Here we first attempt to discuss and define what each of these objects are in general terms before getting a little more formal in defining an intergenerational game and what it means to have a stable convention of behavior in place.

Part II (Chapters 4, 5, and 6) starts our investigation of the impact of advice on the establishment and evolution of conventions of behavior. The experiments discussed in these three chapters all use the exact same design existing of three treatments. In one treatment subjects play an intergenerational game with access to both advice and the history of play, the advice-plus-history treatment; in another they have access to only advice, the advice-only treatment; and finally with access to only history, the history-only treatment. This design is applied to investigate three types of naturally occurring problems that require a convention to solve them: coordination problems with distributional consequences (battle of the sexes games), bargaining in the form of an ultimatum game, and problems of trust in the form of the classic trust game of Berg et al. (1995). We use these games because they are much studied games that have a rich tradition in experimental economics but are never studied in an intergenerational setting. We do that in Part III and ask how behavior differs when such games are played in this context across our three treatments.

The focus in each of these chapters is slightly different, however. In Chapter 4 on the battle of the sexes game, we are interested in what convention of behavior is established for the players in this game and passed on to their successors. As a result, we focus on the time path of behavior and ask whether behavior converges to a stable convention that governs behavior in this situation. However, in the battle of the sexes game, in equilibrium, there is one player who fares better than the other in the sense that the convention established offers her a higher payoff.[9] If a convention is established that favors one type of player, and this is passed down over time, then the players have established what Ullman-Margalit (1977) calls an inequality preserving convention.[10] Obviously the existence of such inequality puts pressure on subjects to rectify it but this can only occur if the convention breaks down and allows new and different

[9] This assumes that the players do not establish an alternate convention in which they alternate taking the better payoff for themselves. Such alternation would equalize payoffs. Given our design, such a convention is hard to establish and was not observed.

[10] Ullman-Margalit uses the term "norm" but we distinguish between conventions and norms and prefer to use the term "convention" to describe actual behavior.

behavior to take its place. We will look to see if such conventions are stable or do, in fact, break down over time.

In Chapter 5, on intergenerational ultimatum games, we look at a slightly different question. Here we are not as interested in what the time path of behavior is but whether behavior is "more conventional" in such games when there is advice as opposed to when there is not. Here the term "more conventional than" will mean a greater consensus among intergenerational players in one treatment that a certain offer is the *conventional offer* and should be adhered to and passed along as advice or punished if not adhered to.

Chapter 6 investigates the trust game using the same experimental design. Here the question turns to whether trust is enhanced by the presence of advice and whether people are more trustworthy in its presence. We will see an interesting result which we also saw in the ultimatum game, which is that advice leads subjects to act in a manner closer to the behavior predicted by the selfish Nash equilibrium. In other words, when advice exists, behavior moves away from that suggested by theories of inequality aversion or fairness and toward the selfish equilibrium theory. Such a result has consequences that are worth investigating further since if, in the real world, people decide with the aid of advice and if that advice is more selfish than what people would do on their own, then laboratory results that do not include advice may suffer from problems of external validity.

In Part III (Chapters 7 and 8) we look at the importance of common knowledge for convention creation. As we discussed in Chapter 3, there are those who believe that conventions can only exist if they are common knowledge in the population adhering to them. This means that everyone knows the convention and their role in it, believes that everyone else knows it, and believes that everyone else believes that everyone else knows it, etc. It is only under such beliefs that people will feel confident in adhering to a convention (especially if doing so is risky).

The two chapters in Part III investigate this common knowledge problem in connection to behavior in the minimum effort game

(Chapter 7) and the two-thirds guessing game (Chapter 8). In these chapters the object that needs to be common knowledge is the advice offered to subjects by others and the issue is how can such advice be made common knowledge.

There are two punch lines here. One is that it is not enough that advice be public to make it common knowledge. What matters is how the advice is made public, i.e., is it read aloud, read aloud and written on a sheet of paper, read allowed and projected on a screen for all to see, etc? It turns out that these three methods are not equivalent. In addition, in both Chapter 7 and Chapter 8 the quality or type of advice also matters. Public advice that urges everyone to behave in a particular way has to be emphatic and meaningful. In other words, any old type of advice if made public will not do the trick. It has to be in some sense relevant for all decision makers. The punch line is that knowledge that is common knowledge in theory may not be common knowledge in practice.

In Part IV (Chapters 9, 10, and 11) we turn our attention to advice in decision problems. In other words we leave the world of game theory and investigate the impact of advice on people making decisions in a world where one's payoff is not tied to the actions of others, or if they are, then everyone's preferences are aligned as they are in the social learning problem we study in Chapter 10.

In Chapter 9 we look at a problem of what we call a meddlesome boss who looks over the shoulder of her workers and offers unsolicited advice that can be ignored but at a cost. In other words, it is a problem where a decision maker has an advisor whose advice she is afraid of ignoring because the advisor is her boss and will resent having her suggestions ignored. The question here is, does such a meddlesome boss get in the way of the decision maker learning the optimal way to behave in the problem she faces? The answer will, miraculously, be no. A meddlesome boss can facilitate learning possibly because it leads the decision maker to think twice about what decisions she would make. To demonstrate this we use an experimental technique called a surprise quiz first developed by Merlo and Schotter (1999,

2003) which effectively can detect how well or what a subject learned after repeatedly engaging in a decision problem.

Chapter 10 also investigates learning and advice but this time in a classic social learning problem of the type first studied by Çelen and Kariv (2004, 2005). In such problems there is a random variable called the state of the world which is unknown to a set of decision makers who are arranged sequentially in a decision line, where the first person in the line makes a binary choice first after receiving a signal about the state of the world. The second person then observes the first person's choice but not their signal and, after receiving her own signal, also makes a binary choice that is observed by the third decision maker, etc. Each decision maker can observe the choice of the person before her but nothing else except their own signal. The payoffs to the decision makers are some positive payoff if their choice matches the objectively true state of the world and zero otherwise.

Although this is the standard problem, in Chapter 10 we introduce a wrinkle in that in some treatments subjects play as described above and can see their predecessor's choice. In others they receive advice from their predecessor but cannot see her choice, while, in a third treatment, she can see both. This design allows us to see the power of advice in contrast to data since we are able to see whether people tend to follow advice as opposed to the actions of their predecessors when they both suggest the same actions. In addition, in the treatment where subjects receive both advice and data, we are able to see which is more powerful in those circumstances where they make opposite suggestions. The punch line here seems to be that advice is preferred to data. People are more likely to follow it and make choices more consistent with it than with the choice they observe their predecessor making. Advice also improves welfare.

Chapter 11 is probably the chapter that is most different from the others in that it is mainly concerned with the market for advice and tries to discover whether people prefer advice from particular types of advisors. As we mentioned above, in the market for advice there is a premium placed on those whose advice is sought after, and it might be informative to investigate what those advisors look like.

The problem presented to subjects in this chapter, like that in Chapter 10, is a Bayesian decision problem. In this problem we can easily see if our subjects suffer from either a conservative or a representative bias by seeing if they place too much or too little weight on their prior beliefs when updating. One interesting question we ask here is how do the biases exhibited by our subject correlate with their willingness to seek and follow advice. Are subjects who update in a conservative manner more resistant to paying for and following advice and are those who suffer a representative bias biased in the opposite direction? These are the questions we ask here.

In Part V we turn our attention to economic mechanisms or more specifically school matching mechanisms and investigate the impact of advice on the behavior of subjects engaged in a matching problem using either the Boston or Gale–Shapley deferred acceptance mechanism. These are the man-made problems we discussed before. In Chapter 12 we look at the influence of what we call horizontal advice which is advice between contemporary participants in the mechanism (parents meeting in the playground and discussing how to behave under the mechanism), while in Chapter 13 we look at vertical advice or advice from previous participants in an intergenerational setting. Here again the question is whether advice spurs learning and is efficiency-increasing. We find our answer is yes and no. While with horizontal advice the existence of advice is welfare-increasing, its impact is much more complex when we embed these mechanisms in an intergenerational setting. More precisely, when the Gale–Shapley mechanism, a mechanism in which reporting one's truthful rankings over objects or schools is a weakly dominant strategy, is placed in an intergenerational setting (a setting that is a very natural one), the fraction of subjects who report the truth declines monotonically over time. This result is almost the only time where advice is welfare-decreasing.

Finally Chapter 14 offers some conclusions about what we have learned in our endeavors here. Let's get started.

REFERENCES

Acemoglu, D. and Robinson, J. A. (2012). *Why Nations Fail: The Origins of Power, Prosperity, and Poverty*. New York, NY: Crown Publishing.

Alesina, A. and Giuliano, P. (2010). The power of the family. *Journal of Economic Growth*, 15(2), 93–125.

Alesina, A. and Giuliano, P. (2015). Culture and institutions. *Journal of Economic Literature*, 53(4), 898–944.

Anderson, L. R. and Holt, C. A. (1997). Information cascades in the laboratory. *American Economic Review*, 87(5), 847–862.

Berg, J., Dickhaut, J. and McCabe, K. (1995). Trust, reciprocity, and social history. *Games and Economic Behavior*, 10(1), 122–142.

Bikhchandani, S., Hirshleifer, D. and Welch, I. (1992). A theory of fads, fashion, custom, and cultural change as informational cascades. *Journal of Political Economy*, 100(5), 992–1026.

Bisin, A. and Verdier, T. (1998). On the cultural transmission of preferences for social status. *Journal of Public Economics*, 70(1), 75–97.

Bisin, A. and Verdier, T. (2000). "Beyond the melting pot": cultural transmission, marriage, and the evolution of ethnic and religious traits. *Quarterly Journal of Economics*, 115(3), 955–988.

Çelen, B. and Kariv, S. (2004). Distinguishing informational cascades from herd behavior in the laboratory. *American Economic Review*, 94(3), 484–497.

Çelen, B. and Kariv, S. (2005). An experimental test of observational learning under imperfect information. *Economic Theory*, 26(3), 677–699.

Chamley, C. P. (2004). *Rational Herds: Economic Models of Social Learning*. New York, NY: Cambridge University Press.

Gale, D. (1996). What have we learned from social learning? *European Economic Review*, 40(3-5), 617–628.

Glaeser, E. L. and Shleifer, A. (2002). Legal origins. *Quarterly Journal of Economics*, 117(4), 1193–1229.

Kiyotaki, N. and Wright, R. (1989). On money as a medium of exchange. *Journal of Political Economy*, 97(4), 927–954.

Kloosterman, A. and Schotter, A. (2016). Complementary institutions and economic development: An experimental study. *Games and Economic Behavior*, 99, 186–205.

Kuran, T. (2012). *The Long Divergence: How Islamic Law Held Back the Middle East*. Princeton, NJ: Princeton University Press.

La Porta, R., Lopez-de-Silanes, F., Shleifer, A. and Vishny, R. W. (1998). Law and finance. *Journal of Political Economy*, 106(6), 1113–1155.

Li, Y. (1995). Commodity money under private information. *Journal of Monetary Economics*, 36(3), 573–592.

Merlo, A. and Schotter, A. (1999). A surprise-quiz view of learning in economic experiments. *Games and Economic Behavior*, 28(1), 25–54.

Merlo, A. and Schotter, A. (2003). Learning by not doing: An experimental investigation of observational learning. *Games and Economic Behavior*, 42(1), 116–136.

North, D. C. (1990). *Institutions, Institutional Change, and Economic Performance*. New York, NY: Cambridge University Press.

Schotter, A. (1981). *The Economic Theory of Social Institutions*. New York, NY: Cambridge University Press.

Todd, E. (1989). *The Explanation of Ideology: Family Structures and Social Systems*. New York, NY: Blackwell Publishing.

Todd, E. (1990). *L'Invention de l'Europe*. Paris, France: Editions du Seuil.

Ullman-Margalit, E. (1977). *The Emergence of Norms*, Oxford, UK: Oxford University Press.

PART I **Background**

2   Advice

Since advice is central to what we are discussing here, it might be worthwhile to spend some time simply thinking about what advice is, what are the different types of advice we might come upon in our daily lives, and how advice is treated by different academic disciplines. That is what we do here. We first define what advice is, then categorize advice into some common-sense categories without expecting our categories to be either exhaustive or mutually exclusive. Finally, we discuss the way advice is treated in the economics and psychology literature and contrast their approaches to the topic.[1]

In our next chapter we turn our attention to conventions of behavior and the intergenerational games determining them.

2.1   WHAT IS ADVICE?

According to the *Oxford English Dictionary* advice is "guidance or recommendations offered with regard to prudent future action".[2] Taking the definition literally suggests that the advisor has the interests of the advisee at heart and wants to give him or her the best advice possible. But, as economists know, the relationship between the advisor and advisee is complicated.[3] For example, person A might

---

[1] There is also a sizable literature in computer science that investigates how advice, when entered into a reinforcement learning algorithm, may enhance its efficiency. For a review of this literature see Garcia and Fernández (2015).

[2] Advice can also be unsolicited. Unsolicited advice, although still advice, tends too many times to be unwelcome, especially when it suggests an unwanted action, and dismissed. For example, a Kibitzer is a Yiddish term for a spectator, usually one who offers (often unwanted) advice or commentary. The term can be applied to any activity, but is most commonly used to describe spectators in games such as contract bridge, chess, and Schafkopf (see Wikipedia, https://en.wikipedia.org/wiki/Kibitzer).

[3] For example, if you are a parent you may have an idea of what is best for your child that differs greatly from what he or she thinks they want as they are influenced by pressure from their peers (see Bisin and Verdier (1998, 2000) for an elegant treatment of this tension). So the guidance a parent gives a child may be furthering the goals of

want to persuade person B into taking an action that is best for person A and actually bad for person B. In doing so she may offer advice, but clearly there is a moral hazard here.

Despite these qualifications, we are going to treat advice as "a suggestion by a person (the advisor) to another person (the advisee) who has partially (mostly) aligned interests".[4] Hence we will consider advice to be given in good faith. The task of the advisee is to evaluate the advice and decide whether to accept it and to what extent. As we will see, however, even if the interests of the advisor and advisee are completely aligned, there are still a host of very interesting questions one can ask about advice giving and receiving, convention creation and stability, and the welfare properties of advice. They are just different questions than those asked in the economics literature.

2.2 TYPES OF ADVICE

Although the type of advice offered by our advisors will typically be straightforward – they just tell their advisee (successor) a strategy to choose in a game – there will be situations where the type of advice offered differs, and hence it might make sense to pause and discuss the different types of advice we see in our daily lives. As you will see, advice comes in many different flavors.

2.2.1 Naive Advice

You're thirty-four years old and deciding to buy your first house. You have a bunch of friends who are also in their thirties and rent apartments. You ask them for advice even though they have never bought a house themselves. Why? What do they know that you don't?

The answer is that they know nothing more than you do. It's the process of asking for advice that's informative. The process of asking

---

the parent and not those of the child, or at least what the parent thinks the goals of the child should be.

[4] There is some work on what may be called advice in one-person decision making with incomplete preferences. Nishimura and Ok (2020) construct a two-self model where an individual has two preference systems, one for easy decisions, things that seem obvious, and one for harder ones, where preferences may be complete but not necessarily transitive. The "hard-problem" self can be interpreted as a consultant or advisor but in their model the two preference systems are aligned but separate.

for advice and the ensuing discussion is useful because it makes you think through your problem once more and that process may be helpful. It's very much like the benefits people derive from their non-responsive psychotherapist who merely sits there and repeats what they say. The process of hearing yourself speak many times leads to new insights.

Put differently, your first approach at a decision may be an emotional response involving what Kahneman (2011) calls System-1 or what Rubinstein (2007) calls an intuitive response, while the process of thinking over the decision a second time, derived from asking for advice, might lead to a more System-2 or contemplative response. Hence we ask for advice in order to allow ourselves to think out loud and maybe arrive at ideas we never thought of before. Asking for advice from naive advisors allows us to engage in a different process of reasoning about the problem we face. We seek the process not the actual advice.

In addition, we sometimes seek naive advice because we are seeking confirmation for a decision we already made either to do something we want to do or to do something we do not want to do but know we should. In this case, advice is what we ask for when we already know the answer but wish we didn't. All too often we ask for advice from a friend and, while they say nothing while we vent, we rethink our decision and change it. When we leave we are amazed at how smart our friend is even though all they did was listen.

In our work here, advice will typically be naive. Those offering advice are barely better informed than those receiving it and typically have the same information sets. The interesting puzzle is how advice from such naive advisors is capable of increasing the welfare of recipients.

2.2.2   Technical Advice

While economics assumes that people are rational decision makers with unbounded cognitive capabilities, we know that we are bounded in our decision-making abilities and as a result need help. Those of us who recognize that fact are the fortunate ones, while those who are both boundedly rational but not self-aware, suffer. But technical advice is just that, technical. Technical advisors are the kind of advisors to whom you present your utility function and the constraints you are facing and ask them for help maximizing. Note that such advice is mechanical. You present the expert with your preferences and your constraints and he or she solves your problem. There are many corporate and financial consulting firms offering technical advice. It's a billion-dollar industry. They come into our organizations, listen to our goals, consider our constraints, and offer a solution (and a bill for services).

Of course, just because someone is billed as an expert does not mean you should listen to them.[5] They may be a bullshit artist whose advice is suspect but whose identity needs to be exposed (see Frankfurt (2005) for a philosophical discussion and Jerrim et al. (2019) for an experimental examination of bullshit).

2.2.3 Wise Advice and Nudges

Wise Advice

In many of the important decisions we make we seek out a wise person for advice. There used to be a notion that old people, those who have been around for a long time, were valuable advisors because they were "wise". But that raises the question of what is "wise" advice and how does it differ from other types of advice, especially technical advice. Put differently, in what sense can advice be wise if it is not utility-maximizing (i.e., the kind of advice you'd get from a technician)? Are the choices prescribed by our decision-theoretic models wise choices or merely technical? Can technically correct choices be unwise?

We will consider advice as wise if it does not merely take the preferences of the decision maker as given and prescribe how to maximize them, but rather questions the decision maker's stated preferences in order to see if he or she should be maximizing something else.

---

[5] An expert has been described as "a jerk from out of town with a PowerPoint presentation".

For example, say you are an 18-year-old and deciding between buying a BMW or a Mercedes. You ask your uncle which car is best and he says neither, you should put your money in the bank and pay for college. He says: "when you are a rich college graduate you can get a fancy car".

I call this advice wise because your uncle did not take the problem presented to him or your objective function as given but asked why you were maximizing that specific objective function.

This is not far from the distinction between wants and needs. Many times we ask people how we can get what we want and they tell us that we should, instead, be looking to get what we need. Wants may be valuable to satisfy in the short term but a wise advisor will suggest that we not be so myopic and think of what we need in the long run. It may also be the case that wise advice tells you to do something different from what others are doing – to not follow the herd. As we know in social learning, people may ignore their own private information and follow what others are doing even if it does not seem right. While sometimes this is rational, it is also possible that people may join an information cascade where people all make the wrong decision.

As it turns out, many times we ask people for advice exactly because we do not know our preferences. For example, say you are offered two jobs, one high-powered high-stress job with big bucks attached to it, and the other a lower-paying job but one filled with nice life amenities. Which job you should take will depend on what you value in life and a wise advisor's job is to help you discover what you care about or perhaps suggest what you should care about. Once that is accomplished, the rest is easy and we can call upon a technical advisor to make our choice.

While we may hate to follow wise advice, because it might tell us to do something other than what we want to do, we tend to value it in retrospect, especially if things turn out right. Sometimes it is worthwhile to reject wise advice since it might be better to learn by one's mistakes in life. A parent who tells their graduating high-school senior not to go to the prom because they turn into drunken debauched events, may be depriving their child of an opportunity to learn from experience, especially when they wake up the next morning with a terrible hangover. As Edna St. Vincent Millay said, "I am glad that I paid so little attention to good advice; had I abided by it I might have been saved from some of my most valuable mistakes." Deciding when to follow advice is tricky.

Nudges: The Best Advice You Never Asked For

If one thinks of wise advice in the terms described above, then there is an interesting connection between such advice and the nudges discussed by Thaler and Sunstein (2009). In some sense a nudge might be considered the best advice you never asked for. It is paternalistic advice but, according to Thaler and Sunstein, minimally so. They advocate libertarian paternalism. According to their definition nudges try "to influence choices in a way that will make choosers better off, *as judged by themselves*" (Thaler and Sunstein, 2009, p. 5). Because nudges do not question the correctness of the preferences of advisees, they are not actually wise advice according to our definition. However, in those cases where people do not have well-formed preferences, nudges may lead them into having preferences the nudger thinks they should have and, when this is true, nudges are wise.

2.2.4   Coaching

One type of advisor is a coach. While often thought of with respect to athletics, a coach is someone who watches your performance and makes suggestions. There are many types of coaches, including speech coaches, drama coaches, athletic coaches, and many others. So while you may be engaged in the heat of athletic battle and learning from direct engagement, your coach is involved in observational learning. He or she is observing the action and taking notes of what you should do.

So the question is how good is observational learning compared to the type of learning the participant is engaged in, i.e., reinforcement

(Erev and Roth, 1998) or belief learning (Nyarko and Schotter, 2002)? If it is superior, then you should listen to your coach or advisor.[6]

As it turns out we humans are some of the few living beings capable of observational learning and we're pretty good at it. Many animals can't do it. One might then ask why would someone who passively watches an event have a better idea of what's going on than the people actually participating? If you're a manager in a boxer's corner you might see what is happening to your guy but you certainly do not feel the power of her opponent's punches nor the true speed of her hands. As it turns out, however, it is precisely because the boxer is engaged that makes it hard for her to stand back and see what is really happening. The manager is there to make sure the boxer does not lose her cool and deviate from the designed plan. As Mike Tyson said, "Everybody has a plan until they get punched in the mouth", and it is at that point that a manager or coach is valuable.

Evidence for the possible advantages of observational learning is offered by Merlo and Schotter (1999, 2003). In their study, laboratory subjects are recruited in pairs with one subject (the doer) performing an experiment 75 times and receiving a payoff after each round while the other (the observer) passively looks over the doer's shoulder. After 75 rounds the two subjects are separated and told to do the experiment once more for rewards that were 75 times the rewards received previously. Since this extra round was not announced before, it was a "surprise-quiz" round. The choice subjects make in this surprise-quiz round should be their best guess as to what the optimal decision is, since they both have experience in the task and are playing for high stakes.

When Merlo and Schotter compared the choices made in that round across doers and observers, they found that observers made far better choices than did doers. In fact the mean choice of observers was remarkably close to the optimum.

---

[6] Of course, you may also want to listen to your coach because she has great experience.

This experiment suggests that observers or coaches may be in a better position than doers to offer advice. The reason is simple and should be obvious. Because a doer is receiving a payoff each round (or getting hit in the head by the opposing boxer), he or she is more focused on responding to the moment-by-moment events of the task rather than sitting back and seeing all that is transpiring. While most economic models describe doers, i.e., agents who make choices, observe the outcome of their choice, receive a payoff, and choose again, such a "learn-while-you-earn" environment is not conducive to learning (see Merlo and Schotter, 2003).[7] If one is placed in the more dispassionate position of an observer or a coach, it is very likely that you would be able to better grasp the full context of what is happening. Put differently, learners learn how to respond and react to incoming information while observers are able to take a more holistic approach and see the forest for the trees.[8]

2.2.5   Narratives

In our daily lives we many times receive advice in the form of societal narratives. Such narratives, as defined by Akerlof and Snower (2016), are stories that people tell each other that take the form

---

[7]   Merlo and Schotter (2003) used the same task but in one treatment they had one set of subjects receive a payoff every round and get feedback (this was the learn-while-you-earn group (LWYE)). This group was then subjected to a surprise quiz as were subjects in Merlo and Schotter (1999). In the other treatment (the learn-before-you-earn treatment (LBYE)) subjects received feedback each period but there were no round-by-round payoffs. Rather, each period subjects were informed of the payoff they would have received if they were paid for their round payoffs. Their 75th round choice was paid at a rate 75 times higher than the round payoffs of the other group. Merlo and Schotter (2003) then compared the choices and payoffs of subjects across these two treatments and found a result similar to what they did in Merlo and Schotter (1999), which was that performance was far better in the 75th round-of-the LBYE treatment than the surprise-quiz round of the LWYE treatment, indicating that getting payoffs round-by-round is a distraction and prevents learning compared to being allowed to freely or hypothetically earn with no distractions. Such learning is more akin to what coaches do.

[8]   We see a similar result when we look at the computer science literature on artificial intelligence reinforcement learning with advice. The reinforcement learning algorithm also does not see the forest for the trees, while the advisor does and offers advice to help solve the algorithm's myopia. See Garcia and Fernández (2015).

of "... a sequence of causally linked events and their underlying sources, unfolding through time, which may be used as a template for interpreting our ongoing experience". In other words, these narratives are what people tell each other at the office water cooler or dinner table when they meet and exchange their views about the world. They may be causal tales about what has caused a current recession (see Shiller, 2019; Benabou et al., 2020), what to do when we experience a hyper-inflation, or why we can expect a certain politician to win an election. If these narratives go viral, they can have a great impact on societal behavior.

Such narratives can serve many purposes. For example, as Akerlof and Snower (2016) say, they can help us to understand our environment, focus our attention on certain aspects of it, be useful in predicting events and motivating us to take action, provide social identities to us, justify the power relationships we are experiencing, and, perhaps more relevant to our concerns here, teach people social conventions and explain why they should adhere to them.

As such, these narratives function like societal advice that helps us understand our world and guide us in our behavior. This advice comes free of charge and is available to us if we engage with others. It is also naive advice since it does not come from experts but simply from those in our social circle. The narratives can play a crucial role in enhancing the stability of social conventions by offering a justification for them to those contemplating a deviation. They can also support a revolution when the narrative works in that direction.

In our work here we will see a type of narrative observed in the advice that generations of players pass on to their successors. As we read the transcripts of this advice we will see our subjects justifying an offer in an ultimatum game, suggesting what to bid in an auction, telling their successors whether it is worthwhile to trust their cohort, suggesting how a school matching mechanism works and how to get your kid into the school of her dreams, etc. Not only will we see this advice being passed on but we will also see that advice and its wording is contagious in that the same words are used and passed down from generation to generation, justifying certain actions and using identical terms to do so. The causal story gets passed from generation to generation almost unaltered.

2.3   ADVICE IN THIS BOOK

In all of the chapters in this book that use the intergenerational-game model, the advice offered is basically naive. This is true by construction since, in almost all intergenerational games we look at, generations play the stage game once and only once. Hence they are certainly not experts and, since they have played rather than observed, they are not coaches. In addition, we are assuming that each generation of player is drawn from the same population of agents and hence none of them, ex ante, have greater technical abilities than the others and hence are not capable of offering technical advice. This focus on naive advice is intentional on our part because, as stated above, we construct the intergenerational game in a way that prevents expertise in the task at hand but also we are focused on advice between real flesh- and-blood players (parents and children) and not investors and financial consultants.

In some chapters, where we do not use the intergenerational-game setup but still have advice, like Chapter 9 on learning with a meddlesome boss, our advice takes the form of coaching and technical advice since in that chapter we have a boss offering advice to her employee. In other chapters, like Chapter 7 on common knowledge in the minimum-effort game, subjects play the game for ten periods before offering advice and hence may have gained some expertise and can be considered experts.

2.4   APPROACHES TO ADVICE GIVING AND FOLLOWING

It is one thing to discuss advice in a common-sense man-on-the-street manner, as we have above, and another to see how different academic disciplines treat it in their research. In this section we look at two different academic disciplines, economics and psychology, and investigate how they incorporate advice into their work.

This exercise is interesting because one way to see the difference in academic disciplines is to take a common problem that each have approached and see how differently they tackle it. For example, on a problem like advice giving and receiving, psychologists are likely to ask what people do, whereas economists are likely either to ask what people should do or to predict what they will do in equilibrium.

For the study of advice this division of labor is natural because, while psychologists tend to look at advice through the lens of one-person decision problems, economists see advice giving and receiving game-theoretically and look for what transpires in the equilibrium of the communication games they construct.[9] Hence the approach to advice differs across disciplines but this is natural and actually useful since each discipline is uniquely equipped to answer the type of questions they individually ask and the answers are complementary.

In the next two subsections I will present a rough overview of the approaches that psychologists and economists take when investigating the question of advice giving and receiving. Our aim here is not to provide two survey papers on the use of advice across these fields. Rather, our aim is to contrast the approaches taken and put their work in context. While the psychology literature is almost exclusively experimental, the economics literature is primarily theoretical, except, of course, for the work related to experiments on intergenerational games that we will describe later in this book.

Let's look at what economists do first.

2.4.1 The Economics Approach

As we mentioned above, the economics literature on advice focuses almost exclusively on the incentive issues existing between the advisor and the advisee. That is, by interpreting what it calls "communication games" as situations of advice giving and receiving, economists are fixated on the strategic relationship between the sender (advisor) and receiver (advisee). The question asked is this: Given the

---

[9] See Sobel (2013).

strategic conflict between sender and receiver, how informative can the sender's communications (advice) be for the receiver? In other words, does their conflict of interest ruin the usefulness of having an advisor?

In such games, advisors here are reluctant communicators only willing to provide information if it increases their payoff. In the canonical model, the sender knows exactly what the receiver should do to maximize her utility since she knows the receiver's preferences and the value of all payoff-relevant variables. It is only when their preferences align that the sender is willing to communicate truthfully or precisely and allow the receiver to make the right choice for her. These are not the type of advisors most people would want to consult with and it is hard to call their communications "advice".

To put some flesh on the bones of this discussion, let us follow Sobel's (2013) elegant survey paper entitled "Giving and receiving advice" and describe the basic model of a "cheap-talk" game (Crawford and Sobel, 1982; Green and Stokey, 2007) that serves as the baseline model for the literature.

In such games there are two actors, a sender and receiver. They differ by the fact that the sender is capable of seeing some unknown but payoff-relevant fact, the "state of the world", and can send a message to the receiver about it. Upon receiving the message the receiver can take an action that affects the payoff of both the sender and the receiver. The message sent by the sender need not be truthful so the sender can lie. The reason the sender would want to lie is because, given the state of the world, she might like the receiver to take a particular action that is not in the receiver's interest. So the sender has an incentive to dissemble. The literature focuses on the equilibria of this communication game.

More precisely, given the setup above, the focus of attention in this literature is how informative equilibria will be in a cheap-talk game, either where there are no constraints placed on communication, or where communications are verifiable so that the sender cannot lie but can withhold information.

The basic problem for cheap-talk games is the existence of what are called "babbling equilibria" which are equilibria where the sender's message has no informational content so that the receiver simply chooses the same action no matter what message is sent and that action is a best response to the prior belief that the receiver held before communication started. Since such non-informative equilibria will typically exist, such games at best have multiple equilibria, only some of which are informative.

This literature is basically a search for conditions under which equilibria in these games can be informative. If multiple equilibria exist, some of which are informative, then it is clear that the receiver would prefer the informative one. One question is when will the sender also prefer to provide more information and hence be a useful advisor. In Chakraborty and Harbaugh's (2010) model, if the sender has a quasi-convex utility function then she would also prefer the more informative equilibria because, in that case, the receiver would vary her action as different information is transmitted, which would create a mean-preserving spread of the outcomes which is preferred by an agent with convex preferences. In such a case, the receiver might find having an advisor useful but only if she selects the informative equilibria.

It is hard for us to view standard cheap-talk games as situations where advice is being transmitted since the advisors in these games are so untrustworthy given their potential conflict of interest. In our experiments, we try hard to align the interests of the advisor and advisee and incentivize the advisor to send honest advice.

For example, what if we knew that, while the sender has preferences different from those of the receiver, she has an aversion to lying or that lying is costly. That could make her trustworthy and informative. This can be introduced into a standard communication game by assuming the existence of behavioral types who are hard-wired to tell the truth (see Chen, 2011). This assumption allows us to select one (informative) equilibrium in the original cheap-talk game (see Chen et al. 2007). Introducing lying costs (see Kartik 2009) has a similar effect.

A related model is that of Agranov et al. (2020) where they model communication games as psychological games where there is a finite set of types, some of whom suffer from either lying aversion, guilt aversion, or both. The guilt on the part of the sender is brought on by the fear of disappointing the receiver, who the sender feels is relying on her for truthful communications. While the introduction of these emotions does not get rid of the babbling equilibrium, it does introduce a set of partially informative equilibria.

Another example of where honesty concerns can lead to informative advisors is Olszewski (2004). In this paper the receiver has her own private information and the sender cares to be perceived as honest. If the honesty concerns of the sender are strong enough, then their model predicts a unique informative equilibrium.

As these papers suggest, in cheap-talk games, senders may be viewed as trustworthy advisors if the receiver has sufficient faith that they are honest types. If not, we are back to the old cheap-talk situation.

The quest for informative advisors can lead us to ask whether we can change the form of the cheap-talk game by designing a different communication institution or a different game form that will allow the receiver to elicit better information from the sender. For example, if the receiver has real doubts about the sender (advisor) she may want to employ the assistance of an arbitrator or mediator. In arbitration, as Goltsman et al. (2009) demonstrate, a third party can ask the sender for information and give her the right to make a decision for the receiver. However, the receiver has the right to constrain the set of actions the sender is allowed to take. If the sender has an upward bias, meaning that for any state she would rather have the receiver make a higher choice than the receiver would want, then, by giving the receiver the right to constrain the sender, she can limit her exposure to extremely high choices which she would like to avoid. Similar results can be obtained through mediation where a third party collects information from the sender and the receiver makes the best choice available to him given the information collected.

While these institutional innovations allow for the existence of a more informative equilibrium for the communication game, the spirit of the interaction between the sender and the receiver is still far from how we view the relationship between an advisor and advisee. In fact, the situation can be even worse since it is possible for the sender to devise a persuasion protocol that will allow it to extract a favorable choice from the receiver. In such Bayesian persuasion situations, the sender designs an information policy that she commits to in the sense that the messages that she states ex ante would be sent, conditional on receiving information about the state of the world, must actually be sent if that state is realized. So the focus here is on the sender who is trying to have the receiver take actions that are best for the sender.

Some settings may provide the receiver with more protection from the strategic actions of the sender because in some situations information may be verifiable. In such a case while the sender cannot lie, she does not have to tell the entire truth. For example, if the true state of the world is θ', the sender can only send sets of messages m that contain θ'. In other words while the sender cannot lie, she can obfuscate the truth.

While the literature has concentrated on situations where the preferences of the sender and receiver differ, there are other circumstances where their preferences are aligned but they hold different priors over the underlying state of the world (see Che and Kartik, 2009). This leads to a difference of opinion between the sender and receiver as to what the optimal action is conditional on any piece of information since their updated priors will differ. Che and Kartik (2009) contemplate the type of sender a receiver would like to engage with, e.g., someone with similar or dissimilar priors. While the results can go either way, they demonstrate that if the receiver has a rich enough choice she might want to choose a sender whose priors are sufficiently different than hers, suggesting a result opposite from the choice a receiver would make if priors were identical but preferences differed.

The information available to the sender may be endogenous and a function of her effort to discover the state of the world. Such senders may be considered experts since they have spent effort in acquiring information. If receivers can choose their expert then one might contemplate what factors go into that choice. Such considerations are the focus of Dewatripont and Tirole (1999) and Dur and Swank (2005) where they focus on how to get the sender to put effort into being an informed expert.

Finally, if the sender has reputation concerns, then one might think that that could create an incentive for truthful communication. Ottaviani and Sørensen (2006) explore professional advice where an expert cares only about her reputation as evaluated by the receiver. In their paper such concerns are only partially successful in providing the receiver with the information she needs since the informativeness of the messages sent is restricted in equilibrium.

In summary, there is a very elegant literature in economics on communication games, cheap talk, and persuasion. The questions asked and answered are extremely interesting and informative. The question we have is whether one would want to call this a literature on advice giving and receiving rather than strategic communication.

As stated before, in the experiments presented in this book we try hard to minimize the strategic tensions between the advisor and advisee. We try to align the interests of the advice giver and receiver. Despite this, however, there may be many reasons why the advisee may reject the advisor's advice. First, while in communication games we have a strategic conflict between the sender and receiver, once the sender sends a message to the receiver, the receiver faces a one-person decision problem which has a uniquely best choice given truthful information. In what we discuss here, after advice is sent, the receiver still has to play a game against an opponent of her generation. Hence, in such situations the receiver may hold different beliefs about the potential actions of her opponent than does the sender, which could lead her to reject the advice received. The receiver might also adhere to a different equilibrium notion or use a different heuristic for her choice. If so, given identical information the receiver may still choose differently than the advisor might want her to. Finally, the choice of the receiver may simply be stochastic. For all of these reasons we will demonstrate in chapter after chapter that life in intergenerational games with advice is somewhat unstable.

2.4.2   The Psychologist Approach

Psychologists investigate behavior in a very different way than economists.[10] Because they are freed from the constraints placed on behavior by equilibrium analysis, they are free to ask questions about behavior that are more wide ranging and perhaps closer to how people actually behave. This makes their results more relatable. This difference is nicely illustrated when we contrast the economics and psychology literature on advice giving and receiving.

The major experimental paradigm for advice giving and receiving in psychology is the judge–advisor system (JAS) (Sniezek and Buckley, 1995) paradigm. In a JAS experiment, participants enter the laboratory and are randomly assigned to the role of "judge" or "advisor". In the experiment the judge is the person who makes a decision while the advisor offers advice or an opinion. In many experiments the judge makes an initial decision without any input by the advisor and then the advisor offers advice. After receiving the advice the judge is free to change her initial choice and make a revised decision which incorporates the advisor's opinion. In some experiments the confidence of the judge in her initial guess is also solicited as is the confidence of the advisor, who might say "I am 75% confident in my advice". This allows the experimenter to investigate the impact of advisor confidence on the decision of the judge. That is, are we more likely to follow the advice of more confident advisors? In most studies there is an objective fact that must be guessed and accuracy is measured by how close the guess of either the judge or the advisor is to the truth.

[10] I will rely on the excellent survey of judge–advisor systems offered by Bonaccio and Dalal (2006) in my discussion.

For example, in one study by Sniezek et al. (2004) the fact that needs to be guessed is the prices of different models of backpacks. The judge's task is to combine the advice she gets from the advisor into a revised guess for the problem. The impact of advice on the judge can be measured by how much the judge's initial decision or guess is altered after receiving the advisors' advice.

In most studies the focus of analysis is on the judge and how she combines her knowledge with that of the advisor. Hence, the motives of the advisor are not examined and, in contrast to the economics literature, they are typically non-strategic actors.

The lack of interest in the strategic relationship between the advisor and the judge is understandable since the literature on advice giving and receiving in psychology stems from a problem in social decision making in an industrial organization context. More precisely, the first study in the psychology literature on advice giving and receiving is attributed to Brehmer and Hagafors (1986). This paper was motivated by a problem faced by all hierarchical organizations where the boss has to rely on a set of experts for advice before making her decision. The question is how does the boss weigh the different opinions of her experts (each specialized in a different area) and aggregate them into a decision for the organization which is made exclusively by her.

Given the JAS paradigm, many questions can be asked that are not part of the economist's agenda. For example, why would a decision maker ever want to get advice in the first place? Do people want advice for its informational content or for non-instrumental reasons? Of course, non-instrumental reasons are not typically dealt with by economists.

For example, some decision makers seek advice in order to share accountability for the outcome of the decision (Harvey and Fischer, 1997) and to improve their accuracy (Yaniv, 2004a,b). Advice may even be sought from non-experts whose naive advice might cause the judge to view the problem she faces in new ways (Schotter, 2003) or to get new information (Heath and Gonzalez, 1995). There is also evidence that seeking advice from multiple advisors leads to better-quality decisions (Budescu and Rantilla, 2000; Yaniv and Kleinberger, 2000; Johnson et al., 2001; Yaniv, 2004a). In such studies the optimal way to weight expert opinions plays a crucial role.

Once advice is received, whether it is solicited, offered in an unsolicited fashion, or paid for, the question arises as to whether the decision maker should listen to it. One prominent finding in the literature is that judges are hesitant to accept the advice of others.[11] This stems from a type of egocentric advice discounting (Yaniv and Kleinberger, 2000; Yaniv, 2004a,b) where people discount the advice of others because, while they understand the thought process they use to think through the problem at hand, they are uncertain about how the advisor came to their conclusion. Others view the discounting of advice as stemming from an anchoring and adjusting heuristic used by the judge in which she anchors her choice using her own decision and then inadequately adjusts it as she receives advice (Lim and O'Connor, 1995; Harvey and Fischer, 1997), while yet others merely think they are better than others (Krueger, 2003) and have an egocentric bias. Despite this tendency for people to dismiss advice, there is an exception to this rule when the advisor clearly has greater expertise or when the judge is aware of her own deficiencies in dealing with the problem at hand. It is also true that judges evaluate the quality of the advisor and the reputation of the advice giver and discount it accordingly. Finally, the characteristics of the advisor may also be relevant, where more weight is given to advisors who are older, more educated, and are seen as wise (Feng and MacGeorge, 2006). Advice is also listened to more often when it is paid for in advance.

Finally the question arises as to whether the presence of advice is welfare-improving. Since this is an efficiency question, it is obviously of interest to economists. In the psychology literature this boils down to whether the judge's accuracy is increased by being

---

[11] As we will see later, this discounting of advice is not a feature of the work we will present here, where, in most of the experiments we will report, advice tends to be followed.

able to solicit or receive advice from an advisor or group of advisors. The answer seems to be generally yes, but with some exceptions. For example, there seems to be a consensus that receiving advice from multiple advisors whose opinions are uncorrelated provides the judge with information that can increase her accuracy of decision making (see Gardner and Berry, 1995; Sniezek et al., 2004; Yaniv, 2004a,b). However, while decision accuracy seems to be enhanced when receiving uncorrelated advice with a potentially large variance across opinions, the confidence in that advice is decreasing in its variance and hence highest when there is a consensus.

For our concerns in this book, the impact of advice is more complex and nuanced. For example, in the JAS the accuracy question boils down to whether collecting and processing advice is beneficial assuming one can find the proper way to combine or weight the advice and information contained in expert opinions (see Budescu and Rantilla, 2000; Budescu et al., 2003). That is a natural concern since in the JAS literature the problems faced by the decision maker are all one-person decision problems with an objectively correct answer or decision. In what we will discuss in this book, however, the advice received is about how to behave in a strategic situation where a person is interacting with other people all of whom have also received advice about what to do from their predecessors in the game they are engaged in and where each person's actions affect the payoffs of all the others. This setting is far more complex and liable to have advice that is welfare-decreasing.

In summary, the psychology literature has provided answers to many of the questions of interest about advice. They investigate whose advice you would like to listen to, what confidence you have in your opinion both before and after receiving advice, and which type of advisors are viewed as more valuable. They are also interested in whether advice increases decision performance, etc. These are probably the questions first and foremost in the minds of people who are interested in advice giving and receiving. As we've seen, economists are interested in a totally different set of questions. This has to do with the need for economists to structure their research differently and do so through the lens of equilibrium analysis. While such a focus has many benefits, it also constrains the type of questions that can be asked and answered.

2.5 WHAT'S NEXT?

This chapter has discussed one of the main ideas of this book – advice. Before we can proceed to our analysis in this book, however, we still need to discuss the three other building blocks of our work – social learning, conventions, and intergenerational games. This is what we turn our attention to in our next chapter.

In Chapter 3 we will try to define what a convention of behavior is, starting with the definition offered by Lewis (1969) and offering some modifications. We then distinguish the type of social learning we use in our work here from the standard approach to social learning in the economics literature. Finally, we offer a formal definition of an intergenerational game and use that game to discuss the stability of conventions of behavior. All of this analysis is presented as a prerequisite for our applications which start in Chapter 4.

REFERENCES

Agranov, M., Dasgupta, U. and Schotter, A. (2020). Trust me: Communication and competition in psychological games. *Working Paper.*

Akerlof, G. A. and Snower, D. J. (2016). Bread and bullets. *Journal of Economic Behavior and Organization,* 126, 58–71.

Benabou, R., Falk, A. and Tirole, J. (2020). Narratives, imperatives, and moral persuasion. *NBER Working Paper.*

Bisin, A. and Verdier, T. (1998). On the cultural transmission of preferences for social status. *Journal of Public Economics,* 70(1), 75–97.

Bisin, A. and Verdier, T. (2000). "Beyond the melting pot": cultural transmission, marriage and the evolution of ethnic and religious traits. *Quarterly Journal of Economics,* 115(3), 955–988.

Bonaccio, S. and Dalal, R. S. (2006). Advice taking and decision-making: An integrative literature review, and implications for the organizational sciences. *Organizational Behavior and Human Decision Processes,* 101(2), 127–151.

Brehmer, B. and Hagafors, R. (1986). Use of experts in complex decision-making: A paradigm for the study of staff work. *Organizational Behavior and Human Decision Processes*, 38(2), 181–195.

Budescu, D. V. and Rantilla, A. K. (2000). Confidence in aggregation of expert opinions. *Acta Psychologica*, 104(3), 371–398.

Budescu, D. V., Rantilla, A. K., Yu, H. T. and Karelitz, T. M. (2003). The effects of asymmetry among advisors on the aggregation of their opinions. *Organizational Behavior and Human Decision Processes*, 90(1), 178–194.

Chakraborty, A. and Harbaugh, R. (2010). Persuasion by cheap talk. *American Economic Review*, 100(5), 2361–2382.

Che, Y. K. and Kartik, N. (2009). Opinions as incentives. *Journal of Political Economy*, 117(5), 815–860.

Chen, Y. (2011). Perturbed communication games with honest senders and naive receivers. *Journal of Economic Theory*, 146(2), 401–424.

Chen, Y., Kartik, N. and Sobel, J. (2007). On the robustness of informative cheap talk. *Econometrica*, 76(1), 117–136.

Crawford, V. P. and Sobel, J. (1982). Strategic information transmission. *Econometrica*, 50(6), 1431–1451.

Dewatripont, M. and Tirole, J. (1999). Advocates. *Journal of Political Economy*, 107(1), 1–39.

Dur, R. and Swank, O. H. (2005). Producing and manipulating information. *Economic Journal*, 115(500), 185–199.

Erev, I. and Roth, A. E. (1998). Predicting how people play games: Reinforcement learning in experimental games with unique, mixed strategy equilibria. *American Economic Review*, 88(4), 848–881.

Feng, B. and MacGeorge, E. L. (2006). Predicting receptiveness to advice: Characteristics of the problem, the advice-giver, and the recipient. *Southern Communication Journal*, 71(1), 67–85.

Frankfurt, H. (2005). *On Bullshit*. Princeton, NJ: Princeton University Press.

Garcia, J. and Fernández, F. (2015). A comprehensive survey on safe reinforcement learning. *Journal of Machine Learning*, 16(1), 1437–1480.

Gardner, P. H. and Berry, D. C. (1995). The effect of different forms of advice on the control of a simulated complex system. *Applied Cognitive Psychology*, 9(7), S55–S79.

Goltsman, M., Hörner, J., Pavlov, G. and Squintani, F. (2009). Mediation, arbitration, and negotiation. *Journal of Economic Theory*, 144(4), 1397–1420.

Green, J. R. and Stokey, N. L. (2007). A two-person game of information transmission. *Journal of Economic Theory*, 135(1), 90–104.

Harvey, N. and Fischer, I. (1997). Taking advice: Accepting help, improving judgment, and sharing responsibility. *Organizational Behavior and Human Decision Processes*, 70(2), 117–133.

Heath, C. and Gonzalez, R. (1995). Interaction with others increases decision confidence but not decision quality: Evidence against information collection views of interactive decision-making. *Organizational Behavior and Human Decision Processes*, 61(3), 305–326.

Jerrim, J., Parker, P. and Shure, N. (2019). Bullshitters, who are they and what do we know about their lives? *Discussion Paper*, IZA DP No. 12282.

Johnson, T. R., Budescu, D. V. and Wallsten, T. S. (2001). Averaging probability judgments: Monte Carlo analyses of diagnostic value. *Journal of Behavioral Decision Making*, 14(2), 123–140.

Kahneman, D. (2011). *Thinking Fast and Slow.* New York, NY: Farrar, Strauss and Giroux.

Kartik, N. (2009). Strategic communication with lying costs. *Review of Economic Studies*, 76(4), 1359–1395.

Krueger, J. I. (2003). Return of the ego – Self-referent information as a filter for social prediction: Comment on Karniol. *Psychological Review*, 110(1), 585–590.

Lewis, D. (1969). *Convention: A Philosophical Study.* Cambridge, MA: Harvard University Press.

Lim, J. S. and O'Connor, M. (1995). Judgmental adjustment of initial forecasts: Its effectiveness and biases. *Journal of Behavioral Decision Making*, 8(3), 149–168.

Merlo, A. and Schotter, A. (1999). A surprise-quiz view of learning in economic experiments. *Games and Economic Behavior*, 28(1), 25–54.

Merlo, A. and Schotter, A. (2003). Learning by not doing: An experimental investigation of observational learning. *Games and Economic Behavior*, 42(1), 116–136.

Nishimura, H. and Ok, E. A. (2020). Preference structures. *Working Paper.*

Nyarko, Y. and Schotter, A. (2002). An experimental study of belief learning using elicited beliefs. *Econometrica*, 70(3), 971–1005.

Olszewski W. (2004). Informal communication. *Journal of Economic Theory*, 117(2), 180–200.

Ottaviani, M. and Sørensen, P. N. (2006). Professional advice. *Journal of Economic Theory*, 126(1), 120–142.

Rubinstein, A. (2007). Instinctive and cognitive reasoning: A study of response times. *Economic Journal*, 117(523), 1243–1259.

Schotter, A. (2003). Decision making with naive advice. *American Economic Review*, 93(2), 196–201.

Shiller, R. (2019). *Narrative Economics: How Stories Go Viral and Drive Major Economic Events.* Princeton, NJ: Princeton University Press.

Sniezek, J. A. and Buckley, T. (1995). Cueing and cognitive conflict in judge–advisor decision making. *Organizational Behavior and Human Decision Processes*, 62(2), 159–174.

Sniezek, J. A., Schrah, G. E. and Dalal, R. S. (2004). Improving judgment with prepaid expert advice. *Journal of Behavioral Decision Making*, 17(3), 173–190.

Sobel, J. (2013). Giving and receiving advice. *Advances in Economics and Econometrics*, 1, 305–341.

Thaler, R. H. and Sunstein, C. R. (2009). *Nudge: Improving Decisions About Health, Wealth and Happiness.* New Haven, CT: Yale University Press.

Yaniv, I. (2004a). The benefit of additional opinions. *Current Directions in Psychological Science*, 13(2), 75–78.

Yaniv, I. (2004b). Receiving other people's advice: Influence and benefit. *Organizational Behavior and Human Decision Processes*, 93(1), 1–13.

Yaniv, I. and Kleinberger, E. (2000). Advice taking in decision making: Egocentric discounting and reputation formation. *Organizational Behavior and Human Decision Processes*, 83(2), 260–281.

3 Conventions, Social Learning, and Intergenerational Games

In addition to advice, which we discussed in Chapter 2, much of what we do in this book revolves around the concepts of intergenerational games, conventions, and social learning. These concepts appear at different times and in different contexts but are ever present in our analysis. In this chapter we start by defining an intergenerational game and its equilibria. We then discuss conventions of behavior, their relationship to intergenerational-game equilibria, and what it takes to make such conventions stable. This is followed by describing the relationship between our use of the term "social learning" and what standard economic theory interprets it to mean. At the end of the chapter we discuss two other types of games, dynastic games (Anderlini et al., 2008) and overlapping-generations games (Kandori, 1992), which also have generational structures.

Throughout the chapter we try to minimize formality whenever possible. In the appendix in Section 3.7 we present a more formal definition of an intergenerational game and its equilibrium. By the end of this chapter we should have all the tools and concepts needed to start to apply our ideas.

3.1 SUPERGAMES AND INTERGENERATIONAL GAMES

As discussed in Chapter 1, the central problem for society is how to solve a set of strategic societal problems (societal games) it faces. The solution to these problems determines a matrix of conventions of behavior that help define a society's culture. Different societies may create different conventions to solve the same set of problems because typically the games defined by these problems have multiple solutions.

The important point, however, is that these societal problems are recurrent, which means that how we behave today in the face of them is dynamic and depends on the advice we receive from previous generations who have engaged in these problems before us.

Since societal games are recurrent games, they are typically viewed by economists as "supergames" or games with infinite horizons played by a set of infinitely lived players. The literature on these games is both elegant and extensive, comprising both theoretical and experimental papers (for classical results on folk theorems and repeated games, see Aumann and Shapley (1994); see Rubinstein (1994) for games with undiscounted payoffs; and see Fudenberg and Maskin (1986) for games with discounted payoffs). A review of the experimental literature on indefinitely repeated prisoner's dilemma games can be found in Dal Bó and Fréchette (2018).

We depart from this literature by making one simple observation, which is that while games may have infinite lives, the people who play them have only finite lives and when their participation in the game ends they must hand their participation over to a new generation of players who will take their place in the game for some finite length of time. When this occurs, because each generation cares about its successor, it passes on advice to them as to how to behave in the game they are about to engage in.

In our work here, we assume that generations are non-overlapping in the sense that all generational players arrive to participate in the game at the same time and leave or die at the same time. Other, overlapping-generations structures could be used, but we restrict our games to having non-overlapping generations in order to place the focus of attention on the advice passed down from generation to generation and not on the, often complicated, generational strategies needed to enforce equilibria in overlapping generations models. We present one such overlapping model later in this chapter when we discuss the work of Kandori (1992) and also another non-overlapping model of generational play when we discuss the theory of dynastic games (Anderlini et al., 2008).

In studying such intergenerational games we are mostly concerned with what happens in the transition between generations. Are the conventions of behavior (or intergenerational-game equilibria) developed by previous players transmitted intact to the next generation or are they modified or even abandoned? Is there continuity across time or is behavior variable? Is there convergence to an equilibrium that corresponds to the equilibrium of the same game played by infinitely lived players? Since these games may have a multitude of equilibria, are different equilibria selected by succeeding generations? These are all questions that we are interested in.

In the intergenerational games we look at, when new generations arrive to engage in the game, they receive advice from those who have just played the game before them, and know their opponents also received advice, but not what it is. They observe all, part, or none of the history of actions of previous generations, and then choose an action for themselves in every period of their participation. Departing generations, after having played the game for K periods, send advice to their successors after observing their own payoff during their lifetime. In other words, when a generation departs they know the history in the game they just engaged in as well as the payoff they, and others, received and, based on that, leave advice for the next generation. In our experiments, advice can be in the form of a full strategy, a free-form essay explaining what to do and why, or both.

To ensure that each generation cares about its progeny and offers them good advice, we will assume that the payoff of player i in generation t, U_{it}, depends both on the material payoff they receive during their lifetime, π_{it}, plus some fraction, λ, of the material payoff of its immediate successor, π_{it+1}. More simply, people care about themselves and their children but not their grandchildren or their successors.[1] Similarly, while people may care about their friends to

---

[1] Note that the utility of a generation t player is defined over her material payoff and the material payoff of her immediate successor but not the utility of her immediate successor. This may introduce a conflict of interest between the advisor and advisee since, while the advisor does not care about the payoff of her generation $t + 2$ successor (her grandchildren), her immediate successor in generation $t + 1$ (her child)

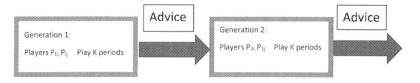

FIGURE 3.1 Intergenerational games.

whom they offer advice, they tend not to care about the friends of their friends. While this can be generalized, we never do so in the experiments we present and hence will simply adhere to this assumption throughout what we do here.

Our generational-game setup can be presented schematically as in Figure 3.1.

As we see in Figure 3.1, each generation plays the game for a finite number, K, of periods, and then passes off its participation to the next generation to whom it offers advice and cares about via the caring parameter λ. This simple structure yields very rich behavior in the lab. When $K = 1$, as will be true for almost all of our experiments, the pay-off for player i in generation t is: $U_{it}(s_t, s_{t+1}) = \pi_{it}(s_t) + \lambda \pi_{it+1}(s_{t+1})$, where s_t and s_{t+1} are the strategy profiles of the generational players in generations t and $t+1$.

In the appendix in Section 3.7 we present a more formal definition of an intergenerational game and its equilibria for those who desire it. However, given our discussion so far we can define an equilibrium to an intergenerational game in the usual way as a combination of intergenerational-game strategies that no player wishes to deviate from under the assumption that the others are also adhering to it. This requires that each player plays her part in the stage game strategy prescribed by the equilibrium and then passes on advice to the next generation to do so as well. In order to be an equilibrium,

does. Despite this possibility we consider the advice offered as being in good faith in maximizing the generation $t + 1$'s agent's material payoff.

however, the players have to have faith that their opponents have received the equilibrium advice and are willing to follow it. Such a set of beliefs we will call a norm and the behavior associated with it (via best responses) a convention.

Given our intergenerational-game setup, there are some features of its equilibrium that are worth discussing. First, we restrict our analysis to the class of strategies where players' advice and actions are a function only of what they observe during their lifetimes and the lifetimes of their immediate predecessor. What this means is that our players do not condition their actions or advice on any part of history that does not involve themselves or their parents. In this sense the strategies are Markovian in the last generation stage-game outcome in that, for any generational player, they depend only on the state of the game (actions chosen) in the generation immediately preceding theirs and on the advice they receive. As a result, our players do not condition their actions on distant history or any action that does not enter directly into their payoff function. An identical assumption is made by Anderlini et al. (2008) in their analysis of dynastic games. They do, however, consider the advice they receive from their predecessor.

Also, unlike players in supergames, players in intergenerational games cannot commit their distant descendants to complex history-dependent strategies or even a grim-trigger strategy since they will not be alive to carry out such strategies and do not even care what their distant descendants do since their actions are not payoff-relevant for them. They can only take actions in the stage game played during their lifetime and advising their immediate successor. In equilibrium, because of the recursive structure of our generational strategies, we could observe behavior that appears equivalent to a grim-trigger strategy since, if any generation deviates from a proposed equilibrium, that deviation can be punished by all generations that follow. However, deviations by generations beyond one's immediate successor are payoff-irrelevant and hence do not factor in to the decision for any player to deviate.[2] They only care about the payoffs of the next generation via their caring parameter λ.

The type of strategies described above are very much like the ones we observe in our experiments in terms of both the actions chosen and the advice offered. For this reason we consider that confining ourselves to these Markov-like strategies makes sense.

Second, because our equilibrium includes a prescription for the advice that one generation is supposed to send to the next, our players must have faith that such advice was sent and will be followed. Such a set of beliefs is not easy to establish and, in the experiments discussed in Chapters 7 and 8, we will see that establishing such beliefs may require that the advice passed on from generation to generation be common knowledge or almost-common knowledge. In this sense the ability to establish the type of self-confirming beliefs required for a Nash equilibrium is slightly more complicated in such games.

Finally, in much of what we do here, a convention of behavior will be a selected equilibrium of the intergenerational game that our players are engaged in. However, conventions may also be something more informal than that and merely be a regularity of behavior that people engage in because they were taught to do so without even thinking of its strategic relevance. It's just traditional behavior.[3]

For such behavior we do not necessarily know why the convention exists or even what purpose it serves, but we are happy to follow it because it at least tells us what to do, which allows us to avoid wasting time thinking about it.

For example, there is an old story of a Jewish mother making pot roast for Passover. Her son-in-law is watching her as she cuts the tip off the pot roast and throws it away. He asks her why she did it and she says "I did it because my mother did it". Because the entire family was gathered for the holiday, the son-in-law asks the grandmother why

---

[2] This may leave future generations free to renegotiate inefficient outcomes but we will not impose any requirement for renegotiation-proof conventions.

[3] In the musical *Fiddler on the Roof*, the opening song is entitled "Tradition", which basically says we do what we do because it is traditional – we do not question it.

she threw the tip of the pot roast away and she said "I did it because my mother did". So luckily the great-grandmother was alive and at the dinner and he asked her why she threw the tip away and she said "My pot was too small".

This story illustrates conventional behavior. It is behavior that people just do because they were taught to do it even if the reason why they do it has vanished. The current mother's pot was more than big enough to cook the pot roast but she followed convention just the same.

We don't judge the reasons for adhering to a convention. While in our formalization conventional behavior is equilibrium behavior, we should not lose sight of the fact that some behavior we consider conventional is merely mindless adherence to what we were taught as a child.

3.2   NORMS AND CONVENTIONS

As our intergenerational games evolve over time there are two objects of interest. One is what we will call a norm which we will define as a set of beliefs, one for each player, defining what choice they expect their generational opponent (or opponents) will take in their stage-game interaction. In other words, norms are beliefs about the behavior of players during their lifetime in the repeated societal game. Norms exist in the space of beliefs.

While beliefs in the stage game are defined over the actions of one's opponent, in the intergenerational game a player has to also define beliefs over what advice she thinks her opponent received and whether her opponent is likely to follow it. Beliefs over actions in the stage game should provide a sufficient statistic for these compound probabilities.[4]

---

[4] When we review the work of Anderlini et al. (2008) we will see that beliefs over advice play a crucial role, but in that case subjects are deprived of the history or play and advice is not a suggestion but a statement about what actions were taken by the previous generation.

Conventions, on the other hand, are the behavioral responses to existing norms. They are what people do when they have expectations about others. They exist in the space of actions.

In the literature on norms and conventions this distinction is many times lost or at least blurred.[5] Scholars tend to use these two terms interchangeably but for our purposes here we make a clear distinction between norms, which are beliefs about behavior, and conventions, which are behaviors chosen in response to beliefs or norms. Further, the beliefs we define are beliefs over the actions of one's opponent. These will be the beliefs that we elicit in our experiments.

Although the term convention is widely used, there is some controversy over exactly what a convention of behavior is. The first person to attempt a formal definition was David Lewis in his famous book *Convention*. In that book Lewis (1969, p. 76) defines a convention as follows:

Definition A regularity R in the behavior of members of a population P when they are agents in a recurrent situation S is a convention if and only if it is true that, and it is common knowledge in P that, in any instance of S among members of P:

- everyone conforms to R;
- everyone expects everyone else to conform to R;
- everyone has approximately the same preferences regarding all possible combinations of actions;
- everyone prefers that everyone conform to R, on condition that at least all but one conform to R;
- everyone would prefer that everyone conform to R', on condition that at least all but one conform to R', where R' is some possible regularity in the behavior of members of P in S, such that no one in any instance of S among members of P could conform both to R' and to R.

This definition has a number of features that have led people to criticize it (see Rescorla, 2019). For example, it appears that this

---

[5] See Bicchieri (2016) and many others for example.

definition is only applicable to pure coordination problems which are self-enforcing and hence do not need punishments to enforce them. As Sugden (2004), Schotter (1981), and others have noted, there are a variety of other problems where conventions are needed that are not pure coordination games and where punishments may be needed.

For example, in public goods games (or prisoner's dilemma games in general), there is a unique equilibrium where free riding (or defection) occurs. If one wants to support other behavior, one has to rely on threatening punishments. However, at least in their finitely repeated game setup, Fehr and Gächter (2000) and many others have noted that such punishments may not be rational (i.e., not subgame perfect and hence should not be observed by a set of rational self-interested agents). The fact that they are observed implies that people have reciprocal preferences that allow for such punishments. It is worth pointing out, however, that these are results from experiments which were not run as indefinitely repeated games. In such games punishments can be features of rational equilibrium behavior and do not require non-standard preferences. (See Cabral et al. (2014) for a discussion of an experiment on indefinitely repeated games where punishments are part of the equilibrium but where subjects do not exhibit reciprocal behavior when punishing others, and the work of Dal Bó and Fréchette (2018) on indefinitely repeated prisoner's dilemma games).

Lewis's definition has also been criticized for requiring that conventions be common knowledge. Binmore (2008), however, has noted that requiring common knowledge may be too strong. For example, among a large population it is very hard for people to achieve it. In addition, common knowledge, even in small groups, may not be necessary for coordination. To illustrate this point he uses Rubinstein's (1989) electronic mail game where two people send messages to each other about coordinating their actions in the future but each message has a positive probability of not being received. As a result, when one player sends a message confirming that he has received the other's message, he is left wondering if his message was received or lost in the mail. This would make common knowledge hard unless people could exchange an infinite number of messages but possibly not even then.

Both Rubinstein (1989) and Binmore (2008) note that, in our daily lives, we often adhere to a coordination plan without all the common-knowledge confirmations or assurances we need. We don't need common knowledge or (as we discuss in Chapter 7) even almost-common knowledge, what Monderer and Samet (1989) call common p-beliefs, to act. What we might call almost-common knowledge may be enough or even less than that. For example, we make plans to meet our friends for lunch after only one email exchange of the following type:

First person: "Want to have lunch tomorrow?"

Second person: "Yes see you at Ernie's Bar at 1."

First person: "OK."

In almost all cases both people show up at Ernie's despite the finite number of messages exchanged.[6]

More recently, a new and very interesting philosophical study of conventions has been written by Vanderschraaf (2018) where he looks at conventions as systems of fairness or at least having fairness consequences. In his definition of a convention he allows social agents to employ correlated equilibria, which allows them to condition their joint actions on random events.

3.3 FORWARD INDUCTION AND STABLE EQUILIBRIUM CONVENTIONS

It is one thing for a convention to exist at a given time t and yet another for that convention to be stable or persistent. To define a stable equilibrium convention for an intergenerational game we need to look at the temptations to deviate from the convention once it is established and the signal that such a deviation conveys to the

---

[6] In fairness to Lewis, he did recognize that full common knowledge might be hard to achieve and offered a definition of a convention which has an "almost-common knowledge" ring to it.

next generation about the intentions of the deviating player and her successors. More precisely, it is not enough that the convention defines a Nash equilibrium. To be stable, it needs to be robust against forward induction arguments.

To be more precise, note that almost all stage games we will look at will contain multiple Nash equilibria. When there are multiple equilibria, each benefiting a different group of players, one must be chosen as *the* convention of behavior defining behavior in the game. As a result, the conventions we consider will most often be a selection of one of the multiple equilibria of the stage game which will be selected and then passed down from generation to generation via intergenerational advice. In order to be stable, however, there must be a set of strategies for the intergenerational game that prevents any player from deviating.

Put differently, a generational player might want to deviate from a convention if she thought that such a deviation might change behavior in the stage game played by her successor and lead them to select an equilibrium that was better for both her and her successor. Since such a deviation would decrease one's material payoff during one's lifetime, it must be the case that such a loss will be compensated for by altering the selected equilibrium in the next generation for which the current generation benefits by $\lambda \pi_{it+1}$, where π_{it+1} is the payoff of the generation $t + 1$ successor of player i in generation t. If this is not possible or likely, then no one will deviate.

To consider how a player might contemplate such a deviation, assume that a player enters a stage game in generation t. Say, the game is a simple 2×2 game with strategy sets $S^1 = (s_1^1, s_2^1)$ for player 1 and $S^2 = (s_1^2, s_2^2)$ for player 2. Further, say there are two pure-strategy stage-game equilibria, $\varepsilon^1 = (s_1^1, s_1^2)$ and $\varepsilon^2 = (s_2^1, s_2^2)$ (we will not consider the mixed strategy equilibrium for ease of exposition) and that at equilibrium ε^1 the payoff for player 1 is greater than that of player 2 while at ε^2 the opposite is true. Assume there currently exists a convention where players play according to the equilibrium ε^2 which happens to be best for player 1's opponent (player 2) and worse for player 1.

To complete our description, assume that there are two subsets of beliefs, Σ^{ε^1} and Σ^{ε^2}, jointly defining the players first-order beliefs about what each player expects their opponent to play in the generation-t stage game. We call these subsets the best-response subsets for ε^1 and ε^2 respectively since, if beliefs jointly are in Σ^{ε^1}, then the best response for each player is to play according to equilibrium ε^1 while, if beliefs jointly are in Σ^{ε^2}, then the best response for each player is to play according to equilibrium ε^2. In other words, beliefs in Σ^{ε^1} support the stage-game equilibrium ε^1 while beliefs in Σ^{ε^2} support the stage-game equilibrium ε^2.

If equilibrium ε^2 is in place in generation t, player 1 might contemplate a deviation since that equilibrium is worse for him and future players of his type.[7] After such a deviation, new beliefs will be held by the next generation and those beliefs will be influenced not only by the deviation itself but also by the advice that all players receive after it occurs and the generation-t outcome determined. The reason for deviating is to influence the beliefs of future generations in an effort to switch the equilibrium convention in the stage game.[8]

Given this setup it should be clear that, in order for a deviation from any equilibrium in the stage game to be beneficial for a player, two things must happen. First, the deviation must shift the equilibrium played in the next generation to one that is better for the deviating player than the existing equilibrium. In order to do this it must shift beliefs sufficiently to move behavior from the current equilibrium to a better one. Second, such a deviation must be profitable in the sense that, since the player is unilaterally deviating from a Nash equilibrium in the generation-t stage game, her payoff

---

[7] A player need not deviate to a stage-game equilibrium strategy since a deviation to any strategy could be entertained. Of course in our example there are only two strategies and each is associated with a particular equilibrium.

[8] This discussion concerns two-player games. Obviously in large communities deviations by one player will not be noticed. Hence, in such communities deviations will have to be carried out via coalitions of players in a coordinated manner. Such coordination, if successful, can lead to revolutions, currency attacks, or coup d'états. They have to alter beliefs sufficiently to lead people to think the deviation (revolution) will succeed.

will be decreased and hence the discounted payoff she receives from the next generation, $\lambda \pi_{t+1}^i$, must be sufficient to compensate her for her generation-t loss. Note that the only payoff-relevant time periods are t and $t + 1$. The players have no interest in outcomes outside of those two periods.

3.3.1 Stable Conventions in the Battle of the Sexes Games

To illustrate the connection between forward induction and stable conventions consider a twice-repeated battle of the sexes game, i.e., not an intergenerational game but rather just a twice-repeated battle of the sexes game played by the same set of people (Table 3.1). Let us use the payoffs of the battle of the sexes game used in Schotter and Sopher (2003) and to be discussed later.

In this twice-repeated version of the battle of the sexes (with no discounting) consider the subgame perfect equilibrium where the equilibrium strategy pair $\varepsilon^1 = \{1, 1\}$ is repeated in each of the two periods. While this equilibrium is subgame perfect, since the prescribed behavior is a Nash equilibrium in both stage games, it is not robust to forward induction.

To see this say that player 2, who is getting the smaller payoff of 50 in each period, decides to deviate in period 1 and play according to the other stage-game equilibrium $\varepsilon^2 = \{2, 2\}$ where both players choose strategy 2. By deviating in this way the column player would receive a zero payoff during her lifetime since the row player would continue to choose row 1. After such a deviation player 1 must conclude that player 2 has rejected playing her part in the $\{1,1\}$

Table 3.1 *Battle of the sexes game.*

		Player 2	
		1	2
Player 1	1	150, 50	0, 0
	2	0, 0	50, 150

equilibrium in period 2 and must be looking to play strategy 2 since, if she continued to play strategy 1 in both periods, she would earn 50 in each but by deviating, and getting 0 in period 1, she must be looking to play strategy 2 in period 2 and get the 150, leaving her with 150 over the two periods rather than 100. Note that such a deviation will be successful if it changes the beliefs of player 1 as to what player 2 intends to do in period 2. In this twice-repeated game such an inference is the only one that player 1 could logically make (if she assumed that player 2 was rational) and hence such a deviation will be successful in ruling out the equilibrium where subjects play ε^1 in both periods. There is no other belief that makes sense for player 1 to hold after player 2's deviation.

The situation is far more complicated when the game is inter-generational. This is true because there is not the same set of players playing across the generations and each is receiving private advice. This creates a great deal more uncertainty as to what the intentions are of player 2 in generation 2 after a deviation in generation 1.

For example, say that the ε^1 has been in place for 100 genera-tions and generational player 101 playing the role of player 2 decides she wants to deviate. She does so and sends advice to her generation-102 successor that she should also play according to ε^2. The question now is what beliefs should player 2 (player 1) in generation 102 hold about the intentions of the generation-102 player 1 (player 2)? Does she think that the generation-102 player 1 (player 2) has concluded that she should abandon the ε^1 convention and play according to ε^2? The answer is not clear. First of all both players may conclude that the deviating player in generation 101 was a nut job who acted erratically. Hence, maybe her deviation will be discounted by both generation-102 players. Remember that in generation 102 we have a new set of players and the generation-102 player 1 is not the same person who deviated in generation 101.

Second, both players in generation 102 will receive advice from their predecessors and both have to form beliefs not only about what the other player has been advised but also about whether they will follow the advice they think their opponent was given. It may be that the generation-102 player-2 type will conclude that the generation-101 player-1 type will advise his successor to ignore the deviation and continue to play according to ε^1. All of these doubts translate into a great deal of uncertainty amongst the generation-102 players about whether the period-t norm has been switched from the belief-best response set Σ^{ε_1}, which supports the ε^1, to the belief-best response set Σ^{ε_2}, which supports ε^2.

Hence, unlike the twice-repeated case, the mere deviation from an established convention in an intergenerational game will not, in general, be enough to switch the norm from Σ^{ε_1} to Σ^{ε_2} and hence the convention from ε^1 to ε^2. If one insists that the post-deviation beliefs or intentions be common knowledge among the set of players in order for the deviation to be successful, this is unlikely to happen when one isolated deviation occurs.

It is this uncertainty that exists in intergenerational games about the intentions of others caused by the introduction of new players each period and the privacy of advice that, ironically, might enhance the stability of conventions by making the interpretation of deviations difficult and less than common knowledge. We will see this same uncertainty existing across generations later in this chapter when we discuss the Anderlini et al. (2008) model where uncertainty is created by private intergenerational messages informing future generations about the history of play of the game. However, it is important to point out that, as might be expected, such uncertainty can also lead to instability as we will soon see in Chapter 4.

3.3.2   Stable Conventions in the Lab

To illustrate the conditions needed for convention stability, consider data from the first thirteen generations of an intergenerational battle of the sexes game discussed in Chapter 4 using the payoffs presented in Figure 3.2.

In Figure 3.2 we have placed generations or time on the horizontal axis and the four possible stage-game outcomes on the vertical

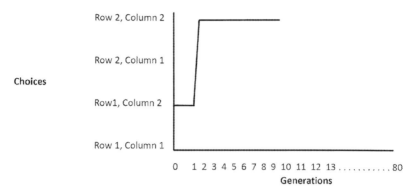

FIGURE 3.2 Path of play of the battle of the sexes game experiment.

axis so the graph traces the time series of behavior across generations of subjects or across time. Note that the outcome {Row 1, Column 1} is the outcome that is best for the row player where she gets the 150 payoff while the column player gets 50, while the {Row 2, Column 2} outcome indicates the outcome that is best for the column player where she gets the 150. Mixed outcomes {1,2} or {2,1} yield zero payoffs.

As we see in Figure 3.2 subjects start out by failing to coordinate their actions in generations 1 and 2 and hence each receives a payoff of zero. However, in generation 3 they coordinate on the {2,2} equilibrium and each generation keeps playing according to that equilibrium for the next 10 periods. According to what we have said above one would have thought that at this point a stable convention of behavior must have been established since no player should want to deviate when playing their stage game nor suggest that their successors do so either.

To demonstrate this, it is obvious that the column player has no incentive to deviate since she is receiving her best payoff of 150 in each generation. So the only player who would want to deviate would be the row player since she is receiving 50 during her lifetime and one half of 50 for her successor's payoff. The question is, can she profitably deviate? The answer is no. If she adheres to the current convention she will received 50 during her lifetime and one half of 50 for the payoff of her successor. Hence her total payoff will be 75. If, however, the row player deviates during her lifetime she will receive 0 rather than 50, so she will suffer by the deviation, but she will hope that that deviation changes the beliefs of her successor's opponent so as to change the stage-game equilibrium in the next generation from {2,2} to {1,1} which would determine a payoff for her successor of 150. If that occurs, then her payoff would again be 75 since she would get 0 during her lifetime but one half of 150 for the payoff of her successor.

Note that such a deviation is unlikely to occur. First, there is no positive benefit from deviating since, given the payoffs we are using, such a deviation can, at best, make the row player indifferent between adhering to the current convention and deviating. More importantly, the row player can only achieve a payoff of 75 if her deviation makes it 100% certain that both her successor and her opponent's successor switch from the {2,2} equilibrium to the {1,1} equilibrium in the next generation. In other words, the next generation norm must predict the {1,1} equilibrium with certainty. Any doubt about the effect of the deviation on the next generation's beliefs (even one where the probability of switching the convention from {2,2} to {1,1} is 0.99) will make the deviation unprofitable. The row player must be 100% certain about the impact of her deviation on the play of her successor and her beliefs.[9]

Of course, things are different if the payoffs are different. For example, say that we increase the big 150 payoff to 200 for both players and leave the 50 payoff intact. This will increase the potential payoff to the row player from deviating since it will increase what the row player receives from the next generation if she is successful in altering norms sufficiently so as to switch the convention from

---

[9] In the experiment generating this data it turns out that, despite the logic of the argument just made, the very next pair of subjects who entered this game both simultaneously deviated from the {2,2} convention. Such deviations are unavoidable since people tend to exhibit stochastic behavior in all aspects of their lives and some are simply contrarians. For these reasons we will observe in our experiments far more variability in behavior than theory might predict. Such variability makes life interesting.

{2,2} to {1,1}. Because of this increased payoff the row player will need less assurance that her deviation will be successful since the benefits of deviation have increased. In fact when the big payoff is 200 the row player will only need to have a probability of 0.75 in order to want to deviate and try to switch conventions. When the big payoff is 300, the probability drops to 0.50. This would suggest, as we might expect, that the greater the benefits of deviating from a convention, the less stable that convention is likely to be. While this is true in theory, our experiments demonstrate that we can observe instability in a convention even when the deviating party has little or no positive incentive to do so. In other words, there is an underlying stochasticity or noise in behavior that is capable of disrupting even the most strongly entrenched convention. Note also that we might expect conventions to be less stable as intergenerational caring extends beyond only the next generation since, in that case, deviations are more lucrative if successful.

Finally, from what we have said it would be expected that any conventions established in large societies are likely to be more stable than those established in small groups since any unilateral deviation by one person in a large society is unlikely to be noticed and hence to affect the beliefs of future generations. To change such beliefs we would need coalitions of subjects to deviate in a coordinated way. Such deviations are possible if there is a device or authority that can coordinate such a collaborative deviation. In the fashion industry this is the role that advertising plays while, as Chwe (2001) describes, in the political realm this may be the role played by large public demonstrations that give people the idea that their planned deviation (a revolution perhaps) may be successful. Demonstrations and marches have had this impact through history in giving people confidence that if they showed their intentions it might sufficiently change existing norms enough to support a new convention or a revolution. We've seen this in the civil rights demonstrations in the American South in the 1960s and during the Black Lives Matter demonstrations in 2020.

3.3.3   Punishments

Note that in our intergenerational games the conventions established need not rely on punishments for their enforcement. As we have just seen, the stability of a convention of behavior can be supported by the uncertainty created by a deviation and the generational players' responses to it in terms of both their beliefs and the advice they offer their successors. Put differently, if it is not certain that your deviation will send a clear enough message about what your successor plans to do in the next generation, then you may not want to deviate now since it is unclear whether the loss you incur today will be paid back tomorrow. In addition, since the games we look at have multiple equilibria, unlike the usual focus on public-goods games with their unique inefficient equilibrium, adherence to the convention need not be supported by punishments since such adherence is an equilibrium. The idea that all conventions need to be policed by punishments in order to be successful follows only if the behavior that needs to be enforced is not an equilibrium.

One final note is that not all conventions are equally stable. That will depend on how strong the norm is supporting them. For example, as we will soon see, if at time t a new generation enters an intergenerational game and all players believe that ε^1 is the established convention with probability 1, it is unlikely that one deviation from that convention will sufficiently shake confidence in it (i.e., change the norms supporting it) so as to flip it to another convention. However, if there is more uncertainty about what to do, i.e., the norms are in the interior of the belief best-response set, then it is possible that a deviation can lead to beliefs jumping from one belief best-response set to another when one deviation occurs and establishes a different convention.

3.4   A NOTE ON SOCIAL LEARNING

As our discussion of intergenerational games suggests, we investigate how the wisdom of the past is passed to the present via intergenerational advice. Not only that but the process we envision is very social in the sense that people actually talk to each other and communicate their suggestions.

This is quite different from the conventional literature on social learning as initiated by Bikhchandani et al. (1992) and Banerjee (1992), and explored in the lab by Anderson and Holt (1997), Çelen and Kariv (2004, 2005), Kübler and Weizsäcker (2003) and others.

The difference between what we do and the standard social learning literature is twofold. In the conventional social learning problem there is an underlying state of the world that is unknown to decision makers but which is payoff-relevant for their decisions. In order to make an optimal choice, people have to infer the true state of the world by observing a noisy private signal about it and the choices made by those decision makers before them (who have also observed a private signal). If they knew the true state of the world their optimal decision would be trivial.

In most of what we do here there is no objectively true payoff-relevant state of the world that needs to be inferred. What there is is a recurrent game played over time by succeeding generations and the question is what convention of behavior governs how any given generation should behave. In other words, generational agents must decide how to behave in a strategic situation where their opponents are trying to figure out the same thing given the advice they received. What needs to be learned is how to behave, what to do, and not what some exogenously determined state of the world is. Note that since generational agents only live for short periods of time, the type of advice offered is typically what we called naive advice since those giving advice have little more experience than those receiving it.

Second, in standard social learning models, there is no intergenerational advice or intergenerational conversations. The only way generations communicate is by later generations being able to observe the actions of their predecessors. In our analysis generations talk directly to each other and suggest strategies as well as offer their thinking about proper behavior in the recurrent game they are all engaged in. If a convention is established they pass it along.

The interesting feature of the social learning literature is that, over time, information may accumulate to the point where no agent in the line of decision makers has an incentive, given the choices of those before her, to update her prior given her private signal but rather just follows the choices of those before them. In other words, the decision makers may enter an information cascade where it is optimal to ignore their signals and follow the pack. Such cascades can herd behavior on the correct or the incorrect decision, yet in either case all decision makers are behaving optimally.

We will arrive at some similar conclusions in what we do here. For example, in Chapter 10 we will look at a standard social learning problem of the Bikhchandani et al. (1992) variety but introduce advice and investigate whether decision makers would rather receive advice from their immediate predecessor rather than see the action she has chosen. Put differently, we investigate whether words speak louder than actions in the sense that, when given a choice, people would rather receive their own signal plus advice from their predecessor rather than their own signal plus the ability to observe their predecessor's action. At the risk of spoiling the punch line, it turns out they prefer advice.

In summation, while we use the words social learning to describe the process of decision making with intergenerational advice, the way we use that term is quite different from its standard usage. As just noted, however, this difference does not prevent us from observing similar types of herding behavior that echoes what we see in the conventional theoretical and experimental literature.

3.5   OTHER GENERATIONAL GAMES

It is important to point out that our work here is not the only work on repeated games with intergenerational agents. Work by Anderlini et al. (2008) and Kandori (1992) also consider such games but from a different perspective. These approaches are interesting and yet, for the most part, untested in the lab so it is important for us to mention them here.[10]

3.5.1   Dynastic Games

Anderlini et al. (2008) have developed a theory of dynastic games which have a structure strikingly similar to what we are discussing here yet was developed independently of our work.

The basic idea behind dynastic games is that the world is composed of dynasties of players who, like intergenerational players, engage in a stage game for one and only one period, receive a payoff, and pass on private messages to their successors. Just as in intergenerational games, the lifetimes of these dynastic players are synchronized so they are born and expire at the same time.

When such dynastic players engage in the stage game, they play a specific role just as our intergenerational agents do, so they are indexed by the role they play in the game, r, and the generation at which they are active, t.

The main way that such games differ from intergenerational games is in their payoff structure. For dynastic games the payoff of a player who engages in the stage game in generation t is equal to the material payoff she receives in her lifetime plus the discounted payoff of all of her successors (players in her dynasty) who take her place and play the game after her. Hence the main difference between these two types of games is that, while in an intergenerational game players care only about themselves and their children, in a dynastic game, when a player enters the game, she views the future in exactly the same way an infinitely lived agent would by discounting future payoffs of her dynasty with a discount rate $\delta \in [0,1]$.

As Anderlini et al. (2008) state, if these dynastic players were allowed to see the history of play before their arrival, then, given the way their payoffs are constructed, infinitely repeated and dynastic

---

[10] While dynastic games have not met with laboratory examination, overlapping-generations games have been explored (see Offerman et al. (2001) for one example).

games would be identical, and the standard folk theorems would apply. To generate a difference Anderlini et al. (2008) deny entering dynastic players the ability to observe the history of play that occurred before their entry. Rather, they receive noisy messages from their immediate predecessors informing them about that history. Because all players are aware that their opponents have also received noisy messages, they are uncertain about what their opponents think the history of play of the game has been before their entry and, as a result, have to define beliefs about what those messages mean.

The final way intergenerational and dynastic games differ is in the messages sent between generations. While in intergenerational games the messages sent across generations are pieces of advice as to how to play, in dynastic games they are messages informing successors about the history of play.

This is similar to the way players in intergenerational games have to define beliefs over the advice their adversaries received even in circumstances where they have access to the entire history of play before them. Interestingly, the uncertainty experienced in these dynastic players allows them to achieve outcomes that would not be possible in standard infinitely repeated games.

In fact, Anderlini et al. (2008) prove what they call a "super folk theorem" which, under mild conditions, states that, when players are sufficiently patient, they can achieve payoffs that are not feasible in the standard supergame with infinitely lived agents. In other words, imposing a generational structure on a standard infinitely repeated game expands the set of attainable equilibria in situations where generational players are not able to observe the previous history of play and must rely on noisy messages from their predecessors.

Rather than go into the details of dynastic games and the proof of the super folk theorem, we will try to explain it using the example Anderlini et al. (2008) offer to motivate their analysis.

This example is simple yet sufficiently rich to provide the intuition about such games. Consider the game shown in Table 3.2. This game will be played twice by two generations of row and column

Table 3.2 *Example dynastic stage game.*

		Dynasty II		
		s_A	s_B	s_C
Dynasty I	s_A	4, 4	−5, 6	1, 3
	s_B	6, −5	3, 3	−10, 2
	s_C	3, 1	2, −10	0, 0

players. At the end of the first period, the two individuals who played the game are replaced by their successors, who play in the second period. There is no discounting. Because there are only two periods the payoff structure is identical to that of an intergenerational game where $\lambda = 1$ so that, as Anderlini et al. (2008) say "each first period 'father' cares about his 'daughter's' payoff as if it were his own". The second-period players only care about their own payoffs since for them there is no tomorrow.

In this example Anderlini et al. (2008) only care about pure strategies. It is clear that, if the daughters could observe the first-period actions, by backward induction, the only subgame perfect equilibrium is one in which (s_B, s_B) is played twice.

Suppose, however, that a daughter cannot observe play in period $t = 1$, but instead receives a private message from her father. With this assumption Anderlini et al. (2008) show that there exists a sequential equilibrium in which (s_A, s_A) is played in the first round, which is not possible if the game was played by the same players twice. In other words, a non-Nash profile is sustainable in the first period. This is so despite the fact that in the standard model the unique stage Nash equilibrium leaves no room for punishment in the second period.

So what Anderlini et al. (2008) are showing is that when we impose a dynastic or generational structure on a standard repeated game, do not allow future generations to observe the actions of their predecessors, and restrict them to relying on messages from their parents about what has occurred, we can expand the set of equilibrium payoffs available to society.[11]

The argument is as follows. Consider a sequential equilibrium in which two messages are used: m^* indicates a message of "no deviation", while m^D indicates "someone's father deviated". The equilibrium prescribes that in the first period each father plays "s_A" and sends m^* to his daughter if (s_A, s_A) was played, and sends m^D otherwise. Each daughter, upon observing the message from her father, plays s_B in the second round if she observes m^* and plays s_C if instead she sees m^D.

The question is, how can each daughter justify playing "s_C" after observing the off-path message m^D? The answer is that this can be done if the player holds the right kind of beliefs when actions are taken that are not expected. This can occur when messages are noisy from father to daughter. For example, say that each father is believed to have erred in the action stage by playing s_B or s_C (instead of s_A) with probability $\varepsilon/4$ each. He is also believed to have sent the wrong message with probability ε. Given these error likelihoods, if a daughter receives message m^D she will believe that her opponent has received m^D or m^* with probability $1/2$ each. Her best response in this case is "s_C". Since (s_C, s_C) provides an effective deterrent in the second period against deviation from (s_A, s_A), each father will choose the prescribed action s_A in the first period.

Note that the example works because there is a societally shared theory of belief formation. Namely, all individuals have a complete and shared theory of the mistakes that might have caused deviations from equilibrium. While this may not be a necessary condition for an equilibrium, this shared belief fills the gap left by generations not being able to view the history before them. Further, note that

---

[11] Note that communication between generations here is not exactly advice but information (albeit noisy information).

while the players share a theory of mistakes, there is a disagreement in the beliefs of fathers and daughters since at the end of their lifetime fathers know what happened in their lifetime but daughters know this only probabilistically and, therefore, hold different beliefs. Hence there is intergenerational disagreement between fathers and daughters. The punch line is that life can be different when games are played across generations.

3.5.2 Overlapping Generations

One feature of intergenerational and dynastic games is that the lives of generational players are synchronized. That means that each generation of player is born and dies on the same date and only interacts with previous players by receiving private advice from them. Since players do not interact across generations, advice is the main vehicle through which they communicate.

There is another way to impose a generational structure on infinitely repeated games played by finitely lived agents, however, and that is to allow asynchronous generations that overlap. In such games the connection to the past is not through advice or messages from previous players but rather through the direct strategic interaction that players of different generations have with each other.

Kandori (1992) depicts the generational structure for such games with three types of players indexed by their type (1,2,3) and the time, t, they are alive and interacting. Each player lives for T periods but they are not synchronized so each new generation arrives K periods after his predecessor and stays in the game for T periods. So at any point in time when a player, of say type 3, enters the game he is playing against players of types 1 and 2 who have entered the game K_1 and $K_1 + K_2$ periods before him.

In this overlapping-generations game, players care only about their own payoffs so there is no intergenerational caring. As a result these games differ from either dynastic games, where players care about the infinite stream of players of their type that will succeed them, or intergenerational games, where players care only about their immediate successor.

What Kandori (1992) wants to demonstrate is that for these overlapping-generations games one can prove the same folk theorems as with infinitely repeated games played by infinitely lived agents, meaning that any feasible and individually rational payoffs can be sustained as a subgame-perfect equilibrium. The condition necessary for the result is that the lifespans and overlapping periods of the lives of generations need to be sufficiently long.

Again we will not explore the proof of this theorem but we will explore its intuition. As Kandori (1992) explains, the problem with maintaining cooperation or adherence to an equilibrium is the fact that when players are about to leave the game their incentives to maintain cooperation decline and ultimately vanish. To maintain their incentives they need to be paid a bonus as they reach retirement to pay them back for previous good behavior. Hence the result is like a bond: players early in their lives have an incentive to police the equilibrium since they face the prospect of a reward at the end of their lives if they do so.

In summation, there are a variety of ways in which one can investigate infinitely repeated games with finitely lived players. Intergenerational games, with its focus on intergenerational advice, is more concerned with the dynamics of conventions of behavior and their stability across generations but both dynastic games and overlapping-generations games do prove that having finitely lived agents is not an impediment to cooperation. Everything, and more, that you can do with infinitely lived agents you can do with finitely lived agents who either communicate over time or overlap strategically.

3.6   CONCLUSION

Our discussion in the first three chapters has put us in a position to start applying our ideas. In Part II we will look at three well-known naturally occurring problems: coordination problems in the form of battle of the sexes games, bargaining problems in the form of ultimatum games, and trust games. All of these games deal with societal problems that we encounter in our daily lives and to which conventions have been established to guide our behavior. We will focus on the transmission of these conventions over time, their stability, and their efficiency.

In general we feel that intergenerational games take a step towards reality. In our daily lives we face recurrent situations or games, some of which are familiar and some not, and we need guidance as to how to behave. These games have infinite lives but we enter them and leave them after a finite amount of time. So there is a tension between the finiteness of our lives and the infinitely lived situations we find ourselves in, and there is a need for some vehicle to connect or tie together the lives of these finitely lived agents with the infinitely lived game they are part of. Advice is that vehicle but we need to understand how the finite–infinite tension mentioned above manifests itself in strategic and learning issues not typically faced by either previous theory or experiments. We aim to take a step in that direction.

3.7   APPENDIX: INTERGENERATIONAL GAMES

We now formally define an intergenerational game and propose a notion of equilibrium for these games. Notice that, in the definitions to follow, we assume that each generation plays the stage game only once. We do this both to simplify notation and because this was the case in most of our experiments. However, the definitions can easily be generalized to cases where the stage game is played more than once. We begin with an auxiliary definition.

Definition   A *n*-players stage game is a tuple $\Gamma = (N, (S_i)_{i=1}^n, (\pi_i)_{i=1}^n)$, where one has the following.

- $N = \{1, \ldots, n\}$ is the set of players.
- For each $i \in N$, S_i is player i's strategy set.

- For each $i \in N$, $\pi_i : S \to \mathbb{R}$ is player i's von Neumann-Morgenstern utility (von Neumann and Morgenstern, 1953), where $S = \prod_{i \in N} S_i$ is the space of strategy profiles.

Definition An **intergenerational game with an a n-players stage game** Γ is a tuple $(\Gamma, \mathcal{P}, (\mathcal{M}_\ell)_{\ell \in \mathcal{P}}, (\mathcal{S}_\ell)_{\ell \in \mathcal{P}}, \lambda, (U_\ell)_{\ell \in \mathcal{P}})$ where one has the following.[12]

- $\Gamma = (N, (S_i)_{i=1}^n, (\pi_i)_{i=1}^n)$ is a stage game.
- $\mathcal{P} = \{it : i \in N \text{ and } t \in \{1, 2, \ldots\}\}$ is the set of players of the intergenerational game, where player it corresponds to the t-th generation of player i in the stage game.
- (Messages) For every $it \in \mathcal{P}$, $\mathcal{M}_{it}$ is the set of messages (advice) that can be sent by player it to player $i(t+1)$. We assume that messages are private. In most cases, we will have $\mathcal{M}_{it} = S_i$.
- (Strategies) For each $t \in \mathbb{N}$, define $H_t = S^t$. These are the sets of possible histories of play up to period t. For every $it \in \mathcal{P}$, we define the **advice function** by $\mathcal{A}_{it} : \mathcal{M}_{i(t-1)} \times H_t \to \mathcal{M}_{it}$ and the **action function** by $\mathcal{B}_{it} : \mathcal{M}_{i(t-1)} \times H_{t-1} \to S_i$. Finally, we define the strategy set of player it as $\mathcal{S}_{it} = \{(\mathcal{A}, \mathcal{B}) : \mathcal{A} \text{ is an advice function and } \mathcal{B} \text{ is an action function}\}$. Therefore, a strategy for player it consists of two parts: Conditional on the advice she receives and the history of play until period t, she decides what advice to pass to her descendants (advice function). Moreover, conditional on the advice she receives from her predecessor and the history of play up to period $t-1$, she has to decide how to play the stage game (action function). When $K = 1$ and $\mathcal{M}_{it} = S_i$, we have that $\mathcal{A}_{it} = S_i \times H_t \to S_i$ and $\mathcal{B}_{it} = S_i \times H_{t-1} \to S_i$. By convention, we fix an arbitrarily chosen symbol $\diamond$ and define both $\mathcal{M}_{i0}\{\diamond\}$ and $H_{i0}\{\diamond\}$. With this convention, it is without loss of generality to say that the strategy set $\mathcal{S}_{i0}$ of role i in generation 0 is simply $\mathcal{M}_{i1} \times S_i$. Notice that we are assuming that players can condition both on the message they receive and on the history of play. This will correspond to the advice-plus-history treatments in the experiments we are going to discuss. If subjects can condition only on the advice they receive (advice-only treatments), the advice function and the action

---

[12] In this definition, we assume that the stage game is played once by each generation. The definition we give here can be generalized to the case in which generations play the stage game more than once, but that would complicate the exposition without adding much to the understanding of the structure of an intergenerational game.

function become, respectively, $\mathcal{A}_{it} = \mathcal{M}_{i(t-1)} \times S \rightarrow \mathcal{M}_{it}$ and $\mathcal{B}_{it} : \mathcal{M}_{i(t-1)} \rightarrow S_i$. Finally, if subjects can only condition on the past history of play (history-only treatments), we define $\mathcal{B}_{it} : H_{t-1} \rightarrow S_i$ and then $S_{it} = \{B : B \text{ is an action function}\}$.

- λ is a measure of intergenerational caring. More specifically, it measures how much generation t cares about the stage payoffs of generation $t+1$.
- For every $it \in \mathcal{P}$, the payoff function of player it, $U_{it} : S^2 \rightarrow \mathbb{R}$, is defined as

$$U_{it}(s_t, s_{t+1}) = \pi_i(s_t) + \lambda \pi_i(s_{t+1}),$$

where $s_t, s_{t+1} \in S$ are the strategy profiles realized in the stage game played by generations t and $t+1$, respectively.

We now define an intergenerational equilibrium for the case where $\mathcal{M}_{it} = S_i$ for all $i \in N$ and $t \in \mathbb{N}$.

Definition   We say that $(a_{it}^{\star}, b_{it}^{\star})_{i \in N}^{t \in \mathbb{N}}$ is an intergenerational equilibrium on strategy profile $\bar{s}$ if:

- (first generation) for all $i \in N$, $a_{i1}^{\star} = b_{i1}^{\star} = \bar{s}_i$;
- (advice following) for all $i \in N$ and $t \geqslant 2$, $b_{it}^{\star}(\bar{s}_i, h) = \bar{s}_i$ for all histories $h \in H_{t-1}$ with $h(t-1) = \bar{s}$;
- (advice giving) for all $i \in N$ and $t \geqslant 2$, $a_{it}^{\star}(\bar{s}_i, h) = \bar{s}_i$ for all $h \in H_t$ with $h(t) = \bar{s}$; and
- (optimization conditional on others playing their part in $\bar{s}$) for all $i \in N$ and $t \in \mathbb{N}$,

$$U_{it}(\bar{s}, \bar{s}) = \max_{(s_i, s_i') \in S_i} U_{it}\left((s_i, \bar{s}_{-i}), (s_i', \bar{s}_{-i})\right).$$

Condition 1 says that the first generation plays the strategy profile $\bar{s}$ and advises the next generation to do so. Condition 2 says that each generation will play their part in the strategy profile $\bar{s}$ provided that they are advised to do so and that the previous generation did so. Condition 3 says that each generation advises the next generation to play their part in the strategy profile $\bar{s}$ provided that the former was advised to do so and in fact did so. Notice that conditions 2 and 3 impose a kind of Markovian structure to the equilibrium. Finally, condition 4 says that payoffs are maximized when every role in every generation plays their part in the strategy profile $\bar{s}$, provided that all other roles in each generation are also doing so. This ensures that no generation wants to deviate from the equilibrium path. Notice that, in any intergenerational-game equilibrium in strategy profile $\bar{s}$, we will only observe the profile $\bar{s}$ in the history of play.[13]

REFERENCES

Anderlini, L., Gerardi, D. and Lagunoff, R. (2008). A "super" folk theorem for dynastic repeated games. *Economic Theory*, 37(3), 357–394.

Anderson, L. R. and Holt, C. A. (1997). Information cascades in the laboratory. *American Economic Review*, 87(5), 847–862.

Aumann, R. J. and Shapley, L. S. (1994). Long-term competition – a game theoretic analysis. *Essays in Game Theory: In Honor of Michael Maschler*, ed. N. Megiddo, pp. 1–15. New York, NY: Springer.

Banerjee, A. V. (1992). A simple model of herd behavior. *Quarterly Journal of Economics*, 107(3), 797–817.

Bicchieri, C. (2016). *Norms in the Wild: How to Diagnose, Measure and Change Social Norms*. Oxford, UK: Oxford University Press.

Bikhchandani, S., Hirshleifer, D. and Welch, I. (1992). A theory of fads, fashion, custom, and cultural change as informational cascades. *Journal of Political Economy*, 100(5), 992–1026.

Binmore, K. (2008). Do conventions need to be common knowledge? *Topoi*, 27(1-2), 17–27.

Cabral, L., Ozbay, E. Y. and Schotter, A. (2014). Intrinsic and instrumental reciprocity: An experimental study. *Games and Economic Behavior*, 87(1), 100–121.

Çelen, B. and Kariv, S. (2004). Distinguishing informational cascades from herd behavior in the laboratory. *American Economic Review*, 94(3), 484–497.

Çelen, B. and Kariv, S. (2005). An experimental test of observational learning under imperfect information. *Economic Theory*, 26(3), 677–699.

Chwe, M. (2001). *Rational Ritual: Culture, Coordination, and Common Knowledge*. Princeton, NJ: Princeton University Press.

Dal Bó, P. and Fréchette, G. R. (2018). On the determinants of cooperation in infinitely repeated games: A survey. *Journal of Economic Literature*, 56(1), 60–114.

[13] It should be emphasized that we do not require that the profile $\bar{s}$ be a Nash equilibrium of the stage game. This implies that an intergenerational equilibrium may be able to support the cooperation as an intergenerational equilibrium (provided, of course, that condition 4 is satisfied).

Fehr, E. and Gächter, S. (2000). Cooperation and punishment in public goods experiments. *American Economic Review*, 90(4), 980–994.

Fudenberg, D. and Maskin, E. (1986). The folk theorem in repeated games with discounting or incomplete information. *Econometrica*, 54(3), 533–554.

Kandori, M. (1992). Repeated games played by overlapping generations of players. *Review of Economic Studies*, 59(1), 81–92.

Kübler, D. and Weizsäcker, G. (2003). Information cascades in the labor market. *Journal of Economics*, 80(3), 211–229.

Lewis, D. (1969). *Convention: A Philosophical Study*. Cambridge, MA: Harvard University Press.

Monderer, D. and Samet, D. (1989). Approximating common knowledge with common beliefs. *Games and Economic Behavior*, 1(2), 170–190.

Offerman, T., Potters, J. and Verbon, H. A. (2001). Cooperation in an overlapping generations experiment. *Games and Economic Behavior*, 36(2), 264–275.

Rescorla, M. (2019). Convention. *The Stanford Encyclopedia of Philosophy*, summer edition. [Original work published 2007].

Rubinstein, A. (1989). The electronic mail game: Strategic behavior under "almost common knowledge". *American Economic Review*, 79(3), 385–391.

Rubinstein, A. (1994). Equilibrium in supergames. *Essays in Game Theory: In Honor of Michael Maschler*, ed. N. Megiddo, pp. 17–28. New York, NY: Springer.

Schotter, A. (1981). *The Economic Theory of Social Institutions*. Cambridge, UK: Cambridge University Press.

Schotter, A. and Sopher, B. (2003). Social learning and coordination conventions in inter-generational games: An experimental study. *Journal of Political Economy*, 111(3), 498–529.

Sugden, R. (2004). *The Economics of Rights, Cooperation, and Welfare*, 2nd ed., pp. 154–165. Basingstoke, UK: Palgrave Macmillan. [Original work published 1986].

Vanderschraaf, P. (2018). *Strategic Justice: Convention and Problems of Balancing Divergent Interests*. Oxford, UK: Oxford University Press.

von Neumann, J. and Morgenstern, O. (1953). *Theory of Games and Economic Behavior*. Princeton, NJ: Princeton University Press.

PART II Coordination, Distribution, and Trust Conventions

Our discussion so far places us in a position to start to untangle the impact of advice and social learning on behavior. To do this we take an experimental approach and use laboratory experiments to try to unravel a set of questions that are of importance to our discussion. For example, we are interested in knowing whether the process of social learning helps or hinders the creation of an efficiently organized world and the social conventions necessary for it. Does it add stability to our daily lives? Are we better off because of it?

In Part II we start with three types of societal problems that call for conventions – coordination, distribution, and trust problems. These problems come in the form of battle of the sexes, ultimatum, and trust games. We will deal with each of them in the next three chapters.

We lump these three problems together for both practical and theoretical reasons. From a practical point of view these experiments share an identical experimental design (in fact they were run simultaneously in the lab) and hence it makes sense to see how the same experimental design works itself out across different types of games. More importantly, these three problems constitute some of the most important types of problems that societies face. All societies need to organize their activities in a coordinated fashion in order to succeed. They must reach a distribution of income that they can tolerate and must learn to trust each other. To do this they must tacitly or explicitly agree that the arrangements or conventions they create to solve these problems are acceptable.

As we will see in the three chapters in Part II, advice can have profound effects on behavior, the type of conventions we create for ourselves, and how stable these conventions are.

For example, in Chapter 4, where we investigate coordination games in the form of intergenerational battle of the sexes games, we find that advice significantly increases the likelihood that subjects coordinate on one of the two pure strategy equilibria that exist in the stage game these subjects play. This leads to a significant welfare increase for subjects in treatments where advice is available as compared to that treatment where subjects must rely on their knowledge of history for guidance.

In the intergenerational ultimatum game presented in Chapter 5 we see the presence of advice facilitating the existence of a bargaining convention but one defined by lower offers.

Finally in Chapter 6, on intergenerational trust games, we again observe a significant effect of advice on behavior. In this game one player, the sender, sends an amount of money to another, the receiver, and that amount is tripled upon receipt. The receiver has to decide how much of the money received to return, if any. Here, sending money is an act of trust, since it is not clear that any of it will be returned, while returning money demonstrates trustworthiness. What we find is that advice leads subjects to be less trusting in that it decreases the amount of money the sender sends to the receiver. However, advice increases trustworthiness since more tends to be returned.

One punch line of Part II of our book is that advice is many times welfare-improving.

Since all of the experiments discussed in Part II share the same experimental design, we will present that design here and now, and not repeat it in every chapter in Part II. Chapter 4 looks at behavior in the intergenerational battle of the sexes game, Chapter 5 in the ultimatum game, and Chapter 6 in the trust game.

Experiment: Design and Procedures

The general features of our intergenerational battle of the sexes, ultimatum, and trust games were as follows:[1] Subjects, once recruited, were ordered into generations. Each generation played the game once

---

[1] The actual experiment performed had three periods. In each period a subject would play one of the three games with a different opponent. For example, in period 1, players 1 and 6 might play the battle of the sexes game while players 2 and 5 play the ultimatum game and players 3 and 4 play the trust game. When they have finished their respective games, we would rotate them in the next period so that in period 2 players 2 and 4 play the battle of the sexes game while players 3 and 6 play the ultimatum game and players 1 and 5 play the trust game. The same type of rotation is carried out in period 3 so that at the end of the experiment each subject has played

and only once with an opponent. After their participation in the game, subjects in any generation t are replaced by a next generation, $t + 1$, who were able to view some or all of the history of what has transpired before them. Subjects in generation t, after receiving their payoff, were able to give advice to their successors by suggesting a strategy and by explaining why such advice is being given.

The payoffs to any subject in the experiment were equal to the payoffs she earned during her lifetime plus a discounted payoff which depends on the payoffs achieved by her immediate successor in the next generation. Finally, during their participation in the game, subjects were asked to predict the actions taken by their opponent (using a mechanism which makes telling the truth a dominant strategy). This is done in an effort to gain insight into the beliefs (norms) existing at any time during the evolution of our experimental society.

All three experiments were run either at the Experimental Economics Laboratory of the C. V. Starr Center for Applied Economics at New York University or at the Experimental Lab in the Department of Economics at Rutgers University. Subjects were recruited, typically in groups of twelve, from undergraduate economics courses and divided into two groups of six with which they stayed for the entire experiment. During their time in the lab, for which they earned approximately an average of $26.10 for about $1\frac{1}{2}$ hours, they engaged in three separate intergenerational games, a battle of the sexes game, an ultimatum game, and a trust game as defined by Berg et al. (1995). All subjects were inexperienced in this experiment.

When subjects started to play any of the three games they faced, after reading the specific instructions for that game, they would see on the screen the advice given to them from the previous generation. In the battle of the sexes game, this advice was in the form of a suggested strategy (either 1 or 2) as well as a free-form message written by the previous generational player offering an explanation of why

each game against a different opponent who has not played with any subject he has played with before.

they suggested what they did. No subjects could see the advice given to their opponent, but it was known that each side was given advice.

In the baseline treatment of each experiment, it was also known that each generational player could scroll through the previous history of the generations before it and see what each generational player of each type chose and what payoff they received. They could not see, however, any of the previous advice given to their predecessors. Finally, before they made their strategy choice they were asked to state their beliefs about what they thought was the probability that their opponent would choose any one of his or her two strategies.

To get the subjects to report their beliefs truthfully, subjects were paid for their predictions according to a quadratic scoring rule. For example, in the battle of the sexes games, they would be asked what the probability was that their opponent would choose a particular strategy while, in the ultimatum game, it would be the probability that the sender (receiver) thought her opponent would accept (send) a particular offer. In the trust game they predicted the amounts sent and returned.

Treatments

The experiments performed can be characterized by four parameters. The first is the length of the history that each generation-t player is allowed to see. The second is the intergenerational caring parameter indicating the fraction of the next generation's payoff to be added to any given generational player's payoff. The third is the number of periods each generation lives for (i.e., the number of times they repeat the game), while the fourth indicates whether advice is allowable between generations. In all of our experiments, each generation lives for one period or repeats the game only once and has a caring parameter of $1/2$. Hence, they only differ on the basis of the length of history the subjects are allowed to view before playing and whether they are able to get advice from their predecessor or not. These differences across treatments are important, since they allow us to isolate the impact of advice and history on behavior and assess their welfare implications.

In the baseline experiment subjects could pass advice to their successor and see the full history of all generations before them. This baseline experiment was run for 81 generations. However, at period 52 we took the history of play and started two separate and independent new treatments with new sets of subjects, which generated a pair of new time series.

In the advice-only treatment (treatment I), before any generation made its move it could see only the advice offered to it by the previous generation and nothing else. This treatment isolated the effect of advice on the play of the intergenerational game. The history-only treatment, treatment II, was identical to the baseline except for the fact that no generation was able to pass advice on to their successors. They could see the entire history, however, so that this treatment isolated the impact of history. Advice-only treatment was run for an additional 80 generations while the history-only treatment was run for an additional 66 generations, each starting after generation 52 was completed in the baseline. Hence, our baseline was of length 81, the advice-only treatment was of length 80,[2] and the history-only treatment was of length 66. Our experimental design is represented by Figure II.1.

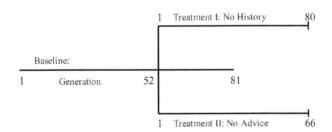

FIGURE II.1 Experimental design.

<hr>

[2] Actually one generation was lost because of a computer crash. The lost generation was the third (last) period of a session. We were able to reconstruct the relevant data files.

Given our experimental design, let us look first at the problem of the evolution of coordination conventions in the battle of the sexes games.

REFERENCES

Berg, J., Dickhaut, J. and McCabe, K. (1995). Trust, reciprocity, and social history. *Games and Economic Behavior*, 10(1), 122–142.

4 On the Evolution of Coordination and Inequality-Preserving Conventions – the Battle of the Sexes Revisited

Coordination is a central feature of economic life.[1] If we do not coordinate our activities we are destined to waste our time and effort. However, often the way we coordinate has distributional consequences – some people receive more benefits than others. Such situations establish what Ullman-Margalit (1977) calls "norms of partiality" where the convention created to solve a problem bestows privileges on one set of people. If you are on the short end of the convention, you may be upset.

Any situation involving a network externality[2] is a candidate for such a convention. For example, the common adoption of the Windows operating system as opposed to Unix bestowed benefits on some people (or firms), who were comfortable with Windows, but hurt those who felt Unix was a better option. The same holds for the QWERTY keyboard which triumphed over the supposedly more efficient Dvorak keyboard[3] and the VHS video format which triumphed over Betamax, etc. The convention that sanctions these formats rather than others has distributional consequences – some people gain and some lose. Continued adherence perpetuates an unequal status quo.

---

[1] This chapter is based on Schotter and Sopher (2003).

[2] A positive network externality exists when the benefits to a person in the network are an increasing function of the number of other users. For example, Facebook has positive network externalities because the more people who use it, the more it is worth to all users.

[3] Dvorak is a keyboard layout for English patented in 1936 by August Dvorak and his brother-in-law, William Dealey, as a faster and more ergonomic alternative to the QWERTY layout (the de facto standard keyboard layout).

This is true of any other situation where privileges or property rights are awarded arbitrarily to some subset of the population and these privileges are maintained over time because they are conventional.

In studying the evolution of conventions, our model of intergenerational games defines a process more Lamarckian than Darwinian[4] in that, while Lamarck had the wrong model of biological evolution, believing that animals could pass on acquired traits to their successors, such a model may be a correct model of social evolution where generations of social agents pass on conventions of behavior they create during their lifetime to their successors.[5] Such conventions may reinforce social inequality as they do in the battle of the sexes game, and such inequality may lay the seeds for the convention's demise or for social strife.

4.1 THE GAME

As stated before, the battle of the sexes is the paradigmatic example of a coordination game with asymmetric payoffs across equilibria. Consider the one we presented our subjects with as described in Table 4.1.[6]

As is true in all battle of the sexes games, this game has two pure strategy equilibria. In one, $(1,1)$, player 1 does relatively well and receives a payoff of 150 while player 2 does less well and receives a payoff of 50. In the other equilibrium, $(2,2)$, just the opposite is true. In disequilibrium, all payoffs are zero. There is a mixed strategy equilibrium as well and, in the repeated instantiation of the game,

---

[4] Our emphasis on this Lamarckian evolutionary process is in contrast to practically all work in evolutionary game theory which is predominantly Darwinian (see, for example, Kandori et al. (1993), Vega-Redondo (1996), Samuelson (1997), and Weibull (1997) just to name a few).

[5] Of course this point has already been made by Cavalli-Sforza and Feldman (1981), Boyd and Richerson (1988), and more recently Bisin and Verdier (1998, 2000, 2001), all of whom have presented a number of interesting models where imitation and socialization, rather than pure absolute biological fitness, is the criterion upon which strategies evolve. We would include Young's (1996, 1998) work in this category as well.

[6] The game was played in "experimental francs". The conversion rate of francs into dollars here is 1fr = \$0.04.

Table 4.1 *Battle of the sexes game.*

		Column player	
		1	2
Row player	1	150, 50	0, 0
	2	0, 0	50, 150

an alternating equilibrium where subjects alternate between the (1, 1) and the (2, 2) equilibria. Since in our data and in the advice statements made across generations there is no evidence that either of these mixed strategy or alternating equilibria occurred, we will ignore them.[7]

The convention creation problem here, therefore, is which equilibrium will be adhered to, and the problem is that because each type of player favors a different equilibrium there is an equity issue which is exacerbated by our generational structure. Each new generation may not want to adhere to a convention established in the past which is unfavorable to them.

As is true of all of the games discussed in Part II, before each generation chooses an action we elicit the beliefs of the subjects about the anticipated actions of their generational opponent using a quadratic scoring rule which gives risk-neutral agents an incentive to report their true beliefs.

4.2   RESULTS

Our experiment is an experiment in social evolution.[8] Given our battle of the sexes game and our experimental design, we are interested in finding out whether our data exhibit the stylized features of

---

[7] In a pilot experiment where generations interacted for ten periods before expiring, there was evidence of a correlated equilibrium which was evident both in the data and in the advice offered across generations. No such advice was observed when generations lasted one period.

[8] For instructions see Schotter and Sopher (2003).

such evolution: equilibrium (behavior from which no agent wishes to deviate and that is passed down from generation to generation), inertia (behavior that is stable and tends to persist once established), and socialization (learning through the process of advice giving and following).

We will concentrate on three aspects of the data our experiment generates. One is the choices our subjects make and the type of equilibrium convention they establish, if any. More precisely, if subjects establish an equilibrium convention for this game, is it one where behavior converges or are there oscillating equilibria where outcomes alternate? Is it a "punctuated equilibrium" where one equilibrium is established, stays in existence for a considerable period of time, only to spontaneously disappear and be replaced by a different equilibrium? If a convention is established, how persistent is it, i.e., how strong is the inertia keeping it in place? Finally, what is the impact of advice or socialization across generations on convention creation, coordination, and welfare?

Since the experimental design we outlined in the Part II introduction allows us to observe not only the actions of subjects but their beliefs and the advice they give each other, we are in a position to measure all the variables necessary to discuss the evolution of a convention of behavior. In addition, the three treatments we ran (the baseline, where subjects have access to both advice and the full history of actions before them, and treatments 1 and 2, where we selectively eliminate either history, leaving subjects with only advice (treatment 1), or advice, leaving subjects with only history (treatment 2)) will allow us to isolate and identify the impact of advice, history, or both on the evolution of a convention for this game.

Since we have described our experimental design in the introduction to Part II, let us jump right in to our results and discuss the behavior of our subjects in the baseline treatment where subjects have access to the full history of the game and to advice.

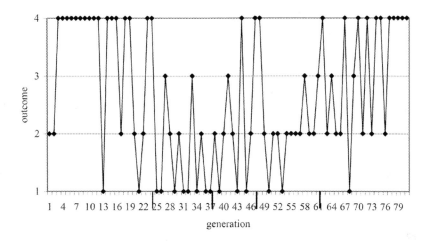

generation

Outcomes: 1 = (Row chooses 1, Column chooses 1)
2 = (Row chooses 1, Column chooses 2)
3 = (Row chooses 2, Column chooses 1)
4 = (Row chooses 2, Column chooses 2)

| Indicates break in Regime

FIGURE 4.1 Outcomes of battle of the sexes games.

4.3 THE EVOLUTION OF CONVENTIONS IN THE BASELINE EXPERIMENT: PUNCTUATED EQUILIBRIA

Figure 4.1 presents the time series of actions generated by our 81-generation baseline experiment. Note that in this figure we have time on the horizontal axis and the actions chosen by our generation pair on the vertical axis. Hence, there are four possible action pairs that we can observe: (o_{11}) = (row$_1$, column$_1$), (o_{12}) = (row$_1$, column$_2$), (o_{21}) = (row$_2$, column$_1$), and (o_{22}) = (row$_2$, column$_2$), where o_{ij} indicates an outcome where the row player chose action i and the column player action j. (In Figure 4.1 we will denote these states as states 1, 2, 3, and 4, respectively.)

As can be seen in Figure 4.1, behavior in this treatment is not the typical pattern in many experiments where there is early learning followed by convergence to some one equilibrium. Rather, for some periods of time, one of our four possible outcomes is observed and appears stable only to disappear and be replaced by a different pattern. Such behavior has been called "punctuated equilibrium" (Gould and Eldredge, 1977) and used to characterize patterns in social evolution.

As can be seen in Figure 4.1, we divide the time series into five regimes as indicated by the marks on the horizontal axis. Each regime exhibits a different type of behavior exhibited by our subjects over time. For the sake of exposition we present the details of our procedure to identify these regimes in the appendix in Section 4.7. Very quickly, however, we estimate the number and location of these regimes by estimating the structural break points in the data using a multinomial logit response model in which the probability of one of our four states occurring in generation t is estimated as a function of the recent history of play by the row and the column players. In the context of such a fitted model, the idea of punctuated conventions suggests a sudden changes (punctuations) in the estimated coefficients on the row and column player choice histories – a structural break.

We employ the likelihood-based estimation procedure proposed by Quandt (1958) to select the best-fitting model with K structural breaks. We estimate break points for different values of K, and then select the number of breaks according to the Akaike information criterion. We then test this "best estimate" of the number of breaks and their locations against the alternative hypothesis of no breaks with a likelihood ratio test.

Our estimates indicate the existence of five distinct regimes. Regime I consists of generations 1–24, regime II generations 25–37, regime III generations 38–46, regime IV generations 47–60, and regime V generations 61–81.

Regime I (generations 1–24) we call the $(2,2)$-convention regime since during this time period we observed 17 periods in which the $(2,2)$ equilibrium was chosen along with one stretch of time where we observed nine consecutive periods of $(2,2)$, the longest run for any stage-game equilibrium in all 81 generations of the baseline game. Regime II (generations 25–37) we call the $(1,1)$-convention regime because while in the first 24 generations we only saw the (1, 1) equilibrium chosen twice, in regime II it is chosen in eight of the 13 generations. In addition, during this time the (2, 2) equilibrium, which was so prevalent in regime I, disappears completely. If we look at the row players in regime II, they choose strategy 1, in 11 of the 13 generations, indicating that at least in their minds they are adhering to the (1, 1) convention in playing this game.

Regimes III and IV (generations 38–60) we call selfish disequilibrium regimes since the generational players spend most of their time in the (1, 2) disequilibrium state with infrequent occurrences of the (1, 1) equilibrium and the (2, 2) equilibrium (four and three respectively). Finally, regime V (generations 61–81) appears to present evidence that the (2, 2) equilibrium is re-establishing itself as a convention after a virtual absence over 35 generations. We say this because during these last 20 generations we see the (2, 2) equilibrium appearing in 10 out of 20 generations while it only appeared three times in the previous 35 generations. Even more surprising, the row players, after a great resistance to playing row 2 (e.g., they only played it seven times in 35 generations between generation 25 and 60), chose it 14 times in the last 20 generations. In total there were 47 periods of stage-game equilibrium played and 34 periods of stage-game disequilibrium. Note finally that there is a great asymmetry in the number of times that the (2, 1) state arises (seven times) as opposed to the (1, 2) state (27 times). This is not a surprise because the (1, 2) state is what we call the selfish disequilibrium state where each player attempts to get the 150 payoff for themselves and as a result both get zero. The (2, 1) disequilibrium one could call the non-selfish disequilibrium since there each player is capitulating to the desires of the other but failing to coordinate for non-selfish reasons.

Advice in the Baseline: Socialization

The type of Lamarckian evolution we are interested in here relies heavily on a process of social learning for its proper functioning. The transmission of conventions and "culture" through advice is

Table 4.2 *Advice offered conditional on state*

State	Row 1	Row 2	Column 1	Column 2
1,1	16	0	14	2
1,2	9	18	15	12
2,1	7	0	2	5
2,2	3	28	0	31

permitted in our experiments and turns out to be extremely important to the functioning of our experimental societies. Hence, it is important to discuss both advice giving and advice following. As you recall, the advice offered was in the form of a strategic recommendation and a free-form essay to between generational subjects of the same type.

To discuss advice we will present a summary of how advice was given in Table 4.2, and under what circumstances it was followed in Table 4.3.

What Advice Was Given[9]

Table 4.2 presents the type of advice that was offered to subjects by their predecessors conditional on the state.

Note the conservatism of this advice. When a stage-game equilibrium state has been reached, no matter which one, subjects overwhelmingly tell their successors to adhere to it. For the row player this occurs 100% of the time (16 out of 16 times) when the stage-game equilibrium is the $(1,1)$ equilibrium, the equilibrium that is best for the row player, while it occurs 90% of the time, 28 out of 30 times, when the state is $(2,2)$. For the column player a similar pattern exists. When the state is $(2,2)$, that state which is best for the column player, we see 100% of the column players (31 out of 31) suggesting a choice of 2, while when the state is $(1,1)$ 87.5% of the subjects suggest that

---

[9] In Schotter and Sopher (2000a) we investigate the content of the advice given by coding it and investigating how it changes depending on the state of the game.. What we find is that the detail with which messages are written depends on the state of the game. When an equilibrium state existed last period that determined a good outcome for a subject, i.e., they received a 150 payoff, they tended to leave low level messages which were not supported by strategic reasoning. However, the subject receiving the low payoff tended to leave more highly reasoned and strategic advice

their successors adhere to the $(1, 1)$ equilibrium despite the fact that it gives the opponent the lion's share of the earnings.

When the last-period state was a disequilibrium state, behavior was more erratic and differed across row and column players. Note that there are two types of disequilibrium states. In one, the $(2, 1)$ state, each subject chose in a manner consistent with that equilibrium which was best for his or her opponent. We call this the **non-selfish disequilibrium** state since both subjects yielded to the other and chose that state which was best for his or her opponent. The $(1, 2)$ state is the **selfish disequilibrium** state since here we get disequilibrium behavior in which each subject chooses in a manner consistent with his or her own best equilibrium.

In the non-selfish disequilibrium state, $(2, 1)$, both the row and column subjects overwhelmingly suggest a change of strategy for their successors in which they suggest a selfish action next period. More precisely, in the seven such instances of the non-selfish disequilibrium state, the row player gave advice to switch and choose row 1 in all seven instances while the column player suggested switching and choosing 2 in five of the seven cases. When the selfish disequilibrium state occurred, advice was more diffuse. In 18 of the 27 occurrences of this disequilibrium state, the row player suggested switching to the non-selfish strategy of choosing row 2 while 9 suggested standing pat and choosing row 1. For the column players 15 suggested switching to the non-selfish strategy (column 1), while 12 suggested standing pat and continuing to choose column 2.

When Was Advice Followed

In order for an equilibrium convention to persist, it must be the case that either all generations advise their successors to follow the convention and their advice is adhered to, or their advice deviates from the dictates of the equilibrium and it is ignored. What we find when we look at the behavior of subjects is that they overwhelmingly tended to follow the advice they were given but not sufficiently strongly to prevent periodic deviations and hence the punctuated

Table 4.3 *Advice adherence conditional on last period's state.*

State last period: $(1, 1)$

		Row player		Column player	
		Followed	Rejected	Followed	Rejected
	1	11	5	5	9
Advice	2	0	0	1	1
Total		11	5	6	10

State last period: $(1, 2)$

		Row player		Column player	
		Followed	Rejected	Followed	Rejected
	1	7	2	10	5
Advice	2	10	8	10	2
Total		17	10	20	7

State last period: $(2, 1)$

		Row player		Column player	
		Followed	Rejected	Followed	Rejected
	1	5	2	0	2
Advice	2	0	0	4	1
Total		5	2	4	3

State last period: $(2, 2)$

		Row player		Column player	
		Followed	Rejected	Followed	Rejected
	1	3	0	0	0
Advice	2	19	8	26	4
Total		22	8	26	4

equilibrium behavior we discussed above. More precisely, Table 4.3 presents the frequency with which advice was followed conditional on the state in which it was given.

Table 4.3 presents some interesting facts. First of all, advice appears to be followed quite often but the degree to which it is

Table 4.4 *Following advice when advice and best response differ.*

	Row		Column	
	Follow	**Reject**	**Follow**	**Reject**
State last period (1, 1)	0	3	3	8
State last period (1, 2)	4	5	11	6
State last period (2, 1)	0	0	0	2
State last period (2, 2)	11	5	3	1
Total	15	13	17	17

followed varies depending on the state in the last period. On average, for the row players it is followed 68.75% of the time while for the column players it was followed 70% of the time. When the last-period state was (2, 2), row players followed the advice given to them 73.3% of the time (strangely agreeing to follow advice to switch to the row 1 strategy three out of the three times), while column subjects followed advice 86.6% of the time (here all advice was to choose column 2). When the last-period state was the (1, 1) equilibrium, column subjects chose to follow it only 37.5% of the time while row player adhered 68% of the time. This suggests that subject types were asymmetric in their willingness to follow advice that led them to disadvantageous outcomes. The column players seemed more resistant to caving in to their row cohorts and this may be one of the reasons they did relatively better.

One question that arises here is how powerful advice is when compared to the prescriptions of best-response behavior. For example, it may be that subjects follow advice so often because the advice they get is consistent with what their best responses are to their beliefs. In such cases, following advice is equivalent to best responding. In our design we are fortunate in being able to test this hypothesis directly since for each generation we have elicited their beliefs about their opponent and hence know their best response and also the advice they have received. Hence it is quite easy for us to compare them and this is what we do in Tables 4.4 and 4.5.

One interesting result seen in Table 4.4 is that when advice and best responses differ, subjects are about as likely to follow the dictates

Table 4.5 *Following advice when advice equals best response.*

	Row		Column	
	Follow	**Reject**	**Follow**	**Reject**
State last period (1, 1)	11	2	3	2
State last period (1, 2)	13	5	9	1
State last period (2, 1)	5	2	4	1
State last period (2, 2)	11	3	23	3
Total	40	12	39	7

of their best responses as they are those of the advice they are given. For example, for the row players there were 28 instances where the best-response prescription was different than the advice given and of those 28 instances the advice was followed 15 times. For the column players there were 34 such instances and in 17 of them the column player chose to follow advice and not to best respond.

These results are striking since the beliefs we measured were the players' posterior beliefs after they had seen both the advice given to them and the history of play before them. Hence, our beliefs should have included any information contained in the advice subjects were given, yet half of the time they still persisted in making a choice that was inconsistent with their best response.

One possible reason why subjects were so willing to follow advice and not their beliefs may be that while they stated a belief, they did not have confidence in it and, as a result, were susceptible to contrary advice.

Finally, the result is even more striking since in this experiment advice was a type of private cheap talk based on little more information than the next generation already possessed. On that basis it could have been easily dismissed, yet it was not.

One reason could be that the costs of cognition are high and people choose to listen to others rather than contemplate themselves. We will see this in Chapter 10 where decision makers in a standard social learning experiment opt to receive advice about their immediate predecessor rather than the choice they made as an input to their choice. If the problem is complex, it might be easier to just follow advice. Another reason, as demonstrated in the psychology literature, is that following advice allows a decision maker to avoid blame if things turn out badly. Finally, our parents have taught us to listen to advice (mostly theirs, of course) and we are used to doing so.

One of the striking aspects to this advice-giving and advice-receiving behavior is how it introduces a stochastic aspect into what would otherwise be a deterministic best-response process. If advice was always followed, or at least followed when it agreed with a subject's best response, and if beliefs were such that both subjects would want to choose actions consistent with the (1, 1) or (2, 2) state, then these states, once reached, would be absorbing. However, we see that neither of these assumptions is supported by our data. Despite the fact that the (2, 2) state was observed nine times in a row in regime 1, and despite the fact that choosing 2 was a best response to a subject's stated beliefs, we observed in generation 13 a completely unexplained deviation. In addition, in three of the 30 rounds where the (2, 2) equilibrium was in place, the row player suggested that her successor deviate, while in two of 16 instances where the (1, 1) equilibrium was in place, the column subject also suggested deviation. Note, however, that to the extent that deviations from established equilibrium conventions occur, they are more likely to be because new generations spontaneously choose to do so rather than them being advised to. In some sense advice appears to be conservative in the sense that, once an equilibrium is established, subjects advise their successors to adhere to it even if they receive the smaller payoff.

4.4 THE ADVICE PUZZLE: SOCIAL AND BELIEF LEARNING IN TREATMENTS I AND II

Starting in generation 52 we introduced two new treatments into our experiment. In treatment I we "took away history" by having successive generations of players play without the benefit of being able to see any history beyond that of their parent generation. What this means is that subjects performing this experiment knew only that the game they were playing had been played before, possibly many times, but that they could only see the play of the generation before them. They could, however, receive advice just as did subjects in our baseline. This treatment was run independently of the baseline and treatment II, except for the common starting point in period 52. In treatment II we "took away advice" by allowing subjects to view the entire history of play before them, if they wished, but not allowing them to advise the next generation.

These treatments furnish a controlled experiment which allows us to investigate the impact of social learning, in the form of advice giving and following, on subjects' ability to attain and maintain an equilibrium convention of behavior in this game. Such learning is in contrast to the more frequently studied belief learning which involves agents taking actions which at any time are best responses to the beliefs they have about the actions of their opponents. In our experiment we can easily test these two types of learning since we have elicited the beliefs of agents at each point during the game. Hence, if each generation forms their beliefs in light of history and then best responds to them, the addition of advice should have no impact on the frequency and persistence of equilibrium behavior among the subjects. This is especially true since in our experiments the people giving advice barely have more information at their disposal than do the ones receiving it. (The only difference in their information sets is that the advice giver has received advice from his or her parental generation which the receiver has not seen.)

More precisely, if advice giving were not essential to convention building, then we should not observe any difference in the number of times our subjects achieved an equilibrium when we compare treatment II (the full history/no-advice experiment) to our baseline experiment, where subjects had access to both. Furthermore, if history was not essential for coordination but advice was, then eliminating history and allowing advice, as we did in treatment I, should lead to identical amounts of cooperation as observed in the baseline.

It turns out that players in intergenerational games appear much more successful in achieving equilibrium behavior (or establishing a convention) when advice is present even if they have no access to the history of play before them. History, with no accompanying advice, appears to furnish less of a guide to coordinated behavior. More precisely, while in the baseline we observe equilibrium outcomes 47 out of 81 times, when we eliminate advice, as we do in treatment II, we only observe coordination in 19 out of 66 periods. When we allow advice but remove history, treatment I, coordination is restored and occurs in 39 out of 81 generations.[10]

The punch line here is that, in the context of the battle of the sexes game, the world is more orderly when advice is present and more efficient as well. People who only have the past to rely on to guide

---

[10] A more formal way to compare the impact of these treatments on the behavior of our subjects is to compare the state-to-state transition matrices generated by our baseline data and test to see if they were generated by the same stochastic process generating the data observed in treatments I and II. More precisely, treating the data as if it were generated by a one-state Markov chain, for each experiment we can estimate the probability of transiting from any of our four states $\{(1,1), (1,2), (2,1), (2,2)\}$ to another. A simple counting procedure turns out to yield maximum-likelihood estimates of these transition probabilities. Doing so would generate a 4×4 transition matrix for each experimental treatment. These transition matrices are presented in the appendix to Schotter and Sopher (2003).

To test if the transition probabilities defined by our baseline data are generated by a process equivalent to the one that generated the data in treatments I and II, we use a chi-square goodness-of-fit test. More precisely, call T the transition matrix estimated from our baseline data and P^k the transition matrix defined by our k-th treatment, i.e., $k = \{I, II\}$. Denote p_{ij}^{pk}, $= \{1,2,3,4\}$, as the transition probability from state i to state j in matrix P^k. To test whether the transition probabilities estimated for any one of our treatments has been generated by a process with transition probabilities equal to those of our baseline experiment, we employ a chi-square test (see Schotter and Sopher (2003) for details). We find that we can reject the hypothesis that the same process that generated the baseline data also generated the data observed in either treatment I ($\chi^2(12\text{d.o.f.}) = 27.6521$, $p = 0.000$) or treatment II ($\chi^2(9\text{d.o.f.}) = 59.4262$, $p = 0.000$) (d.o.f. = degrees of freedom). Hence, if the process generating our data can be considered Markovian, it would appear as if imposing different informational conditions on the subject significantly changed their behavior.

their behavior perform worse than those who have both history and advice. Advice alone is intermediate.

These results raise what we call the "advice puzzle" which is composed of two parts. Part I is the question of why subjects would follow the advice of someone whose information set contains virtually the same information as theirs – a naive advisor. In fact, the only difference between the information sets of parents and children in our baseline experiment is the advice that parents received from their parents. Other than that, all information is identical, yet our subjects defer to their parents' advice almost 50% of the time when the advice differs from the best response to their own beliefs.[11] Part II is the puzzle that, despite the fact that advice is naive, private, and not common knowledge, it still is successful in enhancing coordination.

It is interesting to note that the desire of subjects to follow advice has some of the characteristics of an information cascade since in many cases subjects are not relying on their own beliefs, which are based on the information contained in the history of the game, but are instead following the advice given to them by their predecessor who is just about as much a neophyte as they are. As we will see in several later chapters, when subjects have the choice of relying on naive advice or their own judgments, they often choose advice.

4.5   OTHER-REGARDING PREFERENCES

Since the tension in the battle of the sexes game revolves around inequality of payoffs, one might think that the kind of punctuated equilibria we observe may be the result of subjects not being willing to accept unequal payoffs for their row or column type for long periods of time and deviating simply to rectify the ongoing inequality. Subjects with Fehr–Schmidt preferences (see Fehr and Schmidt, 1999), for example, might be willing to accept zero rather than suffer the inequality prescribed by the convention.

---

[11] There is no sense, then, that parents in our experiment are in any way "experts" as in the model of Ottaviani and Sørensen (2006).

As stated before, the nice aspect of our experimental setup is that we have a data source that can help to confirm or refute proposed models since we have the free-form essays that subjects pass on to their successors. These advice essays reveal the inner thinking of the subjects and therefore can be used to assess if subjects were actually thinking the way a particular model (say, a model with other-regarding preferences) would have them think.

That, of course, raises the question of what types or words or advice could be used as evidence to support this proposed other-regarding preference model. While one might think words like fair, unfair, unequal, etc., would suggest other-regarding preferences, a reading of the actual advice statements makes it clear that such fairness considerations were not evident. To the contrary, the advice offered clearly suggests that all our subjects were worried about was getting the most for themselves as possible and were willing to capitulate if they felt that their opponent was going to be greedy. In addition, much of the advice suggested being greedy oneself since getting the most for oneself appeared to be the overwhelming consideration with no subject ever suggesting that they'd rather have nothing than an unequal something, i.e., no one ever suggested that they would rather get zero than give their opponent the satisfaction of getting 150. More precisely, the words fair, unfair, and unequal were never seen in the advice statements, while the word greedy was used 20 times by the row players alone.

In terms of the actual statements made, a representative sample suggests just what we claimed above. For example, consider the following list of advice statements made by row players. (Spelling and punctuation not corrected.)

Row Player Generation 9: "Both previous advice and previous trends indicate that the pair $(2,2)$ is always chosen. If you look at your history, the pair $(2,2)$ appears everywhere. Your opponent will know that, and won't break the trend by choosing column 2, which is more profitable to him anyway. Stick with row 2 if you wish to make any money. If you want to try to shift the balance to row 1, which is better for us row choosers, take row 1, but be warned that you'll most probably wind up with nothing."

This statement was made right in the middle of the regime I convention when the $(2, 2)$ equilibrium was in place and row players were getting 50. Note that given the history this player is convinced that the convention where everyone chooses 2 is in place and suggests that his successor capitulate and choose 2 as well. However, there is some indication here that this subject views it as arbitrary that the column player is getting the lion's share of the pie and says that if his successor would like to shift the power to the row players he should choose row 1. This is the only suggestion that people make a sacrifice to further equity.

The following statements give an insight into the inner thinking of subjects and their view of the nature of their opponents. As we can see, subjects expect people to be greedy and behave accordingly to maximize their payoffs. Consider the following statements.

Row Player Generation 12: "The History shows it. I found people are greedy so you better choose 2 or you will be left w/ nothing."

Row Player Generation 14: "Your partner is more likely to choose what gives him a higher payoff, so it's better to come out with something than nothing!"

Row Player Generation 23: "the other person will be greedy a lot of the time. look at the history!"

Row Player Generation 29: "if you're greedy, pick row 1 to ensure you get the most or both of you get nothing. If you feel like you don't mind getting less, or think other ppl are generally greedier than you then pick the row 2."

Row Player Generation 33: "don't be nice, take it all ..."

Similar advice was offered by the column players. In the middle of regime I where the $(2, 2)$ equilibrium has been in place for a long time, the column player was so sure the norm suggested the $(2, 2)$ equilibrium that he said:

Column Player Generation 9: "The sure money is on column two."

In regime II, where the $(1, 1)$ regime was in place but where behavior was more variable, we see the following.

Column Player Generation 31: "Hrm …its a question of who is going to think that the other person is going to be selfish. Either way, cover your bets …"

Column Player Generation 39: "predict him/her choosing his/her large payoff with high chance and your high payoff with a low percentage and choosing the box with his/her large payoff!!!"

Column Player Generation 40: "opponent will choose his/her highest payoff. predict this action, while choosing the lower payoff for yourself (i.e. opponent chooses row 1 you choose column 1, and, you predict his/her greediness correctly=high payoff!!!!!!!)."

As we can see, the advice-offered subjects exhibited a keen understanding of the strategic situation they were in and a desire to make as much money for themselves as they could. If they thought their opponent was dedicated to being greedy they suggested capitulation. If they felt their opponent would give in, they suggested going for the big prize. Other subjects' payoffs do not seem to enter into their utility functions.

4.6 CONCLUSION

In this chapter we used an experimental approach to investigate the process of convention creation and transmission in intergenerational games. We have modeled the process of convention creation as a Lamarckian one in which non-overlapping generations of players create and pass on conventions of behavior from generation to generation. These conventions tend to perpetuate social inequality. Since the process is stochastic, however, it exhibits punctuated equilibria in which conventions are created, passed on from one generation to the next, but then spontaneously disappear. In this process several stylized facts appear.

Probably the most notable feature of our results is the central role that the advice, passed on from one generation to the next, plays in facilitating coordination across and between generations. It appears that relying on history and the process of belief learning is not sufficient to allow proper coordination in the battle of the sexes game played by our subjects. For a reason yet left unexplained, advice, even in the absence of history, appears to be sufficient for the creation of conventions, while history, in the absence of advice, does not. This implies that social learning may be a stronger, and belief learning a weaker, form of learning than previously thought.

4.7 APPENDIX: REGIME ESTIMATION

A formal method for determining the number and location of structural break points in the data can be implemented in the context of an estimated econometric model of the process determining the state. To do this, consider a multinomial logit response model in which the probability of state h occurring in generation t is estimated as a function of the recent history of play by the row player and the column player. In the context of such a fitted model, the idea of punctuated conventions suggests sudden changes (punctuations) in the estimated coefficients on the row and column player choice histories. Therefore, if we allow the estimated coefficients on the row and column player history variables to vary over discrete intervals of time, the resulting model can be compared to a "restricted" model in which the coefficients on the row history variables and column history variables (defined for each regime) are restricted to be equal to one another across regimes. We employ the likelihood-based estimation procedure proposed by Quandt (1958) to select the best-fitting model with K structural breaks.[12] We estimate break points for different values of K, and then select the number of breaks according to the Akaike information criterion. We then test this "best estimate" of the number of breaks and their locations against the alternative hypothesis of no breaks with a likelihood ratio test.

---

[12] Though Quandt's article considered a linear model with a single break point, the generalization to multiple break points and a general maximum-likelihood model is immediate. Quandt mentions the multiple break point case in a footnote. The method is based on analysis of the likelihood function only, and is not restricted to linear models.

We first estimated a multinomial logit model for the state on a moving average of the row and column player choices. That is, the probability that any state is observed in period t is a function of the relative frequencies with which the row and column players have used their various strategies over the last m periods. Using a multinomial logit form for this probability yields

$$P_h(t) = \frac{\exp\left(b_o^h + \sum_{k \in S_K} b_{kr}^h r_{t,k} + \sum_{k \in S_K} b_{kc}^h c_{t,k}\right)}{1 + \sum_{j \in J} \exp\left(b_o^j + \sum_{k \in S_K} b_{kr}^j r_{t,k} + \sum_{k \in S_K} b_{kc}^j c_{t,k}\right)},$$

$$h \in J = \{(1,1),(1,2),(2,1)\} \quad \text{and} \quad P_{(2,2)} = 1 - \sum_{j \in J} P_j,$$

where $k \in \{1,2,3,\ldots,K\} = S_K$ indexes the different possible structural regimes, J is the set of states indexed by j, and h is any particular state ($(2,2)$ is the base state). The row history variables, $r_{t,k}$, are defined as follows. Let $f_{t,r}^m$ be the relative frequency with which the row player has chosen action 1 in the previous m periods before t (periods $(t - m - 1)$ to $(t - 1)$), and let d_k be a dummy variable equal to 1 if the observed state in period t is in structural regime k, and equal to 0 otherwise. Then $r_{t,k} = f_{t,r}^m d_k$. The column history variables, $c_{t,k}$, are defined similarly. We call the model "restricted" when we impose the following: $b_{kr}^j = b_{k'r}^j$ and $b_{kc}^j = b_{k'c}^j$ for all k and k', implying that there are no structural regimes. The "unrestricted" model allows these coefficients to vary across structural regimes.[13]

In the estimation we use $m = 5$ to construct the row and column player history variables. We decided on this by comparing the fit for the restricted model for different values of m (from $m = 1$ to $m = 10$) on the basis of the pseudo R-squared measure.[14] We then proceeded

[13] For $K > 1$, we do impose one restriction in the "unrestricted" model, that the coefficients in the first and last regimes are the same. This seemed a natural thing to do, since the data so clearly begin and end with the $(2,2)$ equilibrium being chosen most frequently. This restriction actually improves the fit according to the Akaike information criterion.

[14] Specifically, the pseudo R-squared $= 0.17$ for the five-period moving average, and it declined as one either lengthened or shortened the moving average window, where we allowed the window to range from $m = 1$ to $m = 10$.

Table 4.6 *Structural break estimates.*[a]

K[b]	Log likelihood	Pseudo R^2	Breaks	AIC[c]
0	−81.25	0.17		2.14
1	−73.35	0.25	61	2.25
2	−68.16	0.30	47,61	2.11
3	−62.88	0.35	43,47,61	2.13
4*	**−55.14**	**0.43**	**25,38,47,61**	**2.08**
5	−53.55	0.45	25,34,44,48,61	2.20

[a]Likelihood ratio test for structural change: $\chi^2 = 52.22$ (18 d.o.f.). Prob. $> \chi^2 = 0.00$.
[b] K = number of breaks assumed.
[c] Akaike information criterion.
* K=4 is the best fitting number of breaks

to estimate the break points in the unrestricted model for different values of K, using the five-period moving average, selecting for each K the best-fitting (highest likelihood) set of break points. We do this exercise for $K = 1, 2, 3, 4$, and 5.[15] The results are summarized in Table 4.6.

Table 4.6 shows, for each number of break points, K, the value of the log likelihood function, the pseudo R^2 measure of goodness of fit, the estimated break points, and the value of the Akaike information criterion (used to select the best-fitting number of breaks). The break points are the points at which a new set of coefficients on the regressors take effect. Thus, there are $K + 1$ regimes implied by a set of break points $t_1, t_2, \ldots, t_K$, namely, (1 to $t_1 - 1$), (t_1 to $t_2 - 1$), ..., and (t_K to 81). The best-fitting model according to the AIC is the one with four breaks. It was only at the level of four break points that the rather obvious break in the data at around generation 25 entered the picture, and this leads to a substantial improvement in the fit.

[15] Estimating the break points involves estimating the multinomial logit model discussed above for every possible configuration of the K break points over the sample period, and then selecting the set of break points yielding the highest log likelihood for the multinomial model. This is straightforward enough, though obviously cumbersome. We imposed the restriction in conducting this "grid search" that each regime must be at least four periods long.

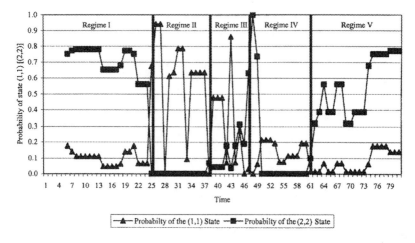

FIGURE 4.2 Estimated probability of equilibrium states.

Since the coefficients are not of particular interest here, we only report the likelihood ratio test for the structural change hypothesis at the bottom of Table 4.6.[16] The likelihood ratio chi-square for the structural change hypothesis is significant: the restriction that coefficients are equal across regimes is rejected at the 0% significance level.

The estimated probabilities for the equilibrium states $(1,1)$ and $(2,2)$ derived from the unrestricted estimated multinomial logit model are presented in Figure 4.2. (See Table 4.7 for estimates.) Figure 4.2 presents strong evidence that behavior changed dramatically as generations moved across our regimes. For example, note that in regime I the probability of being in state $(2,2)$ is consistently high and then drops precipitously as the experiment enters our regime II.

---

[16] Since there are three equations to estimate (one less than the total number of states), there are, besides the constant terms, 2 (row and column history) × 3 (equations) × 5 (regimes) = 30 coefficients to estimate in the unrestricted model, and 2 (row and column history) × 3 (equations) = 6 coefficients to estimate in the restricted model, apart from the constant terms. We imposed the restriction in the models with two or more breaks that the first and last regimes have the same coefficients, so in fact there are only 24 estimated parameters in the so-called unrestricted model. Thus the chi-square statistic for the test of structural change has 24 − 6 = 18 degrees of freedom.

Table 4.7 *Coefficient estimates for test for structural change.*[a]

	Unrestricted model		Restricted model	
	Estimate	Prob. > z	Estimate	Prob. > z
State = Row equilibrium (1, 1)				
Row history, regimes 1 and 5	1.24	0.72	3.27	0.08
Row history, regime 2	56.57	0.00		
Row history, regime 3	16.54	0.20		
Row history, regime 4	105.96	1.00		
Column history, regimes 1 and 5	−4.62	0.45	3.56	0.09
Column history, regime 2	−17.08	1.00		
Column history, regime 3	−20.33	0.32		
Column history, regime 4	−214.57	1.00		
State = Selfish (1, 2)				
Row history, regimes 1 and 5	−1.12	0.68	3.14	0.05
Row history, regime 2	−47.98	1.00		
Row history, regime 3	−0.17	0.98		
Row history, regime 4	106.61	1.00		
Column history, regimes 1 and 5	7.08	0.03	2.73	0.00
Column history, regime 2	86.75	0.00		
Column history, regime 3	5.88	0.56		
Column history, regime 4	−209.85	1.00		
State = Altruist (2, 1)				
Row history, regimes 1 and 5	15.73	0.03	7.21	0.00
Row history, regime 2	74.40	1.00		
Row history, regime 3	21.64	0.33		
Row history, regime 4	197.83	1.00		
Column history, regimes 1 and 5	4.38	0.53	0.95	0.72
Column history, regime 2	−27.42	0.00		
Column history, regime 3	−13.93	0.70		
Column history, regime 4	−621.79	1.00		

[a]Column equilibrium (2, 2) is the baseline state.

In fact, during almost the entire length of our regimes II and III that probability is practically zero. Note, however, the re-emergence of the (2, 2) state in regime V.

The evidence for the (1, 1) state is not so uniformly strong, but is still convincing. Note here that the initial probability of being in state (1, 1) in regime I is practically zero for the first 25 generations and then rises dramatically in regimes II and III only to dwindle away in regimes IV and IV. The abrupt changes in the probability of the $(2,2)$ state as we cross our regime boundaries along with the low probabilities for the $(1,1)$ state in all but regimes II and III supports the idea that there are distinct equilibrium regimes.

REFERENCES

Bisin, A. and Verdier, T. (1998). On the cultural transmission of preferences for social status. *Journal of Public Economics*, 70(1), 75–97.

Bisin, A. and Verdier, T. (2000). "Beyond the melting pot": Cultural transmission, marriage and the evolution of ethnic and religious traits. *Quarterly Journal of Economics*, 115(3), 955–988.

Bisin, A. and Verdier, T. (2001). The economics of cultural transmission and the dynamics of preferences. *Journal of Economic Theory*, 97(2), 298–319.

Boyd, R. and Richerson, P. (1988). *Culture and Evolutionary Process*. Chicago, IL: University of Chicago Press.

Cavalli-Sforza, L. L. and Feldman, M. W. (1981). *Cultural Transmission and Evolution: A Quantitative Approach*. Princeton, NJ: Princeton University Press.

Fehr, E. and Schmidt, K. M. (1999). A theory of fairness, competition, and cooperation. *Quarterly Journal of Economics*, 114(3), 817–868.

Gould, S. J. and Eldredge, N. (1977). Punctuated equilibria: The tempo and mode of evolution reconsidered. *Paleobiology*, 3(2), 115–151.

Kandori, M., Mailath, G. J. and Rob, R. (1993). Learning, mutation, and long run equilibria in games. *Econometrica*, 61(1), 29–56.

Ottaviani, M. and Sørensen, P. N. (2006). Professional advice. *Journal of Economic Theory*, 126(1), 120–142.

Quandt, R. E. (1958). The estimation of the parameters of a linear regression system obeying two separate regimes. *Journal of the American Statistical Association*, 53(284), 873–880.

Samuelson, L. (1997). *Evolutionary Games and Equilibrium Selection*, vol. 1. Cambridge, MA: MIT Press.

Schotter, A. and Sopher B. (2003). Social learning and coordination conventions in intergenerational games: An experimental study. *Journal of Political Economy*, 111(3), 498–529.

Ullman-Margalit, E. (1977). *The Emergence of Norms*. Oxford, UK: Oxford University Press.

Vega-Redondo, F. (1996). *Evolution, Games, and Economic Behavior.* Oxford, UK: Oxford University Press.

Weibull, J. W. (1997). *Evolutionary Game Theory.* Cambridge, MA: MIT Press.

Young, H. P. (1996). The economics of convention. *Journal of Economic Perspectives*, 10(2), 105–122.

Young, H. P. (1998). *Individual Strategy and Social Structure.* Princeton, NJ: Princeton University Press.

5 Conventional Behavior and Bargaining – Advice and Behavior in Intergenerational Ultimatum Games

When people think of bargaining they tend to think of a free-form give-and-take exercise.[1] However, bargaining in many circumstances is actually governed by conventions. For example, in real estate negotiations it is common for the buyers to offer less than the asking price for the house they are interested in. Offering too little, however, can lead to the perception that the buyer is not serious and can ruin the deal. Offering too much is wasteful, at least to the buyer. Depending on the community, a convention exists that dictates which offer is acceptable and which is frivolous, and real estate brokers are typically the repository of such wisdom. Similar conventions exist when buying a car or a rug in a Turkish bazaar, where the bargaining process is very ritualistic.[2]

In this chapter we investigate bargaining through the lens of the ultimatum game (Güth et al., 1982). This game is an extreme type of bargaining situation in which one player, the sender, has 100 units of currency, and must decide how to divide it between herself and a receiver who will receive an offer from the sender. The offer can either be accepted or rejected. If it is accepted, then the money is divided accordingly, while, if it is rejected, each person gets zero.

---

[1] This chapter is based on Schotter and Sopher (2007).

[2] Rubinstein (2012) comments on the conventionality of bargaining in the Jerusalem market where he tried to change the bargaining process used in his negotiations with a seller. Suggesting that they change the standard back-and-forth bargaining into a take-it-or-leave-it ultimatum game drew the following reaction from the seller: "For generations, we have bargained in our way and you come and try to change it?" Bargaining has rules and acceptable outcomes.

If this game is played repeatedly over time by a sequence of generations, then we might expect previous generations to pass on advice to their successors as to how to play and also pass on whatever conventions of behavior pertain to the game, such as what offers they expect will be accepted and what type will be rejected.[3]

In a stimulating paper on the ultimatum game, Roth et al. (1991) make a similar point. They compare the behavior of subjects engaged in ultimatum games in four different countries: the United States, Japan, Israel, and Yugoslavia. They find differences in behavior across countries and ask whether these reflect differences in the type of people inhabiting these countries (i.e., are Israelis more aggressive than Americans by nature?) or simply cultural differences that have emerged which lead them to a different set of mutual expectations about what offers are acceptable (i.e., about the offer convention). They conclude that what is observed are cultural differences (Roth et al., 1991, p. 1092).

> This suggests that what varied between subject pools is not a property like aggressiveness or toughness, but rather the perception of what constitutes a reasonable offer under the circumstances.

Stated differently, what Roth et al. mean here is that, while the ultimatum game may have only one subgame-perfect Nash equilibrium, it has many other Nash equilibria, each one of which defines an offer which is minimally acceptable to receivers. Each one of these Nash equilibria could function as a convention of behavior dictating what offer should be sent and accepted. All that is needed to maintain a non-subgame-perfect equilibrium is a set of beliefs on the part of the senders that the offer contemplated is the minimum that would

---

[3] For example, Young and Burke (2001) and Burke (2015) investigate the creation of conventions determining the terms of sharecropping contracts in southern Illinois and show that such terms appear to be "conventionally" determined in the sense that they are homogeneous within certain spatial areas but differ across space in a manner that cannot be explained by economic fundamentals. In this chapter we aim to present the results of a series of experiments whose purpose is to investigate how such conventions get established and passed on from generation to generation.

be accepted and behavior on the part of the receivers that confirms these beliefs. Hence nothing strange is occurring if we observe one of these non-subgame-perfect equilibrium outcomes at the end of an experiment. We would simply be observing what Robert Aumann has called a "perfectly good Nash equilibrium that just isn't perfect" (see van Damme, 1998).[4]

In this chapter we investigate the ultimatum game played as an intergenerational game using the design specified in the introduction to Part II. Our emphasis will be on whether advice in the ultimatum game leads to a more precisely defined sense of what is an acceptable offer, i.e., does advice lead to a more precise understanding of the bargaining convention.

What we are going to find is that behavior is more "conventional" in intergenerational ultimatum games played with advice. In addition, the offers associated with these conventions are lower when advice exists than when it does not, so not only does advice foster the creation of conventions but it lowers the offers associated with them. This does not mean that advice unambiguously helps the sender in ultimatum games, however, since it also leads receivers to reject more offers as well.

Finally, using the written texts of the advice sent between generations, we will gain some interesting insights into what governs the size of offers and their rejection.

5.1   BARGAINING CONVENTIONS

When we talk about a bargaining convention we mean a convention of behavior that informs the bargainers what to expect when they meet. This implies, however, that the situation they are in has occurred before and a convention has been established. For example, tipping is

---

[4] One could transform a Nash equilibrium outcome in the ultimatum game into a subgame-perfect one by imposing a conventional offer that would serve as a reference point for acceptance behavior. If offers less than the reference point are made and considered losses with respect to the reference point, then under these loss-averse preferences it could be rational to reject positive offers.

a bilateral situation in which a person is supposed to reward another for service rendered. To make things run smoothly and to avoid having to bargain about remuneration with every porter, bellhop, and waiter, a convention is established that says what an acceptable tip is. Hence, in order to find out what you should tip, all you need to do is ask someone or consult a travel guide where they explain what the tipping parameters are. Tipping is an extreme form of conventionalized bargaining, so conventional that there is no need for the parties to talk.[5]

If a convention is firmly established in an intergenerational ultimatum game, and there is no uncertainty about it, then we have what we might call a **strong convention** which would consist of an offer x^* (the "conventional offer") along with a set of beliefs for the senders and receivers, and a pattern of advice, such that:

1. all senders expect offers less than x^* to be accepted with probability 0 and all offers at or above x^* to be accepted with probability 1 and, as a result,
2. send x^* and advise their successors who play the game after them to send x^* as well.

For the receivers when such a strong convention exists:

1. all receivers expect x^* to be sent,
2. reject all offers below x^*, accept all offers at or above x^*, and
3. advise their successors to do the same.

While such a strong convention may get established, it is more likely that behavior, while conventional, may not be so neat. Still, we will judge the conventionality of behavior by the extent to which it conforms to this strong definition. Our claim is that behavior is more conventional in ultimatum games with advice because the behavior we observe is closer to that predicted by a strong convention.

To picture what data generated by a strong convention would look like, assume that a strong convention existed and we are observing the acceptance behavior of receivers by plotting the probability of

---

[5] For a discussion of tipping see Schotter (1979).

acceptance on the vertical axis and the offer made by the sender on the horizontal. When a strong convention is in place, the acceptance function would define a step function such that all offers less than x^* would be accepted with probability 0 and all offers above x^* would be accepted with probability 1. The same function would describe the behavior of our other variables of interest like amount sent, sender and receiver beliefs, and sender and receiver advice. They should all be step functions over the domain of offers with a step at x^*.

For example, consider the functions plotted in Figure 5.1, with amounts of money (offers) on the horizontal axis and probability of acceptance on the vertical. These are the estimated logit acceptance functions. The step function superimposed in each plot is that 0–1 step function that best matches the continuous empirical function, in the sense of minimizing the area between the empirical function and the step function. It can be thought of as the strong convention that most closely approximates actual behavior in the treatment. Note that in each panel there is, in general, a different break point, x^*, in the step function, implying that different conventions were established in each treatment. These are the estimated logit acceptance function for each of our experimental treatments indicating the probability that a given offer is accepted by the receivers.

The step function drawn in each panel of Figure 5.1 is that step function that best fits the data and depicts what behavior we would expect from a strong convention with a conventional offer of x^*. The extent to which the data, as estimated by our logit function, deviates from the step function is the extent to which actual behavior deviated from the strong convention.

While we do not expect behavior to ever settle down to a strong convention, defining such a convention does allow us to create a benchmark and answer a more relevant question, which is what features of the data generated by our experiment would allow us to say that that behavior in one experimental treatment is "more conventional" than that of another?

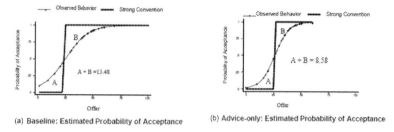

(a) Baseline: Estimated Probability of Acceptance   (b) Advice-only: Estimated Probability of Acceptance

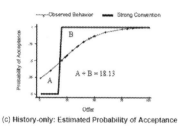

(c) History-only: Estimated Probability of Acceptance

FIGURE 5.1 Acceptance behavior – probability of acceptance.

Given our discussion above, the answer should be obvious. The data generated in treatment A is more conventional than the corresponding data in treatment B if the empirical distribution function is closer to the 0–1 step function characterizing a strong convention.

To illustrate what we mean here, consider the other line (not the step function) plotted in each panel in Figure 5.1, which we described as the estimated logit functions. To measure whether behavior is more conventional in one treatment than the other, we will measure the area between the estimated acceptance function and its associated 0–1 step function. If this area is smaller in one treatment than another, we call behavior in that treatment "more conventional" than that in another.[6]

---

[6] More precisely, we choose the one-step function, increasing from 0 to 1 at the step, to minimize $\sum |f_i - s_i|$, where the sum is over the discrete support of the offer distribution, i.e., from 0 to 100, and where f_i and s_i are the empirical and step

For example, as can be seen by comparing the acceptance functions of the advice-only and history-only treatments, the acceptance function more closely approximates the idealized 0–1 step function in the advice-only treatment. For example, the difference between the step and estimated functions is measured by the sum of the areas between the empirical function and the step function in each panel in Figure 5.1 (see Table 5.2 for the values of the areas). As we can see, that sum is 8.58 in the advice-only treatment while it is 18.13 (or more than twice as large) in the history-only treatment. Further, as can be seen by the shape of the acceptance function for the advice-only treatment in Figure 5.1(b), there is a much sharper change in the probability of acceptance on either side of x^*. In other words, it is much more clear cut in the advice-only treatment what an acceptable offer is since the acceptance function is steeper than in the history-only treatment. Finally, low offers have a small probability of acceptance in the advice-only experiment while they remain viable in the history-only treatment.

Note that a similar result holds when we compare the cumulative frequency of the amounts sent in the advice-only and history-only treatments in Figure 5.2. Here our area metric again indicates that the offer function is more closely step-like in the advice-only treatment, where the area metric equals 8.12, than in the history-only treatment, where the area metric equals 16.21. So, for our two key variables, amount sent and probability of acceptance, it is rather clear that behavior was more conventional in our advice-only treatment than in our history-only treatment. This result holds in general for the other variables such as sender and receiver advice, sender and receiver beliefs, etc. (see Figures 5.3 and 5.4).[7]

---

function values, respectively, at offer $= i$. It is easy to see that the step must occur at a point where the empirical function takes on the value 0.5.

[7] For a more formal analysis see Schotter and Sopher (2007).

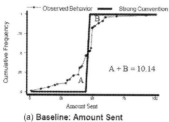

(a) Baseline: Amount Sent

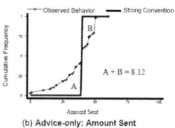

(b) Advice-only: Amount Sent

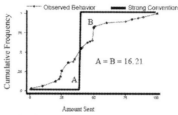

(c) History-only: Amount Sent

FIGURE 5.2 Offer behavior – amount sent.

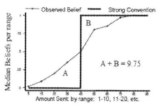

(a) Baseline Sender Beliefs: Acceptable Offers

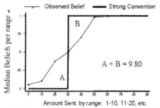

(b) Advice-only Sender Beliefs: Acceptable Offers

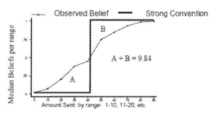

(c) History-only Sender Beliefs: Acceptable Offers

FIGURE 5.3 Sender beliefs – probability of acceptance.

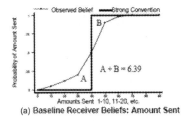

(a) Baseline Receiver Beliefs: Amount Sent

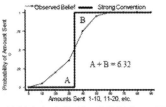

(b) Advice-only Receiver Beliefs: Amount Sent

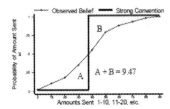

(c) History-only Receiver Beliefs: Amount Sent

FIGURE 5.4 Receiver beliefs – amount sent.

5.2 BARGAINING OUTCOMES WITH ADVICE

Before we examine the impact of advice on the conventionality of bargaining behavior, let us ask how the outcomes of the bargaining process differ when bargainers have access to advice. Does advice make people more likely to exhibit behavior closer to that predicted by the subgame equilibrium? Does it lead them to make lower offers or reject higher ones? While we did see that advice fostered coordination in the battle of the sexes game in Chapter 4, the question here is, what does it do to the behavior of bargainers in the ultimatum game?

In a nutshell, it seems like advice does lead to lower offers and higher rejections of very low offers. To explore this assertion, consider Table 5.1, which presents some descriptive statistics about the offer behavior of our subjects, and Figure 5.5, which shows histograms of the offers made for each treatment. As we see in Figure 5.5(b) and (c), when only advice is present (i.e., not history) the offers are lower and their variance is smaller.

Table 5.1 *Offers by senders.*

Treatment	All generations		Last 40 generations	
	Mean	S.d.	Mean	S.d.
Advice and history	44.70	14.95	45.66	15.95
Advice only	37.16	12.89	33.68	13.53
History only	42.45	21.96	43.90	19.66

To demonstrate this, first note that, by comparing the offers made in the advice-only treatment to those of the history-only treatment, we see that one impact of advice is to truncate the right tail of the offer distribution. In fact, while only 10% of the offers in the advice-only treatment were above 50, in the advice-and-history treatment 17% were above 50, and in the history-only treatment 18% of the observations were above 50. Note also that the distribution is much flatter in the history-only treatment and that there is much less of a spike at the modal choice than in either of the other treatments. In fact, the standard deviation of offers is almost twice as great in the history-only treatment than in the advice-only treatment where subjects have access exclusively to advice (except for a one-period history).[8, 9]

The fact that the variance of offers is greater in those treatments with no advice means that history does not seem to supply a sufficient

---

[8] A series of multiple pairwise comparison tests indicate that there is a significant difference (at the 5% level) between the advice-and-history treatment and the advice-only treatment. There is not a significant difference between the advice-only and history-only treatments, while there is a less significant (at the 10% level) difference between the advice-and-history and history-only treatments.

[9] A series of one-tailed standard deviation tests for binary comparisons between treatments addresses the question of variance. There is a significant difference between the history-only treatment and the advice-and-history treatment $(F_{(65,80)} = 2.16, p = 0.00)$ and between the history-only treatment and the advice-only treatment $(F_{(65,76)} = 2.90, p = 0.00)$. The same test found a difference between the variances of the advice-only treatment and the advice-and-history treatment at only the 10% level.

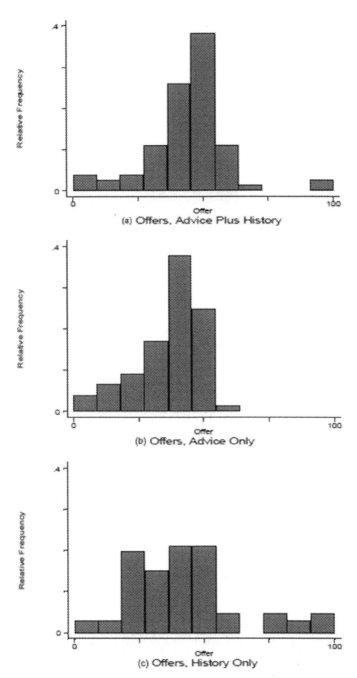

FIGURE 5.5 Offers made for various treatments.

lesson for subjects to guide their behavior in a smooth and consistent manner. Advice seems to be needed. On the other hand, the lower offer variance in the treatments with advice indicates that behavior is "more conventional" there, since it indicates that there is a greater consensus about what are acceptable offers when advice is present. We will substantiate this assertion in greater detail later. Note, however, this is exactly what we saw in Chapter 4 where history was again a poor guide to behavior in that it failed to foster coordination in the intergenerational battle of the sexes game.

With respect to rejection behavior, it appears as if the presence of advice makes receivers tougher in the sense that they are more likely to reject low offers. The estimated logit acceptance functions for these treatments are those presented in Figure 5.1. What we see in Figure 5.1 is that lower offers are least likely to be accepted when only advice exists (the advice-only treatment) and most likely to be accepted when no advice is present but access to history is unlimited (the history-only treatment), and vice versa for higher offers. The advice-and-history treatment, in which both treatments exist simultaneously, is in between. In other words, the advice-only treatment exhibits the steepest acceptance function, and the history-only game the flattest acceptance function.

5.3 CONVENTIONALITY

Our main concern is whether advice fosters bargaining conventions or at least leads to more conventional behavior in those treatments where advice exists. To investigate this we can make use of the conventionality measure we introduced above. Our general claim is that behavior is more conventional when advice exists.

To support our claim, consider Figures 5.1–5.4 again and Figures 5.6 and 5.7. These figures present the behavior of both senders and receivers in each treatment for one of the three types of variables we are analyzing: actions, beliefs, and advice. That is, amounts sent and

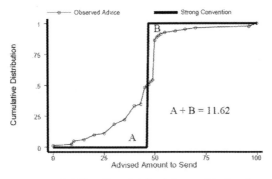

(a) Baseline: Advised Amount to Send

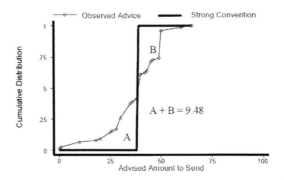

(b) Advice-only: Advised Amount to Send

FIGURE 5.6 Sender advice – advised amount to send.

the corresponding accept/reject decisions, beliefs of the senders about rejection behavior and of receivers about sending behavior, and the advice of senders and receivers to their successors.

For each of the variables in each figure, we have computed a measure of conventionality – the area between the relevant empirical function and the closest idealized (strongly conventional) step function. For each of our relevant variables, we have computed a goodness-of-fit area measure – the distance between the implied break points in the associated step functions for each variable.

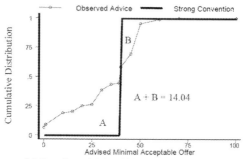

(a) Baseline: Advised Minimum Acceptable Offer

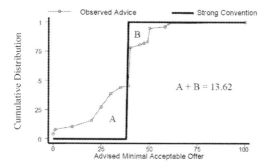

(b) Advice-only: Advised Minimum Acceptable Offer

FIGURE 5.7 Receiver advice – advised minimal acceptable offer.

The same analysis is repeated and portrayed for each variable illustrated in Figures 5.1–5.4, 5.6 and 5.7. Figure 5.1 plots the estimated acceptance functions while Figure 5.2 plots the amount sent using the cumulative distribution of offers. Figures 5.3 and 5.4 plot the median belief of senders and receivers for amounts sent in each of 10 ranges (for values of the amount sent from 0 to 10, 11 to 20, etc.) The horizontal axis indicates the midpoint of each range. The sender belief functions (Figure 5.3) (about likelihood of acceptance) are uncumulated (i.e., they indicate what the sender believes is the likelihood of acceptance for any amount sent in any of our 10 ranges), while the receiver belief functions (Figure 5.4) (over the amount sent) are cumulated, since we elicited the probability that an amount sent in each range would arise and therefore could define for each amount

Table 5.2 *Best-fitting step functions for action, belief, and advice distributions.*

Variable	Advice-and-history		Advice-only		History-only	
	Break	Area	Break	Area	Break	Area
Amount sent	46	10.14	40	8.12	40	16.21
Acceptance function	25	13.48	26	8.58	19	18.13
Receiver beliefs (over amt. sent)	45	6.39	39	6.32	42.5	9.47
Sender beliefs (over acceptance)	45	9.75	35	9.80	47	9.84
Sender advice (amt. sent)	47	11.62	39	9.48	N/A	N/A
Receiver advice (min. acceptable offer)	40	14.04	39	13.62	N/A	N/A
Mean	41.33	10.90	36.33	9.32	37.13	13.41

x what the probability is that an amount less than that x would be sent.[10] Finally, in Figures 5.6 and 5.7, respectively, we present the sender and receiver advice functions. Both of these are cumulative functions representing the frequency with which advice to send or accept amounts less than a specific amount x is observed. Of course, there is no graph for advice for the history-only treatment. The calculated areas are contained in Table 5.2. Also shown are the break points where the step occurs in the benchmark step functions.

A careful look at Figures 5.1–5.4, 5.6, and 5.7 provides support for our main hypothesis that behavior is more conventional when advice is present. For example, the two most important variables constituting a convention of behavior in any ultimatum game are the offers and acceptances. If a convention of behavior is going to be established, then it must be that the acceptance (or rejection) behavior indicates a clear demarcation between what is an acceptable amount to be offered, while the senders must have a clear indication of what

---

[10] We use the median rather than the mean as it reduces the biases that naturally arise for the lower and higher ranges, where it is not possible to err very far in one direction. For the cumulated receiver belief functions, we use the median of the cumulative function, not the cumulation of the medians.

they should send. Figure 5.1 shows that, while such clarity about what an acceptable offer is might have been observed in the advice-only treatment, it certainly was not in the history-only treatment. This is indicated by the difference in the area metrics (8.58 as opposed to 18.13) as well as the shape of the functions. The same can be said about the offer behavior of senders in Figure 5.2. Here, again, the area metric is much smaller in the advice-only treatment as opposed to the history-only treatment (8.12 versus 16.21). Note also the vertical portion of the offer function at the step of 40 in the advice-only treatment. This implies that there is a considerable probability mass exactly at the implied step of 40. Such a mass point is not evident at the step of the history-only offer function.

Further evidence of a convention of behavior in treatments with advice can be seen in the estimated sender and receiver advice functions displayed in Figures 5.6 and 5.7. Here, again, we see a set of functions that very closely approximate a step function. For example, in these figures the empirical functions presented have mass points at or very near the break point of the step function. Again, this indicates that there was a fair consensus about what was a conventional offer and this convention was evidently passed on from generation to generation.

Differences between the beliefs of senders and receivers across treatments were less clearly differentiated and tended to be less step-function-like (see Figures 5.3 and 5.4). This may be because beliefs were measured in a less precise manner than other variables by asking questions about ranges rather than points, and because beliefs are less concrete to subjects than, say, offers or acceptances, which can be made very precise.

Further evidence in support of our claim that advice fosters conventionality can be seen in Table 5.2. Here we see that the area metrics for all relevant variables tend to be smallest in the advice-only treatment than in either of the other two. For example, of the six variables of interest, the area metric is lower in the advice-only treatment for five of the six variables when comparisons are made between the advice-only and advice-and-history treatments, while, for the four variables that are common between the history-only and the advice-only treatments, the area metrics are smaller for the advice-only treatments in all four. The advice-and-history treatment (where both advice and history are available) area measures are uniformly smaller than those in the history-only treatment.[11]

5.4 THE IMPACT OF ADVICE

Our discussion so far suggests that advice affects behavior in our simple bargaining context but it does not suggest how or why it does so. To investigate this, consider Figure 5.8, which plots the time series of the difference between offers and advice in each of the treatments involving advice (in the advice-and-history and the advice-only treatments).

Note from Figure 5.8 the close fit between the advice that senders receive from their predecessors and the offers they make. A simple yet effective model describing the offer behavior of senders would simply be to explain amount sent as a function of the advice received. In other words, senders tend to follow advice. This can also

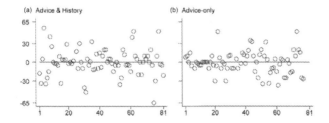

FIGURE 5.8 Deviation of amount sent from advice.

[11] We employ the Kruskal–Wallis test, a non-parametric test for differences in distributions. This test yields a test statistic of 4.57, which is significant at the 10% level, indicating that there is some difference between at least two of the treatments. Multiple pairwise comparisons between the treatments indicate a significant difference, at the 5% level, between the advice-only and history-only treatments, with the area metric significantly smaller in the advice-only treatment. We interpret this as evidence that behavior in the advice-only treatment is more conventional than in the history-only treatment.

be seen by comparing the relevant plots in Figures 5.1, 5.2, 5.6 and 5.7 for the advice-only treatment. As one can see, there is a remarkable similarity between the two, indicating that the offer behavior of senders is closely related to the advice they receive.

5.4.1 What Motivates Our Advisors

When people offer advice in situations like the ultimatum game it might be of interest to know what motivates them. For example, I might offer you advice in an effort to help you get as much of the pie as possible. The ultimatum game, however, has been one of the main vehicles used to argue that people have fairness motives and utility functions that are interdependent in the sense that they take the payoffs of others into account in defining utility (see Fehr and Schmidt, 1999; Bolton and Ockenfels, 2000; Charness and Rabin, 2002). It has also been used to investigate procedural fairness (see Rabin, 1993). As we will see, many of these explanations fail to explain our subjects' behavior.

It is difficult to tease these motives apart. For example, if I am a sender and offer a 50–50 split of $10 to a receiver, it is hard to know whether I did this because I wanted to be fair or simply assumed that you cared about fairness and would reject anything less. Our experimental design, however, allows us to actually observe the motives of subjects since we have access to the advice they offered to their successors, which is a treasure trove of insight into what our subjects were thinking.

There are many ways to rationalize the advice one offers. For example, as just stated, one might advise a particular split (say 50–50) on equity grounds or the same split might just as well rationalize a 50–50 split on payoff-maximizing grounds. Alternatively, one may support offering only 1 by appealing to the notion of backward induction as is expected of subgame-perfect equilibrium arguments. Backward induction arguments, however, need not only be used to support sending 1. One might advise one's successor that 10 is the best offer to make because one thinks that there is a threshold below which one's opponent will reject any offer but above which the offer would be accepted. The argument here is identical to the subgame-perfect argument but the threshold is not zero. This is how a non-subgame-perfect Nash convention can be established. Finally, one can refer to history and look for precedent in what to send or advise one's successor how to make predictions in the experiment since a subject's payoff was also affected by how well they predicted what their opponent would do.

To gain an insight into the thinking of our subject advisors, we took the advice statement they made and coded them according to the following protocol.[12] First, we read each sender and receiver comment. After doing this, we break down the senders' comments into six subgroups: best response advice (BRA), which basically supports an offer on the basis of expected payoff maximization; backward induction advice (BI), which is the type of advice consistent with subgame perfection in that it posits that the receiver will accept any offer and then advises the sender to send as little as possible given that expectation; fairness advice (FA); history-based advice (HBA), which refers to precedent or personal experience in the game; prediction advice (PA), which is advice informing one successor how to make a good prediction; and "other" (OA), which is advice that falls into none of the above categories.

For any text we simply recorded any and all types of advice it contained. For example, if a piece of advice contained references to fairness, backward induction, and payoff maximization, we counted all of them in our coding. Our point was not to define each piece of

---

[12] The coders were a set of three graduate assistants who were not familiar with the experiment or its purpose. They were given instructions to code the advice statements and any conflicts were adjudicated by an additional assistant brought in to break ties.

data as belonging to one and only one category, but rather to count all of the arguments used to bolster the advice given. Hence, in the advice-and-history treatment, where there were 81 generations, there is likely to be more than 81 advice codings since the same text can be counted in many different categories. For example, consider the following advice written by the sender in generation 46 of the advice-only treatment, which includes elements of many different types of advice in extremely pure form:

> The guy before me thought I should send 50. Although, that would be fair, it's not going to maximize your payoff. I was greedy and offered 10, thinking that the other guy would accept anything he got, BUT that wasn't the case. They rejected. So my advice is to be a little more generous, so about 30 should do it. Good Luck

This quote was coded as BRA, BI, FA, and HA, since it included elements of all of these.

For the receiver we proceeded as described above except that we changed the categories slightly given the differing roles of the subjects. We retained the codings BI, FA, HA, PA, and OA but dropped BRA since this was not appropriate to the context. We added a category SP (spite) for all those references which suggested retribution if the amount sent was too small and in doing so indicated that relative payoffs were important, and also BI+ which is basically advice that says accept anything above a strictly positive threshold. Spite and fairness are very close to each other so we have merged them in Table 5.3, but we point out that spite has a much more mean-spirited objective.

A spite statement might read as did this one representing subject 45 in the advice-only treatment, who suggested a minimum acceptable offer of 40:

> You're pretty much at the mercy of the other person, if they try to screw you reject it and get them back, otherwise take the money and be happy.

Table 5.3 *Advice coding.*

	Senders					
Experiment	Type of advice					
	BRA	BI	FA	HA	OA	PA
Advice-and-history	38	4	8	5	10	19
Advice-only	21	6	11	23	6	7

	Receivers						
Experiment	Type of advice						
	PR	BI	BI+	FA/ Spite	HA	OA	PA
Advice-and-history	7	11	3	29	8	11	13
Advice-only	7	10	6	12	5	3	13

Examples of a pure backward induction advice (BI) were seen in the advice given by the receivers in generations 34 and 35 of the advice-only treatment, who all told their successors to accept anything above 1 if it is offered, with the following explanations:

> accept any offer that is offered to you because to reject means that you get nothing. (Generation 34)

> Definitely accept anything, or else you get nothing.
> (Generation 35)

Finally, we added a category PR for prescription, which refers to a statement that simply suggested a cutoff point without any real justification. ("Don't take less than 40" – subject 47 of the advice-only treatment.) These statements are in fact close to BI+ statements and one might be tempted to lump them together, but they did not go all the way and remind their successor that 40 is better than nothing, which is what we expect of backward induction thinking.

The results of this coding are presented in Table 5.3, which present the results of our coding for the advice-and-history and the advice-only treatments. (Note that because we allow a piece of advice to be fit (coded) into many categories, the total number of pieces of advice can vary between senders and receivers.)

One of the most striking features of Table 5.3 is the relatively infrequent use by senders of fairness considerations to support their prescriptions. For example, fairness was not a principle that was invoked often (only eight times in the advice-and-history and 11 times in the advice-only treatments). More interesting, however, is that fact that when 50–50 splits are suggested, they are most often supported by payoff-maximizing arguments and not equity arguments. For example, in the advice-and-history treatment, of the 24 cases in which a 50–50 split is suggested, only seven are supported by references to fairness (a good number leave no written advice, however). In the advice-only treatment, of the 15 times that a 50–50 split was suggested, only three were supported by fairness arguments. Hence, observing a 50–50 split does not appear to offer proof of equity considerations.

It is important to note, however, that the fact that senders did not justify their offers to each other in terms of fairness does not mean that fairness was absent from their thoughts. For instance, they certainly may have feared, and rightly so, that the receivers did care about fairness and hence they better offer more than they'd like. Our point here is not to argue that fairness was not a factor in the minds of senders but simply to say that if they did have such a preference their written advice did not reflect it. Put differently, they did not seem to have the receiver's payoff as an argument in their utility function. Their only motive for offering anything positive seemed to simply be the fear of rejection and not interdependent preferences.

Also notable in Table 5.3 is the infrequent use of pure backward induction arguments. For example, for senders in the advice-and-history treatment, only four pieces of advice relied on subgame-perfect-like arguments while only six such pieces of advice relied on them in the advice-only treatment. The overwhelming bulk of advice had senders suggesting an offer to their successor which, given their assessment of the probabilities of rejection, either maximized their expected payoff or constituted a best offer given their assessment of the minimum acceptable offer on the parts of receivers. For example, there were 38 such pieces of advice in the advice-and-history and 21 in the advice-only treatments. When backward induction is used, it is usually used to support sending a positive amount based on the assumption that anything less than that amount would be rejected for sure. Hence, backward induction-like arguments are used, but not to justify sending zero but rather to justify sending some positive amount.

All of these observations lead us to conclude that we must reject the fairness hypothesis at least for senders.

With respect to receivers, the situation is different. Here recommendations for behavior rely much more on fairness and spite-like arguments. For example, in the advice-and-history treatment, spite and fairness are referred to 29 times to support rejecting low offers while in the advice-only treatment they are used 12 times. Note that pure backward induction arguments are more prevalent as well, used 10 and 11 times for the advice-and-history and the advice-only treatments. Here, being in the position of the receiver probably makes it easier to see how accepting anything positive makes sense.

5.4.2   Unfulfilled Expectations Cause Rejections

In our experiment we have elicited a great deal of information about receivers which can be of great help in describing rejection behavior. For example, we know what they stated as their ex ante minimum acceptable offer, and we can calculate the offer they expect to receive from the sender using their elicited beliefs. In addition, we know what they have been advised to accept by their predecessor. By comparing the offer received to these variables and observing rejection and acceptance behavior, we should be able to learn a great deal about how subjects decide to accept or reject an offer.

Table 5.4 *Rejection and acceptance behavior.*

Variable: Offer–Expected offer

Prediction	Treatment		
	A&H	AO	HO
Acceptance: Offer ≥Expectation	33/66 (0.50)	29/59 (0.49)	19/46 (0.41)
Rejection: Offer < Expectation	14/15 (0.93)	17/18 (0.94)	15/20 (0.75)

Variable: Offer–Minimum acceptable offer

Prediction	Treatment		
	A&H	AO	HO
Acceptance: Offer ≥Minimum	62/66 (0.94)	59/59 (1.00)	43/46 (0.93)
Rejection: Offer < Minimum	4/15 (0.027)	3/18 (0.17)	4/20 (0.25)

Variable: Offer–Advised offer

Prediction	Treatment		
	A&H	AO	HO
Acceptance: Offer ≥Advice	50/66 (0.76)	41/59 (0.69)	N/A
Rejection: Offer < Advice	10/15 (0.66)	13/18 (0.72)	N/A

Table 5.4 describes the rejection and acceptance behavior of subjects on the basis of the difference between the offer they receive and either their minimal acceptable, expected, or advised acceptable offer. Note that if any one of these three variables explains either acceptance or rejection behavior, it must be such that, whenever the offer exceeds any one of them, it is accepted, while when it is below, it is rejected. For example, if expectations matter for behavior, then we would expect any offer below a subject's expectations would be rejected while any offer above would be accepted. Table 5.4 shows the number of cases for which the difference between the offer and the other variables (expectation, minimum acceptable offer, or advice) correctly predicts acceptance or rejection behavior, over the number of possible cases.

A number of things are notable in Table 5.4. First, the difference between what a receiver was offered and what they expected to receive is very good at correctly classifying rejections, but is bad at classifying acceptances. For example, of the 15 rejections in the advice-and-history treatment, 14 occurred when the receiver was not offered at least his expected amount. However, of the 66 acceptances in the advice-and-history treatment, 33 occurred in instances where the amount offered was less than a receiver's expectations. Similar patterns exist in the other treatments as well.

The difference between a sender's offer and a receiver's stated minimum acceptable offer is, in contrast, very good at classifying acceptances but bad at classifying rejections. For example, in the advice-and-history treatment again, of the 66 acceptances, 62 occurred when the offer was greater than the stated minimum acceptable. (It is not surprising that the result here is stronger than that for the expected offer since it is almost always the case that a receiver's expected offer is greater than his or her stated minimum acceptable offer.) However, of the 15 rejections in the advice-and-history treatment, 11 occurred when the offer received was greater than the stated minimum. This seems to imply that rejection behavior is a "hot" phenomenon perhaps triggered for some subjects by a deflation of expectations, while stating a minimal acceptable offer is a more detached "cold" phenomenon (see Brandts and Charness, 2000). Rejection behavior when expectations are unfulfilled is also consistent with Rabin's (1993) idea that kind and unkind acts are defined by the beliefs that people hold about each other which are used to measure their behavior.

The difference between the offer and advice received variable is, perhaps, a good compromise, doing a reasonable, though not outstanding, job of classifying both acceptances and rejections. Hence one could state that advice is important for receivers since it avoids the extremes exhibited by those other variables. Overall, however, our analysis of receiver behavior shows a less dramatic role for advice than was true for senders.

5.5 CONCLUSION

In this chapter we have studied the impact of advice in intergenerational ultimatum games. What our results demonstrate is the overwhelming influence of advice on the behavior of our subjects. As we have seen, advice tends to be followed closely by senders and dramatically lowers the variability of offers when it is present. Hence, games played with advice generate behavior which is more "conventional" than those where advice is absent. Advice is also important for receivers, affecting both their rejection and acceptance behavior. However, for receivers, it appears as if rejection behavior is most affected by a deflation of their expectations, since most rejections occur when they receive an offer that was lower than what they were expecting, even if that offer is above their stated minimal accepted offer.

REFERENCES

Bolton, G. E. and Ockenfels, A. (2000). ERC: A theory of equity, reciprocity, and competition. *American Economic Review*, 90(1), 166–93.

Brandts, J. and Charness, G. (2000). Hot vs cold: Sequential responses and preference stability in simple experimental games. *Experimental Economics*, 2(3), 227–238.

Burke, M. A. (2015). The distributional effects of contractual norms: The case of cropshare agreements. *Working Paper* 15/7, Federal Reserve Bank of Boston.

Charness, G. and Rabin, M. (2002). Understanding social preferences with simple tests. *Quarterly Journal of Economics*, 117(3), 817–869.

Fehr, E. and Schmidt, K. M. (1999). A theory of fairness, competition, and cooperation. *Quarterly Journal of Economics*, 114(3), 817–868.

Güth, W., Schmittberger, R. and Schwarze, B. (1982). An experimental analysis of ultimatum bargaining. *Journal of Economic Behavior and Organization*, 3(4), 367–388.

Rabin, M. (1993). Incorporating fairness into game theory and economics. *American Economic Review*, 83(5), 1281–1302.

Roth, A. E., Prasnikar, V., Okuno-Fujiwara, M. and Zamir, S. (1991). Bargaining and market behavior in Jerusalem, Ljubljana, Pittsburgh, and Tokyo: An experimental study. *American Economic Review*, 81(5), 1068–1095.

Rubinstein, A. (2012). *Economic Fables*. Cambridge, UK: Open Book Publishers.

Schotter, A. (1979). The economics of tipping and gratuities: An essay in institution assisted micro-economics. *Mimeo*, New York University.

Schotter, A. and Sopher, B. (2007). Advice and behavior in intergenerational ultimatum games: an experimental approach. *Games and Economic Behavior*, 58(2), 365–393.

van Damme, E. (1998). On the state of the art in game theory: An interview with Robert Aumann. *Games and Economic Behavior*, 24(1-2), 181–210.

Young, H. P. and Burke, M. A. (2001). Competition and custom in economic contracts: A case study of Illinois agriculture. *American Economic Review*, 91(3), 559–573.

6   Trust and Trustworthiness

6.1   WHAT IS TRUST?

Trust is the lubricant of successful societies.[1] We must rely on others for much of what we do. It is hard to conceive of a successful society where trust levels are low. It is also known that the legal system cannot compensate for a deficit of trust in a society since all contracts are incomplete and hence rely on the good faith of the participants to adhere to them.

The amount of trust existing in society, however, depends on its past and the advice (warnings) people receive about being taken advantage of. Who we trust or under what circumstances is conventional. For example, in the old days, when one picked up one's land-line phone and the person on the line said they were from Chase Bank, you trusted that they were. Today, if you were taught correctly, you say "prove it". When you sign an agreement to have your kitchen remodelled with a contractor, unless you know her well, it is always wise to hold out a portion of the payment until after all the work is done. Paying everything up front can be an invitation to being ripped off. The question is: What is the conventional amount to withhold in order to successfully tamp down the moral hazard existing in the contract? This, of course, will depend on the level of trust existing in the society you inhabit and the conventions created to cope with the problem. If trust levels are high, people may withhold little; if they are low, you try to postpone as much of the payment until the end.

The fact that trust is conventional implies that it varies across cultures and contexts. In societies where people are not trustworthy, small acts of reciprocation can create large reputations

---

[1] This chapter is based on Schotter and Sopher (2006).

for trustworthiness. As we will see later, being trustworthy may mean merely acting in a manner that is more generous than expected and these expectations may be defined by societal norms (beliefs). Convicts released from prison may marvel at the levels of trust existing outside the prison walls which, to us, may seem paltry. Hence, whether I trust you in the future may depend on whether, given the society in which we live, you are more trustworthy than the average person I believe I might come in contact with. Since our experiments elicit these beliefs, we will be able to measure trustworthiness in both absolute and expectational terms.

The willingness to trust others does not just happen, however. We are taught to trust by those who have lived before us and by observing whether it is safe to do so. We are also schooled in the benefits of trustworthiness.

The level of trust existing in a society influences the way life is organized. For example, Fukuyama (1995) contrasts low-trust societies, where businesses take the form of small-scale family enterprises, because managers feel they cannot trust anyone outside of their immediate families, to high-trust societies, where businesses are organized as large-scale corporations because managers feel safe in delegating responsibility to non-related others.

These concerns raise certain questions that we hope to answer in this chapter. For example, how do we learn to trust each other? Once a convention of trust is created, how is it passed on from generation to generation? Does intergenerational communication increase or decrease trust? Does it increase or decrease trustworthiness? Is trust profitable? What is the causal relationship between trust and trustworthiness? In this chapter we use an intergenerational version of the well-known trust game (Berg et al., 1995) to help us answer these questions about how trust is developed and communicated to others.

Our intergenerational game approach provides a unique opportunity to answer these questions since it provides information that is not available when games are played as one-shot games. Combining information on advice and the elicited beliefs of our subjects adds information that can be used to investigate the motives that subjects have for trusting others and being trustworthy.

6.1.1   The Trust Game

When one person trusts, she takes an action that puts her fate in the hands of another, who has the ability to reward this trust or take advantage of it. The trust game of Berg et al. (1995) depicts a canonical situation of trust between two people (the sender and the receiver (truster and the trustee)). The game is very simple. Consider a person (the sender) who has a certain amount of money, say $100, and can either keep it or send a portion of it to another person (the receiver). When the money arrives at the receiver's door, it is tripled, so if the sender sends $15 the receiver receives $45. The receiver can then return to the sender any amount of the $45 she has just received (including nothing).

This game, like the ultimatum game, when played once has a unique subgame-perfect equilibrium where the sender sends nothing and hence the receiver has nothing to return. This is a grim outcome and easily demonstrates why trust is needed in society.

In the context of the static one-shot trust game, trust can be defined as a situation where the sender sends $x > 0$ to the receiver, thereby placing her fate in his hands. A receiver is called "trust worthy" if she returns an amount $y \geq x$ in response. These definitions basically remain the same when we investigate the intergenerational version of the game. One difference, as we will see below, is that while in the one-shot version of the trust game trust is a disequilibrium phenomenon, it can be part of an equilibrium in the intergenerational game.

In the intergenerational version of the trust game, depending on the degree of intergenerational caring and other parameters, one might think of equilibria where in any generation t an amount of money, x^* (the conventional amount), is expected to be sent and if it is then an amount y^* is expected to be returned. If less than x^* is sent in generation t, then nothing is returned by the receiver in that generation in order to maintain trust, while if nothing (or an amount less than y^*) is returned when it is supposed to be in generation t, then nothing is sent by the sender in generation $t + 1$ to maintain trustworthiness.

Note that maintaining trustworthiness requires behavior that spans generations, while a lack of trust can be punished within a generation. In other words, if the sender in generation t demonstrates a lack of trust by sending less than the prescribed amount, nothing will be returned by the generation-t receiver. Such a punishment, if carried out, will maintain trust. A failure of trustworthiness by a receiver in generation t, i.e., returning less than y^*, however, must be disciplined by the next generation by the sender refusing to send a positive amount.[2]

6.1.2   Trust and Trustworthiness

We investigate the relationship between trust and trustworthiness using an intergenerational version of the trust game of Berg et al. (1995).

Using the parameters in our experiment where the intergenerational caring parameter is $\lambda = \frac{1}{2}$ and the sender's endowment is 100, we see that embedding this game into an intergenerational environment expands the set of equilibria. In other words, with these parameters, when the trust game is played as an intergenerational game, there are a multitude of equilibria where the sender sends an amount x^* to the receiver and gets back exactly an amount $y^* = x^*$. Any amount $x^* \geq 0$ can serve as an equilibrium trust convention. However, since the sender gets back only what she sends, her welfare is not changed. For the receiver, however, welfare is an increasing function of x^*.

To illustrate this point, consider an equilibrium to the intergenerational trust game where there is a conventional amount x^* to send

---

[2] This is true because the trust game is played sequentially with the sender moving first and the receiver moving second, and hence if the receiver violates the trust of the generation-t sender, that violation must be punished in generation $t + 1$.

and a conventional amount y^* to return, and the equilibrium specifies that if x^* is not sent in generation t then nothing will be returned in generation t, while if y^* is not returned in generation t then nothing will be sent in generation $t + 1$.[3] Such behavior will be the type we consider here.

We consider such equilibria natural in this setting because the reward and punishments specified only concern players who are connected via their payoff functions. In other words, players are not expected to consider the behavior of players whom they do not care about (players whose payoffs do not enter their payoff function) who acted in non-trusting or untrustworthy ways in the distant past or anticipated distant future. They only care about their payoffs and those of their successors.

Using this type of equilibrium we can demonstrate that the only equilibria to the intergenerational game involve $x^* = y^*$ where $x^* \geq 0$. This means that placing the trust game in an intergenerational context allows positive levels of trust to be equilibrium phenomena and not oddities that can only be explained by non-standard utility functions.

To explain the properties of these equilibria, consider the sender in an intergenerational trust game. Her choice is to send 0 or adhere to the convention and send x^* expecting an amount $y^* = x^*$ to be returned. If she sends 0 and keeps her endowment, then her payoff is $\pi_{keep} = 150 = 100 + \frac{1}{2}(100)$ since she will keep her entire endowment during her lifetime and get $\frac{1}{2}$ of the next generation's endowment as well (since nothing will be sent in generation $t+1$ given the violation of the convention in generation t). With a convention in place where $y = x^*$, if x^* is sent then her payoff will be

$$\pi^S_{send} = 100 - x^* + y + \frac{1}{2}(100 - x^* + y)$$

---

[3] Since this behavior will perpetuate itself in the future, the data will look as if a grim-trigger strategy is being used over time.

where the superscript S indicates the sender. If $\pi_{send}^{S} \geq \pi_{keep}^{S}$, then adhering to the convention $y = x^{*}$ will be beneficial. However, checking this inequality suggests that this can only be true if $x^{*} \leq y$, meaning that the sender will only send x^{*} if she expects getting back at least that much in return.

For the receiver the calculations are similar. She has to decide whether to return something to the sender if she is sent a positive amount. Clearly, returning nothing dominates returning any positive amount less than x^{*} since both will trigger a reprisal in the next generation where nothing will be sent and hence the payoff from the next generation will be zero. If the receiver keeps the entire amount $3x^{*}$ that was sent, her payoff will be $\pi_{keep}^{R} = 3x^{*}$, where the superscript R indicates a receiver. Sending $y = x^{*}$ will mean that the next generation sender will again send x^{*}, and therefore her payoff from returning y which is at least as large as x^{*} will be

$$\pi_{return}^{R} = 3x^{*} - y + \frac{1}{2}(3x^{*} - y).$$

Comparing π_{return}^{R} to π_{keep}^{R} we see that $\pi_{return}^{R} \geq \pi_{keep}^{R}$ if and only if $y \leq x^{*}$, meaning that the receiver will agree to adhere to the convention as long as she is not required to send back more than the sender sent (more than x). However, combining the compatibility constraints for the sender and receiver we see that we must have $y = x$. So in an intergenerational trust game equilibrium the sender must expect to get at least as much as they send back in return and the receiver will adhere to a convention as long as it does not require her to send back more than the sender sent, which requires that $y = y^{*} = x^{*} = x$.

This intergenerational trust game equilibrium is a curious object. As mentioned before, while the welfare of the sender is constant across all equilibria (because she gets back exactly what she sends), the welfare of the receiver is increasing in x^{*}.

To illustrate this, say $x^{*} = 0$, so that in equilibrium nothing is sent or returned. In this case, $\pi_{send}^{S} = (100 - 0 + 0) + \frac{1}{2}(100 - 0 + 0) = 150$ while $\pi_{keep}^{R} = \pi_{return}^{R} = 0$. However, say $x^{*} = 25$, then

$\pi^S_{send} = (100 - 25 + 25) + \frac{1}{2}(100 - 25 + 25) = 150$ while $\pi^R_{return} = (75 - 25) + \frac{1}{2}(75 - 25) = 75$, so we see that, as x^* increases, along the equilibrium path, while the payoffs of the sender remain constant, those of the receiver increase. As a result, trust has a very quixotic implication in this environment, in that, if adhered to, it is a vehicle for the sender to increase the payoff of the receiver without affecting his payoff. Still, the sender will have to trust the receiver because she could be double-crossed.

If the sender has equity concerns there is one situation (not an equilibrium) where the receiver need not reciprocate at all and yet the sender would be content, and that is when the sender cares about equity, sends 25, and hopes that the receiver keeps it all. (We will call 25 the equity threshold.) Such behavior would equalize the payoffs of the sender and receiver at 75 for the stage game and at 112.5 for their intergenerational game payoff over their two-generation horizon with $\lambda = \frac{1}{2}$. If all subjects had fairness preferences, say of the Fehr and Schmidt (1999) type, this could be an equilibrium.[4] Our later discussion of fairness and reciprocity suggests that 25 was a focal amount for some senders as seen in the advice they sent.

Finally, allowing intergenerational caring, λ, to increase introduces equilibria where the receiver returns more than she is sent by the sender. In such situations the incentive compatibility constraints of the sender remain the same so that she will insist on getting back at least what she sent. However, as the receiver cares more about her offspring, she would be willing to send more back to the sender than she received up to a point. In fact, for any given y and x with $y \geq x$, we can find a $\lambda \geq y/(3x - y)$ that will support that exchange as an equilibrium.[5]

---

[4] There are other situations which provide equity and greater efficiency where the sender sends 100 and the receiver sends back 150, but in this situation in order to achieve equity the sender must rely on the receiver whereas the one where he sends 25 and hopes that it is kept does not.

[5] This can be demonstrated as follows. If the generation-t receiver returns y when x is sent and that arrangement is an equilibrium, the same exchange of x for y will happen in generation $t + 1$, and her payoff will be $(3x - y) + \lambda(3x - y)$. If she returns nothing and keeps $3x$ but breaks the equilibrium, then her payoff will be $3x$. So returning is

As we have seen, embedding our trust game in an intergenerational setting has expanded the set of equilibrium conventions that might exist. In the static game typically examined in the lab, there is no room for trust; yet despite that fact, in experiments money is still sent and returned. Our intergenerational setting expands the type of behavior consistent with equilibrium but in a very particular way.

6.2 THE EXPERIMENT: DESIGN AND PROCEDURES

6.2.1 *General Features*

The sequence of events in our trust game experiment is identical to what occurred in the battle of the sexes and ultimatum games. First, subjects were randomly assigned to the role of sender and receiver at the very beginning of the experiment. After reading the experiment's instructions, subjects are shown the advice offered to them by their predecessor. This advice has two parts. A strategy, which is a suggested amount to offer by the sender and a suggested return strategy for the receiver, and a free-form statement offering a justification for the proposed strategy.

Just as in the battle of the sexes game and the ultimatum game, there were three treatments: the advice-only treatment, where subjects could get advice from their immediate predecessor; the advice-plus-history treatment, where subjects could both get advice and can scroll through the history of those who played the game before them to see how much was sent and returned; and finally, the history-only treatment, where subjects had no access to advice but could observe the history of the game up until their participation.

Finally, before they made their strategy choice, subjects were asked to state their beliefs about what they thought was the probability that their opponent would choose any one of her available actions. Senders were asked for a probability distribution over the percentage of the amount received that would be returned (over 10 categories),

---

better than keeping if $(3x - y) + \lambda(3x - y) \geq 3x$. Given an x and y such that $y \geq x$, we see that for any $\lambda \geq y/(3x - y)$ the receiver will be willing to return y. Note that when $x = y$, a λ as small as $\frac{1}{2}$ will work, which is what the have in our experiment.

conditional on the amount actually sent. Receivers were asked for a probability distribution over the amount they thought would be sent (over 10 categories). To get the subjects to report truthfully, subjects were paid for their predictions according to a standard quadratic scoring rule which gave them an incentive to report their true beliefs.[6] After playing the game and learning their payoffs, subjects were then able to leave advice for their descendants.

6.3 TRUST AND SENDER BEHAVIOR

6.3.1 Offers and Advice: Does Advice Increase or Decrease Trust?

The question we address first is what is the impact of advice on trust as measured by the amount sent. As we know, in the ultimatum game examined in Chapter 5, while subjects tended to make positive offers, they sent lower offers in those treatments with advice. Does the same result hold here? As seen in Figure 6.1, the answer is yes.

In Figure 6.1, we see the histograms of all offers made in our three treatments. As was true in the ultimatum game, in all treatments the amount sent is substantially above the zero predictions of the static Nash equilibrium. For example, in all of our treatments 84% of the subjects send something positive. The mean amount sent is 31, and the median amount sent is 25.

The presence of advice, however, has a dramatic impact on sending behavior. As we see, the amount sent is substantially higher in the history-only treatment where there is no advice than it is in either the advice-plus-history or the advice-only treatment. For example, the mean (median) amount sent in the advice-plus-history and advice-only treatments, respectively, is 25.94 (15) and 28.10 (25), while in the history-only treatment, where there is no advice, it was 40.18 (30). See Table 6.1 for results of a set of Wilcoxon rank-sum tests.[7]

---

[6] The procedures used are outlined in Schotter and Sopher (2006).

[7] A set of two-sample Wilcoxon rank-sum tests indicate that while there is no significant difference between the samples of baseline and advice-only treatment

Table 6.1 *Tests for differences in the distribution of the amount sent.*

Pairwise comparison	z-statistic	p-value
Baseline vs. Advice-only	−1.24	0.22
Advice-only vs. History-only	−2.13	0.03
Baseline vs. History-only	−3.03	0.00
Kruskal–Wallace test for all treatments	$\chi^2(2) = 9.93$	Prob.> $\chi^2 = 0.01$

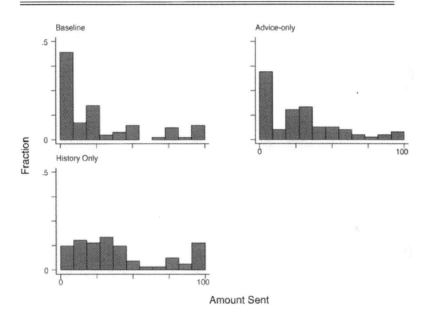

FIGURE 6.1 Histograms of amount sent by treatment.

In addition, while the inter-quartile range of offers in the advice-plus-history and the advice-only treatments were 1–40 and 5–40, respectively, the same range was 15–55 in the history-only treatment. Another measure of trust can be gleaned from the upper end of the offer distribution. For instance, 10% of all offers in the advice-plus-history and the advice-only treatment experiments were greater than

offers, a significant difference did exist between the amounts sent in the history-only treatment and both the baseline and advice-only treatment.

Table 6.2 *Regression of amount sent on advice dummy.*

Dependent variable: Amount sent	Coeff.	t-stat.	Prob. > |t|
Dummy (1 if advice allowed)	−13.18	−2.98	0.00
Constant	40.18	10.82	0.00
Model F Statistic (Prob. > F)	8.90 (0.00)		
Adj. R-squared	0.03		
N	225		

80 and 65, respectively, while 10% of all offers in the history-only treatment were equal to 100, indicating an extreme willingness to "risk it all".

Finally, to demonstrate the impact of advice on amounts sent, we ran a linear regression of the amount sent on a {0,1} dummy variable depicting whether or not advice was allowed in the experiment generating the observation (see Table 6.2). According to this regression, we again observe a significant and negative relationship between the presence of advice and the amount sent. On the basis of these results we conclude that advice lowers the amount of trust in this game by lowering the amount of money sent.

6.3.2 Advice Sent and Followed

Since we found that trust decreased when advice was present, it might be of interest to ask what that advice was. As we might expect, the amount of money advised in both of our treatments with advice was lower than the 40.18 actually sent in the history-only treatment. For instance, in the advice-plus-history treatment the mean amount advised to be sent was 19.42, while it was 28.10 in the advice-only treatment. Ironically, despite this stingy advice, subjects actually sent more than they were advised to.

To illustrate, in the advice-plus-history treatment, while the mean amount advised to be sent was 19.42, the mean amount actually sent was 25.94, with 29 subjects sending more, and 24 sending less

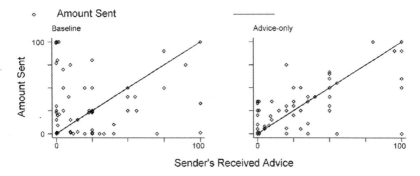

FIGURE 6.2 Amount sent versus amount advised to send.

than they were advised. In the advice-only treatment, while the mean amount sent tended to be no different from the amount advised, 28.10 versus 28.99, 36 subjects sent more than they were advised to, while only 21 sent less.[8]

The difference between what was sent and what was advised to be sent can be seen in Figure 6.2, where we plot for each generation the amount sent corresponding to the advice on how much to send that the sender received. The larger proportion of plotted points lying above the 45 degree line in Figure 6.2, especially for the advice-only game, indicates that there is some tendency for subjects to send more than they are advised to send.[9]

6.3.3 Does Advice Increase Sender Payoffs?

The next question we ask is: Is having access to advice profitable in the sense that it increases the payoffs of senders in the advice-plus-history and advice-only treatments relative to those in the history-only treatment?

---

[8] This difference is significant at the 11% level using a Wilcoxon matched pairs sign rank test ($z = 1.58$, $p > z = 0.11$), suggesting that the distribution of amount sent and advised amount to send may be different (pooled over both games where advice is allowed).

[9] We will see a similar result of advisees being more trusting than their advisors in Chapter 7 where we look at behavior in the minimum-effort game.

Table 6.3 *Tests for differences in sender payoffs.*

Pairwise comparison	z-statistic	p-value
Baseline vs. Advice-only	0.03	0.98
Advice-only vs. History-only	1.55	0.12
Baseline vs. History-only	1.39	0.17
Kruskal–Wallace test for all treatments	$\chi^2(2) = 2.76$	Prob. $> \chi^2 = 0.25$

The data suggests that there is some indication that the presence of advice is beneficial to the sender, but the significance levels for this result are not high. Advice does tend to lower the variance in payoffs to senders, while availability of history, conditional on being able to send advice, tends to raise payoffs.

More specifically, the payoff to senders in the experiments with advice (the advice-plus-history and the advice-only treatments) were higher than those in the history-only treatment where only history was available. For example, while the mean (median) payoffs to senders in the advice-plus-history and advice-only treatments were 91.37 (99) and 90.76 (95), respectively, those same payoffs were 83.85 (88) for the history-only treatment. See Table 6.3 for results of Wilcoxon rank-sum tests.[10]

Figure 6.3 presents histograms of the sender payoffs for each treatment. Note that the tails of the distribution of payoffs for senders in the history-only treatment appear to be thicker than in either the advice-plus-history or advice-only treatment. To be exact, while the

---

[10] Two-sample Wilcoxon rank-sum tests indicate no difference between the treatments with advice (baseline and advice-only treatments) while there is some evidence, though not overwhelming, of a difference between the history-only treatment and both the baseline and advice-only treatments (12% and 17% significance levels, respectively).

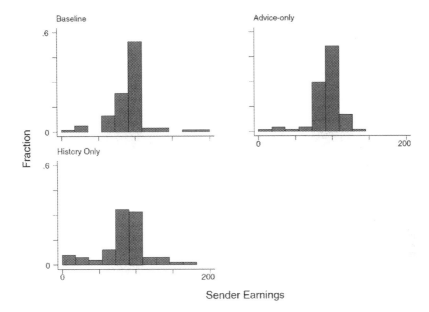

FIGURE 6.3 Sender earnings by treatment.

standard deviation of sender payoffs in the advice-plus-history and advice-only treatments, respectively, are 26.54 and 21.09, it is 32.79 in the history-only treatment. See Table 6.4 for results of F-tests.[11]

It is important to note, however, that while advice leads to higher payoffs for the sender, these payoffs are way below the 150 pay-off they should be earning at the equilibrium of the intergenerational trust game. This is because they are not receiving an amount equal to what they send as the equilibrium suggests. However, if advice suggests less be sent and if that advice is heeded, then the loss they experience by sending any possible amount is mitigated by advice and to that extent advice is beneficial to the sender.

---

[11] F-tests indicate that there are significant differences for all pairwise comparisons of the treatments.

Table 6.4 *Tests for differences in standard deviation of sender payoff.*

Pairwise comparison	F-statistic	p-value
Baseline vs. Advice-only	1.58	0.04
Advice-only vs. History-only	−2.42	0.00
Baseline vs. History-only	−1.53	0.08

6.4   TRUSTWORTHINESS AND RECEIVER BEHAVIOR

6.4.1   *Return Behavior*

While senders exhibit trust in their sending behavior, receivers prove themselves to be trustworthy by what they do in return. Given our intergenerational caring parameter of $\lambda = \frac{1}{2}$ in equilibrium a receiver should return exactly what the sender sent so as to make her whole. A receiver is trustworthy, therefore, if she returns at least as much as she received.[12]

On average, the number of times receivers were trustworthy according to this definition was substantial especially in comparison to the predictions of the static Nash equilibrium prediction of no reciprocity at all. In the advice-plus-history experiment receivers returned an amount greater than or equal to the amount they received 40.7% of the time, while in advice-only treatment and the history-only treatment they did so 38.5% and 37.9% of the time, respectively. These return ratios actually overstate the degree of reciprocation for a number of reasons. First, a large fraction of the time, when money was sent, it was very little money. For example, if cases where the amount sent was 0 (and thus the amount returned was also 0) are not treated as reciprocation, then the rates are roughly halved, to 23%, 21%, and 26% for the advice-plus-history, advice-only, and history-only treatments, respectively. As mentioned above, for the advice-plus-history treatment the median amount sent was 15, while in the

---

[12] We will later alter this definition when we introduce beliefs into our analysis.

Table 6.5 *Average amount returned.*

	Amount returned (# of obs.)		
Amount sent	Advice-plus-history	Advice-only	History-only
0	0(14)	0 (14)	0 (8)
1–10	1(24)	2.1 (15)	6.5 (4)
11–20	7.5(6)	11.2 (5)	7.7 (12)
21–30	14.7(14)	9 (13)	14.3 (10)
31–40	5.8(4)	26.1 (14)	23 (10)
41–50	25(6)	42 (5)	21.4 (5)
51–60	– – –(0)	50 (4)	5 (1)
61–70	30(1)	50 (2)	0 (1)
71–80	60(5)	100 (1)	75 (4)
81–90	20(1)	15 (2)	62.5 (2)
91–100	100.7(6)	86.7 (3)	62 (9)

advice-only and history-only treatments these median amounts were 25 and 30, respectively. Hence, in these circumstances, little trust was shown and little trustworthiness was shown in return.

Our data offers an insight into whether the trust exhibited by senders was reciprocated by receivers. To investigate this relationship we offer Table 6.5, which shows how much of the amounts sent in various intervals was reciprocated by receivers. As we see in Table 6.5, the amounts returned vary depending on the amount sent. There is a roughly monotonic increasing pattern in the average amount returned (note that the number of observations upon which the average is based is often quite small). Overall, sending behavior seems to be unprofitable since the average amount returned is typically less than the midpoint of the interval of amounts sent.

Figure 6.4 graphs the amount returned (on the vertical axis) against the amount sent (on the horizontal axis). Note that while there is a positive relationship between the amount sent and the amount returned, it is typical that less is returned than was sent, since most

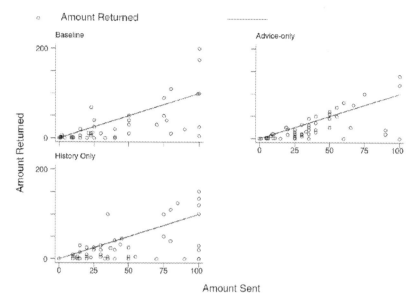

FIGURE 6.4 Amount returned versus amount sent.

of the data lies below the 45 degree line in the figure. On average, sending anything is a losing proposition.

To investigate the relationship between the amount returned and the amount sent in a more systematic manner, we use a censored normal regression, a generalization of the tobit model that allows for variable threshold levels.[13]

The regression results in Table 6.6 indicate that the relationship between the amount returned (AR) and the amount sent (AS) is a significantly positive one for all of the treatments, but is insufficient to ensure reciprocation. The coefficients imply the relationships shown in Table 6.6 and Figure 6.5.

---

[13] The upper censoring threshold level varies because the amount returned an upper limit equal to three times the amount sent. We assume that the amount returned is a reflection of an underlying latent variable, determined by factors which affect trustworthiness. A low level of trustworthiness leads to nothing being returned, while a high level of trustworthiness leads to the return of everything (three times the amount sent). Intermediate levels of trustworthiness result in a positive amount being returned.

Table 6.6 *Relationship between amount returned (AR) and amount sent (AS).*

Dependent variable: AR	Coeff.	*t*-stat.	Prob. > |t|
Amount sent (AS)	1.19	8.70	0.00
Advice-only dummy	6.28	0.67	0.50
History-only dummy	14.39	1.45	0.15
(Advice-only) × (AS)	−0.06	−0.27	0.79
(History-only) × (AS)	−0.37	−1.88	0.06
Constant	−31.70	−4.77	0.00
N	225		
# Left-censored	88		
# Right-censored	4		
Model χ^2 (Prob. > χ^2)	129.48 (0.00)		
Log likelihood	−710.99		
Pseudo-R^2	0.08		

These estimates imply that the sender gets a positive return only when he or she sends above a threshold of 26.64, 22.50, and 21.11 for the baseline, advice-only, and history-only games. These thresholds are all in the neighborhood of the equal-payoff threshold of 25. At levels above the threshold, note that some degree of reciprocation is implied (coefficient on AS >1) only for the baseline and advice-only games. Hence, advice seems to increase reciprocation. This reciprocation seems to be of a qualified sort, however, in that it is evidently conditional on some basic level of equity being achieved. As we will see in our next section, this relationship can be interpreted as one in which the advice offered functions as a lower bound on the receiver's actions by locating a salient anchor from which return payments are adjusted upwards.

The fitted values of the estimated equation, as well as the actual amount returned, are plotted against the amount sent in Figure 6.5. Note in Figure 6.5 that the actual amounts returned are very small

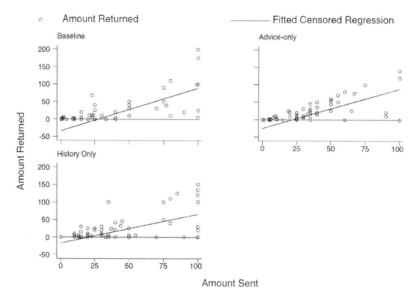

FIGURE 6.5 Fitted versus actual amounts returned versus sent.

or zero and are concentrated to the left of the amount sent when that amount was 25, while the relationship is more clearly positive for values of amounts sent greater than 25.

6.4.2   Does Advice Make Receivers More or Less Trustworthy?

Interestingly, advice appears to lead to higher return rates than those existing in the history-only treatment. For example, consider Table 6.7 where we list the mean and median differences between the amount sent and returned in all three experiments. (Note that a smaller number implies a greater returned amount, relative to the amount sent.)

The median difference between the amounts sent and returned in the history-only treatment is 12 while in the advice-plus-history and advice-only treatments this difference is 0 and 5, respectively, indicating that more is returned in treatments with advice.

Table 6.7 *Trustworthiness (send-return)*.

Treatment	Mean	Median	Std dev.
Advice-plus-history	8.63	0	26.54
Advice-only	9.24	5	21.09
History-only	16.15	12	32.79

Test for difference in means of (send-return)		
Difference tested	*t*-stat.	Prob. > |*t*|
Advice-plus-history vs. advice-only	−0.16	0.87
Advice-plus-history vs. history-only	−1.54	0.13
Advice-only vs. history-only	−1.53	0.13

One interesting result is that, while subjects return more in the presence of advice, they are actually advised to return less. So their observed trustworthiness exists not because of advice but despite it.

To establish this point, consider the results of a censored normal regression of the advised amount to return on any hypothetical amount that could be sent.[14] The dependent variable is constructed from the advice, which was in the form of a percentage of the amount sent to return, and it is regressed on the midpoint of possible amounts that one might be sent. We also include a dummy variable indicating whether advice was present in the experiment generating the observation. Letting ADR stand for the advised amount to return and AS the amount sent, these regressions yield the relationships contained in Table 6.8.

Note that these regressions confirm that subjects in treatments with advice are advised to return less than the amount sent. However,

---

[14] As we did in our regression explaining the amount returned (Table 6.6) we assume that the amount that the receiver is advised to return by her predecessor is a reflection of an underlying latent variable, determined by factors which affect trustworthiness. The idea is that if one has a sufficiently low level of trustworthiness, then one is likely to advise one's successor to return nothing, while if one has a higher level of trustworthiness, then one is more likely to advise that one's successor return a large proportion of what was sent.

Table 6.8 *Relationship between amount advised to return (ADR) and amount sent (AS).*

Dependent variable: ADR	Coeff.	*t*-stat.	Prob. > |*t*|
Amount sent (AS)	0.87	12.31	0.00
Advice-only dummy (AO)	−1.97	−0.33	0.74
(AO) × (ADR)	−0.12	−1.22	0.22
Constant	−30.57	−7.28	0.00
N	1590		
# Left-censored at AS ≤0	608		
# Right-censored at AS ≥100	17		
Model χ^2 (Prob.$>\chi^2$)	239.06 (0.00)		
Log likelihood	−5687.40		
Pseudo-R^2	0.02		

we saw previously that when it comes to actually returning money, advice facilitates it. In particular, the regressions for the amount advised to be returned (Table 6.8) and the actual amount returned (Table 6.6) have essentially the same constant term but the slope coefficient on amount sent is greater than 1 for the actual amount returned, and less than 1 for the advised amount to return. Thus, on average, subjects advise the next generation to return a smaller proportion of the amount they receive, on average, than they actually do. Generation-$(t+1)$ receivers are more generous than the advice they receive from their generation-t advisors.

One explanation for this might be that the advice offered to a subject may function as a lower bound on what the subject thinks is acceptable and she may adjust upwards when she actually plays the game. It is similar to Americans travelling in Europe and advised to leave no tip or just the small change yet finding it hard to do so and leaving more.[15]

---

[15] A similar result was found in Isaac and Plott (1981) where the existence of a non-binding price floor raised prices in a double-oral auction by functioning as a psychological anchoring point for the bidding behavior of subjects.

6.5 RECIPROCITY

Selfish maximizing behavior requires people to maximize their own monetary payoff without regard for the payoffs or actions of others. Alternatively, scholars have come to think that behavior in trust situations is determined by judging the intentions of others and responding or reciprocating to "kind actions" in a positive manner and to "nasty actions" in kind (see Rabin, 1993).

When it comes to looking for evidence of reciprocal behavior, we are fortunate in having data on expectations. More precisely, remember that reciprocal behavior posits that when someone does something kind (unkind) you are likely to respond likewise. For our purposes here we will define a kind act by a sender as one of sending more than the receiver expected to receive.[16] Let DAS denote the difference between the amount sent and the amount the receiver expected to receive in period t. When a receiver receives an amount greater than her expectations we would expect more to be sent back than otherwise. The results of a linear regression of the amount returned on the difference between the amount expected and actually sent are reported in Table 6.9.

As we see from these regressions, it appears that receivers behaved reciprocally in the sense that the coefficient in front of the DAS variable is positive and significantly different from zero. This indicates that when subjects receive amounts greater than they expected to receive, i.e., when their sender acted kindly, they returned more as a result. It is interesting to note, however, that the mean amount expected by the receivers was 27.54, 23.33, and 27.80 for the advice-plus-history, advice-only, and history-only treatments, respectively, which are amounts strikingly close to the equal-payoff threshold of 25 (i.e., that amount which if sent and kept by the receiver would equalize payoffs of the sender and receiver in the stage game). On average when this amount is sent, receivers tended to send

---

[16] Note that given our belief elicitation procedure, we are able to define a quantitative measure of kindness which is less arbitrary than that offered by Rabin (1993).

Table 6.9 *Relationship between amount returned and difference in amount sent (AS) and expected amount sent (EAS).*

Dependent variable: AR	Coeff.	t-stat.	Prob.> $|t|$
AS – EAS (DAS)	0.94	7.02	0.00
Advice-only dummy (AO)	3.75	0.85	0.40
History-only Dummy (HO)	3.30	0.70	0.48
(AO) × (DAS)	−0.09	−0.44	0.66
(HO) × (DAS)	−0.19	−1.07	0.29
Constant	14.86	4.79	0.00
N	225		
Model $F(5,219)$ (Prob.>F)	24.88 (0.00)		
R^2	0.36		

something back instead of keeping it, but as more and more was sent they responded positively although never with a coefficient greater than 1, on average.

Another way to examine the reciprocity issue is to ask how the amount sent relates to the sender's expectations about how much will be returned, since such an expectation is an expectation about how kind the sender expects the receiver to be. Including expectations in our analysis raises questions about what we mean when we call someone trustworthy. In our previous discussion a subject was trustworthy if she returned at least as much as the sender sent. When beliefs are introduced, however, the definition becomes more complex. For example, if I were to give a poor person a "loan" without a big expectation of getting any of it back (an act of disguised charity), and if the person worked hard and was only able to repay a certain percentage of it, I might still call the person trustworthy because, given the circumstances, they paid me back more than I expected or even wanted. In an experiment the sender may feel she was placed in a privileged position in being able to keep or send money and hence when she sends some she may not expect all of it to be returned since she might not do so if they were in the receiver's position.[17] This suggests a definition of trustworthiness that calls an act trustworthy if it was more generous than expected.

To investigate this, we elicited from subject senders their beliefs about what proportion of the amount sent would be returned. Specifically, we asked what the chances were that the amount returned would be between 0% and 10%, between 10% and 20%, etc., of the amount sent. Using these beliefs and the actual amount sent, we are able to construct a measure of the sender's expectation of the absolute amount that will be returned, conditional on the amount sent. We can then regress the amount sent on this measure and derive a relationship of the form amount sent = β(expected amount to be returned), from which one can derive the allocation of payoffs implied by any amount that might be sent. For our data (see Table 6.10), this regression yields a censored normal regression.[18]

The amount sent is increasing in the sender's expectation of the amount that will be returned. In fact, one can try to infer from the estimated relationship how much the sender expected to earn. For example, for the advice-plus-history treatment, the estimated equation implies expected earnings for the sender of 101 + 0.2(ER). The relationship for the advice-only game is 96 + 0.33(ER) and for the history-only game it is 97 + 0.38(ER). The mean expected returns were 35.0, 36.6, and 61.3 for the advice-plus-history, advice-only, and history-only treatments. Evaluated at the means, the regression predicts corresponding amounts sent of 27.12, 28.7, and 41.3. A literal interpretation of these estimates implies that senders plan to send amounts smaller than the amount they expect to be returned to them,

---

[17] See Çelen et al. (2017) for a discussion of blame-free behavior which could be used to provide the expectations of senders in our experiment about the behavior of receivers.

[18] Note that the censoring in this case is purely conceptual. The idea is that one can imagine a very trusting person who would send the maximum of any feasible range of amounts that he or she might be presented with and, similarly, a very untrusting type who would, if it were possible, "send" a negative amount.

Table 6.10 *Relationship between amount sent and expected return (ER).*

Dependent variable: AS	Coeff.	*t*-stat.	Prob. > |*t*|
ER	0.80	16.77	0.00
Advice-only dummy (AO)	5.04	1.55	0.12
History-only dummy (HO)	4.18	1.16	0.25
(AO) × (ER)	−0.13	−1.83	0.07
(HO) × (ER)	−0.18	−2.95	0.00
Constant	−0.88	−0.39	0.70
N	225		
Model χ^2 (Prob.>χ^2)	375.03 (0.00)		
Pseudo-R^2	0.20		

suggesting that senders expected to profit from the game, when in fact they did not. This relationship deserves further study.

6.5.1 Reciprocity and Fairness

The relationship between reciprocity and fairness can be complicated in the trust game. For example, say that I care about fairness and have a preference for equality. In some instances, reciprocation may not even be expected by the sender for small amounts if subjects have fairness preferences. For example, as mentioned before, if 25 were the amount sent then keeping it would equalize the payoffs of the sender and receiver of that generation at 75 each. Hence, amounts below 25 (the equal-payoff threshold), even if kept by the receiver, still determine a distribution of payoffs favorable to the sender and therefore having the receiver keep it all could be justified on fairness grounds. That is, the resulting allocation will be less unfair than if something were returned. So in an effort to be fair, a receiver may look like she is not reciprocating.

The advice statements sent to receivers reflect a mix of motivations for receiver behavior, and they vary from urging fairness and equal payoffs to being purely selfish and urging successors to send back very little. Examples of selfish advice are the following:

- "don't send back anything!!!!!!!!!!!"
- "maximize your own profit"
- "greed is good!"
- "Keep everything! Return nothing!"

Finally a statement showing that trust conventions may vary by geography:

- "this exercise is about powerlessness and frustration. In an ideal world the receiver and the sender would be cooperating, but this is New York, and you shouldn't trust me."

Advice statements urging equal payoffs or fairness appear more complicated and nuanced. Some statements like the ones below appear to suggest reciprocation.

- "you really don't have to send anything back. however if someone trusted me with half their wealth, i would probably send them back what they initially sent me as a goodwill move."
- "Ideally they should send you 100 and you should send them 150, but that doesn't normally happen...If they send you a tiny bit you should just send them 0 but if they send over 25 then give them something...ah well, won't people ever learn. Don't really pay attention to my numbers...just send back what would be fair to try to even the numbers."

Finally, the next subject exhibits a wide variety of thoughts including the idea that small amounts should be punished, moderate amounts rewarded, but if the sender reveals himself to be a "sucker" who sends too much, then everything sent should be kept. This type of U-shaped return advice (keeping everything if the amounts are either low or high and reciprocating in the middle), is supported by a variety of justifications ranging from selfishness to equity. Note, however, that 25 remains a benchmark for our subjects as it was in our regression results.

- "if he's offering below 25 francs don't give anything back if he's trying to cooperate he should be encouraged but always try to keep the amount between yourselves equal if he's a sucker and sends to much punish him and don't give anything back"

6.6 DO INCREASES IN TRUST LEAD TO TRUSTWORTHINESS OR DOES TRUSTWORTHINESS CALL FORTH INCREASED TRUST?

In our final section we try to disentangle a simple riddle: do increases in trust in society lead people to be more trustworthy or does the proven trustworthiness of people lead others to increase their willingness to trust? Put differently, is a person more willing to trust others when they see that others have acted in a trustworthy (reciprocating) manner in the past, or does the causality work the other way, i.e., do increases in the level of trust in the past lead others to be trustworthy today. Note that this question is well suited to being answered by our intergenerational setup.

The idea of trust leading to trustworthiness is, to start, just simple reciprocation from one person to another. The idea of trustworthiness leading to an increase in trust relies on the belief that trust will be reciprocated. In our experiment, reciprocation can occur intragenerationally, but the converse – an increase in trust due to past reciprocation – can only occur intergenerationally.

We define an increase in trust as an *increase* from one generation to the next in the amount sent. We further define trustworthiness as the result that a receiver returns at least as much as what the sender expected (i.e., the expectations of senders are fulfilled). We then can ask whether the probability of an increase in trust is influenced by trustworthiness in the past, and vice versa. A significant (and, in our interpretation, positive) estimated coefficient on the independent variable is interpreted as "causing" the dependent variable, in the sense that the former increases the probability of the latter.

Table 6.11 *Relationship between trust and trustworthiness: Does increased trustworthiness engender increased trust? Marginal effects on the probability that amount sent increases.*

Variable	dy/dx	z-stat.	Prob.>z
Increase in trustworthiness	0.31	3.85	0.00
Advice-only dummy	0.12	1.51	0.13
History-only dummy	0.07	0.81	0.42

Table 6.12 *Relationship between trustworthiness and trust: Does increased trust engender increased probability of trustworthiness? Marginal effects on the probability that (amount returned>amount sent) increases.*

Variable	dy/dx	z-stat.	Prob.>z
Increase in trust	−0.16	−2.73	0.01
Advice-only dummy	0.02	0.28	0.78
History-only dummy	−0.18	−2.79	0.01

The results of this exercise (Tables 6.11 and 6.12 for marginal effects) are that there is causation from trustworthiness to trust, but not the other way around. Specifically, if in the last generation the receiver returned at least as much as the sender expected, the probability that more is sent this generation than last is 0.31 higher.

On the other hand, if the sender in this generation sends more than the sender last period, this does not increase the probability that the receiver in this generation will reciprocate with at least as much as the sender expected.

This suggests that it is possible for past reciprocity to lead to increased trust intergenerationally. On the other hand, increased trust in the current generation tends not to engender reciprocity in the current generation. Thus, it is not hard to see why the "conventional" level of trust shown by subjects (senders) in our experiment is so low, on average. It is not sufficient that one be trusting today to engender more trust tomorrow. One must be trusting today, and others today must be trustworthy, in order for trust tomorrow to increase. Of course, one may be trustworthy even in the face of little trust, but the "target" one must hit to be considered trustworthy is not too difficult to achieve as long as expectations are low.[19]

6.7 CONCLUSION

The results of our trust experiment support our idea that trust is conventional in the sense that how one behaves when facing a situation where trust is involved is influenced by what advice you are given by those who have interacted in that situation before you. As we have seen, however, that does not mean that the advice transmitted was always followed. Our subjects systematically send and return more generous amounts than they are advised to. Despite this, or possibly because of it, the behavior of subjects with advice differs from those subjects in the history-only treatment where advice does not exist.

Using the Berg et al. (1995) trust game as our experimental decision problem, advice seems to decrease the amount of trust that evolves when this game is played in an intergenerational manner in that it decreases the amount of money sent from senders to receivers. Ironically, advice increases trustworthiness in that receivers tend to send more back. Further, we have discovered that subjects appear to follow conventions of reciprocity in that they tend to send more if they think the receivers acted in a "kind" manner, where kind means send more money than they expected them to. Finally, while we find

---

[19] One might think of an equilibrium with increasing trust and trustworthiness where each generation sends more than the last and receives more back, but such an equilibrium may be hard to construct since, if it involves the payoffs of the sender increasing, such an increase will eventually be impossible once the sender sends the entire amount and the upper bound is reached. That may cause any such increasing trust–trustworthiness equilibrium to unravel. If one thinks about an increasing trust equilibrium that keeps the sender's payoffs constant (by merely returning what she sends), it is hard to see the incentive for the sender to send anything let alone increase what she is sending.

a causal relationship between trustworthiness and trust, the opposite cannot be established.

Our results in Chapters 4–6 demonstrate that behavior changes in the presence of advice. Behavior in many instances moves in the direction of that predicted by economic theory and becomes more conventional. The idea that economic agents are proficient at processing historical data and incorporating it into their decision making is cast into some doubt here where we see decision makers performing better in the presence of advice. If, in the world, people typically seek the advice of others before making decisions, our results in this part of our book suggest that designs with advice may have greater external validity than those without it.

REFERENCES

Berg, J., Dickhaut, J. and McCabe, K. (1995). Trust, reciprocity, and social history. *Games and Economic Behavior*, 10(1), 122–142.

Çelen, B., Schotter, A. and Blanco, M. (2017). On blame and reciprocity: Theory and experiments. *Journal of Economic Theory*, 169(1), 62–92.

Fehr, E. and Schmidt, K. M. (1999). A theory of fairness, competition, and cooperation. *Quarterly Journal of Economics*, 114(3), 817–68.

Fukuyama, F. (1995). *Trust: The Social Virtues and the Creation of Prosperity*. New York, NY: Free Press.

Isaac, R. M. and Plott, C. R. (1981). Price controls and the behavior of auction markets: An experimental examination. *American Economic Review*, 71(3), 448–59.

Rabin, M. (1993). Incorporating fairness into game theory and economics. *American Economic Review*, 83(1), 1281–1302.

Schotter, A. and Sopher, B. (2006). Trust and trustworthiness in games: An experimental study of intergenerational advice. *Experimental Economics*, 9(2), 123–145.

PART III The Impact of Public Advice and Common Knowledge

In Chapter 3 we discussed the role of common knowledge in the definition of a convention. While Lewis's (1969) definition suggested that common knowledge is a necessary condition for conventions to be adhered to, Binmore (2008) cast some doubt on that claim, and Rubinstein's (1989) electronic mail game also suggested that common sense would suggest that people should be able to coordinate before full common knowledge is achieved even if theory suggests otherwise.

Most simply, as described by Geanakoplos (1992, p. 54), an event is common knowledge "if each one knows it, if each one knows that the others know it, if each one knows that each one knows that the others know it, and so on. Thus, common knowledge is the limit of a potentially infinite chain of reasoning about knowledge" (and see Aumann (1976) for a formal definition).

Notice that in this definition the object of common knowledge is an event which is a subset of states of the world. People have information in the form of partitions of the states of the world and the question is when, given what people are capable of knowing, will an event be known to them all in the common-knowledge sense.

In our work here, in order for people to adhere to a convention, it may be necessary for them to know what advice is being offered to their opponents. In Chapters 4, 5, and 6 all advice is private and hence it would be impossible for it to attain common-knowledge status. In Chapters 7 and 8, however, we introduce public advice into our experimental designs and look to see how that helps our subjects coordinate their activities.

In Chapter 7 we investigate the minimum-effort game (Van Huyck et al., 1990) and the impact of common-knowledge advice on behavior, while in Chapter 8 we investigate the two-thirds guessing game (see Moulin, 1986; Nagel, 1995; Stahl and Wilson, 1995).

These two games (which we will describe in detail in those chapters) are very different from each other and present very different challenges to the people engaged in them. The minimum-effort game is a coordination problem with Pareto-ranked equilibria, which means, as we will discuss later, that the players all agree on the ranking of the equilibrium as to which is the best; second best, etc. So there is no conflict of interest among the players as to which equilibrium is best; the problem is having faith that your cohorts know this and are aiming to choose that action which is best if chosen by everyone else. The two-thirds guessing game, on the other hand, presents players with a very different challenge. Here one needs to make a choice in a situation where your payoff depends on how strategically sophisticated you think your opponents are. Every level of assumed sophistication on the part of a player's opponents suggests a different choice (best response) for the player.

When both of these games are taken to the lab, they perform badly.[1] In the minimum-effort game, groups of subjects tend to gravitate to the Pareto-worst equilibrium despite the common rankings of the subjects over the game's equilibria. In the two-thirds guessing game, subjects fail to converge to the unique equilibrium defined by the iterative deletion of dominated strategies.[2]

The question we ask in these chapters is whether the existence of advice can help our subjects rectify these mistakes (in the minimum-effort game) or converge to the rational equilibrium (in the two-thirds guessing game), and does that advice not only need to be public advice but delivered in a manner that makes it common knowledge?

In answering this question for both the minimum-effort game and the two-thirds guessing game, we find that there is a trade-off between the quality of the advice being distributed and the way it is delivered. More precisely, in the minimum-effort game we find that the quality of public advice acts as a substitute for the degree to

---

[1] The minimum-effort game performed badly in that subjects selected the Pareto-worst equilibrium while the two-thirds guessing game failed to approach the predicted equilibrium.

[2] In the two-thirds guessing game it is not clear from a welfare point of view why convergence is important since in that game there is one winner who receives a prize and as a result welfare is constant across outcomes. If all players choose the equilibrium, however, then they split the prize, so rewards are spread equally across the population, but the pie is fixed.

which that advice is made common knowledge. Public advice which is very strong in urging coordination on the Pareto-best outcome and which is unanimous among the subjects offering it (what we will call "very good advice") can lead to efficient coordination even if it is delivered in a manner that is less than common knowledge (what we call "almost common knowledge"). However, advice that falls short of this quality threshold must be made common knowledge before it can be successful in helping our subjects coordinate their actions. So, as suspected by Binmore (2008), common knowledge (of advice in this case) may not be a necessary condition for successful coordination.

The same result exists for the two-thirds guessing game but in a modified form. In this game subjects look for a belief about their opponents to best respond to. In the standard analysis of such games, they are assumed to believe that all other subjects are one step below them in terms of strategic sophistication and, under that assumption, choose an action that is a best response to that belief. In the two-thirds guessing game with public common-knowledge advice, subjects will best respond to their beliefs about how their opponents will respond to the common-knowledge public advice that they all have jointly been offered. In such a setting, in order for advice to increase the level of strategic sophistication of our subjects, they have to believe that the advice offered to them is the type of advice that resonates with their opponents or that their opponents think it is worthy of best-responding to. It must be meaningful. Such meaningful advice, however, when made common knowledge, can lead subjects to respond to it in a way that other common-knowledge advice that does not have this quality cannot.

The punch line of this part of our book is that the use of the term "common knowledge" in the definition of a convention is more problematic than we might have thought. The difficulty in making an event (or a piece of public advice) common knowledge would tend to make the process of achieving a convention more difficult except for two things. The first is that if the advice is sufficiently strong or meaningful then it need not be delivered as common knowledge, almost-common knowledge might do. Second, even without this, a convention may be achievable if people have strong enough beliefs (short of common knowledge) that the convention is in place. Common knowledge is great when you can achieve it but life does not stop when you can't.

REFERENCES

Aumann, R. J. (1976). Agreeing to disagree. *Annals of Statistics*, 4(6), 1236–1239.

Binmore, K. (2008). Do conventions need to be common knowledge? *Topoi*, 27(1-2), 17–27.

Geanakoplos, J. (1992). Common knowledge. *Journal of Economic Perspectives*, 6(4), 53–82.

Lewis, D. (1969). *Conventions: A Philosophical Study*. Cambridge, MA: Harvard University Press.

Moulin, H. (1986). *Game Theory for Social Sciences*. New York, NY: New York University Press.

Nagel, R. (1995). Unraveling in guessing games: An experimental study. *American Economic Review*, 85(5), 1313–1326.

Rubinstein, A. (1989). The electronic mail game: Strategic behavior under "almost common knowledge". *American Economic Review*, 79(3), 385–391.

Stahl, D. O. and Wilson, P. W. (1995). On players' models of other players: Theory and experimental evidence. *Games and Economic Behavior*, 10(1), 218–254.

Van Huyck, J. B., Battalio, R. C. and Beil, R. O. (1990). Tacit coordination games, strategic uncertainty, and coordination failure. *American Economic Review*, 80(1), 234–248.

7 The Impact of Private and Public Advice in the Minimum-Effort Game

7.1 DON'T DO WHAT WE DID!

When new generations arrive in the world, they look around and many times remark about what a lousy job their predecessors (parents) have done.[1] The world we leave our children we hope is better than the one we inherited, but that is many times not the case. The question then arises of how, after we have made a mess of things, can we rectify the situation? The answer is to teach our children to do better. Leave them advice that basically says "don't do as we did but do as we say or advise you to do". This chapter investigates how easy this is to do.

In the one coordination problem we looked at before, the battle of the sexes game in Chapter 4, the tension was that there were multiple equilibria with unequal payoffs for the players. Conventions established there were conventions of inequality that justified one group of people faring better than others at the equilibrium defined by the convention. Because the unequal outcome was arbitrary, over time there were pressures built up for the underprivileged to want to change the established convention. This led to the instability we observed.

There are other coordination problems where the issue is different and, perhaps, even more frustrating. In these problems there is a stage game with multiple equilibria where the equilibria are Pareto-ranked so that there is one equilibrium that is best for everyone, one that is second best for everyone, etc. In other words, all players rank the equilibria identically and would all be happiest if they could

---

[1] This chapter is based on Chaudhuri et al. (2006).

achieve the Pareto-best outcome. So why don't they? The answer is that playing according to the best equilibrium is risky and, if you do not have faith that your cohorts will choose along with you, you may choose the safe strategy. If everyone does that, you can end up in a Pareto-worst world.

There are many games with such Pareto-ranked equilibria. In macroeconomics, economies can be trapped in a Pareto-inferior equilibrium (see Cooper et al., 1989; Cooper, 1999). In such instances no firm wishes to expand production unless it can be assured that others will do so, yet not doing so leads to an outcome that is worse for everyone concerned. Kremer (1993), in his O-ring theory of development, proposes extensive coordination failures as the cause of underdevelopment in many countries. Here countries may be caught in a low-level equilibrium "trap" when development requires the simultaneous industrialization of many sectors of the economy but no sector can break even industrializing alone. Similar considerations arise in models of currency crises or speculative attacks (see Morris and Shin, 1998), models of bank runs (see Diamond and Dybvig (1983) and Schotter and Yorulmazer (2009) for an experimental examination of bank runs), and models of political revolution (see Kuran, 1987, 1995) where it is politically risky to attempt to overturn a government unless it is commonly known that others will rise up together. Such coordination problems are ubiquitous and typically characterized by both strategic complementarities and spill-overs. In most instances these phenomena give rise to multiple Pareto-ranked equilibria.

The central question is how to break out of unsatisfactory equilibria when they occur. Obviously, this can only be achieved if some event occurs that convinces people that others have interpreted this event to mean that everyone will coordinate (i.e., increase output or revolt). In a macro context such an event might be an announcement of the central bank to lower interest rates or even some jawboning (public announcement) by a politician. In a revolution it might be a public demonstration (see Chwe, 2001). In other words, it must be common knowledge that such an event is interpreted in an identical manner by all agents.[2]

Because we look at this problem through the lens of an intergenerational game, where advice plays a key role, the object of our common knowledge problem is whether the advice offered from one generation to the next is common knowledge. More precisely, it is hard to act in a risky strategic situation (like the one we place our subjects in) if you know that your opponents have been given advice as to what to do but you do not know what that advice is. In such situations, if a safe action exists it is probably best to choose it unless you are sure that everyone else has been instructed to act responsibly and you expect them to follow that advice. It is at this juncture that common knowledge of advice matters and this is what we investigate in this chapter.

7.1.1 Private, Public, and Common-Knowledge Advice

Advice comes in different forms. For example, it can be private, where each player in a game receives advice only from her predecessor as do all the other players. It can be public, where all the players in generation t receive a sheet of paper listing the advice offered by **all** players in generation $t - 1$. The fact that advice is public does not mean that it is common knowledge, however. In order for advice to be common knowledge, it must be that everyone knows the advice, knows that everyone else knows the advice, and knows that everyone else knows that everyone else knows the advice, etc. The mere existence of a sheet of paper that all players have listing the advice of the previous generation does not make that advice common knowledge because players do not have the knowledge that everyone actually read the advice. All they know is that they received it. We call such a situation "almost-common knowledge" because it is certainly

---

[2] In his book Chwe (2001) discusses the fine points of arriving at common knowledge and investigates various institutional devices that societies commonly use in order to do so.

closer to common knowledge than private advice, but players are still unsure that the infinite hierarchy of beliefs exist that ensure common knowledge.

To make advice common knowledge, it is usual in experiments to read the advice out loud (in addition to handing it out on a piece of paper as we do in one treatment in our experiment). In the experiment discussed in this chapter, we vary the advice offered to subjects across the spectrum just described and also vary its strength as measured by how strongly the subjects in the previous generation urge the current generation to coordinate their actions and whether there is unanimity in the advice offered.

In this chapter we show that (1) common knowledge regarding the expected actions of others can lead to successful coordination, but (2) creating such common knowledge is often challenging, and (3) small deviations from such common knowledge (a small probability that maybe not everyone is on the same page with respect to what they expect to happen) can lead to seriously suboptimal outcomes. More precisely, we find that the strength or quality of the advice offered is a substitute for the degree to which it approaches common knowledge. In addition, if the public advice offered is very strong and unanimous, then it is capable of helping subjects coordinate their actions whether it is distributed as almost-common knowledge or common knowledge. If the advice is less strong, or less than unanimous, however, then in order to coordinate, it must be distributed as common knowledge.

To investigate these questions we use the well-known coordination game called the minimum-effort game (an n-person variant of the stag hunt game) which has a long history in the experimental literature (see Van Huyck et al., 1990; hereafter VBB). Let us look at this game.

7.1.2   The Minimum-Effort Game

In some real-world coordination problems the welfare of a group depends on the group's worst-performing (or least-effortful) member.

For example, before a plane takes off, it must be loaded with luggage, fueled, cleaned, and staffed by its pilots and flight attendants. Since the flight cannot depart until each and every one of these people perform their tasks, the take-off time will be determined by the slowest worker among them. If the airline's reputation depends on its take-off time record, then the entire company will suffer as a result of that one slacking member.[3]

One salient feature of such situations is the fact that, since everyone's welfare depends on the minimum effort of the group's members, putting out a lot of effort is risky since your hard work can be defeated by one lazy coworker. What's needed is a convention of hard work, one that is supported by the faith that everyone knows the convention and the belief that it is common knowledge. Creating such common knowledge may not be easy, but in a world with advice, it becomes important for people to know what advice others have received and know that others know it, etc. This is what we explore in this chapter.

This type of problem was first investigated experimentally by Van Huyck et al. (1990) using the minimum-effort problem, which will be the game we use in this chapter. It can be explained as follows: Say that you work in a firm, that produces a product. The more effort the workers put in, the greater the revenue of the firm and the share of that revenue received by worker i is a_i. In order to produce this revenue each worker must exert effort, c_i, where the effort levels are chosen from the set of integers $\{1, 2, 3, 4, 5, 6, 7\}$. So exerting effort, level 1 is the lowest possible effort, and exerting 7 is the highest. Effort is costly and increases in a linear fashion with a constant marginal cost of b attached to an effort level. Hence the harder you work, the more it costs you, and your marginal effort cost is b.

---

[3] The Knez and Simester (2001) study of the turnaround at Continental Airlines, and the Ichniowski et al. (2004) study of successful steelmills, report that the innovative use of both financial incentives such as bonuses and improved communications – between workers and between management and workers – are crucial to resolving the type of coordination failures seen in the minimum-effort game.

Table 7.1 *Payoff table in Van Huyck et al.'s (1990) minimum-effort game.*

		Smallest value of X chosen						
		7	6	5	4	3	2	1
	7	1.30	1.10	0.90	0.70	0.50	0.30	0.10
	6	–	1.20	1.00	0.80	0.60	0.40	0.20
Your	5	–	–	1.10	0.90	0.70	0.50	0.30
choice	4	–	–	–	1.00	0.80	0.60	0.40
of X	3	–	–	–	–	0.90	0.70	0.50
	2	–	–	–	–	–	0.80	0.60
	1	–	–	–	–	–	–	0.70

The tricky part of the problem is the way effort is translated into output or revenue for the firm, since in this situation the revenue created by the firm is equal to the effort level of the lowest-effort worker. Hence if worker i chooses an effort level of 7 but some other worker chooses an effort level of 1, then worker i's cost is $b \times 7$ but his share of the revenue is $a_i \times 1$.

More succinctly the payoff for each member of the firm is

$$\Pi_i = k + a[\min\{c_i, \ldots, c_n\}] - bc_i,$$

where k is an arbitrary constant. Choosing $k = \$0.60$, $a = \$0.20$, and $b = \$0.10$ defines the game depicted in Table 7.1 which is identical to the payoff table used by VBB. In Table 7.1 the rows depict the choice of player i and the columns the choice of the minimum of all the other players. Entries in the cells are the payoffs to player i.

In this payoff matrix the Nash equilibria are displayed along the diagonal and are Pareto-ranked. The best payoff occurs when all subjects choose 7, but since the cost of one's choice is subtracted from the common payoff to all, higher choices are riskier. In fact, the mini-max or safe strategy choice is to choose $c_i = 1$. Coordination here means everyone choosing the same effort level, but as long as they all choose the same they are in equilibrium.

When this game is played in the laboratory, subjects routinely select the Pareto-worst outcome where everyone chooses $c_i = 1$. While this result seems odd, it is consistent with a large number of game-theoretic papers, all of which demonstrate that Pareto-inferior outcomes are likely in a setting where the Pareto-dominant outcome is also the most risky. For example, Crawford (1991, 1995) demonstrates that the VBB results (and similar results from other studies) are consistent with results in evolutionary game theory and also shows how such results could be the outcome of a learning process which converges to the Pareto-worst equilibrium. Carlsson and van Damme (1993) study 2×2 global games in which risk-dominant equilibria are the unique equilibrium expected to be selected despite the existence of another, Pareto-dominant, equilibrium. Morris et al. (1995) generalize this result and provide conditions under which we would expect that to occur.

7.2 EXPERIMENTAL DESIGN

Our experiment is an intergenerational version of the VBB experiment and is very similar to those run in Part II of our book but there are differences. More precisely, in this experiment groups of eight subjects are recruited into the laboratory and play the same game played by subjects in the VBB paper for 10 rounds.[4] After this, each subject is replaced by another subject, a laboratory "descendent", or "successor", who then plays the game for another 10 rounds with the new group of subjects, so the generations are non-overlapping. Advice from a member of one generation to a successor can be passed along via free-form messages (but not strategies)[5] that generation-t

---

[4] The experimental sessions were conducted at Washington State University, at the Center for Experimental Social Science (CESS) at New York University, the University of Auckland, and Rutgers University. (No subject pool effects were noted, so all observations are pooled.) Inexperienced subjects were recruited from undergraduate courses and participated for about one-and-one-half hours. Average payoffs were approximately $19.00.

[5] It would be difficult to pass on strategies since a 10-period repeated-game strategy is a very complicated object.

players leave for their generation-$(t + 1)$ successors. Finally, payoffs span generations in the sense that the payoff to a generation-t player is equal to what he has earned during his lifetime plus what his successor earns.

In addition, before the first and last of the 10 rounds of any agent's life, we ask them to state their beliefs about frequency with which they expect each of the seven strategies will be played in the eight-person population. This allows us to investigate the relationship between observed actions and (typically) unobserved beliefs or norms.

As we mentioned before, the ability of our subjects to reach an efficient equilibrium will depend on three factors: (1) whether advice is public or private (i.e., whether subjects can observe all of the advice offered to all subjects), (2) whether public advice achieves common-knowledge status, and (3) the quality or strength of advice offered (i.e., how strongly people are encouraged to cooperate). We design our experiment in an effort to be able to identify each of these factors by varying the publicness of advice, its quality, and whether it is common knowledge or not. We do this via two distinct blocks of experiments that we will now describe.

Our Block-I experiments varied the degree to which advice was private or public and the degree to which it was common knowledge. We also varied the access to the history of previous generations but we did not control the quality or strength of advice offered, which we do in Block II.

In treatment 3, the private-advice-plus-history treatment, prior to the first round of any generation, subjects are allowed to view both the history of the previous generations and read the private advice offered by their predecessor. In another treatment, the private-advice-only treatment, they are only allowed to read the advice offered by their own predecessor in the previous generation, but cannot see the history of previous plays from earlier generations.

In other treatments, we also vary whether the advice was public. These are the public-advice treatments, which consisted of the public-advice almost-common-knowledge and the public-advice common-knowledge treatments.

These public-advice treatments were run for nine generations, with the first five generations being the almost-common-knowledge treatment and the last four being the common-knowledge treatment. During the almost-common-knowledge treatment, before play started in the first round of any generation, subjects were given a sheet of paper upon which was written the advice offered by all of the subjects in the previous generation. Each subject in this treatment knew that all other subjects were looking at the exact same advice offered by all the subjects in the previous generation, but any individual subject had no idea if the others in the session actually read the sheet or how carefully they read it. Hence, we call these first five generations the "public-advice almost-common-knowledge" treatment. Starting with generation 6, however, we not only gave the subjects the advice sheets listing all the advice left by the previous generation, but also *read these pieces of advice out loud* so the content of the advice on these sheets was common knowledge. This we call the "public-advice common-knowledge" condition. In none of these generations did subjects receive any information about the history of plays from previous generations.

In addition to these treatments in Block I, we ran two others. Treatment 1, the replicator (no-advice) treatment, aimed to replicate the VBB results (albeit with only eight rather than 14 or 16 subjects), running the minimum-effort game as they did with neither generations nor advice for 10 rounds. This was done, as the name of the treatment indicates, simply to replicate the VBB experiment with four independent groups of subjects. We expected and confirmed that all groups in this treatment would converge over their 10-period lifetimes to the Pareto-worst outcome.

In addition, in an effort to start each treatment off with the same initial conditions, we ran the progenitor treatment in which an initial group of eight subjects played the game once with no advice. This generation was the progenitor of all generations in all the remaining treatments in Block I in the sense that the first generations of all other treatments that followed used the advice of this progenitor generation. This means that the first generation in each treatment started out receiving the same advice and hence we held the advice to first generations constant across treatments.

Our Block-II experiments were run in an effort to isolate the quality of advice subjects received. This was not controlled for in Block I, except for the first generation, as explained above. To do this we ran another set of six treatments using a 2 × 3 design where we varied the quality of advice (good and very good) and the degree to which the public advice offered was common knowledge (common knowledge, almost-common knowledge and projector). As we will see later, advice quality varies by how strongly people are urged to cooperate in the minimum-effort game and how much of a consensus exists among the advisors whose public advice is being distributed.

These treatments differed from those in Block I in an important way. In these treatments each generation that arrived received the exact same advice (either good or very good) and played the game for 10 rounds. The advice they received was taken from previous advice offered to subjects in treatment 3 of Block I, so it was actual advice offered by previous subjects, just not their immediate predecessors. They left advice for the next generation to replicate the experience of subjects in Block I but that advice was not offered to anyone. Hence, each generation in each of the Block-II treatments received the same advice (either good or very good) but received that advice in three different ways. One way was as almost-common knowledge in that all subjects received a sheet of paper with public advice that all subjects knew that all others could see. This advice, depending on the treatment, was either good or very good (as we will define below). In other treatments, they received advice as common knowledge by not only having the sheet of public advice distributed but also by having it read out loud. Finally, in the projector treatment, subjects received good advice and, instead of having it read out loud, it was projected on a screen for all to see. (We did not vary advice quality with private advice since that treatment proved itself to determine Pareto-worst outcomes in a very robust way.)

The advantage of our Block-II treatments is that we are able to control the quality of advice that subjects get as well as the way it is distributed. The disadvantage is that these games are no longer strictly intergenerational since, instead of advice being passed from generation to generation and change over time, each group who enters the experiment receives the same advice. What we get are repeated observations of different groups receiving identical advice and playing the game for 10 rounds with no cross-generation interactions. This is not a serious drawback since one clear and consistent result we will demonstrate is that, once advice in any generation falls below a certain quality threshold, no matter how that advice is distributed, cooperation is very unlikely to be achieved. So the first generation is critical and that is what we concentrate on here. Our focus of attention in these experiments then shifts to the impact of advice quality and distribution method on the first generation receiving it.

The "good" advice was written by generation 3 of the public-advice almost-common-knowledge treatment and failed to spur coop-eration in generation 4, while the "very good" advice was written by generation 7 after we changed to common knowledge and led to consistent coordination in generation 8. The advice we used is presented in Table 7.2.

Note that, while both sets of advice strongly encourage actions that lead to efficient play, the second set (on the right-hand side of Table 7.2) is unequivocal both on what rule to use in playing the game and on what to do in the first round. All subjects in the "very good" advice category urge their successors to choose 7. However, in the "good" advice category (on the left-hand side of Table 7.2) two people equivocate. The first subject says to start with 6 in round 1 and then go down to 5 in round 2, while subject number 6 does not give clear advice as to what to do in the first round. Still, all other subjects unambiguously urge choosing 7.

In order to quantify the quality of advice offered by our subjects we took the pieces of written advice and coded them according to what we think they implied about the suggested course of action for

Table 7.2 *The exact advice given to the subjects in Block II.*

Subject	Good advice	Very good advice
1	Be ahead of everybody, start with a 6, then go down to 5, etc. You will be able to make the most money that way.	Pick 7 every time, EVERY TIME. If everyone picks 7 every time, everyone will make the max per round $1.30 \times 10 = 13.00$), plus you can make the full $1.28 for each of the predictions rounds. Don't be stupid. Pick 7. Honestly, you're here for the money anyway, right?
2	Choose #7. Don't be tempted to deviate but everyone must choose #7.	If you don't start the first round with a 7 then the pattern thereafter will be a 7 or lower. Bottom line – you must begin the first period with a 7|Or else!!!!
3	True, if everyone selects #7, you have max profit. But when you see the smallest # move down, you should follow.	Pick 7 for crying out loud! But if there is a weirdo who picks lower, pick that number too. Pick 7!!! Trust each other it will help you too!
4	If everyone continues to pick 7 you will maximize your profit. Anything else and profit maximization is not possible.	For the first round, you must trust the other participants & choose 7. Choosing 7 gives the maximum payoff. The [sic] adjust your choice by following the trend after the first round. Be consistent!
5	Start with 7! Everyone agree at least once. Once someone starts using one join them.	It would be best for everyone to choose 7 each time. However, if one person consistently chooses a lower number, you will make more profitably conforming to them.

Table 7.2 (Continued)

6	Follow the trend. Ideally you want to maximize at seven but inevitable someone doesn't get it.	Picking 7 will yield the maximum payoff pick 6 if everyone picks 7. So start out picking 7, however, some people are very untrusting and will or 5 – starts picking start picking that also.
7	Stay with 7 unless someone won't use that number. If they insist on a lower number go with it.	Chose 7 & and hope everyone else does. But it is important to follow any trends you notice.
8	Pick #7 until after it is apparent that the number declines and then follow it down.	The thrill of not choosing seven leads only to a smaller payoff than both you and everyone else could earn.
Advice code	6, 7, 7, 7, 7, 0, 7, 7	7, 7, 7, 7, 7, 7, 7, 7

the first round of any generation's life. These codes are listed at the bottom of each column in Table 7.2. For example, if a subject said, "Choose 7 in round 1 and then choose the round $t - 1$ minimum in round t", we coded this with a 7 since it indicated that in the first round 7 should be chosen and then the subject should see what happens and then follow the minimum thereafter.

Using this coding convention we coded our "good" advice as $(6, 7, 7, 7, 7, 0, 7, 7)$ and our "very good" advice as $(7, 7, 7, 7, 7, 7, 7, 7)$. Again, we stress that to most people the good advice listed above would be considered a strong statement in favor of coordination. However, since this is a coordination game, subjects need to know more than that in order to cooperate. They need to know that everyone else knows that everyone else considers this set of advice to be sufficiently strong to act cooperatively and this must be considered

Table 7.3 *Experimental design: Block I.*

No.	Game	No. of generation	Rounds/ generation	Subjects/ generation	No. of subjects
1	Replicator: No advice or history	4	10	8	32
2	Progenitor	1	10	8	8
3	Private advice plus history	6	10	8	48
4	Private advice only	6	10	8	48
	Public advice	9	10	8	71[a]
5	Public advice (not read aloud)	5	10	8	40
	Public advice (read aloud)	4	10	8	31
	TOTAL				207

[a]In the very last session of the public advice game, we only had seven subjects instead of the eight that we used in every other session.

common knowledge. The fact that the very good advice is unanimous is probably also important.

The exact experimental design is summarized in Tables 7.3 and 7.4.

7.3   CAN WE TALK OURSELVES TO EFFICIENCY? RESULTS

Our experimental design reflects the path we needed to take in order to get our subjects to successfully coordinate their activities. What we will find is that it is extremely hard to get agents to coordinate their actions in this game and that the necessary conditions for coordination are that the advice offered be (1) not only extremely positive but also (2) offered publicly. If advice is less exhortative (only of the "good" variety), however, then the manner in which it is distributed does matter, at least for the behavior of subjects in the first generation of their interaction. However, because behavior in succeeding rounds is so path-dependent, first-generation behavior becomes crucial for eventual coordination.

Let's start by looking at behavior in Block I.

7.3.1   Block I Treatments – Minimum Choices

Table 7.5 shows the behavior of the minimum in the Block I treatments of our experiment, while, for comparison, Table 7.6 does the

Table 7.4 *Experimental design: Block II.*

No.	Treatment	No. of groups	Rounds/ group	Subjects/ Group	Advice quality	No. of Subjects
6	CK	4	10	8	Good	32
7	ACK	4	10	8	Good	32
8	Advice projected	3	10	8	Good	24
9	CK	4	10	8	Very good	32
10	ACK	4	10	8	Very good	32
11	Private advice	3	10	8	Very good	24
	Total					176

same for the original (Van Huyck et al., 1990) VBB experiment. In Figure 7.1 we present the round-by-round minimum choices of subjects for each of the five games in Block I along with those of the subjects in the seven groups run by VBB. Here we show the pattern of choices made by each generation in the different games over all 10 rounds. Each block in Figure 7.1 represents one generation and shows the minimum choices that particular generation made over all 10 rounds.

As can be seen from Tables 7.5 and 7.6, the behavior of the group minima in the VBB and our replicator (no-advice) experiments is striking. First, note that in the VBB experiment (Table 7.6), none of the seven groups managed to achieve a minimum greater than 4 and in no group did the minimum remain above 1 for more than three rounds. In two of the seven groups (groups 6 and 7) we observe 1 chosen in each round. This behavior is even more dramatic in our four replicator experiments (treatment 1 in Table 7.5). Here in no round was the minimum greater than 2 and that only occurred in two sessions and only during the first round. Beyond that, all minima were equal to 1.

It was exactly this behavior that we expected would disappear when we introduced private advice into our design. To our surprise we found just the opposite to be true. For example, in the advice-only treatment (treatment 4 in Table 7.3) the behavior exhibited was less coordinated than that in either the VBB experiment or our replicator treatment. In no round of any generation did we ever observe a

Table 7.5 *Observed minimum choices in Block I by round.*

	Rounds									
	1	2	3	4	5	6	7	8	9	10
Treatment 1: Replicator										
Group 1	2	1	1	1	1	1	1	1	1	1
Group 2	2	1	1	1	1	1	1	1	1	1
Group 3	1	1	1	1	1	1	1	1	1	1
Group 4	1	1	1	1	1	1	1	1	1	1
Treatment 2: Progenitor										
Progenitor group	1	1	1	1	1	1	1	1	1	1
Treatment 3: Advice plus history										
Generation 1	1	1	1	1	1	1	1	1	1	1
Generation 2	1	1	1	1	1	1	1	1	1	1
Generation 3	4	4	4	4	4	4	4	4	4	4
Generation 4	1	2	2	2	2	2	2	2	2	1
Generation 5	1	1	1	1	1	1	1	1	1	1
Generation 6	1	1	1	1	1	1	1	1	1	1
Treatment 4: Advice only										
Generation 1	1	1	1	1	1	1	1	1	1	1
Generation 2	1	1	1	1	1	1	1	1	1	1
Generation 3	1	1	1	1	1	1	1	1	1	1
Generation 4	1	1	1	1	1	1	1	1	1	1
Generation 5	1	1	1	1	1	1	1	1	1	1
Generation 6	1	1	1	1	1	1	1	1	1	1
Treatment 5: Public advice										
Generation 1	1	1	1	1	1	1	1	1	1	1
Generation 2	1	1	1	1	1	1	1	1	1	1
Generation 3	6	5	5	4	1	1	1	1	1	1
Generation 4	4	4	3	2	1	1	1	1	1	1
Generation 5	4	3	1	1	1	1	1	1	1	1
Generation 6	7	7	7	7	7	7	7	7	7	7
Generation 7	6	6	6	6	6	6	6	6	6	5
Generation 8	7	7	7	7	7	7	7	7	7	7
Generation 9	7	7	7	7	7	7	7	7	7	7

Table 7.6 *Group minima (VBB; Van Huyck et al., 1990).*

Group	Rounds									
	1	2	3	4	5	6	7	8	9	10
1	2	2	2	1	1	1	1	1	1	1
2	2	1	1	1	1	1	1	1	1	1
3	4	2	2	1	1	1	1	1	1	1
4	4	2	3	1	1	1	1	1	1	1
5	3	2	1	1	1	1	1	1	1	1
6	1	1	1	1	1	1	1	1	1	1
7	1	1	1	1	1	1	1	1	1	1

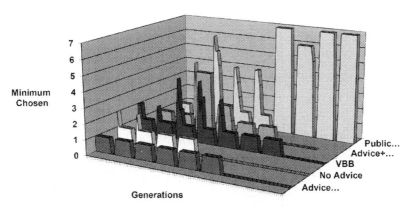

FIGURE 7.1 Behavior of minimum across Block I treatments.

minimum above 1. Hence, it appears that a treatment where subjects cannot observe previous history but can only pass on private advice is hostile to efficiency in a risky environment.

When advice and history are both available, as in treatment 3, we do observe somewhat more improved coordination. Here, as in the advice-only treatment, in four of the six generations (generations 1, 2, 5, and 6) we observed a minimum of 1 in each round. However, in generation 3, we observe the first instance of an interior equilibrium existing for all 10 rounds. Here the minimum starts out at 4 in round 1 and stays at that level for the remainder of the game. In the next generation we also see an elevated minimum of 2 existing from round 2 to round 9. These two generations exhibit behavior different than any seen in the VBB or replicators' games since they exhibit the first instances of a minimum above 1 lasting past round 3. Still, these results cannot be considered evidence of any strong impact of advice on behavior in our intergenerational setup. Finally, in spite of the fact we see a minimum higher than 1 for two generations in this game, subjects find it impossible to sustain that level of coordination and by generations 5 and 6, the minimum is again 1 for all 10 rounds.[6]

In order to find truly different behavior one must look at the results of treatment 5, where public advice is offered from generation 6 on. In generations 1–5 (the public-advice almost-common-knowledge treatment), while all subjects read all of the advice from their eight predecessors, this advice was not read out loud. As one can see, despite some attempts at improved coordination, subjects here were not successful in sustaining efficient coordination. In generation 6 we introduced a treatment change and we read out loud the advice from all the generation 5 subjects (the public-advice common-knowledge treatment). As one can see, this had a large impact, raising the minimum to 7 in all 10 rounds. From this generation on, in no round was the minimum choice below 5. In short, this treatment, with public advice and common knowledge, was successful in breaking the stranglehold that the all-1 equilibrium had on behavior up until this point.

To quantify more precisely the differences in choice behavior among the treatments, we estimate the probability of making various choices, using an ordered probit model with random effects. The details of our estimation are offered in the appendix in Section 7.6.

---

[6] There are very few papers that have been successful in achieving efficiency in the minimum-effort game. Avoyan and Ramos (2020) is a rare exception. In their paper they introduce a dynamic mechanism that allows players to achieve a Pareto-efficient outcome as an equilibrium.

Table 7.7 *Estimated probability of choosing a particular number: Block I treatments (at treatment averages of other variables).*

Choice	Progenitor generation	No advice	Advice-only	Advice-plus-history	Public advice Almost-common-knowledge	Public advice Common-knowledge
1	0.56	0.65	0.76	0.49	0.22	0.00
2	0.22	0.20	0.15	0.24	0.22	0.00
3	0.08	0.07	0.04	0.10	0.13	0.00
4	0.09	0.07	0.04	0.11	0.21	0.01
5	0.03	0.02	0.01	0.03	0.09	0.01
6	0.01	0.01	0.00	0.02	0.07	0.02
7	0.01	0.00	0.00	0.01	0.07	0.96

Table 7.8 *Estimated probability of choosing a particular number: Block I treatments (at full-sample averages of other variables).*

Choice	Progenitor generation	No advice	Advice-only	Advice-plus-history	Public advice Almost-common-knowledge	Public advice Common-knowledge
1	0.45	0.56	0.67	0.42	0.19	0.00
2	0.24	0.22	0.19	0.24	0.21	0.01
3	0.10	0.08	0.06	0.11	0.13	0.01
4	0.13	0.09	0.06	0.13	0.22	0.04
5	0.04	0.03	0.01	0.04	0.10	0.06
6	0.02	0.01	0.01	0.03	0.07	0.09
7	0.02	0.01	0.00	0.02	0.08	0.79

Tables 7.7 and 7.8 provide the fitted (predicted) values for the probabilities of each choice (1 to 7) estimated using our ordered probit.

The fitted values in Tables 7.7 and 7.8 provide a more intuitive picture of the experiment. Table 7.7 contains the estimated choice probabilities with all variables except the treatment dummies held at the treatment average. Thus, these will most closely replicate the raw data averages. Table 7.8 contains estimates with variables held at the full-sample averages. The estimated probabilities are somewhat less dramatically different here (e.g., the probability of choosing 7 is 0.79 in the public-advice common-knowledge treatment in Table 7.8

versus 0.96 in the same treatment in Table 7.7) across the games, probably due to the lower average balance subjects held in the games where advice was not read aloud. Overall, however, the estimation exercise contains no great surprises, confirming what one sees in the raw data. There is a large and significant effect when advice is read aloud, dramatically increasing the probability of choosing 7.

Thus while our experimental agents were finally capable of "talking themselves to efficiency", the process was much harder than we expected and occurred only when advice was public and common knowledge.[7, 8]

7.3.2 Beliefs in Block I

Since beliefs are crucial for behavior, we are interested in comparing the beliefs of subjects in our replicator (no-advice) game to those of subjects in our private and public advice games. Two questions are of interest: First, does the existence of advice change the distribution of subjects' beliefs from what it would be if no advice existed? Second, does advice increase the minimum action upon which there is

---

[7] Note that including advice in our experiments is different from either including cheap talk or allowing free communication amongst decision makers, both of which have been known to increase efficiency (see Dawes et al., 1977; Isaac and Walker, 1988; Cooper et al., 1989, 1992; Charness, 2000; Burton and Sefton, 2004). Blume and Ortmann (2007) look at the impact of costless pre-play communication in the minimum-effort game itself. Blume and Ortmann (2007) find that such costless messages do increase efficiency but subjects still find it extremely difficult to coordinate to the Pareto-dominant outcomes. Cheap talk statements are public, non-binding, and payoff-irrelevant statements made by the players who are actually going to play the game and not their predecessors. In contrast, except for the public-advice treatment, our advice statements are private and made by predecessors. Even when we made advice public and common knowledge, these statements are still not made by the people who are about to play the game. Our advice treatments are different from the communication treatments found in public goods experiments since we only permit one-sided statements to be made and not bilateral or multilateral non-binding discussions.

[8] To demonstrate that the result that common knowledge of advice facilitates coordination to the payoff-dominant outcome is not caused by the fact that in our study a professor reads the advice out loud, Antonopoulos et al. (2022) in a follow-up paper to Chaudhuri et al. (2009), replicate this same discontinuity in behaviour when advice is common knowledge and when it is not using only undergraduate students as experimental administrators.

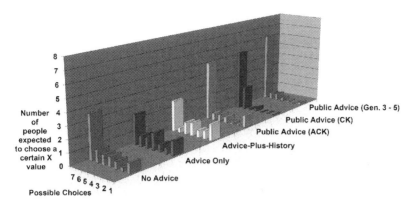

FIGURE 7.2 Comparison of beliefs across treatments in Block I.

positive probability placed? The second question is important since if subjects best respond then the best response rule is trivial: choose that action which you think is the minimum to be chosen by your cohort. Hence, if any subject believes that there will be even one other who will choose 1, then 1 is their best response.[9] If advice can raise this expected minimum, it can succeed in raising subjects' choices.

The answer to both of these questions can be seen in Figure 7.2, which presents the results treatment by treatment. This diagram places the various actions $1, 2, \ldots, 7$ along the horizontal axis and along the vertical axis it displays the mean number of subjects (aggregated over all generations) predicted to choose that action. For example, we see that on average in the no-advice game subjects expected 3.6 people in their group of eight to choose 7, 1 person to choose 6, etc.

Looking across these games there are some interesting results. First, when comparing the beliefs of subjects in the no-advice treatment to those in the private-advice treatments (advice-only

[9] Although a subject's best response can still be 7 even if she thinks that there is some small probability that some other subject (or subjects) will choose 1, our data suggests that that prospect looms large in the strategy thinking of subjects and that even minor doubts can lead to risk-averse choices.

and advice-plus-history), we see that while there appears to be no significant difference (at the 5% level) between these distributions, private advice does seem to lower expectations in the sense that subjects expect more people to choose 7 in the no-advice treatment (mean = 3.6) than in either the advice-only treatment (mean = 2.5) or the advice-plus-history treatment (mean = 2.6).[10]

In addition, subjects in the private-advice treatments predict at least one person will choose 1 (mean = 1.2 for the advice-only treatment and 1.4 for the advice-plus-history treatment) while in the no-advice treatment subjects expect an average of only 0.80 subjects will choose 1. Obviously, the advice offered damaged beliefs in the private-advice treatments and led subjects to think that fewer people are likely to choose 7 and more are likely to choose 1.

The results in the public-advice treatments are quite different, as can be seen from Figure 7.2. For example, in the public-advice common-knowledge (CK) treatment (fifth set of histograms from the left in Figure 7.2), we see that on average subjects expected 5.2 people to choose 7 in round 1 and **no one** to choose either 1, 2, or 3. It is only in the public-advice common-knowledge (CK) treatment that we get beliefs which place zero value on someone choosing 1. In all the other treatments, subjects place a positive (albeit small) probability on someone in the group choosing 1.

The firm belief that no one will choose a low number in the public-advice common-knowledge treatment seems to give subjects the confidence which allows them to choose 7 and maintain efficiency. In addition, the distribution of beliefs for this game is significantly different from the distribution of beliefs in all other games at the 1% level. When we compare the distribution of beliefs in the public-advice common-knowledge and almost-common-knowledge

---

[10] The difference between the distributions of beliefs in the no-advice and advice-plus-history treatments is significant at the 10% level using a χ^2 test (χ^2(7 d.o.f.) = 14.32). A χ^2 test fails to detect any difference in the distributions of beliefs in the no-advice and advice-only treatments even at the 10% level (χ^2(7 d.o.f.) = 8.88).

Table 7.9 *Chi-square test on belief distributions for Block I treatments.*

Treatment	Advice only	Advice + history	Public advice ACK All gens	Public advice ACK Gens 3–5	Public advice CK
No advice	8.88	14.32*	11.84	26.91***	34.24***
Advice only	—	3.84	31.2***	62.45***	64.16***
Advice + history	—	—	31.84***	63.12***	103.92***
Public advice ACK All gens	—	—	—	—	37.92***
Public advice ACK gens 3–5	—	—	—	—	31.19***

[a]Asterisks: * = significant at 10%, ** = significant at 5%, *** = significant at 1%.

treatments, we see that common knowledge has an impact on beliefs. In Figure 7.2 and Table 7.9 (which presents a matrix of statistical tests measuring the differences of beliefs across Block I treatments) the fourth set of histograms from the left presents the results of all five generations of the almost-common-knowledge treatment, the fifth set of histograms presents the beliefs of subjects in the four generations of the common-knowledge treatment and the last (sixth) set presents the beliefs of subjects in the last three generations (generations 3 through 5) of the almost-common-knowledge treatment. The first two generations are eliminated here because the advice offered came initially from the progenitor game and was particularly pessimistic leading the minimum to quickly converge to 1. While the almost-common-knowledge treatment (last three generations only) fostered beliefs that were more like the common-knowledge game than either of the private-advice games, it did not succeed as completely in eliminating the possibility that some subject might choose a low number. As can be seen by the actions taken (Figure 7.1 and Table 7.5), even this small bit of suspicion that someone might choose 1 was enough to ruin cooperation.

The lesson learned here is that any doubt mentioned in advice statements may be enough to lead subjects to fear that others will not act cooperatively and hence cause them to deviate. The mapping from advice to actions seems to be a discontinuous one where the discontinuity arises even when the advice set seems to be rather strong in urging cooperation. The mapping from advice to beliefs, however, is more continuous. Small amounts of doubt lead to small probability weight placed on bad outcomes, and this leads to big changes in behavior.[11]

7.3.3   Block II Games – Minimum Choices and Advice Quality

Because each generation is free to give advice to the next, our experimental design in Block I does not control for advice quality, and thus we cannot say precisely how the way that advice is distributed might affect efficiency. In Block II we isolate the advice quality variable in order to study the interaction between choices and how advice is distributed. To investigate this we ran an additional set of six games (see the experimental design in Table 7.4). Note that, here, our design is different from Block I since here we repeatedly bring in new groups and present them with the same advice distributed in a fixed manner. This allows us to directly compare behavior in groups that received the same advice distributed in different ways, and to see how advice quality matters for a given way of distributing advice. Whereas the Block I games essentially provide us with a single instance of each treatment (albeit with several related generations), the Block II games allow us to collect repeated observations for each "advice quality"– "information condition" combination.

What our Block II experiments do, then, is to hold advice quality constant and ask whether the way this advice is presented to subjects, the information condition, makes any difference to their ability to coordinate on efficient actions. While even the good advice is quite strongly supportive of such coordination, there are differential degrees of success at coordination over different information conditions for the two sets of advice.

---

[11]   This may result if subjects are risk-averse or are averse to being made a sucker of.

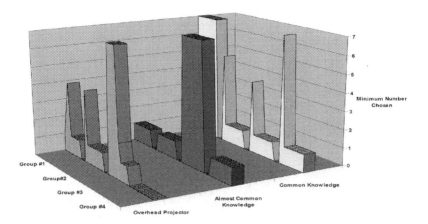

FIGURE 7.3 Behavior of the minimum across Block II games with good advice.

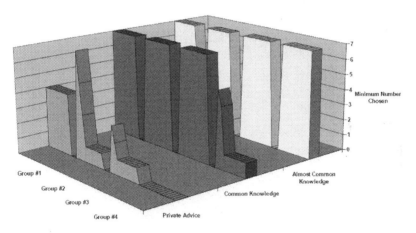

FIGURE 7.4 Behavior of the minimum across Block II games with very good advice.

Table 7.10 and Figures 7.3 and 7.4, present the results of the Block II games. Table 7.10 presents the minima of each group from round 1 to 10. Figures 7.3 and 7.4 are the Block II analogs of Figure 7.1, which presents similar information for the Block I treatments except that here we do not have generations since each group brought into the laboratory receives the same advice and does not communicate

Table 7.10 *Observed minimum choices in Block II games.*

	Rounds									
	1	2	3	4	5	6	7	8	9	10

Good Advice

Game 6: Common knowledge of advice and Good advice

Group 1	7	7	7	7	7	7	7	7	7	7
Group 2	5	1	1	1	1	1	1	1	1	1
Group 3	4	1	1	1	1	1	1	1	1	1
Group 4	7	1	1	1	1	1	1	1	1	1

Game 7: Almost common knowledge of advice and Good advice

Group 1	1	1	1	1	1	1	1	1	1	1
Group 2	1	1	1	1	1	1	1	1	1	1
Group 3	7	7	7	7	7	7	7	7	7	7
Group 4	1	1	1	1	1	1	1	1	1	1

Game 8: Advice on overhead projector for all subjects to see and Good advice

Group 1	1	2	3	4	1	1	1	1	1	1
Group 2	4	1	1	1	1	1	1	1	1	1
Group 3	7	7	7	7	7	2	1	1	1	1

Very good advice

Game 9: Common knowledge of advice and Very good advice

Group 1	7	7	7	7	7	7	7	7	7	7
Group 2	7	7	7	7	7	7	7	7	7	7
Group 3	7	7	7	7	7	7	7	7	7	7
Group 4	5	4	1	1	1	1	1	1	1	1

Game 10: Almost common knowledge of advice and very good advice

Group 1	7	7	7	7	7	7	7	7	7	4
Group 2	7	7	7	7	7	7	7	7	7	1
Group 3	7	7	7	7	7	7	7	7	7	7
Group 4	7	7	7	7	7	7	7	7	7	7

Game 11: Private knowledge of advice and very good advice

Group 1	4	4	4	4	4	4	4	4	4	4
Group 2	7	5	3	1	1	1	1	1	1	1
Group 3	3	2	1	1	1	1	1	1	1	1

across generations. So we have labeled them as "Groups" rather than "Generations". Moreover any temporal sequence of these results is arbitrary since there is no intergenerational structure connecting the groups.

Looking at Figures 7.3 and 7.4, one can see that behavior differs dramatically as we vary the quality of advice offered to subjects. More precisely, when subjects are offered good advice it appears that, no matter how it is presented, it is not sufficient to get them to cooperate over much of the horizon of the experiment. In Figure 7.3 we find that when we have "good" advice the preponderant choice for the minimum is 1. Only one group in the almost-common-knowledge treatment and one group in the common-knowledge treatment manage to sustain a minimum choice of 7 for all 10 rounds. When the advice is "very good", on the other hand, all four groups in the almost-common-knowledge treatment manage to achieve efficiency for all 10 rounds and three out of the four common-knowledge groups manage to do so as well. Clearly, advice quality matters and tends to substitute for the degree of common knowledge.

7.3.4   Path Dependence

Our results from Block I and Block II indicate that behavior in this game is extremely path-dependent, with the choices made (and the minimum chosen) in subsequent rounds being crucially dependent on the **first-round minimum**. For example, there is never a case where the 10th-round minimum winds up being 7 when 7 was not the minimum of the first round. In addition, if the first-round minimum is 1, then the 10th-round minimum is certain to be 1. Put differently, choosing 7 in round 1 is a necessary condition for a round-10 minimum of 7. When the first-round choice is neither 1 nor 7, the evidence is less clear. While it is highly likely that in such cases the 10th-round minimum will be 1, there are several cases where a group winds up at an intermediate level of cooperation in round 10 having started with an intermediate minimum in round 1.

Since round 1 is so crucial to achieving coordination we want to focus on it more intensively here and perform a simulation. In each of the Block II games we had either three or four groups of eight subjects (i.e., either 24 or 32 subjects per game). Note, however, that while group effects (and the choices made in round 1) may affect the choices in later rounds, their round-1 choice is not affected by the group they are randomly assigned to. Hence, all first-round choices are independent of each other. This being the case, if a game has 32 subjects in it, then we are free to form all possible groups of eight from those 32 subjects (and not just the four groups these subjects were randomly assigned to) and then look at *what the minimum would have been if those groups had formed given their first-round choices in Block II*. The minimum chosen in the first round of all the possible hypothetical groups provide us with clues about the path of choices in subsequent rounds. If these hypothetical first-round minima differ, we can expect that the 10th-round behavior evolving from them would be different as well.

We form a "hypothetical" dataset with either $32!/(24! \times 8!) = 10{,}518{,}300$ or $24!/(16! \times 8!) = 735{,}471$ hypothetical groupings for each game and see what behavior would be forthcoming from each of these groups had they formed. The point of this exercise is to be sure that the small number of groups in each game does not mask larger tendencies in the population. This could work in two ways. For example, if there were a large number of players initially choosing small numbers in one of three or four groups of a game, but not in the others, this will show up as a lower expected minimum for round 1 in the hypothetical dataset than is evident from the actual groupings observed. Alternatively, if there are only one or two players choosing small numbers in another game, then there will be many more hypothetical groups with higher minima than in the actual groupings observed. There is too much interdependence to be able to do formal statistical tests with this hypothetical data, but the exercise is useful as a straightforward calculation of what the full set of possible outcomes, in fact, is. Figure 7.5 and Table 7.11 present our results.

Table 7.11 *Probability of observing a first-round minimum by treatment: Block II.*

Game	Minimum						
	1	2	3	4	5	6	7
Private knowledge and Very good advice	0	0	0.33	0.39	0.105	0.14	0.03
Almost common knowledge and Very good advice	0	0	0	0	0	0	1
Common knowledge and Very good advice	0	0	0	0	0.44	0	0.56
Almost common knowledge and Good advice	0.59	0	0	0	0.20	0	0.21
Advice on overheads and Good advice	0.565	0	0	0.16	0.105	0.07	0.10
Common knowledge and Good advice	0	0	0	0.44	0.15	0.11	0.295

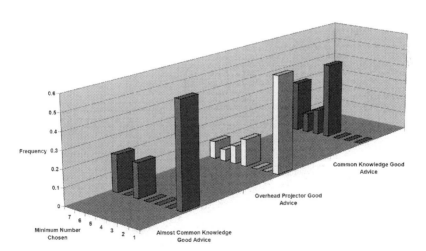

FIGURE 7.5 Probability of observing a particular minimum value in Block II games with good advice using the "hypothetical" dataset.

As we see in Table 7.11 and Figure 7.5, holding advice constant at the good quality level, the manner of information transmission matters. First notice (from rows 5 and 6 of Table 7.11) that in the almost-common-knowledge and overhead-projector treatments with "good" advice, 59% and 56.5% of the hypothetical first-round minima would have been 1. However, **none** of the first-round minima would have been 1 (last row of Table 7.11 and Figures 7.3 and 7.4) in the common-knowledge good-advice game. Since round-1 minima of 1 are sure indicators of round-10 minima of 1, this means that almost 60% of the groups in either the overhead-projector or almost-common-knowledge game would have spent their entire 10-round life choosing 1. While approximately 30% of first-round minima would have been 7 in the common-knowledge good-advice game, only 21% would have been so in the almost-common-knowledge good-advice game, and 10% in the overhead-projector game. Finally, while 100% of the first-round minima in the common-knowledge good-advice game would be 4 or more (last row of Table 7.11), only 41% of the first-round minima would have been 4 or more in the almost-common-knowledge good-advice game (row 5 of Table 7.11). Figure 7.5 highlights the fact that with common knowledge and "good" advice the probability of observing a first-round minimum of 1 is zero.

The effect of the information treatment is less dramatic for very good advice. Even for the private-advice game with very good advice, the probability of a first-round minimum less than 3 is zero. At the same time, the probability of a first-round minimum of 7 with private advice is essentially zero as well (row 2 of Table 7.11), so this game seems doomed to suboptimal outcomes. Both the almost-common-knowledge and the common-knowledge games with very good advice have zero probability of a first-round minimum less than 5. We do not illustrate these probabilities for the "very good" advice games as the differences among games are less dramatic.

Projecting the "good" advice on a screen, in the overhead-projection game, does not result in an average minimum different from the almost-common-knowledge game. Projecting the advice on a screen for all to see evidently does not induce the same degree of common knowledge as reading the advice out loud for all to hear. In short, information affects first-round choices holding advice constant.

These results lead to the following conclusions:

Conclusion 1: *On the basis of our Block II results, we can say that if advice is strong enough (with all subjects in a group strongly exhorting their successors to choose 7), then efficient coordination is achieved regardless of the manner in which the advice is distributed, as long as it is public.*

Conclusion 2: *Also on the basis of our Block II results, we find that when advice is insufficiently strong, then efficient coordination is likely to be established **only if that advice is distributed as common knowledge.***

Of course, there is no guarantee that *any* kind of advice will lead to efficient coordination as long as it is delivered in a way that ensures common knowledge. We have studied the effect of two distinct sets of advice, both generally strong in encouraging efficient actions, but one distinctly stronger than the other, and have uncovered a differential effect of the information condition. Presumably truly bad advice, uniformly encouraging subjects to make choices of 1 in the game, would not be likely to lead to efficient coordination. But we have found that, in practice, the quality of advice is endogenous to the information condition as in the Block I games, so our conclusions are relevant for the generally strong advice that is left in those games with high degrees of common knowledge.[12]

7.4 BELIEFS AND COMMON p-BELIEFS

The problem faced by our subjects is simple. When they hear a piece of advice offered in either one of our public advice treatments (the issues are different for private advice), they must ask themselves whether

---

[12] Chaudhuri et al. (2006) study a voluntary contributions mechanism using a very similar intergenerational paradigm with advice and also find that contributions are significantly higher and closer to the social optimum when the advice from a previous generation is made public and common knowledge.

they believe that all the others heard what they heard and also if they interpreted it to mean what they did. If all people heard it, believe that all others heard it, and believe that all others believe that all others heard it, ad infinitum, then the public advice is common knowledge. They then have to decide whether or not to follow the advice. For example, if it was announced that "you all should choose 7", whether you will actually do so depends on whether you think the other seven people heard what was said, i.e., no one was daydreaming, and whether they all took this statement to be strong enough to lead them to choose 7. However, you may still follow the advice even if your beliefs fall short of common knowledge but you have strong enough p-beliefs, i.e., if everyone believes the advice was heard with probability at least p, everyone believes with probability at least p that everyone believes it with probability at least p, and so on ad infinitum. When $p = 1$, we are back to the event being common knowledge. In other words, if we all share a strong enough common belief (a high enough belief) that these statements will be interpreted identically, then that common p-belief will be enough to get us to coordinate. This is what we think public and strongly exhortative advice achieves. This idea of p-beliefs was first proposed by Monderer and Samet (1989) who formalize the notion.

Prior to round 1 of the actual game, we asked each subject to report the distribution of actions that they believed would result in the subsequent round of play.[13] Figures 7.6 and 7.7 represent these beliefs by presenting the mean number of subjects expected to choose each number between 1 and 7 in each game in Block II with "good" and "very good" advice respectively. These two figures place the various actions $1, 2, \ldots, 7$ along the horizontal axis and along the vertical they display the mean number of subjects (aggregated over all groups) predicted to choose that action.

---

[13] We also elicited beliefs before round 10 but those beliefs tended to simply reflect behavior in round 9.

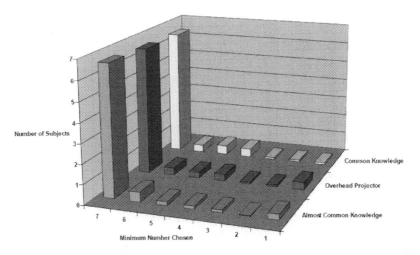

FIGURE 7.6 Comparison of beliefs across Block II games with good advice.

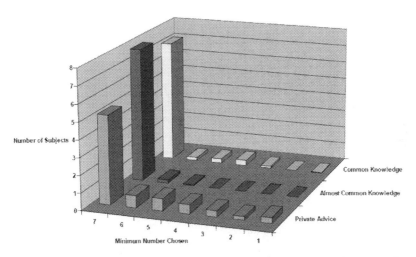

FIGURE 7.7 Comparison of beliefs across Block II games with very good advice.

The key feature of Figures 7.6 and 7.7 to notice is again that advice quality and the way advice is distributed are substitutes. Looking at Figure 7.6, where we only have good advice, it is only when such advice is distributed as common knowledge that no subject expects their opponents to choose 1 in round 1. However, when advice is very good in Figure 7.7, subjects expect none of their opponents will choose 1 in both the almost-common-knowledge and the common-knowledge treatments (clearly, distributing private advice is the worst). While this may seem to be a minor difference, because the payoff function in the minimum-effort game makes subjects vulnerable to the possibility that one's opponents may choose very low efforts, especially 1, even a slight chance that they may do so might be enough to ruin efficient coordination.

The lesson to be learned from these Block II belief distributions is simple. Common knowledge plus strong public advice seems to be a necessary condition for beliefs to be sufficiently positive so as to lead to efficient outcomes. All other settings hold the prospect of someone choosing 1, which leads to a spiral of actions toward 1. Even in the common-knowledge version of the games with good advice, there is a tiny amount of pessimism – a small amount of belief that someone will choose 1 – and there is greater pessimism for the almost-common-knowledge and overhead-projector games. These small amounts of pessimism in the less-than-common-knowledge games seems to have made large differences in behavior.

7.5 CONCLUSION

This chapter was motivated by the conjecture that if we allowed subjects playing a coordination game with Pareto-ranked equilibria to leave advice for their successors, then they would manage, over time, to achieve an efficient outcome. In this sense we thought people could "talk themselves to efficiency" through advice. We found something rather different. If the advice offered by one generation to the next is private advice, then just the opposite occurs. Private advice between a predecessor and her successor, no matter how positive, fails to lead to efficient results.

When advice is public we find that subjects act as if there is a quality threshold with advice. If the advice offered to subjects is sufficiently strong in urging them to cooperate (i.e., above this advice-quality threshold and unanimous), then as long as that advice is offered in a public manner (either as common knowledge or as what we call "almost common knowledge"), we can expect cooperation to follow. However, if the advice quality is below the threshold, then advice is far more likely to result in cooperation if it is not only public but also distributed in a manner that makes it common knowledge.

It is useful to distinguish between **establishing and maintaining** efficiency, on the one hand, and **improving** efficiency, on the other. We found that it is essential that play in the minimum-effort game get started at an efficient level of play if there is to be any hope of efficiency being maintained. To establish efficiency, it seems that subjects have to both get the right advice and take the right actions. When advice is public, subjects seem to leave better advice for their successors, and subjects are more likely to follow this advice. Improving efficiency in the minimum-effort game, either within a given generation or group, or over the course of several generations, seems to be almost impossible. Once play is at a suboptimal level (the minimum less than 7), play can be counted on to deteriorate to the worst outcome with a minimum of 1 within a few rounds. Similarly, once a generation of players has failed to establish and maintain efficiency, play in subsequent generations can be counted on to fail to coordinate as well.

We found the difficulty of achieving efficiency under these circumstances surprising but instructive since it indicates that, if we expect to teach our children the lessons of our experience, we will need to assure them that others in their generation are being taught the same lessons and that fact must be common knowledge. As Chwe (2001) points out, we may, in addition, need to think of how we are going to structure our institutions so as to achieve the common knowledge necessary for the attainment of coordinated action.

7.6 APPENDIX: ESTIMATES FROM ORDERED PROBIT MODEL

An ordered choice model is appropriate in this context as there is a natural ordering of the choices in the game. The intuition is that the factors that determine choice ought to work in a similar way on all the choices, so there is an efficiency gain in estimation from estimating a single coefficient for each independent variable for each of the choices (unlike, say, an (unordered) multinomial model, where there are separate estimated effects for each choice). In other games there need not be an ordering in available stage-game choices, but as we have seen, there are Pareto-ranked equilibria in the minimum-effort game, and there is an evident monotonic structure in the choices. There are seven possible "responses" an individual can make in each period in the minimum-effort game. The choice of $n = \{1, \ldots, 7\}$ are coded as n. Separate "cut-points", which are essentially separate constant terms for each choice, are estimated. The cut-point is an (estimated) threshold parameter between choosing one of two adjacent choices. We use period (round of a game), generation of a treatment, sex ("0" if male, "1" otherwise), and current cash balance of a subject, as well as coefficients on dummy variables for the different treatments, as independent variables.[14]

Table 7.12 contains estimates from the ordered probit procedure. The estimated coefficients in Table 7.12 indicate the direction of the effect of a variable on the estimated choice probabilities, but are difficult to quantify, in terms of the magnitude of the effect on the estimated probabilities of choice. The actual probabilities are calculated via a progressive decumulation of the standard normal distribution, so the estimated probability is a nonlinear transformation of the linear summation of the independent variables weighted by their estimated coefficients. Many variables are significant, including period, balance, and the public-advice treatment dummies.

The period variable has a negative coefficient, consistent for subjects to choose lower numbers in later periods. The generation variable is negative but small and insignificant, consistent with the fact that, in a given treatment, there is generally no trend in choice

---

[14] We used the REOPROB procedure, an "Ado" procedure in Stata authored by Guillaume Fréchette.

Table 7.12 *Estimates from the ordered probit procedure. Dependent variable: number chosen {1–7} by a subject in a particular period.*

Variable	Coefficient	z-statistic	$P > |z|$
Period	−0.53	−13.44	0.00
Generation	−0.04	−0.63	0.53
Sex (0 for male and 1 for female)	−0.10	−0.61	0.54
Balance	0.36	6.67	0.00
G1 No advice	−0.27	−0.90	0.37
G2 Advice only	−0.56	−1.72	0.09
G3 Advice plus history	0.07	0.19	0.85
G4 Public advice	0.75	2.39	0.02
G5 Public advice read aloud	2.96	5.89	0.00
Cut 1	−2.08	−6.92	0.00
Cut 2	−1.46	−4.90	0.00
Cut 3	−1.13	−3.81	0.00
Cut 4	−0.54	−1.84	0.07
Cut 5	−0.19	−0.65	0.51
Cut 6	0.19	0.64	0.53
Rho	0.55	15.73	0.00
Likelihood ratio $\chi^2(9) = 848.19$,	Prob $> \chi^2 = 0.00$,	N = 1860,	Log likelihood = −2086.81

behavior over generations. Instead, there is a similar pattern within each generation (typically more high choices in early periods, lower choices in later periods).

REFERENCES

Antonopoulos, C., Chau, L., Chaudhuri, A., Hahn, E. and Min, S. (2002). Efficiency breakthrough: Conversion from almost common to common knowledge in the minimum effort game. *Working Paper*, Wellesley College.

Avoyan, A. and Ramos, J. (2020). A road to efficiency through communication and commitment. Available at: Social Science Research: https://ssrn.com/abstract= 2777644.

Blume, A. and Ortmann, A. (2007). The effects of costless pre-play communication: Experimental evidence from games with Pareto-ranked equilibria. *Journal of Economic Theory*, 132(1), 274–290.

Burton, A. and Sefton, M. (2004). Risk, pre-play communication and equilibrium. *Games and Economic Behavior*, 46(1), 23–40.

Carlsson, H. and van Damme, E. (1993). Global games and equilibrium selection. *Econometrica*, 61(5), 989–1018.

Charness, G. (2000). Self-serving cheap talk: A test of Aumann's conjecture. *Games and Economic Behavior*, 33(2), 177–194.

Chaudhuri, A., Graziano, S. and Maitra, P. (2006). Social learning and norms in a public goods experiment with inter-generational advice. *Review of Economic Studies*, 73(2), 357–380.

Chaudhuri, A., Schotter, A. and Sopher, B. (2009). Talking ourselves to efficiency: Coordination in inter-generational minimum effort games with private, almost common and common knowledge of advice. *Economic Journal*, 119(534), 91–122.

Chwe, M. (2001). *Rational Ritual: Culture, Coordination, and Common Knowledge*. Princeton, NJ: Princeton University Press.

Cooper, R. (1999). *Coordination Games: Complementarities and Macroeconomics*. Cambridge, UK: Cambridge University Press.

Cooper, R., DeJong, D., Forsythe, R. and Ross, T. (1989). Communication in the battle of the sexes game: some experimental results. *RAND Journal of Economics*, 20(4), 568–587.

Cooper, R., DeJong, D., Forsythe, R. and Ross, T. (1992). Communication in coordination games. *Quarterly Journal of Economics*, 107(2), 739–771.

Crawford, V. (1991). An "evolutionary" interpretation of Van Huyck, Battalio, and Beil's experimental results on coordination. *Games and Economic Behavior*, 3(1), 25–59.

Crawford, V. (1995). Adaptive dynamics in coordination games. *Econometrica*, 63(1), 103–143.

Dawes, R. M., McTavish, J. and Shaklee, H. (1977). Behavior, communication, and assumptions about other people's behavior in a commons dilemma situation. *Journal of Personality and Social Psychology*, 35(1), 1–11.

Diamond, D. and Dybvig, P. (1983). Bank runs, deposit insurance, and liquidity. *Journal of Political Economy*, 91(3), 401–419.

Ichniowski, C., Shaw, K. and Prennushi, G. (2004). The effects of human resource management practices on productivity. *American Economic Review*, 87(3), 291–313.

Isaac, M. and Walker, J. (1988). Communication and free-riding behavior: The voluntary contribution mechanism. *Economic Inquiry*, 26(4), 585–608.

Knez, M. and Simester, D. (2001). Firm-wide incentives and mutual monitoring at Continental Airlines. *Journal of Labor Economics*, 19(4), 743–772.

Kremer, M. (1993). The O-ring theory of economic development. *Quarterly Journal of Economics*, 108(3), 551–575.

Kuran, T. (1987). Preference falsification, policy continuity and collective conservatism. *Economic Journal*, 97(387), 642–665.

Kuran, T. (1995). *Private Truths, Public Lies: The Social Consequences of Preference Falsification*. Cambridge, MA: Harvard University Press.

Monderer, D. and Samet, D. (1989). Approximating common knowledge with common beliefs. *Games and Economic Behavior*, 1(2), 170–190.

Morris, S., Rob, R. and Shin, H. S. (1995). p-Dominance and belief potential. *Econometrica*, 63(1), 145–157.

Morris, S. and Shin, H. S. (1998). Unique equilibrium in a model of self-fulfilling currency attacks. *American Economic Review*, 88(3), 587–597.

Schotter, A. and Yorulmazer, T. (2009). On the dynamics and severity of bank runs: An experimental study. *Journal of Financial Intermediation*, 18(2), 217–241.

Van Huyck, J., Battalio, R. and Beil, R. O. (1990). Tacit coordination games, strategic uncertainty, and coordination failure. *American Economic Review*, 80(1), 234–248.

8 Advice and Common Knowledge in the Two-Thirds Guessing Game: Does Advice Increase Strategic Sophistication?

In most strategic situations and markets, and many other situations where people's fates are connected through their actions, it is not enough to think of what the right action to take is.[1] Rather, one must also think about what others might decide is their best action and perhaps even what others think what others think is the best action to take. John Maynard Keynes in Chapter 12 of his famous book *The General Theory of Employment, Interest and Money* (Keynes, 1936) discussed one such situation where he describes the actions of rational agents in the stock market using an analogy based on a contest that was run in the London newspaper. In this contest, entrants were asked to choose those six faces from 100 photographs of women that were most beautiful. Everyone who picked the most popular faces were entered into a raffle for a prize.

In playing this game, a naive contestant might choose the six faces that she thought most attractive. A more sophisticated contestant, however, would think of what others thought beauty was and choose those faces. However, the thinking need not stop there since one might be drawn to think about what others think others think are the most attractive faces, etc. As Keynes puts it:

> It is not a case of choosing those [faces] which, to the best of one's judgment, are really the prettiest. Not even those which average opinion genuinely think is the prettiest. We have reached the third degree where we devote our intelligence to anticipating what

[1] This chapter is based on Potamites and Schotter (2007).

214

average opinion expects the average opinion to be. And there are some, I believe, who practice the fourth, fifth, and higher degrees.

A stylized version of Keynes's beauty contest is the two-thirds guessing game (Moulin, 1986; Nagel, 1995; Stahl and Wilson, 1995). In this game eight players are asked to choose a number between 0 and 100. The eight numbers are then averaged and two-thirds of the resulting mean is calculated $(\frac{2}{3}\bar{x})$. That subject whose submitted number was closest to $\frac{2}{3}\bar{x}$ receives a prize of \$10 while all other subjects receive nothing. If two or more subjects are equally close, they split the \$10 equally. This is analogous to the Keynes beauty contest because the players must think not only of what they might choose but also think of what others will choose and what others think others will choose, etc.

Despite what appears to require an infinite hierarchy of beliefs, the two-thirds guessing game (as opposed to the Keynes beauty contest) has an equilibrium that can be arrived at by the iterative deletion of dominated strategies which provides a unique equilibrium choice – they all should choose zero.[2] However, when the game is actually played, either in the lab or in the field, a great deal of heterogeneity of choice is observed (see Thaler, 1998). This result has led to a large experimental literature on the two-thirds guessing game – see Nagel (1995), Stahl and Wilson (1995), Ho et al. (1998), Costa-Gomes and Crawford (2006, 2007), and many others.

This heterogeneity has been explained by positing that people vary in their strategic sophistication, with some being unable to think strategically at all (level zeros), some being able to exercise one step of strategic thinking and best respond under the hypothesis that all other subjects are at level zero (level ones), and yet others being able to think at a higher level (level-k thinkers who best respond under the hypothesis that all other subjects are at level $k - 1$).

---

[2] To illustrate the equilibrium, note that the highest that $\frac{2}{3}\bar{x}$ could be is 66, which occurs when all subjects choose 100. So choosing above 66 is dominated. Knowing this and therefore knowing that no rational subjects would choose above 66, the highest $\frac{2}{3}\bar{x}$ could be is 44. Applying this logic iteratively leads the equilibrium to unravel to zero.

In this chapter we ask how would the inclusion of advice, both private and public, alter the distribution of strategic sophistication among the players? Would advice make people more sophisticated and if so why? Would private advice work or would the advice have to be public, and if public what type of public advice would be most effective?[3]

To answer these questions we offer two hypotheses. One, the "focus hypothesis", suggests that people act in a more sophisticated manner when they receive advice because such advice allows them to focus on the problem at hand and, in some sense, lowers their cost of thinking (their cognitive cost), which allows them to be more sophisticated. If this were the explanation, then such a focus effect would exist when advice was private.

Our second hypothesis, the "common-knowledge hypothesis", suggests that if advice were public and common knowledge, then it might give subjects an insight into what others are likely to do since, under the common-knowledge assumption, each subject would know that the others have seen the same advice, and subjects could then best respond to these higher-order beliefs and climb the cognitive ladder. Note that such an explanation would only exist if advice was common knowledge since, if every player saw the same advice and that advice was common knowledge, then that public advice could anchor the beliefs of subjects on that advice and allow all subjects to best respond to it. It would function as a "cognitive anchor" to which subjects could adjust their choices knowing that all others have seen the same advice. For example, if the public advice suggested 33

---

[3] Others, namely, Kocher et al. (2014), Pogrebna (2008), and Sbriglia (2008), have all included advice in different ways into their analysis of the two-thirds guessing game. Kocher et al. (2014) contrast the impact of providing subjects with the history of previous play of the game and contrast it to providing them with written advice from previous subjects. Sbriglia (2008) has a structure somewhat resembling an intergenerational game since the person leaving advice leaves the game just as in our intergenerational game setup, while Pogrebna (2008) looks at the behavior of participants in an Italian game show *Affari Tuoi* where game contestants can ask the audience for advice about whether to accept or reject a deal made to them by the game hosts. Roughly speaking, in all cases, just as in our experiment here, advice enhances the rationality of choices, leads to faster convergence, and is payoff-increasing.

be chosen and if that suggestion were common knowledge, then if subjects were rational they might assume that no one would chose above 33 (since two-thirds of the mean could never be higher than 33 if everyone choose that way) and hence all choices, at a minimum, would be a best response to 33. Some more sophisticated subjects might choose a best response to that best response. So together, these responses would look like an increase in the level of sophistication among our subjects.

As we saw in Chapter 7, however, it is not the case that any old advice will do as long as it is distributed in a manner to achieve common knowledge. The advice has to be strong, or in our case here, meaningful, which means that it offers an insight into what the group is thinking in such a way as to be able to serve as an anchor for their beliefs. While in Chapter 7 meaningful advice plus common knowledge led to coordination in the minimum-effort game, here those same ingredients lead to greater strategic sophistication in the two-thirds guessing game.

8.1 THE TWO-THIRDS GUESSING GAME

The standard models attempting to explain the existence of hetero-geneous types in the two-thirds guessing game assume that subjects are endowed with levels of rationality that form a hierarchy from the lowest type (typically those who choose randomly) to those who either best respond to the type immediately below them (see Stahl and Wilson, 1995) or to some pre-specified distribution of types of lower rationality (see Camerer et al., 2004). Such an explanation implies that a subject's type is predetermined before she comes into the lab so that the distribution of types is exogenous (perhaps fixed in the population). Those with higher levels of cognition (higher cognitive types) enter lower numbers as their guess.

More recent models by Choi (2012) and Alaoui and Penta (2016) relax this assumption by positing that agents actually choose their level of sophistication depending on weighing the cognitive costs associated with different levels of sophistication to the associated benefits. How high a type a subject appears to be is determined by a comparison between the marginal benefits she can expect to receive by choosing a different (higher) rationality level as compared to the marginal cost of doing so. In these models, while people cannot act as if they were smarter than they are capable of being, they can choose to behave in various ways depending on their comparison between the marginal benefit and marginal cost of increasing (or decreasing) their rationality level and (as will be our focus here) their beliefs about the sophistication of their opponents.[4]

This suggests that there are two relevant distributions of cognitive ability that one must consider when analyzing this game. One, which we call the "objective-type distribution", is the distribution of cognitive **maximal** types which accurately describes how many steps of logic players are capable of in the context of the game they are playing. Note that this distribution is unobservable since subjects may decide to behave as if they were a lower cognitive type if they believe that they are playing against a set of less sophisticated opponents.[5] The other is what we will call the "observed-type (or chosen-type) distribution", which measures the distribution of **revealed** cognitive types.

When we introduce advice into our experiments we will see a shift in the distribution of revealed cognitive types. Given our two hypotheses, this shift could occur for two different reasons. If people become more sophisticated when they receive private advice, it may be that, because they have thought through the problem more, they are actually smarter and capable of higher-level thinking. This would suggest that we observe a shift in the distribution of maximal types but that need not be the case if they were acting according

---

[4] Choi's (2012) analysis is an equilibrium analysis so the marginal benefit to increasing one's rationality is definable under the assumption that all other agents are in equilibrium with respect to their level of rationality.

[5] Agranov et al. (2012) inform subjects that they are playing the two-thirds guessing game against players of different levels of sophistication (i.e., undergraduates or graduate students) and see if their play responds to what they perceive as the sophistication of their competitors.

to an artificially low level of sophistication before receiving advice. Such a shift, however, might be consistent with the focus hypothesis. If we offer public advice, which makes people think more about what they think others will do, then a shift here will be consistent with our common-knowledge hypothesis and also can go in any direction, because if they think others are less sophisticated they will exhibit less sophisticated behavior themselves as best response, but such advice may also allow them to act in a more sophisticated manner if they are capable of choosing a best response to the revealed sophistication of their opponents.

Our experiments were designed to investigate these hypotheses. More precisely, in these experiments we have subjects participate in the standard two-thirds guessing game experiment except that before they choose they are given advice from another player. This advice is either private and offered to her alone (knowing that each other subject is being offered similar private advice from another subject) or public, in which case advice is announced for all to hear, and is therefore common knowledge.[6]

Our results provide more support for the common-knowledge hypothesis than for the focus hypothesis. More precisely, providing subjects with private advice as to what to choose leads to only a minimal shift in the distribution of observed types. This would indicate that their revealed behavior was due not to a lack of cognitive ability on their part but rather to diminished expectation about the cognitive abilities of their cohorts. Providing them with public (common-knowledge) advice shifts the distribution significantly but, as in Chapter 7, only if the subjects believe that the advice offered to them is meaningful (or believe that others will believe it is meaningful and think others will as well). This supports the common-knowledge hypothesis because it demonstrates that not all advice revealed publicly is meaningful and can change behavior. The advice must be public and credible and commonly assumed to be credible for others.

---

[6] Although, as we know from Chapter 7, making advice common knowledge may involve more than just making it public.

These results tend to support the view that in any strategic situation people may not choose their most sophisticated strategy if they believe they are not facing very sophisticated opponents. To get them to increase the sophistication of their play, it is not enough to get them to think about the problem more deeply, as in the private-advice case, but rather convince them that others are thinking more deeply about the problem and to make this fact common knowledge, as in our public-advice treatment.

8.2   EXPERIMENTAL DESIGN AND PROCEDURES

Subjects were recruited from the undergraduate student population at New York University and brought into the lab of the Center for Experimental Social Science in groups of 16, where they engaged in a pen-and-paper experiment. Once in the lab they were offered written instructions describing the two-thirds guessing game (we modified the instructions used by Nagel (1995)) and these instructions were read out loud and questions about them answered. In this game eight subjects are asked to choose a number between 0 and 100. The eight numbers are then averaged and two-thirds of the resulting mean is calculated ($\frac{2}{3}\bar{x}$). The subject whose number was closest to $\frac{2}{3}\bar{x}$ receives a prize of \$10 while all other subjects receive nothing. If two or more subjects are equally close, they split the \$10 equally. In all treatments but the control treatment, before the instructions were read, subjects were randomly divided into two groups of eight, with one group being "advisors" and the other "players". As the instructions indicated, the role of the players was simply to play the two-thirds guessing game. They were paid according to the above description and played the game for 10 rounds so their payoffs were the sum of their payoffs in the 10 rounds of the game.

The other group of advisors had the task of offering advice to the players. This was done in several ways. In the private-advice treatment, each advisor was paired with a player and offered her their advice by writing a number to choose on a piece of paper which was anonymously handed to the player's pair member. No one else could see this advice but all subjects knew that such advice was being offered. The advisors were paid in an identical manner as the players. The advisor whose advice was closest to $\frac{2}{3}\bar{x}$ received $10 while all others received zero. Note, however, that the advice offered by advisors did not enter the computation of $\frac{2}{3}\bar{x}$ while the players' choices did. We call this treatment the low-information private-advice treatment (LPri) to distinguish it from another private-advice treatment which was identical to this one except that, in addition to advisors offering advised numbers to choose, they also offered an unstructured text to accompany it explaining why they thought their advice was meaningful. We call this the high-information private-advice treatment (HPri).

In addition to these two private-advice treatments, we also ran two public-advice treatments. In one, called the mean-public-advice treatment (MPub), before each round we collected the eight pieces of advice just as we did for the private-advice treatments, but instead of handing them out individually to subjects, we calculated the mean and announced it publicly to the players so all could hear.[7] In another public-advice treatment, called the random-public-advice treatment (1Pub), we did the same thing, but rather than announce the mean of the advisors' advice, we randomly chose one piece of advice and announced it to all the players. The players were aware of which public-advice treatment they were in, so they knew if the announced advice was the mean or a randomly chosen piece of advice.

Finally, in the first round of all private- and public-advice treatments, after the advisors gave advice to their advisees, they were asked to play the two-thirds guessing game among themselves. Here they chose a number between 0 and 100 and that player whose choice was closest to $\frac{2}{3}\bar{x}$ of the choices of the advisor group received $10. Hence, in the first round of the experiment, and only in the first round, advisors could earn money two different ways. One was to give advice which was closest to $\frac{2}{3}\bar{x}$ of the players' group while the other was to make a choice which was closest to $\frac{2}{3}\bar{x}$ of the choices in their group.

---

[7] What was announced was the mean of the eight pieces of advice and not two-thirds of that mean. It was the mean advice.

Table 8.1 *Experimental design.*

Treatment	Advice	Form of advice	Type of advice	No. of groups	No. of subjects
Low info private	yes	Number	Private	4	64
High info private	yes	Number plus text	Private	4	64
Mean public	yes	Mean of advisors	Public	4	64
Random advice public	yes	Number from one advisor	Public	4	63
Control	no	N/A	N/A	4	62

The results from the advisors' game were announced at the end of the experiment. Having advisors actually play the game allows us to ask which activity, giving or receiving advice, helps to focus attention of subjects most on the game at hand and hence is most likely to shift the observed distribution of choices.

In our final treatment called the control guessing (control) treatment, we again recruited 16 subjects and divided them into two groups. One of the groups were designated as the players and they played a standard two-thirds guessing game without advice among themselves. The task given to members of the other group was to make a guess or forecast in each round about the other group of eight subjects. The subject whose guess was closest to $\frac{2}{3}\bar{x}$ of the players won $10 and everyone else won zero. This "guessers" group was in a separate room and the other players did not know what experiment the "guessers" were doing, so from their perspective they were simply partaking in a conventional guessing game experiment.

In all treatments after each round was over we placed on the blackboard the $\frac{2}{3}\bar{x}$ of the players and the ID numbers of the player and advisor (guesser) who won the $10 prize.

Our experimental design is described in Table 8.1.

8.2.1 Hypotheses

Our experimental design allows us to explore a set of hypotheses about behavior in our private- and public-advice treatments. Let us start with our focus and common-knowledge hypotheses.

If subject behavior is as described by Choi (2012) or Alaoui and Penta (2016), then behavior in our control treatment should be determined by the trade-off between the marginal benefits of higher cognitive processing and its marginal cost. Providing subjects with private advice should lower these costs by offering some benchmark with which to measure one's prior thinking as well as allowing a second round of thinking about the problem. This should cause the subject to focus more on the problem and think at a higher level. Hence we can test our focus hypothesis by comparing behavior in our control treatment with that in both the low- and high-information private-advice treatments (LPri and HPri). If the distribution of choices shifts in the direction of more sophistication as a result of private advice, then this shift would offer support for that hypothesis.

In our experimental design, in both the HPri and LPri treatments, after an advisor offers advice to their advisees in the first round, they play a two-thirds guessing game with each other. As mentioned before, this allows us to ask which activity, giving or receiving advice, helps to focus attention of subjects most on the game at hand and hence is most likely to shift the observed distribution of choices.

Note that even if private advice allows a subject to focus more on the task, it does not follow that she will behave in a more sophisticated manner because she may not believe that her opponents are also capable of thinking in a more sophisticated manner. This is the motivation for our common-knowledge hypothesis.

According to this hypothesis, we would not expect private advice to change the subjects' behavior because, even if they benefit from it, our subjects don't know the private advice that was offered others and hence there is no commonly observed event that can lead them to jointly change their expectations about each other. This is not the case when advice is public and common knowledge, so, under the common-knowledge hypothesis, we expect that the observed distribution of choices should shift when advice is public and lead to more sophisticated behavior.

In our experiment we had subjects give advice under two distinctly different conditions – private and public. This leads us naturally to ask whether the advice offered was different in these two situations.

We might like to know something about the process of advice following. It is our conjecture that advice is more likely to be followed if its logic is spelled out rather than simply receiving a raw number without any explanation. If this is so, we would expect that advice would be followed more in the HPri than in the LPri treatment.

8.3   RESULTS

8.3.1   Private Advice

Let us begin by asking if private advice influences choice. More precisely, as we can see in Table 8.2 and Figure 8.1, when we compare the first-round choices made in the control treatment, where no advice was offered, with those in the HPri and LPri treatments there is no statistically significant difference. More precisely, in Table 8.2 we present the mean choices in round 1 for all of our private-advice experiments as well as our control treatment. As you can see, while the mean of control was 29.2, those of the LPri and HPri were 27.1 and 28.4, respectively. When tested using a Kolmogorov–Smirnov test, none of the distributions of first-round choices were different across these three treatments. This can clearly be seen in Figure 8.1, where we present the empirical cumulative distributions of these first-round choices.

Table 8.2 *Private advice and control.*

Treatment	First-round mean advice	First-round mean choice	Std dev. of first-round choices
LPri	34.5	27.1	10.9
HPri	37.0	28.4	16.4
Control	N/A	29.2	15.6

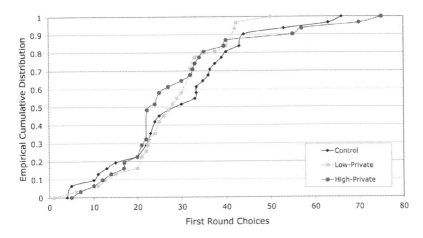

FIGURE 8.1 First-round choice – private advice versus control.

The main import of Figure 8.1 and Table 8.2 is to demonstrate that providing subjects with private advice does not focus their attention on the task at hand more than it already is in the control treatment. In other words, it appears as if subjects had already chosen their level of sophistication the way they wanted to, and merely presenting them with one piece of private advice did nothing to lead them to want to change their choice.

This result leaves open the possibility that while *receiving* private advice does not lead to a change in the choices made by subjects, *offering* advice may in fact focus the attention of subjects in a manner that causes them to act at a higher cognitive level. For example, if one struggles to give good advice, it very well may be that the process of thinking could lead a subject to realizations about the game she would not have, had she not been forced to give advice or passively receive it.

Our data allows us to answer this question. The mean choice of advisors after they gave advice in LPri and HPri was 35.1 and 32.2, compared to the mean choices of receivers, 27.1 and 28.4, respectively. The means in LPri are significantly different when tested using a Mann–Whitney U-test ($z = 2.179, p = 0.029$). In the cumulative

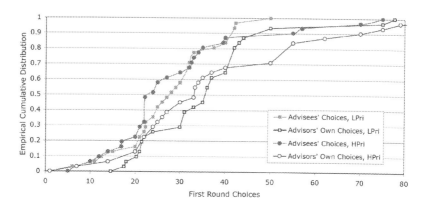

FIGURE 8.2 Advisor and advisee choices – private advice.

distribution functions of the choices in both treatments, the advisees' choices are shifted to the left relative to the advisors' choices (see Figure 8.2) and this difference is significant when tested using the Kolmogorov–Smirnov test in the LPri case. Hence, it appears that those who offered advice chose higher numbers (behaved in a less sophisticated manner) when they actually played the game than those who received it.

This result is somewhat surprising since considerably more thinking is involved in offering advice than passively receiving it (and perhaps ignoring it). Hence we originally thought that it might have an impact on how advisor subjects made their first-round choices. Here again we can only conjecture that, since such advice does not change a subject's expectations about her cohorts, it has no impact on behavior. It may also be that, since the advisee receives two opinions, her own and that of the advisor, she might perform better.

8.3.2   Public Advice

Public (common-knowledge) advice may affect behavior differently than private advice since, being common knowledge, once all subjects hear the announced advice they may start to conjecture that others will respond to it. For example, once a piece of public advice is

Table 8.3 *Public advice and control.*

Treatment	First-round mean advice	First-round mean choice	Std dev. of first-round choices
MPub	36.1	23.7	9.3
1Pub	33.0	30.7	15.5
Control	N/A	29.2	15.6

announced it might make little sense to choose a number above it since a subject knows that others know, that others know etc., that they all heard the same announcement. Hence public advice may provide a "cognitive anchor" from which all subjects commonly adjust their choice downward as a best response and hence shift the distribution of types upward.

Table 8.3 presents the mean results from the first round of our public-advice treatments while Figure 8.3 presents the cumulative distribution functions of the choices. As we can see, there appears to be no difference between first-round choices in the control treatment and the random public-advice treatment (1Pub) (29.2 versus 30.7), while the first-round choices in the MPub treatment are much lower (29.2 versus 23.7). Using a Mann–Whitney U-test the difference between the control and MPub is significant at the 7% level ($z = 1.767, p = 0.077$).

It appears, therefore, that the only type of events (advice) that lead to a significant shift in the level of strategic sophistication are events which are not only common knowledge but are perceived by subjects to be meaningful to others. More precisely, the only difference between the 1Pub and MPub experiments is that in the MPub experiment subjects are offered public advice which is the mean of the advice from the pool of advisors while in the 1Pub experiment they are offered advice which, while public and common knowledge, is merely a random choice of one piece of advice from the pool of eight advisors. We consider this to mean that, while the random public advice was commonly observed, it was not commonly considered

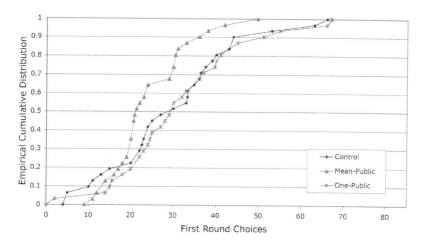

FIGURE 8.3 First-round choices – public advice versus control.

to be meaningful to all others by the subjects and hence failed to
serve as a common cognitive anchor for their thinking. On the other
hand, public advice that was the mean of the advisors' group in the
MPub treatment appears to have struck our subjects as something to
consider as meaningful and which others will take into account when
they make their choice of a number. Under these circumstances, a
best response is to respond to that advice as well.

One explanation of why public advice of the mean has an impact
on behavior where other types of advice do not may be that seeing it
was equivalent to having seen a round of play of the game you are
engaging in (since you learn the mean of the advisors' choices), so
what we observe in the first round of our MPub treatment is actually
the second round of play of other games. In fact, this was far from the
truth. In the control treatment the second round mean was 16 (std
dev. 5.98) while in the MPub treatment the first-round mean was 23.7.
We can reject the hypothesis that these means came from the same
population at the 1% level using a Mann–Whitney U-test. This again
supports our common-knowledge hypothesis.

Our discussion up until now has involved choices and not
advice. One question that is natural to ask is whether the advice

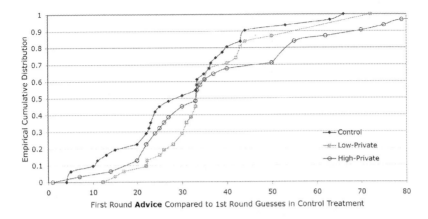

FIGURE 8.4 Private advice versus guesses.

offered in the LPri and HPri treatments differed significantly from merely the best guesses of the advisors as to what the mean of the players would be. To investigate this we compared the guesses made by our guessing subjects in the control treatment with the advice given by advisors in our two private-advice treatments. Figure 8.4 presents these results.

As we can see in Figure 8.4 the guesses in the guess-control treatment appear to be shifted to the left (toward lower numbers) compared to the advice given in private-advice treatments. While the mean guess in the control treatment (31.4) is not significantly lower than the mean advice in LPri and HPri treatments (34.5 and 37, respectively) using the Mann–Whitney U-test, a Kolmogorov–Smirnov test confirms that the distribution of guesses or forecasts is significantly different than the distribution of advice in the LPri case $(p = 0.057)$.

This result suggests that advisors in the private-advice treatments seem to offer advice which is of a lower level of sophistication than are the guesses of subjects in the guess-control treatment where they are asked to forecast the mean of an independent group of subjects and are paid for their accuracy. This is a curious result but similar to what we saw in Chapter 7 where private advice made things worse for subjects in the minimum-effort game.

Table 8.4 *Private and public advice.*

Treatment	First-round mean advice	Std dev. of first-round advice
LPri	34.5	12.0
HPri	37.0	22.1
MPub	36.1	17.7
1Pub	33.0	15.8

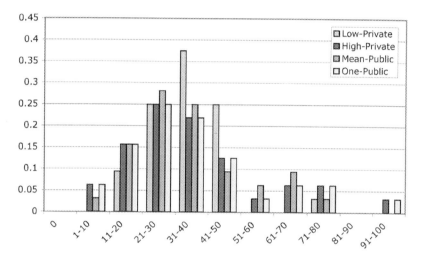

FIGURE 8.5 First-round advice – public versus private.

The advice discussed above was the advice provided in the private-advice treatments. However, it may be that the advice offered in public-advice treatments differed from that offered in the private-advice treatment because it was known that such advice would be made public.

Table 8.4 presents the means (and standard deviations) of the advice given in each of our two private- and public-advice treatments. Figure 8.5 presents the disaggregated information behind these means as histograms. As we can see, the advice given did not vary much by treatment.

Table 8.5 *Advice following.*

Treatment	Above advice	Follow advice	Below advice
LPri	28%	28%	44%
HPri	16%	28%	56%
1Pub	38%	0%	62%
MPub	9%	3%	88%

Up until now we have not commented on how influential advice was in determining the actions of subjects. In other words, did players follow the advice of their advisors? Did they do it more often in public rather than private treatments? All of the questions can be tested by comparing the relationship between the advice given and action taken in our private- and public-advice treatments.

To get some answers to these questions, consider Table 8.5, which indicates, treatment by treatment, how subjects reacted to the advice offered them. More precisely, it presents the percentage of subjects who chose more than, less than, and approximately equal the advice offered them.

Some of these numbers are informative. For example, compare the first and last rows of Table 8.5, which present the following behavior of subjects in our MPub and LPri treatments. As should be obvious, it appears that subjects in the MPub treatment tend to use the public advice as a cognitive anchor and best respond to it. This is supported by the fact that 88% of choices are below the announced mean. For the LPri only 44% of subjects chose below the advice they were given. Further, note that practically no subjects followed the advice offered in the MPub treatment (only 3%) while 28% did so in the LPri. This is all consistent with our main findings that, in order to raise the observed distribution of cognitive types, an event (like advice giving) must be common knowledge and meaningful.

To further strengthen this point, consider the 1Pub treatment and the fraction of subjects (38%) who chose numbers that were greater than advised (note that 28% did so in the LPri). The fact that only 9% of subjects did this in the MPub treatment indicates that subjects in the 1Pub treatment did not consider the advice announced to be meaningful to all the players since a logical consequence of common knowledge and backward induction in this game is to choose below a number announced if you believe that all others heard that number and that their cohorts will treat it seriously. This is what we mean by a cognitive anchor. Finally, notice that while 84% of subjects made choices equal to or less than the advice they were given in the HPri experiment, only 72% did so in the LPri experiment, indicating that advice was more persuasive in that treatment or more suggestive about the backward induction needed to think oneself to the Nash equilibrium.

8.4 COGNITIVE HIERARCHIES

Since our main focus is on how the distribution of cognitive types changes as we vary the type of advice subjects receive, we need to have a method to measure or at least describe these distributions in order to meaningfully discuss their changes. To do this we employ the often used cognitive hierarchy model of Camerer, Ho, and Chong CHC; Camerer et al., 2004. This model posits that the distribution of types is a Poisson distribution, $f(k) = e^{-\tau} \times \tau^k / k$, where k is the number of steps of thinking that players do and τ is a parameter indexing the mean number of thinking steps done by players in the game. Hence, higher τ would imply that subjects in the game are behaving according to a higher level of rationality on average.

According to this model, a player of type k, i.e., a player who does k steps of iterative thinking, best responds to the belief that the other players are distributed by this same Poisson distribution truncated (and normalized) over all steps of thinking up to $k-1$. Given a set of choices in the two-thirds guessing game, one can estimate the distribution of types by simply finding the τ which, when used in the Poisson, predicts a mean choice that best matches the mean choice in the data. Our estimate of τ describes the predicted distribution of types parameterized as a Poisson.[8]

To fully specify the model, the behavior of the level-zero players must be described. In CHC, level-zero players are assumed to choose randomly between 0 and 100. Level-one players, who by definition believe that everybody else is level zero, think that the average choice will be 50 and respond accordingly. Level-two players best respond to the distribution of level zeros and ones that they believe exist in the population. The expected actions of the level zeros define the responses of the rest of the hierarchy.

To get a first approximation to how our treatments change the distribution of types, let us estimate the CHC model as they do by specifying the level-zero type as one who chooses actions uniformly over the interval $[0,100]$. Table 8.6 shows our estimates of τ across each treatment. Several things are of interest. Figure 8.6 compares the distributions of thinking steps predicted by these different estimates of τ.

First note that, in terms of τ, the biggest impact on our estimate of the type distribution occurs in our MPub treatment, where advice is the mean advice of the advisors and it is made public. While the estimated τ in the control is 2.02 and in the private-advice treatment it is 1.99 and 2.17 in the HPri and LPri treatment, respectively, it is 2.71 in the MPub treatment. (It actually falls to 1.68 in the 1Pub treatment but that fall is due to one session where it is 0.39.) Put differently, the addition of credible public advice leads subjects to take 0.69 more thinking steps on average compared to the control group. Note also that the standard deviation of the choices made is smaller in the MPub treatment than in any other treatment.

---

[8] CHC offer a detailed explanation of why a Poisson distribution is a good choice of functional form and also present a set of desiderata for such a function which they demonstrate are satisfied by the Poisson.

Table 8.6 *The Camerer, Ho, and Chong (CHC) model.*

Treatment	Session	Mean choice	Std dev. of choices	τ	Predicted Mean	Std dev.
MPub	1	19.2	6.5	3.59	19.2	9.0
	2	23.2	10.8	2.80	23.2	11.3
	3	26.2	7.6	2.31	26.2	13.1
	4	26.3	11.4	2.29	26.3	13.2
MPub treatment avg.		23.7	9.3	2.71	23.7	11.6
1Pub	5	25.9	9.5	2.36	25.9	12.9
	6	25.9	12.0	2.35	25.9	12.9
	7	27.1	17.1	2.18	27.0	13.6
	8	44.0	16.3	0.39	43.9	25.3
1Pub treatment avg.		30.7	15.5	1.68	30.7	16.0
LPri		27.1	10.9	2.17	27.1	13.7
HPri		28.4	16.4	1.99	28.4	14.5
Control		29.2	15.6	2.02	28.2	14.3

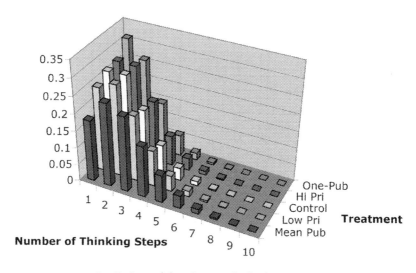

FIGURE 8.6 Estimated distribution of "thinking steps" per treatment.

To calibrate the impact of various types of advice, we can relate our τ values to those estimated on data from various different subject pools. Consider Table 8.7 (modified from Camerer et al. (2004, p. 36)) which presents the estimates of τ for various guessing games run with different values of N (the number of subjects playing).

Table 8.7 *Previous beauty contest results.*[a]

Subject pool	Source	N	Sample size	Mean	τ
Pasadena City College	Camerer et al. (2004)	3	24	47.5	0.10
Caltech Board	Camerer et al. (2004)	73	73	42.6	0.50
CEOs	Camerer et al. (2004)	20	20	37.9	1.00
German students	Nagel (1995)	14–16	66	37.2	1.10
70-year-olds	Kovalchik et al. (2005)	33	33	37.0	1.10
US high school	Camerer et al. (2004)	20–32	52	32.5	1.60
Econ. PhDs	Camerer et al. (2004)	16	16	27.4	2.30
Portfolio managers	Camerer et al. (2004)	26	26	24.3	2.80
Caltech students	Camerer et al. (2004)	17–25	42	23.0	3.00
Newspaper	Bosch-Domènech et al. (2002)	1460–3696	7884	23.0	3.30
Game theorists	Bosch-Domènech et al. (2002)	27–54	136	19.1	3.70

[a]This table is an abbreviated version of Table II in Camerer et al. (2004).

Note that our control group's τ of 2.02 puts the NYU students between US high school (1.60) and PhD students in economics (2.30), but after receiving credible public advice in the MPub treatment, NYU students look more like portfolio managers (2.80).

The estimates above are done under the assumption that the level-zero types choose uniformly between [0, 100]. While this may be a correct assumption in the information-poor environments that the two-thirds guessing games are typically run in, when public advice is added it may be that those same zero-level types decide to use the announced advice as an anchor and adjust their choices accordingly, especially when the advice is common knowledge and credible. In fact, in such circumstances level-zero types may decide to blindly follow advice and choose what is announced. Since everyone knows that everyone heard the announced number, the assumption of random choices by the level zeros is less plausible.[9] However, there still may be some fraction of zero-level types who do choose randomly despite the existence of advice.

To capture this possibility we estimate a generalized (two-parameter) CHC model where we add a second parameter, p, where p is the percentage of level zeros who ignore advice and choose randomly. The remaining level-zero types are assumed to follow the announced advice (or at least have a mean choice equal to the advice announced). Estimating p is a natural way to measure one of our main contentions, that people paid more attention to the advice when the mean was announced than when one advisor's suggestion was announced, since we would expect that the observed p for the MPub treatment would be lower than that of the 1Pub treatment where, although advice is public, it is not necessarily credible.

This conveniently nests both the CHC model and our advice-following modification of it. When $p = 1$ we are back in the CHC model, while when $p < 1$ we have a mixture model. Since the behavior of the level zeros is crucial for the actions of the rest of the distribution, we feel that the addition of an extra parameter to the model is more than justified.[10] Further, the addition of p is necessary in those cases when a piece of advice is announced and the mean choice of subjects is greater than the announced mean, since if all zero-level types simply followed advice, then all higher-level types would have to choose numbers which were lower than the announced mean, which would be impossible if the actual mean were above that which was announced. (This happened in one of the 1Pub treatment sessions where the announced advice was 13 and the mean chosen was 25.9.

[9] We apply this modification only to our public treatments because level ones can only respond to level zeros if they know the advice that they receive. While one could assign beliefs about the advice received by other players in the private treatments (for example, we could assume all players know at least the mean of the advice distribution), we choose to focus on the public-advice treatments where the advice received by all is directly observed.

[10] We would like to thank Colin Camerer for suggesting adding p to the model in order to address this problem.

Table 8.8 *The Potamites and Schotter modification of CHC.*

	Public advice	Mean choice	Std dev. of choices	p	τ	Predicted Mean	Predicted Std dev.
MPub	31.7	19.2	6.5	0.01	1.76	19.2	6.5
	28.6	23.2	10.8	0.18	1.12	23.14	10.8
	46.5	26.2	7.6	0.00	2.02	26.2	9.1
	37.6	26.3	11.4	0.29	1.53	26.3	11.4
1Pub	30	25.9	9.5	0.08	0.62	25.9	9.5
	13	25.9	12.0	1.00	2.59	24.4	12.0
	33	27.1	17.1	0.72	1.18	31.7	17.1
	73	44.0	16.3	0.24	1.45	44.0	16.2

Obviously forcing all zero-level types to choose 13, and hence all higher types to choose below, could not explain this observation.)

To estimate p and τ in our modified model, we search over τ and p in an effort to match both the mean choice and the standard error in each public advice session.

Table 8.8 presents our results. While there is a large degree of heterogeneity across sessions, p, the percentage of level zeros that ignore the advice, is much lower when the mean advice was announced (in the MPub treatment), 12%, as compared to the 51% who ignored advice in the 1Pub treatment. This fact reinforces our interpretation of the data since it confirms that mean public announcements are not only common knowledge but also perceived as credible announcements since they appear worthy of being followed at least by zero-level types. The fact that p averaged 51% in the 1Pub treatments indicates that such announcements were often ignored.

8.5 CONCLUSION

In this chapter we have attempted to explain the endogenous choice of rationality levels for subjects in two-thirds guessing games. We have argued that the distribution of cognitive types revealed in an experiment may not be identical with the true distribution of types that the subjects walk into the lab with. What differentiates the two is the belief on the parts of the subjects of how rationally their cohorts are likely to behave. If these beliefs can be altered by having subjects observe some outside event, offering them advice in various ways, then we would expect that the distribution of revealed types could change. We hope to have demonstrated that a necessary condition for such a distributional change is that the external event (advice) be both public (and common knowledge) and credible. If either of these elements is missing, then it is unlikely that we will observe a change in the observed cognitive hierarchy.

Finally, this chapter provides yet another example of the impact of advice on behavior. In line with what we learned in Chapter 7, the impact of private advice appears to be minimal as compared to public (common-knowledge) advice, but the type of information contained in that advice made public matters.

REFERENCES

Agranov, M., Potamites, E., Schotter, A. and Tergiman, C. (2012). Beliefs and endogenous cognitive levels: An experimental study. *Games and Economic Behavior*, 75(2), 449–463.

Alaoui, L. and Penta, A. (2016). Endogenous depth of reasoning. *Review of Economic Studies*, 83(4), 1297–1333.

Bosch-Domènech, A., Montalvo, J. G., Nagel, R. and Satorra, A. (2002). One, two, (three), infinity, ...: Newspaper and lab beauty-contest experiments. *American Economic Review*, 92(5), 1687–1701.

Camerer, C. F., Ho, T. H. and Chong, J. K. (2004). A cognitive hierarchy model of games. *Quarterly Journal of Economics*, 119(3), 861–898.

Choi, S. (2012). A cognitive hierarchy model of learning in networks. *Review of Economic Design*, 16(2), 215–250.

Costa-Gomes, M. A. and Crawford, V. P. (2006). Cognition and behavior in two-person guessing games: An experimental study. *American Economic Review*, 96(5), 1737–1768.

Costa-Gomes, M. A. and Crawford, V. P. (2007). Studying cognition via information search in two-person guessing game experiments. *Berkeley Psychology and Economics Seminar*, March.

Ho, T. H., Camerer, C. and Weigelt, K. (1998). Iterated dominance and iterated best response in experimental "p-beauty contests". *American Economic Review*, 88(4), 947–969.

Keynes, J. M. (1936). *The General Theory of Employment, Interest and Money*. London, UK: Macmillan.

Kocher, M. G., Sutter, M. and Wakolbinger, F. (2014). Social learning in beauty-contest games. *Southern Economic Review*, 80(3), 586–613.

Kovalchik, S., Camerer, C. F., Grether, D. M., Plott, C. R. and Allman, J. M. (2005). Aging and decision making: A comparison between neurologically healthy elderly and young individuals. *Journal of Economic Behavior and Organization*, 58(1), 79–94.

Moulin, H. (1986). *Game Theory for Social Sciences*. New York, NY: New York University Press.

Nagel, R. (1995). Unraveling in guessing games: An experimental study. *American Economic Review*, 85(5), 1313–1326.

Pogrebna, G. (2008). Naïve advice when half a million is at stake. *Economics Letters*, 98(2), 148–154.

Potamites, E. and Schotter, A. (2007). Endogenous cognitive types: An experimental study. *Mimeo*, New York University.

Sbriglia, P. (2008). Revealing the depth of reasoning in p-beauty contest games. *Experimental Economics*, 11(2), 107–121.

Stahl, D. O. and Wilson, P. W. (1995). On players' models of other players: Theory and experimental evidence. *Games and Economic Behavior*, 10(1), 218–254.

Thaler, R. (1998). Giving markets a human dimension. *Financial Times*, June 16, Mastering Finance Section, Sec. 6, pp. 2–5.

PART IV   **The Value of Advice**

Nobody forces us to follow advice or seek it. Doing so is a choice we make. If there are other sources of information out there and we rely on advice in preference to them, then it suggests that people either suffer from an advice bias – a preference or need to be advised – or we simply prefer to follow it for some other reason. Why might this be the case?

First, people may be cognitively lazy and prefer to follow advice rather than work things out for themselves. Second, although it is commonly thought that people are overconfident, many of those statements of overconfidence are not made in situations where money is on the line.[1] Hence, when it comes to actually risking real money in a decision, people may want to rely on others, possibly because they think other people (even randomly drawn other people who have barely more experience than they do in the task, as is true in most of our experiments) may be better than they are.

Finally, people may opt for advice because it allows them to avoid responsibility if things turn our badly (see our discussion of the work of psychologists in Chapter 3).

In the chapters in Part IV, we investigate whether unsolicited advice from a meddlesome boss can still be welfare-increasing (Chapter 9), whether people actually do prefer advice over other sources of information that might be inputs into their decisions (Chapter 10), and finally, in Chapter 11, which type of advisors are we most interested in receiving advice from.

The chapters in Part IV are different from the others in that none of them use the intergenerational-game framework employed in our other chapters. In addition, in all of these chapters, the problems faced by our decision makers are one-person decision problems and not games, which means that our emphasis in these chapters will

---

[1] For example, when people are asked whether they are better than the average driver, most people will say yes. Yet if asked whether they would choose to enter a driving contest where they could lose (or win) money based on the results, those same people might opt to allow someone else to take the wheel. Putting one's money where one's mouth is, is the true mark of confidence.

not be on the evolution of conventions of behavior but rather on the impact and desirability of advice.

Finally, in each of our chapters in Part IV, we observe one of the different types of advice discussed in Chapter 2. In Chapter 9 advice takes the form of advice from a coach who makes suggestions that are costless or costly to ignore. In Chapter 10 we have naive advice offered by subjects with little more experience than the advisee, while in Chapter 11 advice is offered by experts or at least by subjects who have performed the experiment many times themselves before they offer advice.

9 Learning with the Advice of a Meddlesome Boss

Much to their chagrin, most people at work have bosses who are responsible for their compensation and promotion.[1] Pleasing such bosses can be a full-time job if they are constantly poking their noses into your business and offering advice.

One example of such a relationship comes from sales-force management where a worker is paid a fixed salary and any raises are determined by her supervisor who works closely with the worker. Typically these raises are a function of how well the organization does as a whole. In such settings, however, if the supervisor offers suggestions, a problem is created for the worker – she cannot completely ignore the advice (even when she knows it to be wrong) for fear of displeasing the person who determines her compensation. The worker is caught between pleasing her boss and making what she feels are the best decisions. Such a trade-off can affect worker performance and learning-by-doing.

In this chapter we explore the dynamics of such trade-offs within a laboratory experiment wherein advisors and advisees make repeated decisions. We ask a question that is critical for such settings – does the relationship between worker (agent) and supervisor (advisor) interfere with the learning abilities of the worker?[2] In other words, are intrusions by the advisor so distracting that the agent fails to learn the essentials of her job?[3]

---

[1] This chapter is based on Iyengar and Schotter (2008).

[2] We use supervisor, advisor, and boss interchangeably. Similarly, we use agent, advisee, and worker interchangeably.

[3] Overbearing parents who smother their children with directives also have to fear that they may stunt the ability of their children to learn how to function independently and make good decisions on their own.

Surprisingly the answer is a resounding no. In fact, subjects in our experiment who have bosses advising them actually learn better than those with no laboratory bosses. This result is true even when the given advice can be ignored with no cost. Interestingly, we find that advisors also learn better than advisees or agents with no bosses. The reason, we conjecture, is that advice forces both advisors and advisees to think deductively about the problem. This reflection on the problem is different from the more inductive trial-and-error process that people typically go through on their own. Past research can give an indication of why such reflection might occur in the presence of advice.

The work on accountability suggests that when people are accountable, they engage in a more effortful, self-critical search (Tetlock, 1983; Lerner and Tetlock, 1994). This search can lead participants to pay greater attention to the information that they use and also develop a greater awareness of their cognitive processes (Lerner and Tetlock, 1994). In our setting, we have advisors who are giving advice and advisees who are evaluating the given advice and then making a decision. The reward structure (discussed later) is such that both are affected by each other's actions. Such a setting makes both advisors and advisees accountable for their actions. It is this accountability that can lead subjects to reflect on the problem more and gain a better assessment of the situation.

An increase in reflection and its benefits have been pointed out in past research on problem solving and learning.[4] For instance, Chi et al. (1989) found that good learners reflected on the problem in a way that went beyond the information that was given. In contrast, bad learners merely considered just the given information and did not make any other inferences. Such self-explanation and abstraction

---

[4] This result is similar to that reported by Weber (2003) where he allows subjects to play Nagel's (1995) two-thirds guessing game repeatedly without any feedback information. He finds there that behavior is more convergent toward the equilibrium despite the fact that no information is received. The explanation, however, is the same: forcing people to reflect on their behavior leads them to treat the problem they face differently.

has also been found to improve learning in many domains (Ferguson-Hessler and de Jong, 1990; Pressley et al., 1992). Hence, we surmise that it is the process of accountability and reflection that enhances learning in the presence of advice.

Note that our results are extensions of the results of psychologists using the judge–advisor system (Sniezek and Buckley, 1995) as described in Chapter 2. As you may recall, in that paradigm an advisor offers advice to a judge who makes an independent decision based on their own inclinations and the advice received. The advisor in that paradigm, however, is not a boss who needs to be pleased. In fact, in that literature the advisor is typically depicted as a member of the judge's staff who offers advice that the judge has to evaluate and include in her decision making if she deems it valuable. In our work here, just the opposite is true. The boss offers advice to the staff member who is in charge of the decision that needs to be made.

Finally, past work has in fact shown that subjects, when acting alone, have a difficult time learning in environments where decisions are repeated and there are rewards at the end of every round (Merlo and Schotter, 1999, 2003). More precisely, in their work Merlo and Schotter (1999, 2003) show that the standard environment employed in most economic models, where decision makers choose an action, get a payoff based on that action, and then, in light of that feedback, choose again (what they call a learn-while-you-earn environment),[5] is a poor one for learning. The question we ask here is whether advice (whether by a meddlesome boss or advice that is costless to ignore) can improve learning in this same environment.

Our results suggest that it can. When advice is introduced into the same learn-while-you-earn environment used by Merlo and Schotter (1999, 2003), performance improves even when it is costly to ignore the advice of the boss.

In terms of the types of advice discussed in Chapter 2, meddlesome bosses are like coaches who watch from a distance and intervene

---

[5] This is in distinction to a learn-before-you-earn environment where learning takes place for free before payoff-relevant decisions need to be made.

when they think they need to. Ignoring one's coach has consequences even when you think she is offering bad advice. Such advice is also similar to a noisy nudge or a very heavy-handed paternalistic intervention.

9.1 DECISION PROBLEM

All the experiments performed to investigate learning in the principal-agent context were identical to those used in Merlo and Schotter (1999, 2003) and discussed in Chapter 2. In those experiments, subjects played a simple game against a computerized opponent. In each round, the subject has to choose a number, e between 0 and 100 called their decision number. They were told that their computerized partner would always choose the number 37. After this number is chosen, a random number is independently generated from a uniform distribution over the interval $[-a, +a]$ ($a = 40$ in the experiment) for both the subject and her computerized opponent. This number represents random luck or noise in the decision for both the subject and her computerized opponent and the interval $[-a, +a]$ represents the support for this noise component. As the size of this interval increases, luck becomes a more important component for the subjects' payoffs and their choice of e less important. These numbers (the decision number and the random luck) are then added together and a "total number" is defined for each of the real and computerized players. Payoffs are determined by comparing the total numbers of the real and computerized subjects and awarding the real player a fixed payoff of M if her total is larger than that of the computerized opponent. If her total number is smaller, then she receives a payoff of $m, m < M$.

The cost of the decision number chosen is given by a convex function $c(e) = e^2/r$, where r is a constant. This amount is then subtracted from these fixed payments to determine a subject's final payoff. Hence, in these experiments, there is a trade-off in the choice of decision numbers: higher numbers generate a higher probability of winning the big prize but, at the same time, also imply a higher decision cost. By letting $r = 500$, $a = 40$, $M = 29$, and $m = 17.2$, and holding the computerized player's choice fixed at 37, our subjects face a rather simple decision problem with a quadratic payoff function whose peak is at 37.[6]

9.2 EXPERIMENTAL PROCEDURES

The experiments performed are an extension of those of Merlo and Schotter (1999, 2003) briefly discussed in Chapter 2. The difference is that in those experiments there was no advisor offering advice in every period. Other than that, however, the designs are very similar.

In these experiments, subjects were brought into a computer lab and were all handed a common set of instructions. The instructions had the description of the entire experiment, the roles played by the principal and the agent during the experiment, and determination of their respective payoffs. (Subjects were called decision makers of type A and type B and not principal or agents.) After the subjects read the instructions, they were randomly paired up in groups of two. One member of the group was assigned to the role of the principal or advisor (called subjects of type P for the remainder of this chapter) while the other was the agent (or advisee) (called subjects of type A). Thereafter, pairs were escorted to computers where they began the experiment seated next to each other.

In these experiments, the type-A subjects repeated the experiment for 75 rounds. Before every round, the type-P subjects wrote down what he or she thought is the right number for the type-A subjects to choose. The type P's suggestion would be her advice to the type-A subject. There was absolutely no other form of communication between the subjects, i.e., they were not allowed to speak, or make any verbal or facial expressions to each other. They were, in fact, not allowed to even react to the feedback they were getting from the computer. Total silence was strictly enforced.

---

[6] See Bull et al. (1987) and Schotter and Weigelt (1992) for a version of this problem where both subjects are real players.

The payoffs in each round depended on the treatment run: In the costly advice treatment, type-A subjects received a payoff from the decision problem in round t, π_t, that was composed of three parts. First, they received a fixed payment of either M or m depending upon whether their total number was above or below that of the computer. From that fixed payment a decision cost $C(e_i) = e_{it}^2/500$ was deducted, and finally an amount equal to $0.025(e_{it} - a_{it})^2$ was further deducted, where e_{it} is the decision number chosen by subject i in round t and a_{it} is the advice he or she received in that round from the type-P agent. This last term is a disagreement cost specifying a cost to disagreeing with the type-P subject equal to a constant, 0.025, times the square of the difference between the type A's decision number in period t and the advice they received from their type-P advisor. In the no-cost treatment this last term was set to zero, so there was no cost to following or ignoring type-P advice. Type-P subjects received a payoff equal to three-quarters of the payoff of their type-A counterpart. This payoff was inclusive of their disagreement cost, so the P-type subjects lost money if their A-type pair did not follow their advice.[7]

After each round of the experiment, both subjects received some information which was shown on the screen they both observed. In the costly advice treatment, both subjects saw the decision number chosen, the advice given, the advice cost, the payoff (inclusive of decision costs) of type-A subjects before the advice cost was deducted, the net payoff (inclusive of both decision costs and advice costs) to type-A subjects, and the net payoff to the type-P subjects (three-quarters of type A's net payoff). In the no-cost treatment, there was no advice cost and the net payoff of type-A subjects included only the decision cost. Thus, in the no-cost condition, both subjects saw the decision number chosen, the advice given, the net payoff to type-A subjects (inclusive of decision cost), and the payoff to type-P subjects (three-quarters of the net payoff to type-A subjects).

---

[7] Note that the incentives of the principal and agent are aligned, so the only reason for the agent not to follow the advice of the principal was the belief by the agent that the principal (boss) was not as knowledgeable about the problem as she was.

Following Merlo and Schotter (1999, 2003), after the 75 rounds of the experiment were over, we administered a "surprise quiz". To do this we first asked the type-P subjects to leave the room, leaving only the type-A subjects. These subjects were told that they would be participating in one more round of the experiment which involved making the same decision that they made for the past 75 rounds but with a few changes. One, there was no advice given for this round (i.e., no type-P subjects). Second, this round was worth 75 times the value of the previous rounds. In other words, this one choice was worth exactly as much as was the sum of the 75 previous choices. Thus, since they were playing for quite big stakes in this "surprise-quiz round" the choice they made there should serve as a sufficient statistic of how much the agents learned during the past 75 rounds. After the agents made their surprise-quiz decision, they were then taken out of the room, given a questionnaire, paid, and let go. The type-P subjects were then ushered into the room and given the same surprise quiz, paid, and let go. Hence, when we ask questions about how well our subjects learned over the course of the experiment, we will be comparing the results of their surprise-quiz choices over different treatments.

Finally, to make an inference about the impact of costly and costless advice, we compare the results of our experiment to those of Merlo and Schotter (1999), where subjects performed the exact same experiment but without the presence of an advisor

Table 9.1 lists the three treatments just described.

Table 9.1 *Experimental design.*

Treatment	Description	No. of pairs	Data
1 (NA)	No advisor	24 subjects	Merlo and Schotter (1999)
2 (CA)	Advisor, **Costly advice**	19 pairs	Iyengar and Schotter (2008)
3 (NCA)	Advisor, **No-cost advice**	14 pairs	Iyengar and Schotter (2008)

9.2.1   The Optimal Action

Given the computerized partner's choice of 37 and the uniform distributions for the random terms, the expected payoff function[8] for a type-A subject takes the form

$$E\pi_t(e_t) = \alpha + \beta_1 e_t + \beta_2 e_t^2 - k(e_t - a_t)^2, \qquad (9.1)$$

where e_t is the choice made by the type-A subjects, a_t is the advice offered by his type-P pair member at time t, and k is a known constant. In this expression, the first three terms constitute the payoff function associated with the decision problem while the last term is the disagreement cost function. The agent must trade off his need to satisfy his boss's desires and his desire to maximize his payoff from the decision problem he faces. When k equals 0, we are back to the payoff function in the no-advice case studied by Merlo and Schotter (1999, 2003).

If at any time t during the experiment the agent can use the data from the past $t - 1$ rounds to estimate the values of α, β_1, and β_2 in his or her payoff function (k is known with certainty at the start of the experiment), then he or she can use those estimated coefficients, $\hat{\alpha}_t \hat{\beta}_{1t}$ and $\hat{\beta}_{2t}$, to decide on the optimal choice of e_t by simply maximizing $E\pi_t$. Taking the derivative of $E\pi_t$ with respect to e_t and equating it to zero, and solving for e_t, we find

$$\frac{\mathrm{d}\pi_t}{\mathrm{d}e_t} = \hat{\beta}_{1t} + 2e\hat{\beta}_{2t} - 2ke_t + 2ka_t = 0, \qquad (9.2)$$

$$e_t^{optimal} = -\frac{\hat{\beta}_{1t}}{2(\hat{\beta}_{2t} - k)} - \frac{2ka_t}{2(\hat{\beta}_{2t} - k)}.$$

Second-order conditions are satisfied if $\hat{\beta}_2 < 0$ or $\hat{\beta}_2 < k$. If these conditions fail, then we get optima at the corners, either 0 or 100.

Note that when $k = 0$ the optimal e_t simply becomes that choice which, given the current estimates of the payoff function coefficients, maximizes the subject's payoff in the decision task without any disagreement-cost trade-offs. With $k > 0$, the optimal e_t

---

[8] Under risk neutrality.

becomes one which optimally trades off the choice which maximizes a type-A subject's payoff from the decision problem against his or her disagreement cost given a_t.

The objectively true coefficients are $\alpha = 18.94$, $\beta_1 = 0.079$, and $\beta_2 = -0.0011$. Hence when $k = 0$ we find the optimal choice is

$$e_t = -\frac{\hat{\beta_1}}{2(\hat{\beta_2})} = -\frac{0.079}{2(-0.0011)} \cong 37.$$

Without knowing the true coefficients, the optimal choice for an A-type subject at any round t depends on the advice given and the subject's best estimate of $\hat{\alpha}_t, \hat{\beta}_{1t}$, and $\hat{\beta}_{2t}$, given the data through round $t - 1$.

9.3   RESULTS

We will present our results in two parts. In the first part, we will look at the surprise-quiz round choices of our subjects in our three treatments. This is the data we will use to make statements about the ability of our subjects to learn in these four environments. This will be followed by a discussion of the advice-giving and advice-following behavior of our subjects.

9.3.1   Surprise-Quiz Behavior

Table 9.2, 9.3, and 9.4 present the choices of our subjects in the surprise-quiz rounds in each of our three treatments. In the Merlo and Schotter (1999) experiment, subjects performed our task alone. In that experiment, the mean and median surprise-quiz choices of subjects who did the experiment for 75 rounds was 51 and 50, respectively (Table 9.4).

A median test rejects the hypothesis that 37 is the median of Merlo and Schotter (1999). The message of Merlo and Schotter (1999) is that people fail to learn appropriately when they repeat experiments in which they receive payoffs after each period and the task is repeated often. The question is whether the presence of advice can alleviate this problem?

Table 9.2 *Surprise-quiz choices: costly advice treatment.*

Pair	A	P
1	40	47
2	38	50
3	38	38
4	37	38
5	23	38
6	64	51
7	23	29
8	48	47
9	65	38
10	52	51
11	23	20
12	60	60
13	25	17
14	23	82
15	19	3
16	1	1
17	50	25
18	21	1
19	36	1
Mean	**36.10**	**33.52**
Median	**37**	**38**

Table 9.3 *Surprise-quiz choices: no-advice-cost treatment.*

Pair	A	P
1	37	50
2	39	45
3	40	44
4	10	38
5	10	63
6	1	37
7	1	20
8	50	40
9	66	57
10	1	1
11	40	50
12	61	80
13	42	42
14	40	40
Mean	**31.2**	**43.35**
Median	**39.5**	**43**

In our experiments here, however, we find a remarkable result, which is that the process of giving advice (and receiving it) enhances the learning ability of both the type-A and the type-P subjects. For example, in the costly advice experiment the mean and median choices of the type-A and type-P subjects, were 36.1 and 37 for the type-A subjects and 33.5 and 38 for the type-P subjects, respectively. Neither of these medians are significantly different from 37 using a median test at any meaningful level of significance ($p \leq 1$ for the type-A agents and $p \leq 0.648$ for the type-P subjects). For the no-cost advice experiment, the situation is slightly different. Here the mean

Table 9.4 *Surprise-quiz choices: Merlo and Schotter (1999).*

Subject	Surprise-quiz choice	Subject	Surprise-quiz choice
1	65	13	0
2	45	14	44
3	100	15	68
4	77	16	0
5	0	17	70
6	45	18	69
7	41	19	50
8	68	20	50
9	70	21	45
10	65	22	50
11	45	23	30
12	35	24	100
		Mean	**51.33**
		Median	**50**

and median choices of the type-A and type-P subjects were 31.28 and 39.5 for the type-A, and 43.35 and 43 for the type-P subjects. Only the type-A subjects had a median that was not significantly different from 37. For the type-P subjects we had to reject that hypothesis at the 2% level. However, while this might indicate that advisors whose advice was ignored did not learn as well as those who received this advice (which they were at liberty to ignore), the type-P advisors still learned better than those in the Merlo and Schotter (1999) experiment who actually did the experiments. For example, a Wilcoxon test indicates that we can reject the hypothesis that the sample of type-P surprise-quiz rounds came from the same population as those of the subjects in Merlo and Schotter (1999).

Another feature of the learning experience subjects have when advice is given is that advice seems to diminish the number of subjects who choose dominated strategies. For example, in the surprise-quiz rounds of experiments where there are no disagreement costs, any choice of 65 or more is dominated by choosing 0. While in Merlo and Schotter (1999) 10 out of 24 subjects chose a dominated strategy in their surprise-quiz round, in our no-cost advice experiment only one type-P subject and one type-A subject made dominated choices. In other words there were only two out of 28 such choices. For the costly advice experiment the results are the same. Only one type-P subject and no type-A subjects made surprise-quiz choices strictly greater than 65. This is a very strong difference and indicates that these subjects clearly learned some minimum lesson that seemed not to be learned by others in the no-advice treatments.

The punch line then is that learning is fostered when advice is given even if there is no cost to ignore it. Those who learn well are both the people who give the advice and those that receive it.

9.3.2 Advice Giving and Following

The surprise-quiz data just discussed presents a snapshot of what was learned by our subjects. It says nothing, however, of the process they went through. In this section we analyze the advice-giving and advice-following strategies used by our subjects. We ask several questions. First, was advice followed by our type-A subjects? Second, was the advice offered them accurate in the following sense? Say that we assume that our type-P subject was an amateur (or professional) econometrician and knew that the payoff function was quadratic so that it was fully defined by three coefficient, α, β_1, and β_2. At each point in time t, by observing the choices made up to round $t - 1$ they could use the choice-payoff data to estimate each of these three coefficients $\hat{\alpha}, \hat{\beta}_1$, and $\hat{\beta}_2$, calculate the payoff-maximizing choice given those estimates, and offer that decision number as their advice. This should yield advice of $a_t = -\hat{\beta}/2\hat{\beta}_2$ at any time t since this is the period-t best guess about the peak of the payoff function. Does such a model explain the advice-giving behavior of our type-P subjects?

Finally, since the optimal choice for a type-A subject is to trade off his/her decision payoff against his/her agreement cost, we can ask if it appears as if that is what type-A subjects do. In other words, just like the type-P subjects, at any time during the experiment, our type-A subjects should have an estimate of the payoff-optimal decision

$$e_t = -\frac{\hat{\beta}}{2\hat{\beta}_2}$$

formed by estimating $\hat{\alpha}, \hat{\beta}_1$, and $\hat{\beta}_2$. Given the advice, a_t, they receive, they should modify this choice and choose

$$e_t = -\frac{\hat{\beta}_1}{2(\hat{\beta}_2 - k)} - \frac{2ka}{2(\hat{\beta}_2 - k)}$$

as described above. A question we ask is: does this process furnish a good model of type-A advice-following behavior?

9.3.3 Advice Following

To answer the question of whether type-A subjects follow advice, we ran a regression on the 19 type-A subjects regressing their 75 decision choices on the advice they were offered. We call this model the advice model. We estimated the parameters of this model using ordinary least-squares (OLS) but, as the data is of a time-series nature, there is a possibility of autocorrelation of the errors. This autocorrelation can cause a bias in the OLS-estimated standard deviations. To address this issue, we used the Newey–West (Newey and West, 1987) estimator. The Newey–West estimator provides a robust, consistent estimator for the covariance in the presence of autocorrelated disturbances with an unspecified covariance structure. The advice model is specified as

$$e_{it} = a + ba_{it} + \varepsilon_t,\tag{9.3}$$

where a_{it} is the period-t advice received by subject i, and ε_t is a disturbance term, which can be correlated with the previous disturbances.

Tables 9.5 and 9.6 show the regression results. The results for the costly advice treatment show that the advice model is extremely well specified. For example, 75% of the subjects had R^2 values of 0.69 or greater for these simple regressions, while the median R^2 was 0.82.

Table 9.5 *Advice-following regression results: costly advice treatment.*

Pair	$\hat{a}$	$\hat{b}$	R^2
1	−0.02(1.05)	1.04(0.017)	0.98
2	5.36(3.23)	0.93(0.07)	0.82
3	4.52(1.88)	0.82(0.08)	0.70
4	0	1.00	1.00
5	7.99(16.7)	0.82(0.382)	0.34
6	4.54(2.22)	0.89(0.05)	0.79
7	2.19(1.60)	0.96(0.03)	0.93
8	25.97(5.25)	0.44(0.12)	0.57
9	20.02(3.08)	0.66(0.05)	0.80
10	3.49(10.49)	0.91(0.25)	0.11
11	5.37(3.07)	0.98(0.08)	0.70
12	12.77(6.47)	0.82(0.09)	0.69
13	2.19(1.60)	0.96(0.03)	0.93
14	11.04(3.57)	0.6(0.08)	0.56
15	0	1	1
16	0.03(0.02)	0.97(0.02)	0.89
17	8.96(1.93)	0.81(0.05)	0.89
18	0.71(0.23)	0.97(0.008)	0.99

In addition, about 25% of the subjects had an R^2 0.98 or more. Clearly this implies that this simple model does a good job of explaining behavior.

The results for the advice no-cost experiment are worse. Here the mean R^2 was 0.585 while 75% of the subjects had R^2 values greater than only 0.34 (only 25% have R^2 values of 0.80 or more). Obviously, when it was free to ignore advice, subjects did it but, as we have seen, as a group they still learned far better than those subjects – in Merlo and Schotter (1999) – who did not receive advice.

Table 9.6 *Advice-following regression results: no-advice cost treatment.*

Pair	$\hat{a}$	$\hat{b}$	R^2
1	20.49(2.45)	0.43(0.06)	0.58
2	12.57(3.39)	0.66(0.09)	0.61
3	−0.13(8.62)	0.96(0.22)	0.21
4	6.74(5.55)	0.64(0.17)	0.16
5	28.17(7.07)	0.45(0.13)	0.20
6	2.00(9.23)	0.90(0.59)	0.37
7	0.95(1.01)	0.99(0.02)	0.95
8	29.25(2.35)	0.24(0.06)	0.34
9	22.25(5.95)	0.69(0.09)	0.59
10	−0.83(1.29)	0.80(0.07)	0.61
11	12.31(4.17)	0.59(0.05)	0.43
12	0.00	1.00	1.00
13	−0.33(1.16)	1.01(0.03)	0.94
14	−0.42(1.49)	0.98(0.03)	0.83

An alternative to the advice model posited above is that subjects optimally trade off payoff maximization versus disagreement cost minimization by choosing

$$e_t = -\frac{\hat{\beta}_1}{2(\hat{\beta}_2 - k)} - \frac{2ka}{2(\hat{\beta}_2 - k)}.$$

We have to be careful here, however, because the first-order conditions for a maximum are only necessary conditions and, given any $t - 1$ period history, it is possible that $\hat{\alpha}_t, \hat{\beta}_{1t}$, and $\hat{\beta}_{2t}$ defines a local minimum instead. In such cases, the best advice is at the corners of the feasible set, either 0 or 100. As time evolves, however, these estimates can change rapidly, with the estimated payoff function changing repeatedly from being concave to convex and back again.

To alleviate this problem we look at the behavior of only those subjects (call them "concave A-type subjects") who, during the last 20 rounds, consistently had estimated payoff functions that were concave and hence defined interior maxima. We look at the behavior of these subjects only and, further, restrict the analysis to only the last 20 rounds of the experiment.

By regressing the choices of our concave type-A subjects on their optimal choice of e given their disagreement costs, we specify the following model (optimal-action model):

$$e_{it} = a + b\hat{e}_{it}^* + \varepsilon_t, \tag{9.4}$$

where $\hat{e}_{it}^*$ is the period-t estimated best choice for agent A, and ε_t is a white noise disturbance term. In other words, $\hat{e}_{it}^*$ is that choice that is best for the concave type-A subject given his estimates of the coefficients of the payoff function and his disagreement costs.

Tables 9.7 and 9.8 show the regression results for the costly advice as well as the no-advice cost treatments, respectively.

These results show that the advice model outperforms the optimal-action model. We get further corroboration when we estimate the optimal-action model after pooling data from subjects in the costly advice treatment for the last 20 rounds and find that the overall R^2 for this model is 0.45 whereas the R^2 for the advice model is 0.77. We find a similar result (i.e., the advice model outperforms the optimal-action model) within the no-advice-cost treatment as well.

In summary, it appears as if subjects follow advice rather closely in both of our experiments, although they do so more often when it is costly not to deviate.

9.3.4 Advice Giving

Now that we know something about advice following behavior, we need to ask how was advice offered. One model suggested above was that advice was informationally optimal in the sense that type-P

Table 9.7 *Advice following: costly advice treatment.*[a]

Pair	Category	$\hat{a}$	$\hat{b}$	R^2
1	good	44.2(14.70)	0.18(0.28)	0.02
2	bad			
3	good	25	0	1
4	bad			
5	bad			
6	good	61.82(12.70)	−0.29(0.27)	0.06
7	good	15.39(7.12)	0.49(0.22)	0.21
8	good	13.63(13.40)	0.65(0.27)	0.23
9	good	52.99(16.80)	0.11(0.27)	0.01
10	good	−3.93(4.49)	1.11(0.10)	0.86
11	good	1.59(3.80)	0.93(0.20)	0.55
12	good	35.43(16.30)	0.46(0.25)	0.15
13	bad			
14	good	49.31(13.50)	−0.03(0.25)	0.01
15	bad			
16	bad			
17	good	9.30(13.51)	0.68(0.36)	0.16
18	bad			
19	good	−0.45(8.91)	1.07(0.19)	0.63

[a]Good = concave advisee. Bad = not-concave advisee.

subjects offered that advice that was their best guess of the peak of the payoff function conditional on their information set at any time t. For the same reasons as stated above we only look at concave type-P subjects (these coincide with their concave type-A counterparts as we use the same criterion).

We regressed the advice offered by concave type-P subjects over the last 20 rounds of the experiment on the estimated peak of their

Table 9.8 *Advice following: no-advice-cost treatment.*[a]

Pair	Category	$\hat{a}$	$\hat{b}$	R^2
1	bad			
2	bad			
3	bad			
4	good	−1.09(37.50)	1.20(1.01)	0.07
5	bad			
6	good	22.81(24.85)	0.37(0.87)	0.01
7				
8	bad			
9	good	183.79(33.72)	−2.91(0.81)	0.41
10	bad			
11	good	−4.54(48.27)	0.98(1.85)	0.01
12	good	−76.23(67.55)	3.83(1.92)	0.18
13	good	60.27(19.05)	−0.39(0.39)	0.05
14		57.72(16.30)	−0.39(0.31)	0.08

[a]Good = concave advisee. Bad = not-concave advisee.

payoff function and tested to see if the right-hand side coefficient was significantly different from 1. Tables 9.9 and 9.10 show the estimated coefficients and the results of the hypothesis test.

From Tables 9.9 and 9.10, it is evident that most concave type-P advisors are offering advice that is informationally optimal. In the costly advice condition, we cannot reject the null hypothesis of the right-hand side coefficient equal to 1 for 11 out of the 12 concave advisors. In the no-cost-advice treatment, there were only two out of the seven concave type-P advisors for whom we could reject the null hypothesis.

This result enforces the results of Merlo and Schotter (1999, 2003) and our discussion above that learn-while-you-earn environments, where decision makers repeatedly make decisions and are immediately rewarded or punished, are not conducive to learning.

Table 9.9 *Advice giving: costly advice treatment.*

Pair	Category	$\hat{a}$	$\hat{b}$	R^2	Null hypothesis $b = 1$
1	good	19.37(31.96)	0.79(0.73)	0.06	Accept null
2	bad				
3	good	25	0	1	Reject null
4	N/A				
5	bad				
6	good	34.13(95.40)	0.34(2.32)	0.00	Accept null
7	good	26.41(34.46)	0.15(1.49)	0.00	Accept null
8	good	−8.71(82.40)	0.90(1.38)	0.02	Accept null
9	good	−105.52(154.80)	3.12(2.92)	0.06	Accept null
10	good	−24.93(34.77)	1.62(0.82)	0.18	Accept null
11	good	−20.44(25.66)	1.49(0.99)	0.11	Accept null
12	good	−75.06(99.61)	2.47(1.76)	0.09	Accept null
13	bad				
14	good	13.69(106.87)	0.93(2.91)	0.09	Accept null
15	bad				
16	bad				
17	good	−45.08(36.07)	1.89(0.85)	0.21	Accept null
18	bad				
19	good	−216.45(186.03)	6.77(4.79)	0.10	Accept null

However, when advisors are introduced into those environments – advisors who do not receive period-by-period payments and are therefore in a more detached relationship to the decisions being made – the performance of the decision makers improves. What is added by our results here, however, is how good advisors are in using the information generated by their advisees in offering good advice to them and how faithfully this advice is followed.

Table 9.10 *Advice giving: no-advice-cost-treatment.*

Pair	Category	$\hat{a}$	$\hat{b}$	R^2	Null hypothesis $b = 1$
1	bad				
2	bad				
3	bad				
4	good	1.59(13.10)	0.90(0.35)	0.27	Accept null
5	bad				
6	good	13.28(14.04)	0.74(0.49)	0.11	Accept null
7	bad				
8	bad				
9	good	−102.85(120.44)	3.79(2.90)	0.08	Accept null
10	bad				
11	good	−55.51(82.49)	3.49(3.16)	0.06	Accept null
12	good	−76.23(67.55)	3.84(1.92)	0.18	Accept null
13	good	60.27(19.05)	−0.39(0.39)	0.05	Reject null
14	good	42.25(2.03)	−0.06(0.03)	0.14	Reject null

9.4 CONCLUSION

In this chapter we investigated a setting where a decision maker attempts to learn the optimal way to behave in the presence of a meddlesome boss who repeatedly makes suggestion as to how to behave which are either costly or costless to ignore.[9] Our results suggest that the presence of advice forces both advisors and advisees to think deductively about the problem. This reflection of the problem leads to insights that may not be gleaned by a subject involved in a learning task in which he is constantly getting payoff feedback. Such a stimulus–response atmosphere tends to lead subjects to act myopically as opposed to sitting back and seeing the forest for the trees. However, it is precisely these types of environments that exist

---

[9] In some sense it is a paper on the welfare consequences of costly and costless kibbitzing.

when people function in markets and make choices repeatedly which are reinforced by an immediate payoff. Put differently, one benefit of advice is to make us think twice before we act.

Finally, note that in this experiment the advice received is in some sense that of a coach as discussed in Chapter 2. A meddlesome boss is like a meddlesome coach whose advice (or orders) can be ignored at the risk of being admonished or benched if we are talking about a sports coach. When a player is told to do something in a game that he thinks is wrong, he faces the same dilemma as the salesman who motivated our discussion does when ignoring his supervisor. He must do so at his own risk.[10]

REFERENCES

Bull, C., Schotter, A. and Weigelt, K. (1987). Tournaments and piece rates: An experimental study. *Journal of Political Economy*, 95(1), 1–33.

Chi, M. T., Bassok, M., Lewis, M. W., Reimann, P. and Glaser, R. (1989). Self-explanations: How students study and use examples in learning to solve problems. *Cognitive Science*, 13(2), 145–182.

Ferguson-Hessler, M. G. and de Jong, T. (1990). Studying physics texts: Differences in study processes between good and poor solvers. *Cognition and Instruction*, 7(1), 41–54.

Iyengar, R. and Schotter, A. (2008). Learning under supervision: An experimental study. *Experimental Economics*, 11, 154–173.

Lerner, J. S. and Tetlock, P. E. (1994). Accountability and social cognition. *Encyclopedia of Human Behavior*, vol. 1, ed. V. S. Ramachandran, pp. 3098–3121. San Diego, CA: Academic Press.

Lerner, J. S. and Tetlock, P. E. (1999). Accounting for the effects of accountability. *Psychological Bulletin*, 125(2), 255–275.

Merlo, A. and Schotter, A. (1999). A surprise-quiz view of learning in economic experiments. *Games and Economic Behavior*, 28(1), 25–54.

Merlo, A. and Schotter, A. (2003). Learning by not doing: an experimental investigation of observational learning. *Games and Economic Behavior*, 42(1), 116–136.

---

[10] In sports it might even be harsher since a disobedient player may be benched even when his disobedience is successful. Discipline may ultimately be more important for the coach in the long run.

Nagel, R. (1995). Unraveling in guessing games: An experimental study. *American Economic Review*, 85(5), 1313–1326.

Newey, W. K. and West, K. D. (1987). A simple, positive semi-definite, heteroskedasticity and autocorrelation consistent covariance matrix. *Econometrica*, 55(3), 703–708.

Pressley, M., Wood, E., Woloshyn, V., Martin, V., King, A. and Menke, D. (1992). Encouraging mindful use of prior knowledge: Attempting to construct explanatory answers facilitates learning. *Educational Psychologist*, 27, 91–109.

Schotter, A. and Weigelt, K. (1992). Asymmetric tournaments, equal opportunity laws, and affirmative action: Some experimental results. *Quarterly Journal of Economics*, 107(2), 511–539.

Sniezek, J. A. and Buckley, T. (1995). Cueing and cognitive conflict in judge–advisor decision making. *Organizational Behavior and Human Decision Processes*, 62(2), 159–174.

Tetlock, P. E. (1983). Accountability and complexity of thought. *Journal of Personality and Social Psychology*, 45(1), 74.

Weber, R. A. (2003). "Learning" with no feedback in a competitive guessing game. *Games and Economic Behavior*, 44(1), 134–144.

10   Advice and Social Learning

Social learning theory (Bandura and McClelland, 1977) is a theory of the learning process and social behavior which proposes that people are capable of learning by observing and imitating others.[1] When people engage in social learning they observe others and experience their rewards and punishments vicariously rather than directly as with reinforcement learning or operant conditioning (see Skinner, 1938).[2]

But we can also learn by being advised by others. People who have experience in the past could simply share their experience with us and advise us what they think we should do. Both of these methods can be called social learning because people are in the presence of others who offer (intentionally or unintentionally) assistance.

More concretely, say that there is a set of decision makers each of whom has to choose between two actions $\{A, B\}$ when facing an identical problem. The decision makers choose sequentially starting with the first person and continuing to the last and everyone can see only the action of the person before them. However, since each person knows that the person before them could see the action taken by their predecessor, such actions may contain information about all previous choices.

Alternatively, let's say that we have the same problem but instead of being able to see the actions taken by the person before them, decision makers are able to receive advice from their immediate predecessor as to what to choose without being able to see what their predecessor actually chose.

---

[1] This chapter is based Çelen et al. (2010).
[2] See Banerjee (1992), Bikhchandani et al. (1992, 1998) for the seminal applications of social learning to economics.

Given this setup we ask three questions in this chapter:

Question 1. *Do subjects tend to follow advice more often than action when each is observed under identical circumstances?*

Question 2. *Which information – advice or actions – is more valued by the subjects? Under what circumstances do subjects offer advice that is different from their actions?*

Question 3. *Do subjects make the right decisions more often in treatments with advice than in those with only actions?*

These questions get at the heart of how we value advice. In the problem we look at in this chapter, if all decision makers are rational and that fact is known, then, in equilibrium, the informational content of advice and actions is the same, so there is no rational reason to prefer one to the other, yet, as we will see, people tend to prefer receiving advice to observing and perhaps copying the actions of others.

In the real world, the power of advice is seen online where people buy goods sequentially and offer their opinions and advice about the goods to later consumers. In addition, there is a great deal of consumer-generated advertising where consumers take it upon themselves to blog about the quality of various products. Such consumer-generated advice has become influential in online purchasing and may carry more weight than knowing which product is most popular.

In our treatments with advice, the subject offering advice is rewarded as a function of the actions taken by their successor so that there are incentives in our design to offer payoff-maximizing advice just as there was in our intergenerational game setup. In addition, in our experiments here subjects are ordered into generations (or at least choose sequentially one after the other) again, as was true in our intergenerational-game experiments.

Let us describe our experimental design.

10.1   EXPERIMENTAL DESIGN

In each round of the experiment, eight subjects were assigned to one of eight decision turns and made decisions sequentially starting with the first subject.[3] A round began with the computer drawing eight numbers (each with two decimal places) from a uniform distribution over $[-10, 10]$. The numbers drawn in each round were independent of each other and of the numbers in any of the other rounds. If the sum of the random numbers drawn was positive, then the payoff-maximizing choice for any subject was A, while, if it was negative, then the payoff-maximizing decision for any subject was B. Since each subject only received one of the eight randomly drawn numbers, they each received only a partial signal about the payoff-relevant sum. There were 15 rounds in each session so subjects repeated the experiment 15 times before the experiment was over.[4,5]

As in Çelen and Kariv (2004b, 2005)), we used a strategy method: after receiving this information, each subject was asked to select a number between -10 and 10 (a cutoff) that would result in the subject taking action A if their random signal was above the cutoff and action B if the signal was below the cutoff. As mentioned above, action A was profitable if and only if the sum of the eight numbers was positive and action B otherwise. The subject was informed of the value of her private signal only after she submitted her decision. Then the computer recorded her decision as A if the signal was higher than the cutoff she selected. Otherwise, the computer recorded her action as B.

The experiment had three treatments, the action-only, advice-only, and action-plus-advice treatments. In all treatments, upon being

[3] Our data come from experiments conducted at the Center for Experimental Social Science (CESS) at NYU and at the Experimental Social Science Laboratory (Xlab) at UC Berkeley, as well as from the earlier experiment of Çelen and Kariv (2005). Çelen and Kariv (2005) provide us with much of our design and all of the theory. In fact, our experiment here is identical to theirs except for the introduction of advice.

[4] In each of the treatments we have observations from 40 subjects (in one case, 48 subjects) who had no previous experience in advice or social learning experiments. Each subject participated in only one experimental session, and eight subjects were recruited for each session. The treatment was held constant throughout a given session. After subjects read the instructions, they were also read aloud by an experimental administrator. Participation fees and subsequent earnings for correct decisions were paid in private at the end of the session. Throughout the experiment, we assured anonymity and an effective isolation of subjects in order to minimize any interpersonal factors that might have caused a tendency toward uniform behavior.

[5] Sample instructions for the advice-plus-action treatment can be downloaded at: https://pubsonline.informs.org/doi/suppl/10.1287/mnsc.1100.1228/suppl_file/mnsc .1100.1228-sm-ec.pdf.

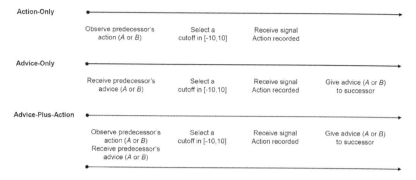

FIGURE IO.I Experimental design and procedures.

called to participate but before being informed of her private signal, the subject received some information relevant to decision making (either the predecessor's action, the predecessor's advice, or both, depending on the treatment). The advice was in the form of a decision to make {A, B} and not a cutoff.

After all subjects had made their decisions, the computer informed everyone what the sum of the eight numbers actually was. Everyone whose decision determined that their action would be A earned $2 if the sum of the subjects' private signals was positive (or zero), and nothing otherwise. On the other hand, everyone whose decision that determined their action would be B earned $2 if the sum was negative, and nothing otherwise. In addition, in the treatments containing advice, everyone earned $1 if their successor took the correct action. This was paid to induce subjects to give advice that was their best guess as to what the correct action was.[6] At the end of a session, subjects were paid in private. Figure 10.1 summarizes our experimental treatments and procedures.

10.2 THEORY AND PREDICTIONS

Social learning has a long tradition in economics – see Gale (1996), Bikhchandani et al. (1998), and Chamley (2004) for surveys of the

---

[6] Subjects in the action-only treatment did not receive a payment if their successor chose the correct action.

theoretical literature, and Anderson and Holt (1997) for an early experimental analysis. Çelen and Kariv (2004a) provide an extensive analysis of a general version of the action-only case. As we will see, we will demonstrate that, in the advice-only case, it is optimal to offer advice equal to the action chosen. As a result, substituting advice for actions in our experiment cannot convey more information. This implies that the environment in the advice-only treatment is not informationally richer than the environment in the action-only treatment.

10.2.1 *Preliminaries*

To more formally present the decision problem our subjects faced, suppose that the eight agents receive private signals $\theta_1, \theta_2, \ldots, \theta_8$ that are independently and uniformly distributed over the support $[-10, 10]$.

In the problem presented to our subjects, $\sum_{i=1}^{8} \theta_i$ defines the set of the payoff-relevant states of the world which are partitioned into two decision-relevant events, $\sum_{i=1}^{8} \theta_i \geq 0$ and $\sum_{i=1}^{8} \theta_i < 0$. The decision problem involves incomplete and asymmetric information: agents are uncertain about whether the realization of the underlying decision-relevant event will be $\sum_{i=1}^{8} \theta_i \geq 0$ or $\sum_{i=1}^{8} \theta_i < 0$, and the information about it is shared asymmetrically among them.

In what follows, we will first discuss the theory behind the action-only case that constitutes the backbone of all three treatments and then extend this analysis to the advice-only and advice-plus-action treatments. Proofs will be relegated to the appendix in Section 10.6. For a more complete discussion of the intricacies of the underlying action-only model, see Çelen and Kariv (2004a).

10.2.2 *Action-Only*

The Decision Problem In the action-only case, except for the first agent, everyone observes only her immediate predecessor's action. Since agents do not know any of their successors' actions, agent n's optimal decision rule – conditional on the information available to her – is the following cutoff rule:

$$x_n = \begin{cases} A & \text{if} \quad \theta_n \geq \hat{\theta}_n, \\ B & \text{if} \quad \theta_n < \hat{\theta}_n, \end{cases} \tag{10.1}$$

where

$$\hat{\theta}_n(x_{n-1}) = -\mathbb{E}\left[\sum_{i=1}^{n-1} \theta_i \mid x_{n-1}\right]. \tag{10.2}$$

This cutoff accumulates all the information revealed to agent n from her predecessor's action. Thus, $\hat{\theta}_n$ is sufficient to characterize agent n's behavior and the sequence of cutoffs $\{\hat{\theta}_n\}$ characterizes the social behavior. That is why we take the *cutoff equilibrium* (an equilibrium in which all agents follow the cutoff strategy (10.1) and (10.2)) as the primitive of the experimental design and of our analysis.

Note that this cutoff says that whether the n-th decision maker chooses A will depend on what she thinks is the sum of the signals decision makers have received up through the $(n - 1)$-th. No information about the future is available and hence not relevant for agent n. The obvious conceptual issue is how can subjects estimate $-\mathbb{E}\left[\sum_{i=1}^{n-1} \theta_i \mid x_{n-1}\right]$ if they only have information about the choice of their immediate predecessor, x_{n-1}. To illustrate how, let us describe the cutoff process for the parameterized example used in our experiment.

The Cutoff Process – Action Only To demonstrate how these cutoffs are determined, let us use the example that our subjects will face in our experiment.

As stated above, the optimal history-contingent cutoff rule is

$$\hat{\theta}_n = -\mathbb{E}\left[\sum_{i=1}^{n-1} \theta_i \mid x_{n-1}\right].$$

To see how this rule is determined, let us start with the first decision maker and work recursively.

The first agent's decision is based solely on her private signal and thus her cutoff will be $\hat{\theta}_1 = 0$. If she gets a positive signal she will choose A and if she gets a negative signal she will choose B. Knowing this, the second decision maker will be able to detect if the first saw a negative or positive signal by observing her action. If she saw the first decision maker choose A she knows that the first decision maker must have seen a positive signal and, given the uniform distribution over signals, she will expect that the signal was 5, i.e., the expected value of the signal conditional on the first decision maker choosing A.

The second agent's cutoff rule is therefore

$$\hat{\theta}_2 = \begin{cases} -5 & \text{if} \quad x_1 = A, \\ 5 & \text{if} \quad x_1 = B. \end{cases}$$

What this says is that if the first decision maker chose A and hence had an expected signal of 5, the second decision maker will choose A only if the signal she receives is greater than -5 since only then will the sum of the first two signals still be positive.

By the time it is the third agent's turn to make a decision, the information inherent in the first agent's action is suppressed, but she can still draw a probabilistic conclusion about it by Bayes' rule. That is, by observing the action of the second agent, x_2, the third assigns probability to the actions that the first agent could have taken. For example, by observing $x_2 = A$, she assigns probability $3/4$ that $x_1 = A$ and probability $1/4$ that $x_1 = B$. A simple computation shows that $\mathbb{E}\left[\theta_1 + \theta_2 | x_2 = A\right] = 6.25$, which implies that if $x_2 = A$ it is optimal for the third agent to take action A for any signal $\theta_3 \geq -6.25$.

A similar analysis shows that if $x_2 = B$ it is optimal for her to take action A for any signal $\theta_3 \geq 6.25$. Thus, the third agent's cutoff rule is

$$\hat{\theta}_3 = \begin{cases} -6.25 & \text{if} \quad x_2 = A, \\ 6.25 & \text{if} \quad x_2 = B. \end{cases}$$

The dynamics of the cutoff rule $\hat{\theta}_n$ is described in a closed-form solution recursively as follows:

$$\hat{\theta}_n(x_{n-1}) = \begin{cases} -5 - \dfrac{\hat{\theta}_{n-1}^2}{20} & \text{if} \quad x_{n-1} = A, \\[3mm] 5 + \dfrac{\hat{\theta}_{n-1}^2}{20} & \text{if} \quad x_{n-1} = B, \end{cases} \qquad (10.3)$$

where $\hat{\theta}_1 = 0$.

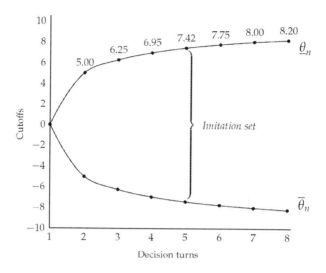

FIGURE 10.2 Process of cutoffs and imitation sets.

Figure 10.2 defines the following sequence of cutoffs. As we can see from Figure 10.2, the cutoff rule partitions the signal space into three subsets: $[-10, \overline{\theta}_n)$, $[\overline{\theta}_n, \underline{\theta}_n)$, and $[\underline{\theta}_n, 10]$. For high-value signals $\theta_n \in [\underline{\theta}_n, 10]$ and symmetric low-value signals $\theta_n \in [-10, \overline{\theta}_n)$, agent n follows her private signal and takes action A or B, respectively. In the intermediate subset $[\overline{\theta}_n, \underline{\theta}_n)$, which we call an *imitation set*, agent n ignores her private signal when she makes a decision, and all agents imitate their immediate predecessor's action. Furthermore, as Figure 10.2 illustrates, since $\{\overline{\theta}_n\}$ and $\{\underline{\theta}_n\}$ are decreasing and increasing sequences, respectively, the imitation sets $[\overline{\theta}_n, \underline{\theta}_n)$ monotonically increase in n regardless of the actual history of actions. Hence, over time, it is more likely that imitation will arise, as agents tend to rely more on the information revealed by the predecessor's action, rather than on their private signal.[7]

---

[7] Çelen and Kariv (2004a) show that this has an important implication: beliefs and actions are not convergent but cycle forever. Despite this instability, over time, private information is increasingly ignored and decision makers become increasingly likely to imitate their predecessors. Consequently, behavior is typified by longer and longer periods of uniform behavior, punctuated by (increasingly rare) switches.

10.2.3 Advice-Only

Since our interests are in the role or impact of advice in social learning, it is of interest to us to replicate the analysis above using advice rather than observable actions. In other words, we want to contrast the advice-only and action-only treatments in terms of their theoretical predictions. Our purpose in this section is to demonstrate that in the advice-only case, advice cannot convey more information than action. This is because in the only relevant equilibrium of the advice-only case, it is optimal to send advice equal to the action taken since subjects are rewarded for their advice only if their successor chose the correct action.

The complication we face in proving the equivalence of the action-only and advice-only treatments is that in the advice-only treatment other equilibria may arise because it is possible for a decision maker to choose one action for herself but offer different advice to her successor. In the action-only treatment this was not possible since there was no advice and each decision maker could see what their predecessor did. In the advice-only treatment there are three types of equilibria.

One equilibrium, which we call the truthful equilibrium, entails each decision maker offering advice to her successor equal to the action she took during her turn and this fact is known to all decision makers. Since in this equilibrium advice = action, this equilibrium exactly replicates that of the action-only treatment.

A second equilibrium, the mirror equilibrium, also exists where agents advise their successor to take the opposite action to theirs, $a_n \neq x_n$; the successor believes that the advice given to her by the predecessor is opposite to her predecessor's action; and she sets her cutoffs optimally according to (10.2), given her beliefs. This equilibrium is the mirror image of the truthful equilibrium. Clearly, this equilibrium and the truthful equilibrium define the same process of cutoffs $\{\hat{\theta}_n\}$ given by (10.2) and depicted in Figure 10.2. However, for this equilibrium to be selected, it must be common knowledge that all agents are switching the meaning of the advice they get. We consider that unlikely and hence will ignore this equilibrium in what we do.

Finally, there is a babbling equilibrium, where agents give noisy advice that is uncorrelated with their action and thus independent of the available information. In such an equilibrium, subjects would believe that the advice they receive is so noisy that they will ignore it and set their cutoffs optimally at zero.

In the appendix in Section 10.6, we provide a proof that these three equilibria are the only types that exist. We will concentrate our analysis on the truthful equilibrium, so we assume, in essence, that the incentives of the advisor and advisee are aligned.

The Truthful Equilibrium As we stated above, in a truthful equilibrium of the advice-only treatment, all subjects offer advice equal to the action they took and hence behavior in the advice-only equilibrium is identical to that in the action-only treatment. Hence advice contains exactly the same information as actions.

10.2.4   Action-Plus-Advice

In the action-plus-advice case, agents are able not only to receive advice from their immediate predecessor, but also to observe her action.

Here agent n's optimal decision takes the form of the cutoff strategy given by (10.1), where

$$\hat{\theta}_n(a_{n-1}) = -\mathbb{E}\left[\sum_{i=1}^{n-1} \theta_i \mid x_{n-1}, a_{n-1}\right] \tag{10.4}$$

is the optimal cutoff that accumulates all of the information revealed to agent n from her predecessor's action and advice.

Observing action and advice enables agents to engage in more sophisticated, and hence informationally richer, strategies. These strategies combine all four available action–advice pairs (x_{n-1}, a_{n-1}) to partition their signal space into four subsets and thus convey more information to an agent's successor. Hence, the informational pipeline in this case is less constrained and there exists more informationally rich equilibria, which we call *signaling equilibria*, than in the action-only and advice-only cases.

Despite the possibilities of new equilibria here, the truthful equilibrium in the advice-only case, in which agents simply advise their successor to do as they did ($a_n = x_n$), is also an equilibrium in the action-plus-advice case. In particular, when a convention exists such that agents ignore conflicting advice and make decisions solely on the basis of the action observed, then the resulting equilibrium is, of course, the truthful equilibrium.[8]

10.3   DO ACTIONS SPEAK LOUDER THAN WORDS?
EXPERIMENTAL RESULTS

Our original research questions asked whether advice is a more powerful tool in influencing behavior than actions. Are people more likely to do as you say than do as you did?

10.3.1   *Question 1*

Do subjects tend to follow advice more often than action when each is observed under identical circumstances?

The question here is how powerful is advice? Our experiment presents a controlled comparison of the strength of advice and actions by comparing behavior in our advice-only and our action-only experiments. (We will look at the advice-plus-action treatment later.)

At any turn n, the data generated in our experiment are the cutoffs $\tilde{\theta}_n$ set by our subjects, the actions taken $x_n = \{A, B\}$, and, in the advice-only treatment, the advice given $a_n = \{A, B\}$. To organize these data, following Çelen and Kariv (2005), we first define decisions made by subjects as *concurring decisions* if the sign of their cutoff agrees with the action observed or advice received. For example, when

---

[8] To illustrate signaling equilibria, consider an equilibrium in which everyone with a cutoff leading to action A (B) advises her successor to take action A (B) if the realization of her signal is closer to 10 (-10) than to her cutoff; she advises her successor to take action B (A) otherwise. Assuming consistent beliefs, such a strategy is clearly more informative than the equilibria we discussed in the advice-only or action-only cases, because agents use a finer signaling partition here to convey information about their signals.

Table 10.1 *Concurring, contrary, and neutral decisions in the action-only and advice-only treatments.*

	Concurring	Neutral	Contrary
Action-only	44.2%	16.6%	39.2%
Advice-only	74.1%	9.1%	16.8%

a subject observes that her predecessor took action or gave advice A (resp. B) and adopts a negative (resp. positive) cutoff, she demonstrates concurrence, since by selecting a negative (resp. positive) cutoff she adopts a higher probability of taking action A (resp. B). Similarly, if a subject observes action or receives advice A (resp. B) and selects a positive (resp. negative) cutoff, then she disagrees with her predecessor. We say that such decisions are *contrary decisions*. Finally, *neutral decisions* are carried out by choosing a zero cutoff, which neither agrees nor disagrees with the predecessor's action or advice but simply entails a choice based on private information.

Table 10.1 presents the percentages of concurring, contrary, and neutral decisions in the action-only and advice-only treatments. The most notable pattern in Table 10.1 is that advice is followed far more often than actions. Over all decision turns except the first, subjects tend to set a cutoff consistent with the advice they receive 74.1% of the time in the advice-only treatment, but only 44.2% of the time in the action-only treatment. Together with the neutral cutoffs, subjects tend to weakly agree (set a concurring or neutral cutoff) with advice 83.2% of the time in the advice-only treatment but only 60.8% of the time in the action-only treatment. These distributions of the concurring, contrary, and neutral decisions in the action-only and advice-only treatments are significantly different according to a Kolmogorov–Smirnov test (p-value 0.000).

One possible explanation of why subjects tend to follow their predecessor's advice more in the advice-only treatment than they imitate their predecessor's action in the action-only treatment is that the advice was offered after the predecessor observed her signal, while her action was determined by her cutoff, which was set before she observed her signal.

To investigate this claim, Çelen et al. (2010) conducted a fourth treatment, the post-signal action-only treatment, where subjects observe both their private signal and their predecessor's action before taking their own action. If advice is followed more often in the advice-only treatment than actions are copied in the post-signal action-only treatment, then we can conclude that advice is more persuasive than actions even in those situations where they are based on identical information. No significant differences were found, which suggests that the preference for advice was not caused by an asymmetry in information across treatments.

While Table 10.1 presents data on the number of decisions that were concurring, neutral, or contrary, the histograms in Figure 10.3 show the distribution of concurring, neutral, or contrary decisions disaggregated to the subject level. The horizontal axis measures the number of contrary decisions (the percentage of subjects who disagreed with the observed action (advice) in less than two rounds, three to five rounds, and so on) and the vertical axis measures the percentage of subjects corresponding to each interval. In the advice-only treatment, 67.5% of the subjects disagreed with the advice they received only in one or two rounds. In the action-only treatment, subjects tended to disagree far more often: only 20.0% of the subjects disagreed in one or two rounds, and 40.0% of the subjects disagreed in six to eight rounds. The distributions presented in Figure 10.3 are significantly different according to a Kolmogorov–Smirnov test (p-value 0.000).

10.3.2 Observed and Predicted Cutoffs

While the sign of the cutoffs indicates agreement and disagreement, it ignores the actual cutoff set and the strength of her agreement or disagreement with their predecessor's action or advice. For example, if a subject observes action or receives advice A and sets a cutoff close to

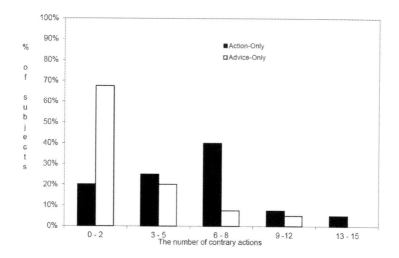

FIGURE 10.3 The distribution of contrary subjects.

-10, then not only does she agree with the action observed or advice received, but she also does so very strongly since she will then almost surely take action A.

In contrast, selection of a negative cutoff that is closer to zero clearly indicates a much weaker agreement. Since the cutoff strategy is symmetric around zero, the strength of agreement or disagreement is independent of the actual action observed (A or B) or advice received (to choose A or B).

To present this strength of agreement (or disagreement), we use the fact that the cutoff strategy is symmetric around zero and proceed as per Çelen and Kariv (2005) and, in the action-only treatment, transform the cutoffs in any turn $n > 1$ using the *mirror image transformation*:

$$\tilde{\theta}_n = \begin{cases} |\hat{\theta}_n| & \text{if } x_{n-1} = A \text{ and } \hat{\theta}_n \leq 0 \text{ or } x_{n-1} = B \text{ and } \hat{\theta}_n > 0, \\ -|\hat{\theta}_n| & \text{otherwise.} \end{cases}$$

Analogously, we define the mirror image transformation in the advice-only treatment by replacing x_{n-1} with a_{n-1}. That is, we take the absolute value of the cutoffs in concurring decision points, and the negative of the absolute value of the cutoffs at contrary decision

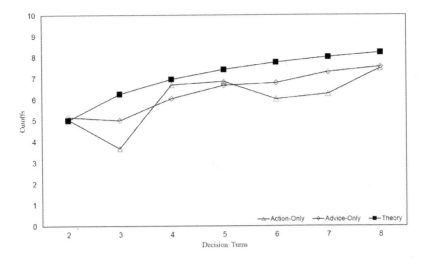

FIGURE 10.4 Mean cutoffs: all concurring decisions. Conditional means where the conditioning is done on whether the subject's decision was a concurring decision.

points. For example, if a subject observes action A or receives advice to choose A and selects a cutoff of -5, we take it as 5, since she acts in a concurring manner. On the other hand, if she sets a cutoff of 5, we take it as -5, since she acts in a contrary manner. In the remainder of our discussion, we will refer to this as mirror image transformation.

Since our theory predicts the optimal cutoffs for each subject at each decision turn, we can use our mirror image transformation to judge how close our subjects came to setting their optimal cutoffs. Figure 10.4 depicts, turn by turn, the theoretical cutoffs θ_n in the truthful equilibrium and the mean cutoff after mirror image transformation $\tilde{\theta}_n$ in the subset of concurring decisions in the advice-only and action-only treatments. It is evident from Figure 10.4 that there is little difference in the magnitude of the cutoffs set by subjects when they strictly agreed with either the advice offered or the action observed by their predecessor. In other words, once a subject has decided to follow the advice offered or imitate the action taken, she does so with equal intensity. Also note that there is a substantial degree of conformity with the theory in the magnitude of the cutoffs

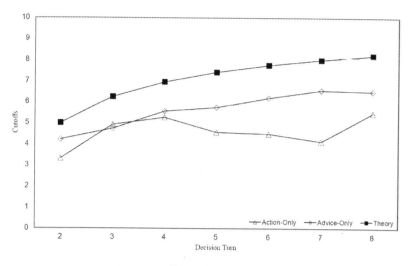

FIGURE 10.5 Mean cutoffs: weakly concurring decisions. Conditional means where the conditioning is done on whether the subject's decision was weakly concurring.

chosen by subjects when they agree with the action observed (advice received). However, Figure 10.5 shows that the situation is reversed in the action-only treatment, particularly in late decision turns, when we include neutral decisions in our sample.

These mirror image cutoffs can be used to compare the actual cutoffs chosen by our subjects to these predicted by the theory by simply combining our concurring and contradictory cutoffs and calculating an unconditional mean. Figure 10.6 does just that.

Figure 10.6 presents the mean cutoffs of subjects regardless of whether the subjects agreed or disagreed with the action observed or advice received. It appears overall that there is a significant difference between the mirror image of the cutoffs set in the action-only and the advice-only treatments. Subjects appear to set cutoffs that are closer to those predicted by theory when in the advice-only treatment. However, this result is an artifact of a compositional difference. As we saw, when a subject agrees with the advice or action they get, they tend to set a cutoff close to the theoretical cutoff no matter whether they are in the action-only or advice-only treatment. When they disagree, however, the strength of disagreement is far stronger

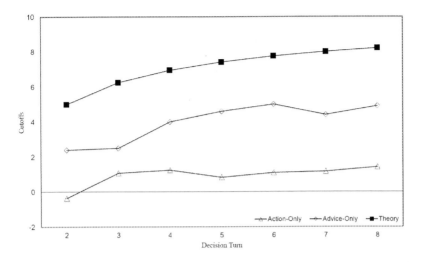

FIGURE 10.6 Unconditional mean cutoffs.

in the action-only treatment where subjects tend to set significantly lower cutoffs, ones that are further from the optimal cutoffs predicted by the theory. Because subjects tend to agree with or follow advice more than they do with actions, when all choices are combined, as in Figure 10.6 we see that overall the cutoffs set in the advice-only treatment are closer to our theoretical predictions.[9]

These results are confirmed by a regression analysis provided in the appendix in Section 10.6.

10.3.3   Question 2

Which information – advice or action – is more valued by the subjects? Under what circumstances do subjects offer advice that is different from their action?

---

[9] Turn by turn, Wilcoxon rank-sum (Mann–Whitney) tests detect statistically significant differences between the cutoffs $\bar{\theta}_n$ in the advice-only and action-only treatments in all decision turns. However, none of these differences are significant if we focus on the subset of concurring or contrary decisions. We note that the Wilcoxon test requires independence. The outcomes of games in which the same subjects appear are not independent. This biases the standard errors downward, increasing the likelihood of finding a significant treatment effect. We use the null of independence and recognize that there is no simple adjustment that will take care of the possible dependence problem.

Our action-plus-advice treatment provides a perfect platform upon which to measure the relative value of advice and actions. This treatment is identical to the action-only and advice-only treatments with the exception that each subject observes the action chosen by her immediate predecessor and also receives her advice. Hence this treatment allows us to separate the impact of advice from the impact of actions on behavior since, if the predecessor's action and advice differ – for example, if the predecessor chooses A and advises B – then the successor subject must decide which suggestion to follow – advice or action. Overall, such contradictory behavior, $x_{n-1} \neq a_{n-1}$, is relatively rare, accounting for only 17.5% of the data from the action-plus-advice treatment, which is only marginally higher than the 15.8% from the advice-only treatment.

To organize the data from the action-plus-advice treatment, we adopt the convention that decisions made by subjects are defined as concurring or contrary decisions with respect to *advice*. That is, decisions are defined by whether the sign of the cutoff agrees or disagrees with advice received. A neutral decision is again defined as choosing cutoff zero, which does not favor any action, A or B.

Table 10.2 presents the percentages of concurring, contrary, and neutral decisions in the action-plus-advice treatment and compares them with the analogous percentages in the action-only and advice-only treatments reported in Table 10.1. In the action-plus-advice treatment, subjects set a cutoff consistent with the advice they receive 84.2% of the time when $x_{n-1}=a_{n-1}$, but only 60.2% of the time when $x_{n-1} \neq a_{n-1}$. Hence, advice is more likely to be followed when backed by an action. In addition, as the second line in Table 10.2 suggests, when advice and actions differ, subjects are far more likely to follow advice than copy any actions (60.2% versus 24.1%). The distributions of the concurring, contrary, and neutral decisions in the action-plus-advice treatments are significantly different according to a Kolmogorov–Smirnov test (p-value 0.000).

Figure 10.7 shows the distribution of contrary decisions (the percentage of subjects who disagreed with the observed action (advice)

Table 10.2 *Concurring, contrary, and neutral decisions in the action-plus-advice treatment.*

	Concurring	Neutral	Contrary
Action-plus-advice $(x_{n-1} = a_{n-1})$	84.2%	7.0%	8.8%
Action-plus-advice $(x_{n-1} \neq a_{n-1})$	60.2%	15.7%	24.1%
Action-only	44.2%	16.6%	39.2%
Advice-only	74.1%	9.1%	16.8%

in less than two rounds, three to five rounds, and so on) in the action-plus-advice treatment aggregated at the subject level and compares them with the corresponding distributions in the action-only and advice-only treatments depicted in Figure 10.3. We present the distribution for *all* decisions, as well as the distribution for the subset of decisions where the advice received was consistent with the action observed, $x_{n-1} = a_{n-1}$. The horizontal axis measures the number of concurring decisions and the vertical axis measures the percentage of subjects corresponding to each interval. For the subset of consistent decisions $x_{n-1} = a_{n-1}$, 80.0% of the subjects disagreed with the advice they received only in one or two rounds. This distribution is significantly different from the analogous distributions in the action-only and advice-only treatments using Kolmogorov–Smirnov tests (p-values 0.000). For the full sample, only 62.5% of the subjects disagreed with the advice they received in one or two rounds, and 35.0% disagreed in three to five rounds.

Figure 10.8 depicts, turn by turn, the mean cutoff after the mirror image transformation $(\tilde{\theta}_n)$ in the action-plus-advice treatment. We present the mean cutoffs for all decisions, as well as the mean cutoffs for the subset of decisions where the advice received was consistent with the action observed $(x_{n-1} = a_{n-1})$, and compare the cutoffs to those in the action-only and advice-only treatments. Figure 10.8 shows that the magnitude of the cutoffs set in the action-plus-advice treatment does not differ much from the magnitude of the cutoffs set in the advice-only treatment. Hence, when backed up by action, the impact of advice is to increase the number of times that a

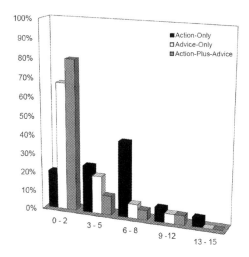

FIGURE 10.7 Distribution of contrary subjects: action-only, advice-only, and action-plus-advice treatments.

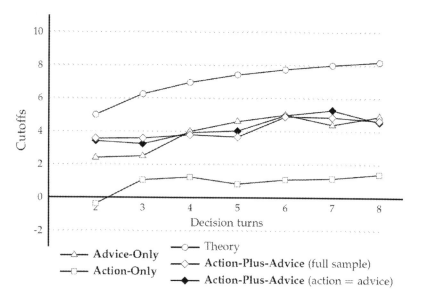

FIGURE 10.8 Mean cutoffs for all decisions.

predecessor's decision is followed. But once it is followed, the strength of commitment to the predecessor's decision is practically identical.

In the appendix in Section 10.6, we present a regression analysis that supports these results.

Table 10.3 *The likelihood of correct actions by treatment.*

	Prop.	Std err.	95% conf. interval
Action-only	0.625	0.020	[0.586–0.663]
Advice-only	0.720	0.018	[0.684–0.756]
Action-plus-advice	0.768	0.017	[0.734–0.802]

10.4   QUESTION 3

One final question is whether advice is welfare-increasing

> *Do subjects make the right decisions more often in treatments with advice than in those with only actions?*

The answer is yes.

Table 10.3 presents the results (note that uninformed random actions will be correct half the time). Most interestingly, the likelihood of correct actions is significantly higher in the treatments involving advice – the advice-only and the action-plus-advice treatments – than in the action-only treatments. Hence, as we have seen before, advice aids decision making.

10.5   CONCLUSION

This chapter suggests that people might prefer the advice of others over their ability to see what others have done when making a decision. This result is not that strange, however. Recent evidence suggests that consumer reviews of products and films are quite influential in affecting consumer choices. Perhaps it's the human voice speaking to you rather than cold inanimate data or statistics that is so persuasive. Perhaps you can relate to a person more easily than to data. It also may be that the person making the recommendation actually had experience with the product (or decision problem) and has thought about it before making a suggestion that so impresses you. It is also hard to deny that when you contradict advice the phrase "I told you so" rings in your ears if things turn out badly.

As we stated in Chapter 2, where we reviewed the work of psychologists (Harvey and Fischer, 1997), following advice may allow a decision maker to escape responsibility for the decision made (or at least share accountability) since the decision maker can always say that she was merely following advice.

The experiments described here allowed decision makers to actually talk to each other (make recommendations) rather than merely observe the actions of those before them. Since we found welfare to increase in such circumstances, one might say that the efficiency of social learning in the field may be higher than previously thought since in the real world, in many circumstances, decision makers do communicate.

Finally, it might be considered ironic that subjects prefer to listen to advice rather than follow the actions of their advisor since, in equilibrium, the informational content of advice should be equivalent to that of actions. Subjects should actually offer advice equal to the actions they took. This is not always the case.

10.6 APPENDIX: PROOF OF UNIQUENESS AND REGRESSIONS

10.6.1 Proof: No Other Equilibria Exist

Here, we show that there are no other equilibria in the advice-only case. If any other equilibria existed, they would take the form of agent n advising her successor to take the same action as she did, $a_n = x_n$, with some probability $0 < p_n < 1$, and the opposite action, $a_n \neq x_n$, with probability $1 - p_n$. In the truthful equilibrium, $p_n = 1$, while in the mirror and babbling equilibria, $p_n = 0$ and $p_n = 1/2$, respectively. With a consistent belief system (agent $n + 1$ believes that the advice given to her by agent n is indeed the same as the chosen action with probability p_n), it is obvious that it is optimal for agent n to always advise her successor to take the same action she took, $a_n = x_n$, if $p_n > 1/2$ and always to advise her to take the opposite action, $a_n \neq x_n$, if $p_n < 1/2$.

We can prove this result by contradiction. Suppose there is an equilibrium in which the first agent sets her optimal cutoff $\hat{\theta}_1 = 0$ but advises the second agent to take the same action that she did, with some probability $1/2 < p_1 < 1$, and the opposite action with probability $1 - p_1$. With a consistent belief system, the second agent conditions her decision on p_1 and on whether the advice received is A or B. If the advice received is $a_1 = A$, then a simple calculation shows that $\mathbb{E}\left[\theta_1 \mid p_1, a_1 = A\right] = 10p - 5$. Thus it is optimal for the second agent to take action A if and only if $\theta_2 \geq 5 - 10p$. Likewise, if the advice received is $a_1 = B$, it is optimal for the second agent to take action A if and only if $\theta_2 \geq 10p - 5$. Thus, after adding noisy advice to the model, the second agent's cutoff rule is

$$\hat{\theta}_2(p_1, a_1) = \begin{cases} -5 + 10p & \text{if} \quad a_1 = A, \\ 5 - 10p & \text{if} \quad a_1 = B. \end{cases}$$

Because $\bar{\theta}_2 < 0$ and $\underline{\theta}_2 > 0$ (where $\bar{\theta}_2 = -\underline{\theta}_2$, as in the action-only case), the second agent may still follow the advice given to her, even though she would have made the opposite decision had she based her decision solely on her own signal. But in that case the first agent is better off if she never offers advice which differs from her action. An analogous argument also applies if $0 < p_1 < 1/2$. This is a contradiction.

10.6.2 Regression Analysis of Cutoffs: Advice-Only and Action-Only

Let $\tilde{\theta}_n$ be the data generated by the choices of subjects at decision turn $n > 1$, and let χ and χ_n be indicator variables for the advice-only treatment and decision turns, respectively. Our econometric specification has the form

$$\tilde{\theta}_n = [\alpha_n + \beta_n \chi]\chi_n + \epsilon_n,$$

where ϵ_n is assumed to be distributed normally with mean zero and variance σ_n^2. We generate estimates of the α and β coefficients using a tobit model that accounts for the censored distribution (the cutoffs

Table 10.4 *The impact of advice: action-only and advice-only.*[a]

			Decision turns					Full sample
	2	3	4	5	6	7	8	$(n > 1)$
α	−0.372	1.201	1.722**	1.022	1.306*	1.432*	2.109**	1.181***
	(0.71)	(0.74)	(0.82)	(0.72)	(0.75)	(0.79)	(0.94)	(0.30)
β	3.183***	1.585	3.145***	4.134***	4.704***	3.966***	4.057***	3.566***
	(1.01)	(1.04)	(1.17)	(1.02)	(1.07)	(1.13)	(1.34)	(0.42)

[a]The figures given above are the estimates generated by tobit regressions using robust standard errors that allow for clustering at the level of the individual subject. Standard errors are in parentheses. Asterisks *, **, and *** indicate 10%, 5%, and 1% significance levels, respectively.

are bounded between −10 and 10), and use robust standard errors that allow for clustering at the level of the individual subject.

Table 10.4 reports the estimation results. The last column presents the results for the full sample. There are marked differences between the α and β estimates. Except for the third decision turn, all the β estimates are significantly positive. This implies that the later a subject's turn is, the more she relies on the information revealed from advice, and that subjects are more likely to follow their predecessor's advice than to imitate her action. The magnitudes are very large, implying an overall shift in cutoffs $\tilde{\theta}_n$ from approximately 1.18 to 3.57. This is roughly consistent with the effect implied by the summary statistics presented above.

10.6.3   Regression Analysis: Action-Plus-Advice Treatment

We now turn to regression analyses that examine the patterns in the data from the action-plus-advice treatment more systematically. The regressions run here are similar to those presented in Section 10.6.2, where we looked at cutoffs in the advice-only and action-only treatments.

Let χ^c and χ^i be indicator variables for the action-plus-advice treatment when the predecessor's action is consistent or inconsistent with her advice, respectively. This generates the following econometric specification:

$$\tilde{\theta}_n = [\alpha_n + \beta_n \chi^c + \delta_n \chi^i] \chi_n + \epsilon_n,$$

where ϵ_n is assumed to be distributed normally with mean zero and variance σ_n^2. We again generate estimates using a tobit model that accounts for the censored distribution, and use robust standard errors that allow for clustering at the level of the individual subject.

Tables 10.5 and 10.6 report the estimation results. In Table 10.5, we focus on the data from the advice-only and action-plus-advice treatments. In Table 10.6, we repeat the estimations using the data from the action-only and action-plus-advice treatments. The last column in each table presents the results for the full sample. The most apparent cross-sectional feature of the beta series is that,

Table 10.5 *The impact of advice: action-only and action-plus-advice.*[a]

	Decision turns							Full sample
	2	3	4	5	6	7	8	(n > 1)
α	−0.372 (0.65)	1.192* (0.70)	1.708** (0.81)	1.013 (0.69)	1.296* (0.72)	1.379** (0.68)	2.140** (0.97)	1.163*** (0.28)
β	3.534* (2.08)	2.104 (1.90)	1.290 (2.09)	0.169 (1.92)	2.073 (1.91)	1.745 (1.90)	1.317 (2.37)	1.765** (0.77)
δ	4.234*** (0.95)	3.026*** (1.04)	2.776** (1.19)	3.504*** (1.02)	4.888*** (1.09)	4.624*** (1.01)	4.884*** (1.48)	3.946*** (0.42)

[a]The figures given above are the estimates generated by tobit regressions using robust standard errors that allow for clustering at the level of the individual subject. Standard errors are in parentheses. *, **, and *** indicate 10%, 5%, and 1% significance levels, respectively.

Table 10.6 *The impact of advice: advice-only and action-plus-advice.*[a]

	Decision turns							Full sample
	2	3	4	5	6	7	8	(n > 1)
α	2.811*** (0.72)	2.739*** (0.66)	4.682*** (0.69)	5.225*** (0.65)	5.900*** (0.71)	5.269*** (0.72)	6.217*** (1.00)	4.673*** (0.28)
β	0.351 (2.27)	0.513 (1.78)	−1.751 (1.78)	−4.043** (1.78)	−2.570 (1.82)	−2.131 (1.98)	−2.760 (2.38)	−1.758** (0.75)
δ	1.083 (1.04)	1.439 (0.98)	−0.288 (1.01)	−.751 (0.95)	0.228 (1.04)	0.775 (1.06)	0.806 (1.49)	0.414 (0.41)

[a]The figures given above are the estimates generated by tobit regressions using robust standard errors that allow for clustering at the level of the individual subject. Standard errors are in parentheses. *, **, and *** indicate 10%, 5%, and 1% significance levels, respectively.

for each decision turn, the estimated δ coefficients in Table 10.5 and the estimated α coefficients in Table 10.6 are monotonic and significantly positive. The other coefficients in Tables 10.5 and 10.6 are not significantly different from zero in most turns. This implies that, for a fixed decision turn n, the cutoffs $\tilde{\theta}_n$ in the action-plus-advice treatment when the advice received is consistent with the action observed, $x_{n-1}=a_{n-1}$, are the same as the cutoffs in the advice-only treatment and higher than the cutoffs in the action-only treatment. For the full sample, the estimates show that the cutoffs $\tilde{\theta}_n$ are lowest in the action-only treatment, higher in the action-plus-advice treatment when the advice received is inconsistent with the action observed, $x_{n-1}\neq a_{n-1}$, and highest in the advice-only and action-plus-advice treatments when the advice received is consistent with the action observed.

REFERENCES

Anderson, L. R. and Holt, C. A. (1997). Information cascades in the laboratory. *American Economic Review*, 87(5), 847–862.

Bandura, A. and McClelland, D. C. (1977). *Social Learning Theory*. Englewood Cliffs, NJ: Prentice Hall.

Banerjee, A. V. (1992). A simple model of herd behavior. *Quarterly Journal of Economics*, 107(3), 797–817.

Bikhchandani, S., Hirshleifer, D. and Welch, I. (1992). A theory of fads, fashion, custom, and cultural change as informational cascades. *Journal of Political Economy*, 100(5), 992–1026.

Bikhchandani, S., Hirshleifer, D. and Welch, I. (1998). Learning from the behavior of others: Conformity, fads, and informational cascades. *Journal of Economic Perspectives*, 12(3), 151–170.

Çelen, B. and Kariv, S. (2004a). Observational learning under imperfect information. *Games and Economic Behavior*, 47(1), 72–86.

Çelen, B. and Kariv, S. (2004b). Distinguishing informational cascades from herd behavior in the laboratory. *American Economic Review*, 94(3), 484–498.

Çelen, B. and Kariv, S. (2005). An experimental test of observational learning under imperfect information. *Economic Theory*, 26(3), 677–699.

Çelen, B., Kariv, S. and Schotter, A. (2010). An experimental test of advice and social learning. *Management Science*, 56(10), 1687–1701.

Chamley, C. P. (2004). *Rational Herds: Economic Models of Social Learning*. New York, NY: Cambridge University Press.

Gale, D. (1996). What have we learned from social learning? *European Economic Review*, 40(3-5), 617–628.

Harvey, N. and Fischer, I. (1997). Taking advice: Accepting help, improving judgment, and sharing responsibility. *Organizational Behavior and Human Decision Processes*, 70(2), 117–133.

Skinner, B. F. (1938). *The Behavior of Organisms: An Experimental Analysis*. New York, NY: Appleton-Century-Crofts.

11 The Market for Advice

This chapter asks and attempts to answer a set of questions we have not dealt with previously.[1] More precisely, in all of our previous chapters (except for Chapter 10 on social learning) people had no choice as to what information they received before they made a decision. They just received advice. We now ask whether there are other types of information they might prefer. We have also never asked whether people have preferences over who gives them advice. Are there types of people that are perceived as good advisors and other types that are perceived as unreliable? If so, who are those "good advisors" and what characteristics do they share?

The first question is important because it asks how important is advice to decision makers. If people consider advice only when they have no other source of information, then its influence will be diminished when they are given access to alternatives. However, if advice has an inordinate sway over people, if they seek it out, then we need to understand why advice is so desirable or persuasive. The second question is also important because if certain types of people are considered good advisors, then this perception may confer rents on them which may or may not be warranted.

To answer our first question we set up a market for information and let people bid for advice versus other types of information. For example, in our experiment, subjects have to make a binary choice whose payoff depends on an unobserved state of the world. The advisors (expert subjects with previous experience with the problem) have seen data and experienced the data-generating process offering signals about the true state of the world and have also updated their

---

[1] This chapter is based on Nyarko et al. (2006).

prior over what the true state is given the data they observed. Hence, given their experience, these laboratory advisors or experts can offer three types of information to their advisees (clients): advice about which binary choice they think the advisee should make, a report of their updated (posterior) beliefs about the true state of the world, or the unprocessed raw data they have observed. The question is, which type of information is valued most by the clients?

Second, to discover who our subjects value advice from (our second question), we set up a market for advice. Since our subjects are students, we have them bid for advice from economics, science/math, or humanities majors. We use these categories since, as undergraduates facing a decision-making problem, these might be the most relevant categories in their minds. Hence we are asking them if they want advice from someone with their major or a different one? Would they prefer advice from a male or female? How much do they value the expertise of their advisor as measured by their previous performance on the task at hand or their GPA (grade point average), etc.?

In this market for advisors, however, there may be a perception that certain people or types of people are worth listening to. These perceptions amount to broad stereotypes that may bestow rents on some of the agents in the market. For example, Feng and MacGeorge (2006) find evidence that older people, more highly educated people, and people considered to be "wise" are more highly valued advisors. Such stereotypes may be accurate assessments of the abilities of advisors but sometimes they may be inaccurate. Either way, such stereotypes, if they persist, can lead to what we will call "perception rents", which can be valuable to those who can collect them. In order for such rents to exist, however, there must be a consensus that such advisors are truly talented.

An alternative to perception rents is what we will call the "chauvinistic bias". Here, people tend to believe that advice from people like themselves is the best and hence tend to bid higher amounts for advice from people with characteristics like theirs, whether or not those types give the best advice. As we mentioned in Chapter 2, where we discussed the work of psychologists (Yaniv, 2004a,b), people who exhibit a chauvinistic bias value advice from people like themselves because they are familiar with the way people like them think through a problem and may therefore value such advice. Strangers, using an unknown heuristic, may be too exotic to listen to. When chauvinistic biases exist, there is obviously no consensus as to who are the best advisors, since each group thinks they are best.[2]

The problems our decision makers face in this chapter are basically problems of Bayesian updating and decision making. It is commonly known, however, that when engaging in Bayesian updating some people are subject to a "conservative bias" in that they place too much weight on their prior as opposed to the new data or sample they observe. Others suffer a "representative bias" which leads them to do the opposite, i.e., place too much importance on the sample. Such people fail to take base rates or priors sufficiently into account.

The fact that such different types of decision makers exist begs us to ask if such biases affect the willingness of our subjects to pay for and follow advice? More precisely, if conservatives are reluctant to update their priors on the basis of new information, are they also less inclined to pay for advice and also follow it once it is given?

In this chapter we study an experimental market for advice in an attempt to measure both the informational content of advice and the market for it. To do this we create a set of "experts" by having some of our subjects get experience with a simple investment problem (a game against nature) a large number of times. These experts are surveyed to obtain information about their gender, GPA, major, and year in school. Advice is elicited from these experts and is then sold to a new set of subject "clients" who play the game once and only once. The prices generated by this market for advice furnish us with an opportunity to measure potential perception rents in the market.

---

[2] This chauvinistic bias is the flip side of the egocentric bias (Yaniv, 2004a,b) since, there, people reject advice or discount advice from people unlike themselves.

There are some interesting findings and ones that, for the first time in our discussion here, raise the question of whether advice is undervalued relative to data. In general, we find that subjects bid significantly more for data than they do for either advice or beliefs. We also find some evidence for perception rents for economics majors and a certain amount of support for what we call the "chauvinistic bias", meaning that subjects tended to bid more advice from people sharing the same major as themselves than for people of other majors.

11.1   EXPERIMENTAL DESIGN

11.1.1   The Investment Game

The decision problem that both our experts (advisors) and clients (advisees) play is what we call the investment game. In this game, a game against nature where one's opponent is a random device and not a real person, there are two actions, and in each period an individual is required to make a decision to either invest (the investment option) or not invest (the "safe option"). The financial market has two possible states, profitable or unprofitable, in each period. The investment option yields a total return which depends upon the state, while the return to safe option is independent of the state. The payoffs are described in Table 11.1.[3]

The probability of the profitable state is equal to θ. The value of θ is unknown to subjects. If the subject chooses the safe option, the

Table 11.1 *The payoff matrix.*

State	Profitable Prob $= \theta$	Unprofitable Prob $= (1 - \theta)$
Investment option	$10	$0
Safe option	$5	$5

[3] We denominate everything in this chapter in US dollars. Subjects performed the experiment in units denominated by "experimental" francs at the exchange rate of 10 francs to a dollar.

subject receives a return of 5. If she chooses the investment option, she will receive 10 when the state is profitable and 0 otherwise. Assuming risk neutrality, the value function is therefore given by

$$V = \max\{5, 10E\theta\}, \tag{11.1}$$

which implies that if $E\theta > 0.5$ investing must be the correct value-maximizing decision.

We choose the probability distribution from which θ is drawn such that the optimal Bayesian updating rule follows a simple rule of thumb which we will describe later. More specifically, we suppose that θ is drawn from a beta distribution. The beta distribution is parameterized by a constant α which we vary across treatments. We use three different values of α. One of these results in the uniform distribution for θ ($\alpha = 1$); the remaining two will result in, respectively, a U-shaped density function ($\alpha = 1/4$) and an inverted U-shaped density function ($\alpha = 4$). For all of our analysis, we will only use the distribution where $\alpha = 1$ and hence the distribution of θ is uniform. We will not discuss the other cases which are exclusively used in that part of our experiment dealing with experts.

11.1.2 Creating Experts or Advisors

As stated above, in our experiment we have two types of subjects – experts and clients. We are not interested in the behavior of our experts and hence will not discuss their behavior very much. They are in the experiment primarily to offer information (advice, beliefs, or data) to their clients. In addition, while in our expert treatment different subjects will play the investment game under different parameter values, in the client treatment they will only face $\alpha = 1$ or a uniform distribution of θ.

To create our experts we ran sessions at the experimental laboratory at Rutgers University during the spring and summer of 2002, and at the Center for Experimental Social Science at New York University in the fall of 2002. Subjects were recruited primarily from undergraduate courses. Before the students began the experiments, we recorded information on their gender, age, class, major, and GPA. They were paid $5.00 simply for showing up. The subjects were then given the instructions for the game.

Before their experiment began, they were shown graphically the distribution function corresponding to the value of α for their game, and they were informed of how θ would be chosen for their experiment, but not told its actual value. Payoffs in the expert games were denominated in experimental dollars and converted into US dollars at a rate of 1 experimental dollar = $0.05.

While, in our expert treatment, we had subjects play our investment game with a variety of α and θ values, our clients only played their investment game with θ values drawn from the uniform distribution ($\alpha = 1$). Hence we will concentrate only on those experts who played the investment game using a uniform distribution over θ.

The experts played the investment game for either three or 25 rounds with a fixed θ.[4] So after they were done, each expert had a posterior belief about the θ they faced in the game they played.

At the end of the experiment, expert subjects were asked what they believe the probability of the profitable state is (what θ did they face). They were rewarded for this decision via a *quadratic scoring rule* (see Nyarko and Schotter, 2002). We call these beliefs the *elicited beliefs*.

After obtaining the elicited beliefs of our experts, they were then asked to give an "investment option" or "safe option" recommendation to be used by other future subjects who would play the investment game under the exact circumstances they did. Note that we did not reward subjects for their recommendation. We refer to this as the subject's advice, although sometimes instead of offering advice in the form of recommendations we simply offered the client the experts beliefs over θ.

---

[4] We actually ran this particular game for 24 rounds (rather than three) or for 75 rounds (rather than 25), with updating of beliefs every three or 25 periods. We only pass on beliefs or advice to clients based on the first three or 25 periods.

In our design there were many experts with different subjects playing the investment game with a different θ. For example, there were 11 subjects having a $\theta = 0.586$ drawn from a uniform distribution. Each one of those 11 subjects were ranked from 1 to 11 indicating how well they did monetarily in their experiment. Hence, for each θ and for each expert subject in the set of subjects having that θ, we have a "pay rank" for that subject – their ranking in terms of money earned among their cohort. We use these rankings as well as other characteristics of these experts to describe the experts that our client subjects will bid for in their part of the experiment.

II.2   CREATING CLIENTS OR ADVISEES: THE BELIEF–PRICE ELICITATION GAME

Our client subjects first played what we call the belief elicitation game which was followed by the price elicitation game. The belief elicitation game had two parts. The belief elicitation part was run as a diagnostic tool to see how our client subjects updated their beliefs given specific information offered to them. Their responses were used to type them as to their updating style – conservative or representational.

To see how our client subjects updated their priors, we told all subjects that the θ they faced was drawn from a uniform distribution $(\alpha = 1)$. Subjects then saw three draws from the distribution using that θ. The three draws were (profitable, profitable, profitable) for all subjects. In the second period all subjects received advice. This advice was from a 21-year-old male senior economics major with a GPA of 3.7 and payoff rank of fourth out of 10 who played the investment game with the same θ. The advice given was "invest". We elicited beliefs before each period so we could see how the subject updated their beliefs from their prior to a posterior after seeing three pieces of data (profitable, profitable, profitable) and then from that posterior to a new one after seeing the advice "invest". This updating exercise, as stated above, was diagnostic and used to test whether subjects updated their beliefs in a conservative manner (putting excess weight on their prior) or a more representative one (putting more weight on the sample). We offered subjects skewed data (profitable, profitable, profitable) since we are interested in how conservative they are in updating and hence gave them a sample that was rather representative of a high θ to see how much they updated after seeing that sample. Finally, after this belief elicitation exercise, all subjects played the investment game once.

After the subjects played the belief elicitation game they then played the price elicitation game. Subjects were told that the θ for this experiment was an independent observation drawn from the same prior distribution (the uniform or $\alpha = 1$ case) as was used in the belief elicitation part of the experiment. They were also told that they would be matched with an expert who had played the investment game with exactly this same θ. Subjects then bid on data, beliefs, and advice from the expert they were matched with. More precisely, subjects bid on 12 different experts. For each expert (advisor) they were told some information (gender, age, GPA, year, major, and pay rank), and they placed bids on the advisor's data, beliefs, and advice. They were told, as indeed was the case, that 10 of the experts were "hypothetical" and that only two were actual subjects who had played the investment game. (They did not know which was which, so truthful bidding was optimal.) After the bids were entered, we applied the Becker–DeGroot–Marschak (BDM) procedure (Becker et al., 1964) to determine what information, if any, is made available to the advisee. In particular, since there are only two real advisors, each with three types of information (data, beliefs, advice), there are six possible information alternatives. One of these was randomly chosen and the BDM mechanism was applied to determine whether that information alternative would be observed by the advisee. Subjects were told that only their bids on the real experts would be chosen for the actual BDM mechanism.

11.3 RESULTS

Our experimental design allows us to answer two sets of questions, one dealing with the market for advice and the second with the way in which subjects update beliefs and their willingness to accept advice. For example, we ask: Do people seek advice from people like themselves (a chauvinistic bias) or do perception rents exist where people tend to think some types of advisers are best and the market reflects these perceptions through the prices it sets? Are certain types of information deemed preferable to others by our subjects and is this preference reflected in market prices?

Our second set of questions deals with the relationship between how people update their beliefs and the value they place on advice. For example: Are people who suffer from a conservative bias in the way they update beliefs less willing to pay for advice than others who update in a Bayesian manner or who suffer from a representative bias? Do they find advice less persuasive? Let us start with investigating the market for advice.

11.3.1 The Market for Advice

Our first question is whether there are perception rents or a chauvinistic bias in the market for advice? In other words, is there a consensus as to who is the best advisor, as we have suggested is a prerequisite for perception rents to exist, or do people prefer to receive advice from people like them – a chauvinistic bias?

The raw data from the bids that client subjects made for expert data, beliefs, and advice are contained in Table 11.2. On the face of it, it appears that there are perception rents in the advice markets we set up since, on average, subjects bid more for the advice of economics students followed by scientists, humanists, and social scientists.

More precisely, in terms of means, subjects tended to bid 0.893, 0.800, 0.637, and 0.637 to hear the advice of economics students, science students, humanists, and social science (other than economics) students, respectively, and 1.07, 0.865, 0.75, and 0.71 to observe the beliefs of these same types of subjects. From these means it would seem as if economics students are perceived to be the best, followed by scientists, humanists, and social science majors. Also it appears that people are willing to pay more for beliefs than the binary advice invest/not invest. This seems intuitive. If all agents are rational and

Table 11.2 *Client bids for data, beliefs, and advice by major:*
belief–price elicitation game.

Client major	Means	Expert major				
		Econ.	Sci.	Hum.	Soc. Sci.	Total
Econ	Data	1.49	0.871	1.02	1.18	1.20
	Beliefs	1.14	0.550	0.609	0.678	0.815
	Advice	0.902	0.388	0.495	0.625	0.655
	N	99	59	43	60	261
Sci	Data	2.32	2.51	2.14	1.74	2.18
	Beliefs	1.48	1.41	1.38	0.806	1.28
	Advice	1.31	1.40	1.05	0.665	1.12
	N	49	24	28	32	133
Hum.	Data	0.998	1.01	1.98	1.17	1.20
	Beliefs	0.600	0.404	0.640	0.553	0.544
	Advice					
	N	63	50	32	47	192
Soc. Sci.	Data	1.83	1.88	1.69	2.62	1.97
	Beliefs	0.997	0.939	0.484	0.484	0.761
	Advice	0.657	0.889	0.428	0.348	0.581
	N	83	38	50	45	216
Other	Data	1.42	1.89	0.889	1.57	1.45
	Beliefs	1.34	1.98	1.02	1.65	1.49
	Advice	1.41	2.01	1.05	1.67	1.52
	N	36	23	19	18	96
Total	Data	1.60	1.43	1.56	1.62	1.56
	Beliefs	1.07	0.865	0.750	0.713	0.865
	Advice	0.893	0.800	0.637	0.637	0.767
	N	330	194	172	202	898

there is common knowledge of the rationality of others, then the amount one would be willing to pay for beliefs and data should be the same since, given that all subjects start out with the same priors and rationality is common knowledge, one should be able to invert the expert's posterior beliefs to uncover the data she must have observed. Hence, in these circumstances, the value of beliefs should be the same as data. Advice, however, because it is binary, conveys less information and hence is less valuable, which could account for its being undervalued in the market. Hence a client might say that she would simply prefer the experts' beliefs and make the choice on her own.

But perception rents only exist if there is a consensus by all types of subjects that certain types of people are best at a given task. This is different from the mean amount of money willing to be paid for advice being higher for one type of advisor than another. For example, assume that each type of person prefers advice from their own kind but economists are willing to pay more for the advice they receive from other economists than are other types of subjects. In that case the mean amount of money people are willing to pay for economists' advice would be the greatest but in such a case there is really a chauvinistic bias rather than a perception rent.

This can be seen in Table 11.2. For beliefs and advice, we see some tendency for economics and/or science majors to receive higher bids (e.g., from social science majors) yet humanists persist in bidding more for advice from other humanists than from any other type of advisor. Of course, there really is no reason to bid more for data from a particular expert since the expert has no role in generating this information – it is furnished by the computer and independent of which type of subject receives it.

As we see, there is certainly no strong consensus among the subject types as to which expert types (major) are the best advisors. This apparently refutes the perception rent hypothesis. Still, there is some evidence pointing to economics majors being favored in the bidding for beliefs and advice. We investigate this question more formally with regression analysis of bidding behavior below.

While our results so far indicate which type of subjects receive the highest price in the market, we still might be interested in knowing what determines the level of prices, i.e., how the attributes of experts are priced.

To investigate this, consider experts as bundles of characteristics (age, major, GPA, gender, rank on experts experiment, etc.). Under this interpretation, we can expect that each of these factors could contribute to the price a given subject would be willing to pay for advice from such an agent. To explore this relationship, we ran a hedonic type of regression, in which we estimate the contribution of

Table 11.3 *Determinants of bid price: belief–price elicitation game.*[a]

Dep. var.: Bid	Pooled reg.	Econ. reg.	Sci. reg.	Hum. reg.	Soc. sci. reg.
Expert female	−1.27*	−0.99	−3.71*	−0.03	−0.69
	0.51	0.98	1.21	0.70	1.09
Expert economist	1.57*	2.52*	4.19*	1.12	0.01
	0.68	1.28	1.49	0.91	1.50
Expert scientist	0.89	1.31	1.27	0.82	0.34
	0.77	1.49	1.77	0.98	1.77
Expert humanist	−0.19	−0.05	2.85**	0.20	−0.67
	0.78	1.57	1.69	1.08	1.64
Expert GPA	0.29	−1.11	4.36*	0.82	1.62
	0.53	1.00	1.31	0.73	1.12
Expert age	−0.14	0.20	−0.72**	−0.09	−0.00
	0.18	0.32	0.41	0.27	0.40
Expert payoff rank	−7.16*	−8.89*	−14.77*	−3.80*	−10.64*
	0.86	1.65	2.05	1.18	1.94
Belief bid dummy	−6.77*	−3.89*	−8.95*	−6.66*	−12.14*
	0.59	1.14	1.32	0.80	1.26
Advice bid dummy	−7.95*	−5.42*	−10.59*	−7.09*	−13.95*
	0.59	1.14	1.32	0.80	1.26
Constant	21.29*	15.96*	27.94*	12.82*	20.64*
	4.22	7.84	9.76	6.09	9.07
N	2693	782	399	576	648
R^2	0.06	0.04	0.17	0.09	0.16
ρ	0.50	0.49	0.56	0.41	0.40

[a]Asterisks: *, 5% significance; **, 10% significance. Number on the bottom in each cell is the standard error.

expert characteristics to the bid price. We report results for the pooled regression (with all bidder types) and with disaggregated regressions (one for each bidder type). The results of these regressions are contained in Table 11.3.[5]

The estimation results substantiate much of our previous analysis and add some new insights as well. Note that the bids in these regressions are denominated in the experimental currency, or one-tenth the actual dollar value. In the pooled regression, economists

[5] The regression treats the data as a panel (repeated observations of a cross-section of bidders), with a generalized least squares random effects error structure. Note that this structure, since it takes into account individual-specific effects, should control for the effect of individuals who bid systematically higher than others. Thus, the effect of outliers here should not be a concern, as it was in examining the raw bid data.

get a significant premium over other majors. Neither scientists nor humanists garner bids that are significantly different from those of social scientists (the default category in the regression). The dummy variables for bids on beliefs and advice are both negative and significant, confirming the fact that less is bid for beliefs and advice than for data. There is a significant penalty to female experts. Neither the expert's GPA nor the expert's age are significant, but the ranking of the expert based on his or her performance relative to others who played the same investment game is an important factor. This variable ranges from roughly 0.1 (for the highest ranked) to 1 (for the lowest ranked). Thus, there is a significant penalty for being a low-earning expert.

In the disaggregated regressions, if we find that all bidder types pay a significant premium for one expert type category, this can be interpreted as support for the perception rent hypothesis. The results do not support this. Both economist and scientist bidders pay a significant premium for economists experts, but humanists and social scientists do not. There is a consensus that the payoff ranking of the expert is important. All types also agree in paying less for beliefs and advice than for data. With respect to gender, we find that only scientists pay significantly less for female experts which would indicate that the result in the pooled regression was driven by this subgroup. These separate or disaggregated regressions then tend to cast doubt on the perception rent hypothesis without providing compensating strong evidence for the chauvinistic hypothesis.

Now that we know how much subjects are willing to pay for the advice of various types, it is of interest to know how rational these bids are, i.e., are the bids consistent with how accurate our expert types really are. To answer this question, we use the data of the expert treatment.

To characterize the performance of our experts, we use three different performance measures. In metric 1 our accuracy measure is **simply** the fraction of subject experts who provided the correct advice (invest, don't invest) (i.e., the advice that a Bayesian decision maker would have provided, given her observations) in round $N = 3$ or

$N = 25.$[6] Metric 2 asks how different are the actual beliefs provided from the "correct" beliefs that should be provided given the observations of the individual. This is simply the distance from the Bayes-optimal posteriors. Finally, metric 3 is slightly more complex and deals with the case where the client receives the expert's beliefs as advice. If you were to receive an advisor's beliefs, and if you believe that your advisor has updated her beliefs correctly, then you would choose the invest option when the beliefs exceed 0.5, and the don't-invest option when beliefs are less than 0.5. One can then compute the number of times that the actual beliefs of advisors, given their observed data, results in the same answer that a Bayesian decision maker would have arrived at. This measure of accuracy of beliefs just checks whether the announced beliefs agree with Bayesian beliefs. Note that this measure uses the announced beliefs of the expert that are observed by the client. That is the input into this metric.

We score the accuracy as $1/2$ when elicited beliefs are exactly 0.5 while rational beliefs are either strictly above or below 0.5. Table 11.4 contains the results of these calculations for the expert game.

As we see, if we were to lump experts by major into three categories, economics majors, science/math majors, and others, we can see that science/math majors appear to make the best advisors. For example, for the $N = 25$ expert game they outperform each of the other types on all three metrics. In fact, they are the only group that offered the correct advice all of the time in the sense of suggesting investing when the state of the world was profitable. There is a significant difference in the means of economics and science/math majors at the 6% and 5% levels for metrics 1 and 2, respectively. There is no significant difference for metric 3. In the $N = 3$ expert game their advantage is less clear, and there is essentially no difference between

---

[6] Six out of the 10 advisors who gave the incorrect advice had data for which the correct beliefs are between 0.44 and 0.56. (For the entire data, only 16 out of 87 had data resulting in beliefs in the same region.) In particular, the six out of 10 advisors who gave the incorrect advice may not have been too far off in their decisions.

Table 11.4 *Performance of advisors by major in expert games.*

		Expert game ($N = 25$)			Expert game ($N = 3$)		
Major		Metric 1	Metric 2	Metric 3	Metric 1	Metric 2	Metric 3
Econ.	Mean	0.87	−0.07	0.83	0.68	−0.03	0.64
	S.d.	0.34	0.11	0.38	0.48	0.27	0.49
	N	53	53	53	22	22	22
Sci./math	Mean	1	−0.02	0.94	0.67	−0.02	0.78
	S.d.	0	0.03	0.24	0.50	0.31	0.44
	N	17	17	17	9	9	9
Other	Mean	0.82	−0.08	0.59	0.67	0.06	0.66
	S.d.	0.39	0.09	0.51	0.47	0.25	0.48
	N	17	17	17	58	58	58
Total	Mean	0.89	−0.06	0.80	0.67	0.03	0.66
	S.d.	0.32	0.10	0.40	0.47	0.26	0.48
	N	87	87	87	89	89	89

the economic majors and the other majors, except for metric 2. None of the differences are significant.

11.4   BELIEF BIASES

Up until now we have discussed the market for advice. We now want to dig down to a more micro-level and ask how our subjects processed the information they received in an effort to update their beliefs about their profitability of investment. We are interested in this for a number of reasons, but mostly we are interested in correlating their updating method (which we can estimate from our belief elicitation game) to how willing subjects are to buy either advice, data, or beliefs, and also how willing they are to follow advice once received.

11.4.1   Optimal Updating of Beliefs

In our belief elicitation game a subject will state her prior, see a sample of observations, update her beliefs on the basis of this information, and then be given either the beliefs of an expert or some invest/don't-invest advice from their expert and update once more. In particular, in the belief elicitation game, we observe three beliefs: the prior, the belief after observing data, and the belief after receiving either beliefs or advice. (In some experiments the order is reversed and the subject will get advice first.)

The updating rule when using data is simple because it prescribes an optimal way to place weight on the data a subject observes with the remaining weight placed on her prior.[7] More precisely, before seeing any data, given the description of the distributions from which θ is drawn, we would expect the prior probability over the profitable state to be $b_0^* = 0.5$ for all subjects. Suppose that in each round the advisee sees N observations, with a fraction m_1 profitable in the first round ($(1-m_1)$ being negative), and m_2 being profitable in the second. Then after the first round, when $m_1 N$ profitable observations are seen, the Bayesian posterior will be

$$b_1^* = \frac{N}{2\alpha + N}(m_1) + \left(1 - \frac{N}{2\alpha + N}\right)(b_0^*).$$

Note what this updating formula says. If we let $\psi_0^* = N/(2\alpha + N)$, then ψ_0^* is the weight the subjects should optimally place on the data observed, with the remaining weight placed on their prior, b_0^*. If there is a second period where data is observed with Nm_2 profitable observations, then the updated posterior after both periods will be

$$b_2^* = \frac{N}{2\alpha + 2N}(m_1) + \left(1 - \frac{N}{2\alpha + 2N}\right)(b_1^*).$$

In our belief–price game subjects observed three profitable observations taken from a distribution where $\alpha = 1$. We purposefully chose these parameters since this choice offers subjects a limited number of observations (after seeing, say, 25 observations, the optimal weight to put on the sample is practically 1, so it is hard to differentiate who is Bayesian from who is representative). Also, seeing three positive observations and using the updating formula above for b_1^* defines a posterior belief of

$$0.8 = \frac{3}{2(1) + 3}(1) + \left(1 - \frac{3}{2(1) + 3}\right)\left(\frac{1}{2}\right).$$

---

[7] In order to derive an updating rule for advice, one has to assume that one's advisor is using the optimal Bayesian rules and invert their advice to infer its informational content. We do not get involved with that here but refer the reader to Nyarko et al. (2006) for analysis.

If we denote the optimal weight to place on the sample Ψ^B (B for Bayesian), then we will call subjects "conservative" if they place a weight $\Psi_i < \Psi^B$ on the sample and "representative" if they place a weight $\Psi_i > \Psi^B$ on the sample, with a perfectly representative person setting $\Psi_{i=1}$. Our design is efficient since it allows us to differentiate Bayesian, conservative, and representative subjects.

With this background, we can ask whether subjects tend to update their beliefs in a Bayesian manner or, if not, do they tend to give more or less weight to data than is optimal, i.e., do they suffer from a representative bias or are they conservative?

To answer this question, we focus on the belief–price experiments where subjects observe three observations taken from a distribution where $\alpha = 1$. We focus first on the Ψ_0 they use to update their prior after observing three positive observations in a row indicating that the state is profitable, remembering that $\Psi_0 = 0.6$ is the optimal Bayesian weight.

Table 11.5 presents the results of our calculations. It presents the person-by-person weights that subjects used in their updating. As we can see, the median weight that subjects used was 0.6, so the median subject updated using perfectly Bayesian weights. (The mean was 0.55, which is not far off.) In addition, note that subjects are almost equally split between being conservative, using a weight less than 0.6 on data, and representative, using a weight greater than 0.6. Interestingly, 21 subjects proved themselves to be perfectly representative and placed a weight of 1 on the data they saw. This was the modal choice. However, the next two most frequently used weights were the Bayesian weight, which was chosen by eight subjects, and the perfectly conservative weight of 0 chosen by four subjects. So while Bayesian weighting seems to be the center of gravity for the subject population, there is a very wide distribution of subjects, with some acting as if they were conservative and others being representative (with a large number totally representative).

Since our main focus in this book is not Bayesian updating but rather advice and its impact on decision making, we need to ask what

Table 11.5 *Values of Ψ_0 in the belief–price elicitation game.*

Ψ_0	Frequency	Ψ_0	Frequency
−1.64	1	0.48	1
−0.5	2	0.5	9
−0.34	1	0.52	1
−0.33	1	0.555	1
0	4	0.6	8
0.085	1	0.625	1
0.142	1	0.657	1
0.2	1	0.666	1
0.249	2	0.7	3
0.285	2	0.749	1
0.3	1	0.75	1
0.333	1	0.8	4
0.375	2	1	21
Mean = 0.550, Median = 0.6			

are the consequences of the way people update their beliefs on how they value information and advice and their willingness to follow advice once received. More precisely, we ask: are clients who are more representative in their updating more likely to bid more for advice and data?

In general the answer to this question is yes. The Ψ_0 that subjects exhibited in the belief elicitation part of the belief–price game is a measure of the weight given to new information (whether from data, beliefs, or advice). Table 11.6 contains the average bids made for data, advice, and beliefs conditional on whether a subject is categorized as being Bayesian $\Psi_0 = 0.6$, conservative $\Psi_0 < 0.6$ or representative $\Psi_0 > 0.6$.

Note that, while there is not strict monotonicity exhibited in Table 11.6, it is clearly true that subjects who are representative,

Table 11.6 *Mean bids by type – conservative, Bayesian, or representative: belief–price elicitation game.*

Type of subject	Type of information		
	Data	Beliefs	Advice
Conservative, $N = 27$	0.99	0.69	0.57
Bayesian, $N = 8$	2.04	1.07	0.62
Representative, $N = 33$	1.91	1.09	1.02

$\Psi_0 > 0.6$, bid more for all types of information, data, advice, or beliefs, than do subjects who are conservative, $\Psi_0 < 0.6$. It is only in the case of data that Bayesians bid more than representative types. In general, representative types seem to respect data more and bid more for it. The bids of conservatives are significantly lower than those of representative types for all types of information according to a t-test on the means. The distributions of bids by conservatives also differ from those by representatives according to a non-parametric Wilcoxon rank-sum test. The bids of Bayesians are not significantly different from those of representatives for data or beliefs, nor from those of conservatives for advice, by either type of test. The significant tests are all highly significant (1% level or better).

As we can see in Table 11.6, subjects who suffer a representative bias appear to be most willing to pay for advice. The question, however, is whether the high value they place on advice leads them to update their priors more when they receive it?

To answer this question, remember that in our experiment subjects have seen three positive (profitable) observations from the relevant distribution and have updated their priors once. The weight they used in this initial updating was their Ψ_0. We then offered them advice in the form of a binary suggestion about whether they should invest or play it safe. In fact all the advice they received was positive, i.e., all were told to invest. We then measured the change in their beliefs after receiving this advice and take that as a proxy of the impact

Table 11.7 *The impact of advice on change in beliefs: belief–price elicitation game (N = 73, R² = 0.54).*

Variable	Coef.	Std err.	t	P > |t|
Ψ_0	−0.212	0.045	−4.68	0.00
Dummy	0.374	0.073	5.15	0.00
Constant	0.096	0.030	3.20	0.002

of advice on them. Those who change more are more affected by the advice. (We do not look at whether subjects followed the advice they were given, since there is little variance in this, as most people chose the invest option.)

To examine this question we ran a regression where the left-hand variable was the change in a subject's belief after receiving advice. We regressed this on the person's Ψ_0 and a dummy variable which took the value of 1 if the advice offered was counter to the best-response choice of the subject to his updated beliefs (updated after seeing three observations). The results of this regression are contained in Table 11.7.

This regression reveals a negative sign for Ψ_0. While this might lead one to think that subjects who are highly representative are less likely to follow advice, it is interesting to note why this is true. To explain, take the extreme case. Say that I am completely representative and observe three plus signals during my observation of data. In this case I would update my prior to 1. Now when I get a piece of advice to invest, as we have indicated before, unless I also think that my advisor is as perfectly representative as I am, I would invert his advice for its informational content and assume that he probably saw a less optimistic sample than I did. In this case, ironically, his advice to invest is actually treated as bad news, since it implies that the sample he saw was less positive than mine. Decreasing one's posterior after such advice is therefore not as perverse as one might think and explains the negative coefficient on the Ψ_0 variable. Note that 21 subjects were fully representative, so that this result applies to many people in the sample.

11.5   CONCLUSION

The results described in this chapter are of interest to our enterprise here since, in the world outside the lab, there is a market (perhaps informal) for advice in the sense that different types of people's advice is sought after and listened to with different degrees of enthusiasm. Influence, esteem, and power follow from being the type of person others want to listen to.

Perception rents, if they exist, can be lucrative. In our small experiment, however, such rents were hard to identify possibly because of the limited variation across student advisors and the lack of meaningful dimensions across which they differed (i.e., everyone was almost of the same age, for example), yet we did find some significant results. In the real world, however, results similar to ours might be stronger since the variation across advisors should be more meaningful.

How receptive people are to following advice may be related to how conservative or fixed they are in their current beliefs. Those that put a great deal of weight on the past or on their prior may be resistant to new information or advice suggesting change. Those who may be most easily influenced, however, may be those who suffer from base-rate neglect or a representative bias. In future research, it may be of interest to try to correlate such biases with the willingness of people to follow unconventional theories or cult leaders. In other words, are such biases good diagnostic tools for the willingness of people to be influenced by new ideas that diverge greatly from the past or base rates existing currently?

REFERENCES

Becker, G. M., DeGroot, M. H. and Marschak, J. (1964). Measuring utility by a single-response sequential method. *Behavioral Science*, 9(3), 226–232.

Feng, B. and MacGeorge, E. L. (2006). Predicting receptiveness to advice: Characteristics of the problem, the advice-giver, and the recipient. *Southern Communication Journal*, 71(1), 67–85.

Nyarko, Y. and Schotter, A. (2002). An experimental study of belief learning using elicited beliefs. *Econometrica*, 70(3), 971–1005.

Nyarko, Y., Schotter, A. and Sopher, B. (2006). On the informational content of advice: A theoretical and experimental study. *Economic Theory*, 29(2), 433–452.

Yaniv, I. (2004a). The benefit of additional opinions. *Current Directions in Psychological Science*, 13(2), 75–78.

Yaniv, I. (2004b). Receiving other people's advice: Influence and benefit. *Organizational Behavior and Human Decision Processes*, 93(1), 1–13.

Yaniv, I. and Kleinberger, E. (2000). Advice taking in decision making: Egocentric discounting and reputation formation. *Organizational Behavior and Human Decision Processes*, 83(2), 260–281.

PART V Advice and Economic Mechanisms

In our introductory chapter we made a distinction between naturally occurring and man-made societal problems. What we mean by this distinction is that some of what we face in our daily lives are problems that exist simply because, as people, we come in contact with each other and our fates are intertwined as a result. Because of this we are forced to create conventions to help us navigate these interactions and guide our behavior. But some of the problems we face are designed for us by economic planners or mechanism designers. These mechanisms define games that are designed to help us solve problems that may be intractable or too difficult for us to solve by ourselves. In Chapters 12 and 13 we will look at the impact of advice and convention creation in school matching mechanisms, which are mechanisms (or game forms)[1] designed by bureaucrats (or smart economists) whose aim is to help us match students with schools. Other such matching mechanisms exist to help medical students get internships when they graduate medical school, to match students to dorm rooms, or to match kidney donors to kidney patients. In all of these situations, there is an underlying problem that needs a solution, and a mechanism is designed to solve it.

The problem, however, is that, while the mechanisms designed to solve these problems typically define a static one-shot game for the participants to play, the problem people face is a recurrent one played repeatedly by a series of generations of players. For example, the school matching problem occurs every year, and every year a new set of students arrive to be matched with schools. The parents of these students, however, talk to each other and exchange advice on how to strategize in the mechanism they face. In the playgrounds, while their children play, these parents are chatting about how to solve for the Nash equilibrium of the matching mechanism or investigating whether there is a dominant strategy for them to use (a slight joke here). Such chatting, investigated in Chapter 12, can affect the

---

[1] A game form consists of all the rules of the game (its extensive form) exclusive of assigning utilities or preferences for the players over outcomes (terminal nodes).

strategies parents use and affect the matches that occur. The question is, does chatting affect behavior and is this change beneficial? In addition, we ask whether it matters to whom you chat, in the sense whether you chat in a homogeneous network with others of your type or a heterogeneous network with people who are different from you.

But in the playground where parents congregate there are also parents of older children who engaged in the match before and have experience with it. These parents are the object of study in Chapter 13, where we treat the school matching problem as an intergenerational game and ask if the conventions of behavior established in the past increase the stability or efficiency of the match.

In that chapter we contrast the social learning that exists in intergenerational games with the reinforcement learning that occurs when our matching problem is repeated 20 times with the same set of subjects. This exercise is similar to the one performed by Chaudhuri et al. (2006a) with respect to public goods games and by Chaudhuri et al. (2006b) on tournaments. As we will see, social and experiential (reinforcement) learning can produce very different results, with subjects being more able to learn when they face the matching problem repeatedly over time as compared to the social learning that exists in intergenerational games, where each generation plays only once and passes on advice. Here dysfunctional conventions can be established and passed on from generation to generation.

REFERENCES

Chaudhuri, A., Graziano, S. and Maitra, P. (2006a). Social learning and norms in a public goods experiment with inter-generational advice. *Review of Economic Studies*, 73(2), 357–380.

Chaudhuri, A., Schotter, A. and Sopher, B. (2006b). Learning in tournaments with inter-generational advice. *Economics Bulletin*, 3(26), 1–16.

12   Chatting and Matching

Your child has finally grown old enough to go to school and part of you is delighted.[1] The other part dreads having to go through the school application and matching process, which you fear will place little Johnny or Debbie in a school that is just not right for him or her. After digging for information you find out that the way kids are matched with schools is by having parents list their preferences for schools in terms of a ranking stating which school you rank first, second, third, etc., and then an algorithm or mechanism takes all of the parent preferences and school availabilities and matches them.

You read the instructions for the match, which you do not quite understand, and also the publicly stated advice that it is in your best interests to reveal your rankings truthfully, but you don't believe it. You reason that if they are telling you what they want you to do it must be best or easiest for them and not you. You might also figure that if other parents believe the advice and follow it (like the suckers you think they are), it opens the door for a clever person like yourself to try to game the system and do better for your kid. All of this makes you confused.

Before you act or submit a ranking, you do what you always do when you have to make an important (or unimportant) decision, you ask around for advice. But who do you ask? Probably you ask those people who you are connected to in a social network. These are your relatives, friends, and people you chat with in the playground. They may be people like yourself or people very different from you. In any case, who you chat with and receive advice from may affect your behavior in the match.

---

[1] This chapter is based on Ding and Schotter (2017).

In this chapter we compare the performance of two frequently used matching mechanisms, the Boston and the Gale–Shapley mechanisms, in the presence of chatting through social networks. We want to know whether chatting, and who you chat with, affects your strategic behavior in the match compared to those who do not have access to others (are in isolated networks).

In the experiment, when subjects enter the lab they are assigned to a chat network, which may connect them to people of their own type (same preferences over schools or objects), people of different types, or no one at all. We then have them play the "matching game" twice, once before they are allowed to chat (phase 1) and once after they chat (phase 2) and compare their rankings. The difference will measure the impact of advice on their decision.

As you might recall, this is similar to the design psychologists used in the judge–advisor system (see Chapter 2 for a discussion) where they have subjects make a guess as to the correct answer to a question, receive an opinion from another subject, and then submit another guess in light of the advice they received. Clearly, in that design, the influence of advice is measured by the difference in their guess between the before-advice and after-advice situations. In our design we also measure the impact of advice by looking at how subjects change their submitted ranking after receiving advice by comparing their phase 1 and phase 2 rankings. We also look at who is offering advice (people like themselves or people different from them) to see how that affects their behavior.

Very succinctly, we find that chatting influences both the behavior of our subjects and their welfare. This suggests that including chat into an experimental design on matching enhances its external validity since in the real world chatting is ubiquitous. We also find that those subjects who communicate with people of their own experimental type (i.e., who have the same induced preferences and priorities) tend to change their submitted preference rankings more between phases but their payoffs increase less, indicating that sometimes the beneficial aspect of chatting should be to persuade subjects who are already using good strategies not to change.[2]

It is important to point out that the object of chat in our experiment is the strategies of subjects but not the quality of schools or objects. While, in the world outside of the lab, parents are very likely to talk about the quality of the schools which they might send their children to or the fit between the schools and their children, in our experiment, because subjects know the values of the objects to them precisely, there is no scope for such discussion. We have done this intentionally to focus the attention of subjects on strategic issues.

12.1   THE SCHOOL CHOICE MATCHING PROBLEM

In this section we will closely follow Pathak (2011) in describing the school choice problem. A school choice model with I students and N schools consists of a triple (P, q, π) where

- $P = (P_1, \ldots, P_I)$ are the preferences of students,
- $q = (q_1, \ldots, q_n)$ are the school capacities, and
- $\pi = (\pi_1, \ldots, \pi_n)$ are the school priorities.

The last of these is a list of students, one list for each school, indicating which students have priority for that school (we define priority below).

---

[2] There are a few other papers that study what you might call top-down advice given to people by those who administer the mechanism, in which they suggest various strategies. In the experiments conducted by Braun et al. (2014), people (subjects) receive strategic coaching before submitting their preferences: in strategy-proof mechanisms, subjects are told to submit truthful preferences, while in the non-strategy-proof mechanism, subjects are offered a suggested manipulation. They find that subjects in their experiment are likely to follow advice. The results of Guillen and Hakimov (2014), however, are mixed. They deploy the top trading cycles mechanism and have three advice treatments: right advice recommending truth-telling, wrong advice suggesting misrepresentation, and mixed advice that offers both right and wrong advice. They find that the fraction of subjects telling the truth in all three advice treatments is significantly lower than that in the control group where no advice is provided.

The preferences of the students express their rankings over schools, the school capacities state the number of seats in each school, while the school priorities express information about how applicants are ordered at schools. A strategy for a student is a ranking of the schools that is submitted to the mechanism. In this paper we investigate only the school choice problem in which students are free to choose their strategies while schools are constrained to accept students on the basis of their exogenously defined priorities. Hence we will be looking at the "one-sided" version of the matching problem.

The outcome of a school choice problem is a student assignment, or a matching $\mu : I \rightarrow S$, where $\mu(i)$ indicates the school assignment of student i. A matching is **Pareto-efficient** if there is no way to improve the allocation of a student without making another student worse off. (Note that only the welfare of students is considered in this definition.) A matching is **stable** if there is no student–school pair $(i; s)$ such that (1) student i prefers school s to her assignment $\mu(i)$, and (2) there is another student j with lower priority than student i assigned to s under μ, or school s has slots unfilled. Finally, a mechanism is **strategy-proof** if truth-telling is a dominant strategy for all students, i.e., a strategy that is best for the student no matter what rankings other students submit.

12.1.1 Boston Mechanism

The Boston mechanism (a mechanism formulated in response to a court order to integrate Boston schools) works as follows:

Step 1: Only the first choices of the students in their submitted rankings are considered. For each school, consider the students who have listed it as their first choice, and assign the seats in the school to these students one at a time following the school's priority order until either there are no seats left or there are no students left who have listed it as their first choice.

In general, at

Step k: Consider the remaining students. Only the k-th choices of these students are considered. For each school with still available seats, consider the students who have listed it as their k-th choice, and assign the remaining seats to these students one at a time according to priority until either there are no seats left or there are no students left who have listed it as their k-th choice.

This mechanism, while widely used, is not strategy-proof.

12.1.2 Gale–Shapley Deferred Acceptance Mechanism

The Gale–Shapley deferred acceptance mechanism works as follows:

Step 1: Each student proposes her first choice. Each school tentatively assigns its seats to its proposers one at a time following its priority order until either there are no seats left or there are no students left who have listed it as their first choice.

In general, at

Step k: Each student who was rejected in the previous step proposes to her next choice. Each school considers the students who have been held together with its new proposers, and tentatively assigns its seats to these students one at a time according to priority, until either there are no students left who have proposed or all seats are exhausted. In the latter case, any remaining proposers beyond the capacity are rejected. The mechanism terminates either when there are no new proposals, or when all rejected students have exhausted their preference lists.

The Gale–Shapley mechanism is strategy-proof. Though it generally does not guarantee Pareto-optimal results for students, it does determine student-optimal stable matches when students and schools have strict preferences (Dubins and Freedman, 1981; Roth, 1982), i.e., no other stable assignment Pareto-dominates the outcome produced by the Gale–Shapley mechanism, although this outcome might be Pareto-dominated by some unstable assignments. However, when schools have coarse priorities, in the sense of not being able to express a strict order over students, the welfare consequences change, as the Gale–Shapley mechanism may not always produce student-optimal stable matches. In our experimental design we consider coarse priorities.

12.2 EXPERIMENTAL DESIGN

All our experiments were conducted in the experimental laboratory of the Center for Experimental Social Science at New York University.[3] Five hundred and ten students were recruited from the general undergraduate population of the university using the CESS recruitment software. The experiment was programmed using the z-tree programming software (Fischbacher, 2007). The typical experiment lasted about an hour, with average earnings of $23.52. Subjects were paid in an experimental currency called Experimental Currency Units (ECUs) and these units were converted into US dollars at a rate specified in the instructions.

12.2.1 The Matching Problem

Our experiments are designed with an eye toward integrating the school choice mechanisms with social networks.[4] To evaluate the impact of chat, we ran a static school choice matching experiment twice, once before (phase 1) and once after (phase 2) allowing chatting via networks. Subjects were paid for either phase 1 or phase 2, but not for both. At the end of the experiment, the computer randomly determined which payoff, phase 1 or phase 2, would be paid. Subjects did not receive any feedback about their decisions or the decisions of other participants until the very end of the experiment, so the results of phase 1 were not known until after the experiment. We used neutral language so schools were called "objects" and students were designated "subjects".

---

[3] For instructions see the online appendix of Ding and Schotter (2017).

[4] In the experiment, subjects participated in three distinct decision tasks, and the monetary payoffs they received were the sum of their payoffs in each task. The first task was the matching experiment to be described below, while the second task was one play of the two-thirds guessing game, and the third was the Holt and Laury (2002) risk aversion task. We used the beauty contest game as a diagnostic tool to evaluate their strategic sophistication, and we had subjects perform the Holt–Laury task for the obvious reason of eliciting their attitudes to risk aversion. For the sake of brevity, we will not discuss the results of these diagnostic tests. The two-thirds beauty contest had no effect on our results, and we will discuss our risk aversion results in the text below when necessary.

Table 12.1 *Preferences.*

	Student preferences				
Type	1	2	3	4	5
First choice	C	C	C	A	A
Second choice	A	A	B	B	C
Third choice	B	B	A	C	B

Phase 1

In both phases of the experiment there are 20 subjects. At the beginning of phase 1 we randomly assign subjects to types, in the sense that among these 20 subjects four are designated type 1, four type 2, four type 3, four type 4, and four type 5. In addition to these 20 subjects, there are also a set of 20 objects, grouped into three types, which are called object A, object B, and object C. In total there are eight units of object A, eight units of object B, and four units of object C.[5]

Table 12.1 presents the full preference matrix of our subject types. These preferences are the same for all our experimental sessions, although the cardinal utilities associated with these objects vary across treatments.

In terms of payoffs, in six of our nine treatments that use either what we call the Boston 16 or the Gale–Shapley mechanism, if a subject is matched to her first-best she will receive 24 ECU, if she is matched to her second-best she will receive 16 ECU, and if she is matched to her third-best she will receive only 4 ECU. In the remaining treatment, using the Boston 10 mechanism, we lower the value of the second-best object to each subject from 16 ECU to 10 ECU. We did this because the closer the payoff of the second-ranked option is to the first, the less incentive a subject has to think

[5] The numbers of subjects in the isolated network treatment, defined in Section 12.2.2, vary from 10 to 20. In each session the number is a multiple of 5, and then the number of subjects for each type and objects change accordingly. For example, when there are 15 subjects in one session, we have three subjects for each type, six units of object A, six units of object B, and three units of object C.

328 PART V ADVICE AND ECONOMIC MECHANISMS

strategically since less is riding on their decision. Making the second-best object worth less increases the benefit of thinking hard.

In all treatments, it is common knowledge that types 1 and 2 are given priority for object A, while type 3 is given priority for object B, and types 4 and 5 are not given priority for any objects. When a subject has priority for an object, she will be admitted in preference to a subject with no priority if there is only one remaining object available. When the number of subjects of equal priority applying for an object is greater than the number of objects available, the mechanism employs a lottery to break ties.[6] Note that types 1 and 2 are identical with respect to both their preferences and priorities.

Subjects are told their own types and matching payoffs for each object as well as a priority table, but they do not know the types or the object payoffs of any subject other than themselves. They are then required to state their rankings over objects. Based on the information subjects provide, one of the matching mechanisms (either the Boston or the Gale–Shapley mechanism) determines the allocation outcome. Each subject is matched to one and only one object.

There are six possible preference orderings or rankings that subjects can submit in either phase 1 or phase 2: 1–2–3, 1–3–2, 2–1–3, 2–3–1, 3–1–2, and 3–2–1, where the numbers in each ranking are the subject's first-best, second-best, and third-best objects. So strategy 1–2–3 is a truth-telling strategy since the subject submits her first-best object first, her second-best object second, and her third-best object last.

Phase 2

To measure the impact of chat on matching, we run phase 2, which allows subjects to submit their preference rankings after they communicate with each other via chat boxes. By comparing the submitted preference rankings of subjects in phase 2 to those of the same subjects

---

[6] In our experiment we used a single lottery instead of object-specific lotteries to break ties.

in phase 1, we are able to observe the impact of chatting on subject behavior and welfare.[7]

At phase 2, subjects face the same matching problem as at phase 1. Their types and matching payoffs for each object do not change. However, at phase 2, before subjects enter their rankings, they are assigned to some subnetwork and allowed to talk with other subjects in their subnetwork for five minutes via chat boxes. The size of subnetworks range from one to five subjects. If a subject is assigned to a subnetwork with only one subject, she cannot talk to anyone but is asked to enter into the chat box what factors influence her decision in phase 2. In other words, we ask her to write in the chat box what she thinks of as she contemplates her ranking.[8] All communication goes via chat boxes. After five minutes all chat boxes become inactive and subjects have to submit their rankings again, i.e., they have to enter into the computers which objects they rank first, second, and third, just as they did in phase 1. The exact types of subnetworks used will be described later.

Payoffs in phase 2 are determined in the same way as they were in phase 1. At the end of the experiment, the computer randomly determines which payoff, phase 1 or phase 2, will be paid to subjects.

12.2.2 Networks

In investigating whether chatting impacts the behavior of subjects, it is important to ask with whom a subject chats. Does she talk to someone who has similar preferences and priorities, or someone quite different? While the subjects in our experiment, when being placed into subnetworks, do not know the types of others with whom they are networked, this information could be revealed during the chat (and our chat records show that it indeed is). In addition, subjects do

---

[7] All advice in this experiment is from peer to peer (subjects to subjects). Li (2021) runs an experiment where subjects are offered advice both from their peers and from the experimental administrator (or mechanism designer) and looks to see which type of advice subjects desire most.

[8] See Cooper and Kagel (2016) for a similar "self-advice" feature.

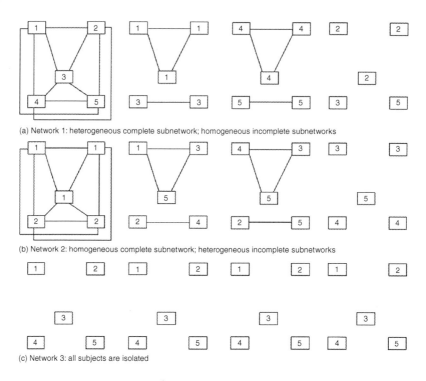

(a) Network 1: heterogeneous complete subnetwork; homogeneous incomplete subnetworks

(b) Network 2: homogeneous complete subnetwork; heterogeneous incomplete subnetworks

(c) Network 3: all subjects are isolated

FIGURE 12.1 Networks.

not know the global network structure in the sense that they do not know the types of subnetworks other subjects are allocated to. We designed three different types of networks, which we call networks 1, 2, and 3, and these three networks are illustrated in Figure 12.1.

Both networks 1 and 2 are composed of four distinct five-person subnetworks, some of which are complete and some incomplete. More precisely, the first subnetwork on the left in these two treatments is complete in the sense that each subject can send and receive messages from all the others, while the other subnetworks are incomplete. The subnetwork on the far right is "isolated" because no subject can communicate with any other. When chatting is allowed, these subjects can only talk to themselves. Note that subjects in the complete subnetwork of network 2 have the same preferences and

Table 12.2 *Experimental design.*

Treatment	Pref. intensity	Network	Mechanism	No. of sessions	No. of subjects
1	24–16–4	1	Boston	4	80
2	24–16–4	2	Boston	4	80
3	24–16–4	3	Boston	2	40
4	24–16–4	1	Gale–Shapley	4	80
5	24–16–4	2	Gale–Shapley	4	80
6	24–16–4	3	Gale–Shapley	3	45
7	24–10–4	1	Boston	2	40
8	24–10–4	2	Boston	2	40
9	24–10–4	3	Boston	2	25
				Total: 27	Total: 510

priorities (types 1 and 2) while those in the incomplete subnetworks are all of different types, while in network 1 the opposite is true. In network 3, all subjects are isolated.

12.2.3   Treatments

Using the experimental procedures described above, we run a set of nine treatments. These treatments differ by changing the matching mechanisms used while holding preferences and priorities constant, or changing the preference intensities while holding the mechanisms and priorities constant, or changing the network structures while holding all else constant.

Our design is summarized in Table 12.2.

12.3   RESULTS

For the purpose of our discussion here, we are interested in the impact of chat on subject behavior. Because phase 1 has no chatting, the results there simply report on the performance of our two mechanisms in the absence of chat, we will discuss our results in phase 1 minimally (see Ding and Schotter (2017) for a fuller analysis).

12.3.1 Strategy Classification

In our analysis we classify a subject's strategy on the basis of what she places first in her submitted ranking. For example, we classify a strategy as "truthful" if a subject submits her first-best choice first, "strategic" if she submits her second-best choice first, and "irrational" if she submits her third-best choice first.

We use this classification for three reasons. First, our main goal is to investigate how subjects change their submitted preference rankings as a result of chat. If we used a very disaggregated way to categorize strategies, each subject would have six possible strategies, and, across phases 1 and 2, would contain 36 possible transitions between them. Because many of these transitions would occur infrequently or be non-existent, statistical comparisons would be difficult. In contrast, under our definitions, the transition matrix is 3×3 and is much easier to handle. Second, we believe that this aggregation has a cognitive justification since we consider what a subject states as her first choice (among three objects) as more indicative of her strategy than how she ranks other objects. A subject who ranks her second-best object first is clearly strategizing, while a subject who places the third-best first is being irrational since there is no scenario, in either mechanism, where that strategy can be beneficial. If a subject had to rank more than three objects it might be myopic to look only at her first choice, but, for a three-object world, little is lost since there are not many manipulations one can do after the first choice is fixed. There are relatively few subjects using strategies such as 1–3–2 and 2–3–1.[9]

When the Gale–Shapley mechanism is used one might suggest that all strategies other than truth-telling are irrational. For the sake

---

[9] In our data only a small fraction of subjects use strategies 1–3–2 and 2–3–1. Among all treatments in phase 1 there are 2.75% of subjects playing 1–3–2 while 8.63% play 2–3–1. In phase 2 the respective fractions are 2.16% and 10.00%. The fractions of subjects using irrational strategies are also small, 6.67% in phase 1 and 4.17% in phase 2. Therefore, if we use the disaggregative way to categorize strategies, some cells of the transition matrices would contain few observations.

of consistency, however, across treatments we will continue to use "irrational" to categorize strategies 3–2–1 and 3–1–2.[10]

12.3.2 Phase 1: A Quick Summary of Results

If the behavior of our subjects and the performance of our two baseline (Boston 16 and Gale–Shapley) mechanisms were identical in phase 1, one might be tempted to conclude that these mechanisms were equivalent and hence interchangeable. Such a conclusion could be misleading if chat changes behavior, since, in the real world, chatting via networks is the norm. To properly examine the impact of chatting on mechanism performance and subject behavior, we will first examine how our dual baseline mechanisms performed in phase 1 (the Gale–Shapley and the Boston 16) where there was no chatting to see if we conclude that they were equivalent. We will then proceed to phase 2 and investigate the impact of chatting on changes in behavior and welfare in order to make what we consider to be the most telling comparisons.

In short there is little difference in submitted preferences between the Boston 16 and the Gale–Shapley mechanisms in phase 1. While there are 37.00%, 58.00%, and 5.00% of subjects submitting truthful, strategic, and irrational preference rankings in the Boston 16 mechanism, in the Gale–Shapley mechanism these percentages are 39.51%, 53.66%, and 6.38%, respectively (see Tables 12.9 and 12.10 in the appendix in Section 12.5). These percentages are not significantly different (using a set of t-tests) either when we pool subjects across types or when we compare the strategies chosen subject type by subject type except for the use of the irrational strategy by Type 1 subjects.[11]

---

[10] To ensure our strategy classification does not create a bias in our results, we also do our analysis using the more conventional definition with six strategies in which the truthful strategy is defined as only submitting preference 1–2–3, and then rerun our main regressions concerning strategy changes across phase 1 and phase 2. See Ding and Schotter (2017, appendix B).

[11] The high-frequency use of the irrational strategy in Gale–Shapley, though, is hard to explain given truth-telling is the dominant strategy.

In terms of welfare, since the actual outcome of the mechanism is the result of both the submitted rankings and the lottery used to break ties when they exist (i.e., when the number of students with priority exceeds the capacity of the school), we need to simulate the expected matches of our subjects by randomly drawing a large number (2500) of lottery orders while holding the stated preference rankings of subjects constant at their submitted preferences. We will refer to the results of this simulation often, especially when we consider our results on welfare.

Doing this (as Table 12.10 in the appendix in Section 12.5 suggests) indicates that there are no statistical differences in the matching outcomes across the two baseline mechanisms in either aggregate or type by type. In each simulation iteration we run a χ^2 test with the null hypothesis that the outcomes across the two mechanisms are identical. In the last column of Table 12.10 we report the fraction of times when the null hypothesis is not rejected.

With these simulated outcomes, we also calculate the fraction of the first-best surplus that is captured by our subjects. Our results show that in the Boston 16 mechanism the subjects are able to capture 84.77% of the potential payoffs available to them, while in the Gale–Shapley mechanism they capture 85.62%. These fractions are not statistically different (the p-value is 0.6898). In summary, in the absence of chat, there is little difference in the behavior of subjects as well as the performance of these two baseline mechanisms.

Since our design includes the Boston 10 treatment where the value of the second-ranked object was reduced from 16 to 10, it is of interest to us to investigate whether there were differences between the performance of this treatment and those of our dual baselines. The short answer here is yes. Subject behavior in phase 1 of our Boston 10 mechanism differs from that of both the Boston 16 and Gale–Shapley mechanisms. This can be seen most easily in Figure 12.2 where we present the use of truth-telling, strategic, and irrational strategies across our three mechanisms in phase 1.

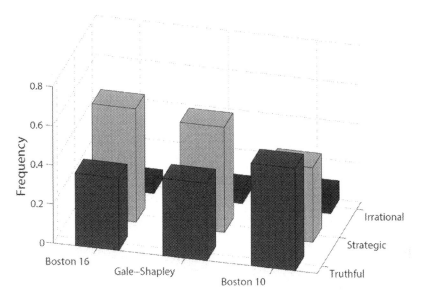

FIGURE 12.2 Phase 1 submitted preference rankings.

Looking at Figure 12.2, notice that, while there is little difference between the submitted rankings across the Boston 16 and Gale–
Shapley mechanisms, there is a marked increase in the use of truthful
strategies in the Boston 10 mechanism as well as an increase in the
use of irrational strategies. When we compare the stated preference
rankings of subjects in the Boston 10 mechanism with those in our
dual baseline mechanisms, we find that there is a significant increase
in the submission of truthful preferences for all subjects who have
priority rights and for the pooled set of subjects.[12] Meanwhile we
find a decrease in the use of the strategic strategy for all types when
comparing the Boston 10 to our dual baseline mechanisms, and the
decrease is significant not only for the subjects who have priority
rights but also for those who do not. Finally, similar to what we
find in the Boston 16 mechanism, in the Boston 10 mechanism there

[12] A similar impact of preference intensity is found in Klijn et al. (2013).

are no subjects with priority rights who use the irrational strategy (i.e., stating their third-best objects as their first choices), while a non-negligible fraction of subjects without priority rights do so.

In terms of welfare, in aggregate, subjects using the Boston 10 mechanism are more likely to receive their first-best, less likely to receive their second-best, and more likely to receive their third-best. Using a set of χ^2 tests, the null hypothesis that the allocations are identical is rejected in 86.40% of the 2500 simulation runs when we compare across the Boston 10 and Boston 16 mechanisms, and in 93.88% of the simulation runs when we compare the Boston 10 and the Gale–Shapley mechanisms.

12.3.3   Impact of Chat: Differences between Phase 2 and Phase 1

To investigate the impact of chat, we examine the behavior of our subjects and the performance of our mechanisms in phase 2 and compare it to phase 1. In particular, we check whether the changes in behavior and matching outcomes of the non-isolated subjects are different from those of the isolated subjects. In addition, we are interested in how chat influences the changes in submitted preference rankings when we condition on whether subjects have priority rights and on the preferences they stated in phase 1.[13]

---

[13] Note that our focus is on the changes in submitted preferences and outcomes across phases 1 and phase 2 and between subjects who chat and those who do not chat, but not on the aggregate distribution of preferences or outcomes in these two phases. Comparing the distribution of submitted preferences across phases 1 and 2, but not their change, may mask what is really going on, since preference changes may cancel each other out and leave the impression that chatting has no impact. For example, say that in phase 1 half the subjects submitted truthful preference rankings and half submitted strategic rankings. After chat, say all those who told the truth in phase 1 submit strategic rankings in phase 2, while all those who submitted strategic rankings in phase 1 tell the truth in phase 2. Furthermore, say for the subjects who are isolated, half of them chose to tell the truth and the other half entered strategic preferences in phase 1, and no one changes in phase 2. Then, while the phase 1 and phase 2 distributions would remain 50–50 for both the isolated and the non-isolated subjects, we could not claim that chatting has no impact, since it leads all non-isolated subjects to change but simply in a counterbalancing direction. As we will see later, while our data does exhibit this cancelling-out property to some

Table 12.3 *Fraction of strategy changes.*

	Boston 16	GS	Boston 10	Difference Boston 16 – GS Boston 16 – 10 Boston 10 – GS	*p*-value
All	0.2750	0.3512	0.3714	−0.0762	0.0985
	(0.4476)	(0.4785)	(0.4855)	−0.0964	0.0922
				−0.0202	0.7278
Isolated	0.3000	0.2706	0.2444	0.0294	0.6782
	(0.4611)	(0.4469)	(0.4346)	0.0556	0.5039
				−0.0262	0.7474
Non-isolated	0.2583	0.4083	0.4667	−0.1500	0.0136
	(0.4396)	(0.4936)	(0.5031)	−0.6694	0.0075
				0.2084	0.4620
Difference	0.0417	−0.1377	−0.2223		
(*p*-value)	(0.5245)	(0.0387)	(0.0172)		

Changes in Submitted Rankings

Our first question concerns the frequency of changes in submitted preference rankings across our two baseline mechanisms among subjects who chat (i.e., the non-isolated subjects) as compared to isolated subjects who do not. Later we will investigate the direction of those changes, and will condition on the subjects' priority rights and what strategies they used in phase 1. To start, we examine unconditional aggregated changes.

To start, let us examine the fractions of subjects who change their submitted rankings from phase 1 to phase 2 across our three mechanisms, and check whether chat leads non-isolated subjects to change their preference rankings differently from those who are isolated.[14] The answer to these questions can be found in Table 12.3.

---

extent, these cancellations do not negate the impact of chat on the performance of the mechanisms.

[14] Here we aggregate over subjects who are isolated in treatments 1 and 2 and those in treatment 3 where all subjects are isolated.

As Table 12.3 indicates, a substantial fraction of subjects change their preference rankings in phase 2. In the Gale–Shapley mechanism, while 40.83% of the non-isolated subjects change their submitted rankings, only 27.06% of the isolated subjects do so. For the Boston 16 mechanism, the percentages are 25.83% and 30.00%, respectively, and for the Boston 10 mechanism, the fractions are 46.67% and 24.44%. A set of t-tests show that the non-isolated subjects change their strategies more often than those isolated in the Gale–Shapley and the Boston 10 mechanisms (the p-values are 0.0387 and 0.0172, respectively). However, in the Boston 16 mechanism, there is no significant difference in strategy changes between subjects who chat and those who do not (the p-value is 0.5245). The result of the Boston 16 mechanism may not be surprising if chatting convinces subjects that they have made the right choices in phase 1 and so they should not change. For example, in phase 1 a non-isolated subject in the Boston 16 mechanism may have submitted strategic preference ranking and, during chatting, become convinced that she need not change. On the other hand, an isolated subject, after submitting strategic preferences in phase 1, may convince herself to change. We will, in fact, see that this is indeed the case from our chat records in Section 12.3.5.

It is also interesting to note that, even when some subjects are not allowed to chat, they still change their submitted preference rankings in phase 2.[15] As shown in our chat records, these isolated subjects change their strategies possibly because they realize their

---

[15] The fact that subjects who are isolated change their strategies indicates that there are two sources of learning taking place amongst our subjects: introspective and social. Introspective learning (Rick and Weber, 2010) is that learning that takes place amongst subjects where the experiment they are engaged in is repeated without feedback (as between phase 1 and phase 2 in our study). Here subjects learn by introspection and second thinking. When chatting takes place, however, learning is social. Our results indicate that, while both types of learning take place, social learning seems to have a larger impact on subjects, in the sense that there is a significant difference in the fraction of subjects who change their strategies between those who chat and those who do not. Still, introspective learning is non-negligible. It is not the case that those who do not chat keep their phase 1 preference in phase 2.

mistakes in phase 1 or they believe the subjects who chat will change their strategies in phase 2, so they should also change as a response. (A similar phenomenon is found in Guillen and Hing (2014) which finds that subjects are more likely to deviate from truth-telling, the dominant strategy in the top trading cycle mechanism, when they learn that other players misrepresent their preference rankings.)

When comparing across the mechanisms, we find that there is no statistical difference in the fraction of subjects changing their submitted preferences when chat is absent. In contrast, when subjects are allowed to chat, the fractions of subjects changing their strategies are significantly greater in the Gale–Shapley and the Boston 10 mechanisms when compared to that in the Boston 16 mechanism (the p-values are 0.0136 and 0.0075, respectively). This indicates that chat has a differential impact on behavior conditional on the mechanism used or the preference intensities within a mechanism.

To further investigate the impact of chat, we run four logit regressions to investigate not only whether chat has a differential impact on strategy changes but also whether whom you chat with (i.e., people like yourself or different than yourself) matters (see Table 12.4). In all four regressions, the dependent variable is a binary {0,1} variable indicating whether a subject changes her strategy across phases. The independent variables include dummy variables indicating a subject's type, whether she is allowed to chat (or to whom she chats), and the mechanism used. The coefficients measure the changes away from the default situation, which is an isolated subject of type 5 in specifications 1 and 3, and an isolated subject of type 5 using the Boston 16 mechanism in specifications 2 and 4.

The regression results substantiate what we stated above. As we see in specifications 1 and 2, the presence of chat increases the likelihood that subjects change their submitted preference rankings. Furthermore, subjects who use the Gale–Shapley and the Boston 10 mechanisms are more likely to change their strategies after chat than those using the Boston 16 mechanism. In specifications 3 and 4, where

Table 12.4 *Strategy change, chat, and network type.*[a]

Variables	Specification 1 Coeff. (std err.)	Specification 2 Coeff. (std err.)	Specification 3 Coeff. (Std. Err.)	Specification 4 Coeff. (Std. Err.)
Type 1	−0.3413	−0.0358	−0.1468	−0.1497
	(0.3091)	(0.3104)	(0.3204)	(0.3218)
Type 2	0.2258	0.2285	0.2096	0.2122
	(0.3044)	(0.3056)	(0.3049)	(0.3062)
Type 3	0.1809	0.1832	0.1646	0.1668
	(0.3058)	(0.3067)	(0.3060)	(0.3073)
Type 4	0.3575	0.3605	0.3217	0.3245
	(0.3000)	(0.3012)	(0.3015)	(0.3029)
Chat	0.4274**	0.4395**	—	—
	(0.2008)	(0.2017)	—	—
G–S	—	0.3665*	—	0.3683*
	—	(0.2170)	—	(0.2175)
B 10	—	0.4614*	—	0.4637
	—	(0.2585)	—	(0.2591)
Homo.	—	—	0.6171***	0.6313***
	—	—	(0.2411)	0.2423
Hetero.	—	—	0.2627	0.2352
	—	—	(0.2342)	0.2352
Constant	−1.1361***	−1.3937***	−1.1097***	−1.3684***
	(0.2524)	(0.2863)	(0.2529)	(0.2860)

[a] Asterisks: * = significant at 10%, ** = significant at 5%, *** = significant at 1%.

we divide the non-isolated subjects into homogeneous and hetero-geneous groups, we find that talking to subjects via heterogeneous subnetworks appears not to increase the incidence of strategy changes above that of isolated subjects. However, subjects communicating in homogeneous subnetworks tend to change their phase 1 submitted preference rankings more than isolated subjects.[16]

The results just stated are unconditional results. Since some of our subjects have priority rights for objects (namely types 1, 2, and 3)

[16] To ensure our results are not sensitive to the way we classify strategies, we rerun the above four regressions using a disaggregated definition, which allows six possible strategies of preference rankings and 36 possible changes between phase 1 and phase 2. The results are presented in the online appendix of Ding and Schotter (2017).

Table 12.5 *Strategy change, chat, and priority rights.*[a]

Variable	Specification 5 Strategic → Truthful Coeff. (std err.)	Specification 6 Truthful → Strategic Coeff. (std err.)
Non-priority	−0.6343*	−0.3407
	(0.3324)	(0.3126)
B 16 × Chat	−0.1038	−0.3451
	(0.4994)	(0.5027)
G–S × Chat	0.9708**	−0.0492
	(0.4211)	(0.4503)
B 10 × Chat	0.9756*	0.4350
	(0.5526)	(0.4729)
G–S × Iso.	−0.1518	−0.3749
	(0.5575)	(0.5280)
B 10 × Iso.	−0.5302	−0.9582
	(0.8423)	(0.6432)
Constant	−1.2947***	−0.2260
	(0.3796)	(0.4151)

[a]Asterisks: * = significant at 10%, ** = significant at 5%, *** = significant at 1%.

and some do not (types 4 and 5), we would like to investigate whether chat has a differential impact on the fraction of subjects changing their preference rankings across phases conditional on whether a subject has priority or not and also on the strategies they used in phase 1.

To answer this question, in Table 12.5 we aggregate subjects of types 1–3 into a priority group and subjects of types 4 and 5 into a non-priority group, and run two logit regressions in which specification 5 examines the subset of subjects who submitted strategic preference rankings in phase 1 and the dependent variable is a dummy variable indicating whether a subject switches from a strategic to a truthful preference submission, while specification 6 investigates whether subjects who initially submitted truthful rankings switch to strategic preference rankings.[17] In both the specifications, the independent variables include an indicator of whether a subject has a priority right and the interaction terms across mechanisms and an indicator of whether a subject is allowed to chat.

When examining subjects who initially submitted strategic preference rankings, we find that subjects without priority rights are less likely to switch to truth-telling in phase 2 than those with priority rights. However, when we look into the subset of subjects who initially submitted truthful preference rankings, the behavior difference with regard to priority rights disappears. In addition, our regressions show that the chat effect that we find from the pooled data only remains significant if subjects initially submitted strategic preference ranking in phase 1, but it is not significant if subjects initially report their preferences truthfully.[18]

Stability

School matching mechanisms are primarily focused on stability, because if the matches generated by the mechanisms are not stable, then there are likely to be disgruntled parents whose children were not placed in schools who would have accepted them. Given the preferences and priorities of our subjects, an outcome will be stable as long as no subjects of types 1–3 are awarded their third-best objects.[19] Using this criterion to search for stable outcomes, we find

---

[17] Here we do not examine the changes from (to) the irrational strategy because only few subjects use the irrational strategy in our experiment.

[18] As we did above, we check whether the above results are sensitive to our classification of submitted preference rankings. More precisely, we examine whether subjects are more likely to change their strategies conditional on whether they submitted strategy 1–2–3 in phase 1. The results are presented in the online appendix of Ding and Schotter (2017).

[19] This can easily be established. The claim is that a match is stable if and only if no subjects of types 1–3 are awarded their third-best objects.

Proof: (i) Stability $\Rightarrow$ No subjects of types 1–3 are awarded their third-best objects.

that chat increases the stability of matches in both the Gale–Shapley and Boston 10 mechanism but not in the Boston 16 mechanism. More precisely, in the Boston 16 mechanism, 56.48% of the phase 1 matches are stable while 56.99% of the phase 2 matches are stable. The corresponding numbers for the Gale–Shapley mechanism are 68.75% and 85.45%, respectively (p-value is 0.0000), while for the Boston 10 mechanism they are 17.16% and 49.65%, respectively (p-value is 0.0000).

The reason we find no increase in the stability of matches across phases for the Boston 16 mechanism is probably because, as we know, there was no significant change in the submitted preferences of subjects across phases. However, notice that for the Gale–Shapley and Boston 10 mechanisms the frequency of stable matches increases considerably across phases. This is particularly true in the Boston 10 mechanisms where in phase 1 very few stable matches were created. This is probably the result of the fact that subjects in phase 1 of the Boston 10 mechanisms submitted a large number of truthful preferences and those submissions lead many subjects to receive their third-best objects – exactly the circumstances where instability is likely to occur. Chat appears to have rectified this situation to some extent.

Suppose a subject with priority right is allocated into her third-best. For the ease of exposition, say this subject is of type 1 who has priority for object A. Then (a) this subject prefers object A to her current assignment, and (b) another subject who has a lower priority order than this subject is currently awarded object A (because there are enough objects A to satisfy the demand of type 1), which violates the condition of stability.

(ii) Stability $\Leftarrow$ No subjects of types 1–3 are awarded their third-best objects.

Suppose the match is not stable. Then there exists a subject–object pair (i, s) such that (a) subject i prefers object s to her current assignment, and (b) there is another subject with lower priority ranking than this subject assigned to object s. Notice, given our design, subject i cannot be of type 4 or type 5 who have no priority for any objects because condition (b) cannot be satisfied. Furthermore, subject i cannot be of type 1, 2, or 3 because we assume no subjects of types 1–3 are awarded their third-best objects. Suppose subject i is type 1 (or 2 or 3) and she is not allocated into her first-best object; condition (b) cannot be satisfied because no one has priority for object C, the first-best school for types 1–3.

12.3.4   Welfare Changes

A standard welfare measure for experimental markets (of which matching is one example) calculates the fraction of the available surplus (i.e., the first-best payoff sum) that is captured by subjects in an experimental session. In our experiment, however, we care about the impact of chat on welfare and hence would like to compare the welfare of subjects who chat to that of those who do not, as well as the change in welfare across phases. This is not easily accomplished using the surplus measure, since that measure is an aggregate market measure encompassing both the isolated and the non-isolated subjects and there is no way to impute the changes in aggregate market welfare across phases separately to each group. To compensate for this difficulty, we will compare how the payoffs of the isolated and the non-isolated subjects change across phases, which we will do below.

To do this, we employ two different payoff measures and run regressions that investigate the impact of chatting on these payoff measures. The first measure, payoff difference, is simply the mean payoff difference of subjects between phase 1 and phase 2, while the second, payoff difference dummy, is a discrete measure which assigns a −1 for any subject whose payoff decreases from phase 1 to phase 2 , a 0 for any subject whose payoff stays the same, and a +1 for any subject whose payoff increases. These differences are calculated for each subject using the mean payoff determined by our simulation, which takes account of the possibility that some outcomes are determined randomly by lottery draws.

We find that allowing subjects to chat either increases their payoffs across phases or, as is true in the Boston 10 mechanism, when payoffs decrease, they decrease less among those who chat. In addition, when we condition on whom the subjects chat with, we find that only when subjects chat with subjects unlike them, i.e., in heterogeneous networks, do their payoffs increase.

To support this conclusion, note that across our three mechanisms the payoffs among those who chat increase by 0.7229 and

0.3128 in moving from phase 1 to phase 2 in the Boston 16. For those who do not chat in the Gale–Shapley mechanisms, however, they decrease (the payoff differences are −0.2097 and −0.6392, respectively). In the Boston 10 mechanism, payoffs decrease both for subjects who chat and for those who do not by −0.4974 and −0.7376, respectively. Note, however, that while the payoffs for subjects who chat decrease in the Boston 10 mechanism, the decrease is greater for those who do not chat. These mean payoff differences across subjects who chat and those who do not are significant for subjects using the Boston 16 and the Gale–Shapley mechanisms (p-values are 0.0159 and 0.0289), but insignificant for the Boston 10 mechanism (p-value is 0.4140).

We further substantiate these results in a regression analysis where we use our two payoff measures (payoff difference and payoff difference dummy) as dependent variables and employ our usual set of right-hand dummy variables such as a subject's type, a dummy designating whether she is allowed to chat, and the mechanisms used. For the payoff difference regression, we use an OLS regression, while for the discrete payoff difference dummy variable, we use an ordered logit regression.

The impact of chat on welfare may be influenced by a number of factors, such as whom one chats with (heterogeneous versus homogeneous subnetwork), whether a subject chatting has a priority, and the type of matching mechanism used. Table 12.6 demonstrates several interesting facts. First, the chat variable is significantly positive in all regressions where it appears. That is, chat increases the average payoffs across phase 1 and phase 2, and also the likelihood that one's payoff will increase. Second, when we break the chat variable down by checking to whom subjects chat, it appears that only those who chat with people different from them increase their payoffs significantly. This result is interesting because we find that subjects in the homogeneous subnetworks are more likely to change their phase 1 strategies. Hence, while speaking to people of one's own type

Table 12.6 *Chatting and payoff differences.*[a]

Variables	Specification 7 Differences Coeff. (std err.)	Specification 8 Differences Coeff. (std err.)	Specification 9 Differences Coeff. (Std. Err.)	Specification 10 Differences Dummy Coeff. (Std. Err.)	Specification 11 Differences Dummy Coeff. (Std. Err.)	Specification 12 Differences Dummy Coeff. (Std. Err.)
Type 1	−0.0508 (0.5861)	−0.5048 (0.5852)	−0.4541 (0.6047)	−0.6955 (0.2694)	−0.0688 (0.2969)	0.0438 (0.2789)
Type 2	−0.9576 (0.5824)	−0.9591 (0.5816)	−0.9516 (0.5825)	−0.4053 (0.2712)	−0.4030 (0.2707)	0.3855 (0.2709)
Type 3	−0.7440 (0.5824)	−0.7455 (0.5816)	−0.7380 (0.5825)	−0.1229 (0.2706)	−0.1182 (0.2707)	0.1108 (0.2706)
Type 4	−2.002*** (0.5812)	−2.000*** (0.5804)	−1.983*** (0.5829)	−0.3961 (0.2730)	−0.4107 (0.2732)	0.3731 (0.2740)
Chat	0.7559** (0.3827)	0.7398** (0.3822)	– –	0.4432** (0.1692)	0.4398*** (0.1694)	– –
GS	– –	−0.4209 (0.4119)	−0.4210 (0.4123)	–	−0.3070* (0.1830)	−0.3059* (0.1831)
B10	– –	−0.9289* (0.4996)	−0.9291* (0.5000)	–	−0.1303* (0.2245)	−0.1310 (0.2249)
Homo	– –	–	0.6489 (0.4681)	–	–	0.2466 (0.2090)
Hetero	– –	–	0.8168* (0.4454)	–	–	0.6023*** (0.1989)
Constant	0.3779 (0.4686)	0.7478 (0.5227)	0.7355 (0.5244)	–	–	– –

[a] Asterisks: * = significant at 10%, ** = significant at 5%, *** = significant at 1%.

may lead a subject to change her preference ranking, such changes do not necessarily lead to payoff increases. This might imply that there are some circumstances where not changing one's submitted preferences is advantageous and listening to people of a similar type may be damaging.

Our design has subjects who have priority in the mechanisms (types 1–3) and those who do not (types 4 and 5). In heterogeneous networks there is chat across these types and one might be curious to ask if chatting has a different impact on subjects who do and do not have priority. This may be important on equity grounds since parents in disadvantaged communities many times do not have priority for high-quality schools given housing segregation and hence, even if they chat, they may still not be able to place their children in high-quality schools.

To answer this question, we run a simple OLS regression to examine the payoff difference across phases 1 and 2 for subjects with and without priority rights. We do this by running three separate regressions, one for each mechanism, where the dependent variable is the average payoff difference of subjects across phases, and the independent variables are interaction terms across an indicator of whether a subject has priority and an indicator of whether she is allowed to chat. The default situation is a subject with priority who is allowed to chat.

As Table 12.7 indicates, the impact of priority on the payoff differences varies across mechanisms. Among subjects who are allowed to chat in the Boston 16 mechanism, the subjects without priority appear to experience a greater increase in their payoffs than those with priority. However, among subjects who are allowed to chat in the Gale–Shapley or the Boston 10 mechanism, there is no significant payoff difference between subjects who have priority and those who do not. Rather, in these two mechanisms, the chat has an impact when subjects have no priority and are isolated, in which case their payoffs decrease.

Table 12.7 *Payoff difference, chat, mechanism, and priority rights.*[a]

Variable	Boston 16 Specification 13 Coeff. (std err.)	Gale–Shapley Specification 14 Coeff. (std err.)	Boston 10 Specification 15 Coeff. (std err.)
Non-priority × Chat	2.1623*** (0.7248)	−0.4761 (0.6541)	−2.0551 (1.4560)
Non-priority × Iso.	0.0122 (0.8264)	−1.8594** (0.7305)	−2.6960* (1.5950)
Priority × Iso.	−0.1207 (0.7248)	−0.6645 (0.6425)	0.0269 (1.4067)
Constant	−0.1421 (0.4584)	0.5032 (0.4137)	0.3247 (0.9209)

[a] Asterisks: * = significant at 10%, ** = significant at 5%, *** = significant at 1%.

This result may be of interest for policy makers since, if we consider subjects without priority (or with priority in substandard schools) to basically be those who inhabit lower-income areas, it would appear that, if the city they lived in used the Gale–Shapley mechanism, they would benefit from being included in a better social network with others who could discuss the strategic elements of the mechanism they were using or a consumer education program that could advise them on what to do.

12.3.5   The Content of Chat

Up until now we have investigated the impact of advice on behavior in school matching mechanisms. What we have not looked at, however, is the content of that advice: What did subjects say to each other? This is what we turn our attention to now.

To do our analysis, we recorded all the messages exchanged among subjects during chat periods, and had two independent research assistants code the records. There were nine different categories that the chat text could be classified by. More precisely, a statement was coded with a T (truthful) if it mentioned revealing one's truthful preference and a T– if it urged against doing so. Likewise, a message was coded as S (strategic) if it encouraged listing one's second-best object first, and S– if the statement urged against being strategic. An I (irrational) statement suggested an irrational submission, such as placing one's third-best first, and an I–T statement warned against doing so. If a statement mentioned the lottery, it was coded as L, and if a statement mentioned the scarcity of the objects in comparison to the possible demand, it was coded as SC. Finally, a statement was coded with a C if subjects simply mentioned that chat might have an impact on the results. We allowed chat statements to be categorized by as many of the nine categories as was appropriate. When a subject repeated the same opinion several times, we counted every statement.

After our two research assistants coded each statement with as many labels as they saw fit, their codings were given to a third assistant, the judge, who compared them and, when they were in conflict, the judge decided which codings were best. There are surprisingly few conflicts between the coders.

Table 12.8 presents the percentage of each message type sent by those subjects who chat and those who are isolated across mechanisms. We find that, in the Boston 16 mechanism, subjects discuss strategic preference submission almost twice as often as truthful preference rankings. For example, chat statements coded as S and T– constitute 45.8% of the meaningful chat statements, while those coded as T and S– constitute only 26.0%. (Here we lump S and T– (T and S–) together, since an S– statement warning against being strategic is almost equivalent to suggesting that a subject report truthfully, and the same is true for T– and S.) For the isolated subjects, these percentages are 41.6% and 22.0%, respectively. This may explain why subjects in the Boston 16 mechanism chose not to change their

Table 12.8 *Chat records: message type.*

	Boston 16		Gale–Shapley		Boston 10	
	Chat	Isolated	Chat	Isolated	Chat	Isolated
T	0.2418	0.1883	0.2915	0.2184	0.2606	0.2091
T–	0.0293	0.0779	0.0404	0.0825	0.0493	0.0455
S	0.4286	0.3377	0.3184	0.2573	0.2113	0.1727
S–	0.0183	0.0325	0.0224	0.0388	0.0352	0.0545
I	0.0440	0.0584	0.0717	0.0631	0.1197	0.1182
I–	0.0110	0.0260	0.0224	0.0728	0.0141	0.0455
SC	0.0769	0.0909	0.0538	0.1359	0.0423	0.2000
L	0.0879	0.1753	0.1525	0.1311	0.2535	0.1545
C	0.0623	0.0130	0.0269	0.0000	0.0141	0.0000

strategies especially when they listed their second-best objects first in phase 1, since chat served to reinforce the efficacy of submitting strategically. In contrast, subjects who chat in the Gale–Shapley mechanism talk about truthful and strategic preference submission with almost equal frequency (31.8% and 35.9%, respectively), while in the Boston 10 mechanism these percentages are 29.6% and 26.0%, respectively.

The differences between our two baseline mechanisms are accentuated when we examine chat statements among subjects who communicate through homogeneous, heterogeneous, and isolated subnetworks. For example, when subjects using the Gale–Shapley mechanism talk through homogeneous subnetworks, they discuss truth-telling (strategic) preference ranking 34.2% (26.7%) of the time, while, when they talk to others via a heterogeneous subnetwork, they discuss truth-telling (strategic preferences) 23.3% (37.9%) of the time. Finally, it is worthy of note that even when we pool all chat massages across all mechanisms and all types of subjects, we find that subjects who chat, whether in a homogeneous or heterogeneous subnetwork, chat in a different manner than those who are isolated. (The *p*-values are 0.00 for the comparison between both the heterogeneous and homogeneous subnetworks and the isolated subnetworks.)

What a subject chats about may, of course, depend on whether she has priority or not. We find that for each of our three mechanisms there is a significant difference in the distribution of chat messages sent by subjects with and without priority. These differences vary across mechanisms, as we see in Figure 12.3.[20]

A few more aspects of these distributions are of interest. First, note that subjects appear more concerned about the possibility of facing the lottery in the Gale–Shapley and Boston 10 mechanisms than in the Boston 16 mechanism. This is particularly true in the Boston 10 mechanism, where about 21.3% (20.6%) of the messages of subjects who chat concern the lottery for subjects with (without) priority.[21] Also, when scarcity is mentioned, it is more likely to be mentioned by subjects without priority, since they are the ones who cannot guarantee themselves an object by acting strategically and hence have to worry about being frozen out of a preferred item. The dramatic difference across priority and non-priority subjects in their reference to irrational strategies, i.e., submitting one's least-preferred object first, is puzzling but consistently higher for subjects without priority than those with it. For example, while in the Boston 16 mechanism 7.7% of the messages of non-priority subjects mention irrational preferences, only 3.1% of the messages of subjects with priority do so. For the Gale–Shapley and the Boston 10 mechanisms, the percentages are 1.9% versus 14.6% and 4.0% versus 23.5%,

---

[20] The p-values associated with the χ^2 tests under the null hypothesis that there are no differences in the distribution of chat statements across our nine categories for subjects with and without priority are 0.023, 0.000, and 0.000 for the Boston 16, Gale–Shapley, and Boston 10 mechanisms, respectively.

[21] Remember that there are 12 subjects who have object C as their first choice and only four such objects available. Hence, if many subjects were to report truthfully, there would be a great scarcity of object C and many subjects would face a lottery since no subjects have priority for that object. This finding may explain why the fraction of subjects telling the truth significantly decreases after chat in the Boston 10 mechanism.

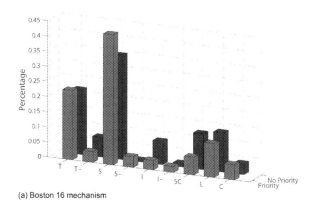

(a) Boston 16 mechanism

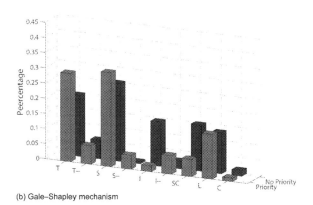

(b) Gale–Shapley mechanism

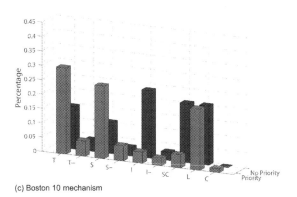

(c) Boston 10 mechanism

FIGURE 12.3 Content of chat messages.

respectively. It is hard to explain the use of irrational strategies and the differential reference to them by subjects with and without priority. One explanation is that, since subjects without priority could not guarantee themselves their second-best objects by being strategic, they entertained exotic (and irrational) strategies.

Another relevant question is whether the messages that people send are related to the strategies that they used in phase 1. In other words, do people who submitted truthfully in phase 1 tend to suggest truth-telling and do those submitted strategic preferences suggest that strategy to their cohorts? The answer is yes, as Figure 12.4 suggests.

As we see in Figure 12.4, while the convention among chatters seems to be to offer advice that is identical to the strategy they just used, this is by no means the only advice offered. For example, in the Gale–Shapley mechanism, among those subjects who reported truthfully in phase 1, almost 46% of the chat statements were coded as suggesting truth-telling in phase 2. This rises to almost 50% if one adds the advice S–, which is warning against being strategic. The next largest category is for statements that urge strategic play in phase 2 (15.8%). After these two categories, the rest of the advice is scattered over the remaining categories, including a remarkable 12.9% urging the submission of the irrational strategies.[22] Similar results are found for those who played strategically in phase 1, where, in the Gale–Shapley mechanism, 34.4% suggest using that strategy in phase 2. Comparable results are found for the other treatments where the Boston mechanisms are used.

Finally, one might ask what the rationale is that subjects use when urging the various strategies they do. For example, do those who suggest truth-telling in the Gale–Shapley mechanism do so because they have discovered it is a dominating strategy? Do subjects urging playing in a strategic manner understand that if one has priority then

---

[22] Remember, these percentages are calculated based upon chatting statements that fall into these categories. It is possible that one person may have uttered several of these statements, so this is not equivalent to saying that, of the subjects who submitted truthfully in phase 1, x% urged truth-telling in phase 2.

Figure 12.4: Messages Condition on Strategies used in Phase 1

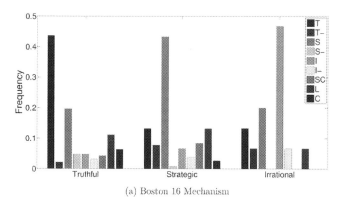

(a) Boston 16 Mechanism

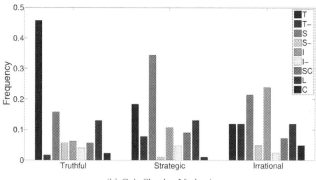

(b) Gale-Shapley Mechanism

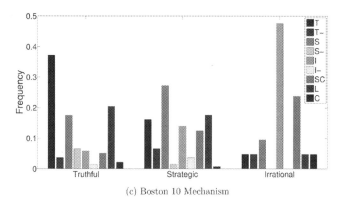

(c) Boston 10 Mechanism

FIGURE 12.4 Messages condition on strategies used in phase 1.

submitting one's second choice first guarantees getting one's second choice? The answer is basically that only a few subjects who urge truth-telling do so because it is dominant. Across all mechanisms, the rationale for being honest seems to be one of striving to get one's first-best choice despite the risks involved (this is especially true in the Boston 10 mechanism), while playing strategically is more associated with settling for one's second choice or playing it safe. This fact should not imply that subjects did not understand the mechanisms: they offer substantial evidence that many of them do. But despite this fact their strategies appear to be influenced by their desire to get their first-best objects or to settle for their second-best objects.

12.4   CONCLUSION

This chapter has commented on the role of advice between people engaged in a man-made game in the form of a school matching mechanism. As we have said before, examining the performance of economic mechanisms should be done in the environment in which they are used in the real world in addition to the way they exist in theory. Mechanisms may perform well when tested using the game form defined by theory, only to falter when exported to the real world because of the way they are implemented there. If the performance of mechanisms differs when placed in a real-world context (i.e., one where advice exists), then designers need to take this into account.

In our experiment we have found a number of results relevant to mechanism design. First, chatting increases the likelihood that subjects will change their submitted preferences compared to those subjects who are isolated and do not chat. Second, chatting leads to an increase in the fraction of stable outcomes, which is important from a policy point of view. With respect to welfare, chatting appears to influence welfare differently for subjects with and without priority rights. Though there is little welfare change among subjects with priority rights between phases, chatting does significantly change the welfare of those without priority rights. Furthermore, our results show that, among subjects who chat, those chatting with others of a different type appear to increase their payoffs between phases more than those chatting with others like themselves. Combined with the result that subjects who chat with others like themselves tend to change their submitted preference rankings more between phases, this suggests that some of those preference changes are not beneficial. (Sometimes chat is beneficial if it persuades people not to change their already beneficial strategies.)

In terms of policy, our results indicate that the advice received through chatting via social networks can influence a subject's behavior and also the performance of the mechanism used. It is of more interest that being isolated when using the Gale–Shapley mechanism leads to a decrease in average payoffs when that isolation is combined with a lack of priority. As we noted before, this result may be of interest for policy makers since, if we consider subjects without priority (or with priority in substandard schools) to basically be those who inhabit lower-income areas, it would appear that, if the city they lived in used the Gale–Shapley mechanism, they would benefit from being included in a better social network with others who could discuss the strategic elements of the mechanism they were using or a consumer education program that could advise them on what to do.

Our conclusions would have been very different if we found that chatting was deleterious to welfare since, in that case, the problem for mechanism designers would have been to design chat-inclusive (or chat-combatting) designs or designs that anticipate the impact of advice. The fact that chat is welfare-increasing suggests that the original design can be left intact and chat encouraged (perhaps people will convince others that submitting truthful preferences in the Gale–Shapley mechanism is the right thing to do). While this seems correct here, in our next chapter we see just the opposite, since intergenerational advice or chat has dramatic negative effects for truth-telling in the Gale–Shapley mechanism.

12.5 APPENDIX: STATED PREFERENCES AND WELFARE

Table 12.9 *Stated preference (%) in all three mechanisms: Phase 1.*

	Truthful						Strategic						Irrational					
	Boston 16	G-S	Boston 10	p-value G-S vs Boston 16	Boston 16 vs 10	G-S vs Boston 10	Boston 16	G-S	Boston 10	p-value G-S vs Boston 16	Boston 16 vs 10	G-S vs Boston 10	Boston 16	G-S	Boston 10	p-value G-S vs Boston 16	Boston 16 vs 10	G-S vs Boston 10
All	37.00	39.51	52.38	0.6040	0.0107	0.0324	58.00	53.66	38.10	0.3803	0.0009	0.0009	5.00	6.83	9.52	0.4361	0.1680	0.4260
Type 1	35.00	31.71	47.62	0.7570	0.3568	0.2416	65.00	58.54	52.38	0.5552	0.3568	0.6537	0.00	9.76	0.00	0.0440	NA	0.0440
Type 2	40.00	48.78	61.90	0.4328	0.1097	0.3342	60.00	51.22	38.10	0.4328	0.1097	0.3342	0.00	0.00	0.00	NA	NA	NA
Type 3	47.50	34.15	66.67	0.2268	0.1548	0.0160	52.00	60.98	33.33	0.4478	0.1548	0.0404	0.00	4.88	0.00	0.1598	NA	0.1598
Type 4	27.50	48.78	57.14	0.0496	0.0305	0.5420	60.00	43.90	14.29	0.1509	0.0001	0.0100	12.50	7.32	28.57	0.4407	0.1687	0.0619
Type 5	35.00	34.15	28.57	0.9366	0.6143	0.6599	52.50	53.66	52.38	0.9181	0.9931	0.9260	12.50	12.20	19.05	0.9676	0.5273	0.5059
Priority	40.83	38.21	58.73	0.6775	0.0218	0.0083	59.17	58.91	41.27	0.7229	0.0218	0.0442	0.00	4.88	0.00	0.0137	N/A	0.0137
Non-Priority	31.25	41.46	42.86	0.1786	0.2169	0.8834	56.25	48.78	33.33	0.3442	0.0150	0.0975	12.50	9.76	23.81	0.5818	10.425	0.0630

Table 12.10 *Outcome distributions in all three mechanisms: phase 1 (%).*

	Truthful			Strategic			Irrational			% H_0 not rejected by a χ^2 test Boston 16 vs. GS Boston 16 vs. 10 GS vs. Boston 10		
	First-best	Second-best	Third-best	First-best	Second-best	Third-best	First-best	Second-best	Third-best			
All	23.08	63.83	13.09	22.57	65.63	11.79	31.10	48.09	20.80	0.9928	0.1360	0.0612
Type 1	18.93	77.16	3.91	16.84	73.43	9.73	18.25	64.72	17.04	0.9452	0.6028	0.9624
Type 2	19.38	72.80	7.81	27.40	72.60	0.00	25.13	48.61	26.26	0.6348	0.3628	0.0032
Type 3	27.86	71.33	0.81	16.89	80.86	2.25	25.47	74.53	0.00	0.8432	0.9712	0.9140
Type 4	22.90	70.56	6.54	27.86	67.28	4.86	57.15	32.15	10.70	0.9904	0.0044	0.1140
Type 5	26.33	27.29	46.38	23.87	33.99	42.13	29.53	20.45	50.02	0.9732	0.9760	0.9132

REFERENCES

Braun, S., Dwenger, N., Kübler, D. and Westkamp, A. (2014). Implementing quotas in university admissions: An experimental analysis. *Games and Economic Behavior*, 85(3), 232–251.

Cooper, D. J. and Kagel, J. H. (2016). A failure to communicate: An experimental investigation of the effects of advice on strategic play. *European Economic Review*, 82(3), 24–45.

Ding, T. and Schotter, A. (2017). Matching and chatting: An experimental study of the impact of network communication on school-matching mechanisms. *Games and Economic Behavior*, 103(3), 94–115.

Dubins, L. E. and Freedman, D. A. (1981). Machiavelli and the Gale–Shapley algorithm. *American Mathematical Monthly*, 88(7), 485–494.

Fischbacher, U. (2007). z-Tree: Zurich toolbox for ready-made economic experiments. *Experimental Economics*, 10(2), 171–178.

Guillen, P. and Hakimov, R. (2014). Monkey see, monkey do: Truth-telling in matching algorithms and the manipulation of others. *Working Paper*.

Guillen, P. and Hing, A. (2014). Lying through their teeth: Third party advice and truth telling in a strategy proof mechanism. *European Economic Review*, 70(3), 178–185.

Holt, C. A. and Laury, S. K. (2002). Risk aversion and incentive effects. *American Economic Review*, 92(5), 1644–1655.

Klijn, F., Pais, J. and Vorsatz, M. (2013). Preference intensities and risk aversion in school choice: A laboratory experiment. *Experimental Economics*, 16(1), 1–22.

Li, P. (2021). School choice with multiple advice sources: An experimental study. *Mimeo*, New York University.

Pathak, P. A. (2011). The mechanism design approach to student assignment. *Annual Review Economics*, 3(1), 513–536.

Rick, S. and Weber, R. A. (2010). Meaningful learning and transfer of learning in games played repeatedly without feedback. *Games and Economic Behavior*, 68(2), 716–730.

Roth, A. E. (1982). The economics of matching: Stability and incentives. *Mathematics of Operations Research*, 7(4), 617–628.

13 School Matching and Learning under the Influence of Intergenerational Advice

In this chapter we return to intergenerational games and apply them to the school matching mechanisms we explored in Chapter 12.[1] As you recall, these mechanisms are designed to match students with schools and do so by having parents enter rankings over schools for their children into a computer algorithm that matches the students with the school. The strategic question for parents is what preferences to submit.

Our focus here is very different from that in Chapter 12, however. First, we look at what we called "vertical" advice or advice from one generation of players to their successors. This is in contrast to the "horizontal" advice used in Chapter 12 where contemporaneous players exchange advice amongst themselves.

Second, this chapter introduces a comparison across treatments that we think is very important to our work here. More precisely, in most experimental work in economics, the experimentalist takes her experiment to the lab and, in order to allow her subjects to learn the underlying problem of the experiment (or the underlying theory), she repeats the experiment numerous times looking for behavior to ultimately converge as people learn and, hopefully, converge to the equilibrium behavior predicted by the theory. This is standard stuff. In these papers, the first few periods are many times dismissed as a learning stage, while the last few periods are treated as a learning-inclusive sample encapsulating all that subjects have learned during their repeated play.

---

[1] This chapter is based on Ding and Schotter (2019).

In this chapter we take a different approach. In keeping with our intergenerational approach, we ask not whether subjects can learn when repeating a recurrent stage game but rather can they learn when the same game is repeated by sets of non-overlapping intergenerational players who engage in the game once and pass on advice to their successor. Put differently, we ask: Is intergenerational social learning superior or inferior to the type of reinforcement, belief, or adaptive learning so often used in theory and in the lab?

We do all of this in the context of the same matching problem we examined in Chapter 12. Here, however, there is no chatting across social networks but rather chatting over time between predecessors and successors. As it turns out, the school matching problem exactly fits our intergenerational-game framework, since in each period a new generation of players (parents) arrive to engage in the school matching problem, interact in it for one period, and then are replaced by a new generation to whom they offer advice. So if learning occurs here, it is the type of intergenerational social learning we have examined before and not the typical reinforcement or adaptive learning so often used in the lab. Our design allows us to directly compare these two types of learning.

There is also a policy lesson in this chapter for mechanism designers. The lesson is simple. When a mechanism designer designs a mechanism that can be used to match students with schools, allocate goods via auction, manage contributions to a public good, etc., it is not enough to simply write down the rules of the mechanism, prove that they are incentive-compatible or lead to stable outcomes, pat oneself on the back, and walk away. The reason is that, once the mechanism is used, it takes on a life of its own as advice passed on from generation to generation may steer people away from the mechanism's equilibrium. For example, in the Gale–Shapley mechanism, subjects are supposed to submit their true preferences since that is a weakly dominant strategy – no matter what the other people do, they can do no better than submitting truthful preferences. However, it has been shown repeatedly that people do not do that, in part because a convention is created where subjects think they can game the mechanism and advise their successors to try to do so as well. Since the counterfactual of what their outcome would have been if they had reported truthfully is not accessible to them, they have no way of knowing that they could have done better and, if their current outcome is acceptable to them, they will advise others to do as they have done. For example, if by strategizing I get my second-best alternative in a match, an alternative that I am pretty happy with, and do not see any evidence that I could have received my first-best if I had reported my preferences truthfully, then I may very well tell my successor to do as I did, since it turned out pretty well for me.

To illustrate this point, Rees-Jones (2018) surveyed 558 graduating medical students who participated in the 2012 US medical residence match, a strategy-proof mechanism, and 17% of them misrepresented their preferences, even though the matching mechanism has been in practice for a decade and the participants are well educated. Similarly, Hassidim et al. (2017) examined the 2014 and 2015 Israeli Psychology Master's Match and also found that a significant fraction of applicants misrepresented their preferences in the applicant-proposing Gale–Shapley deferred-acceptance mechanism. This defection from truth-telling is ubiquitous despite the advice participants get from the mechanism organizers telling them that truth-telling is what they should do. Clearly, there is a folk wisdom passed down from generation to generation suggesting dissembling and corrective action needs to be taken to rectify the misperceptions that are passed down from generation to generation.[2]

---

[2] Several recent experiments have examined how public advice and factual information influence the strategies that subjects choose in school choice programs. Braun et al. (2014) provide strategic coaching before subjects submit their preferences, and find that subjects are prone to accept advice. Guillen and Hing (2014), in contrast, find that subjects are less likely to tell the truth in the top trading cycles mechanism (where truth-telling is a weakly dominant strategy) when they receive public advice, regardless of whether they are advised to tell the truth or to be strategic. Bo and Hakimov (2020) test an iterative Gale–Shapley mechanism in which subjects are informed of the tentative acceptance decisions or the tentative cutoff values for acceptance in schools at each round, and find that subjects are more likely to tell the truth when they learn the tentative decisions between rounds. Zhu (2015)

Given this fact it is apparent that the job of the mechanism designer is not over when the mechanism is designed. The behavior of people using it must be monitored consistently since, in the game played in the real world, advice is part of the strategy set of people and poor advice can be responsible for poor mechanism performance.

To make the comparison between repeated and intergenerational play, we run two school matching mechanisms, the Gale–Shapley deferred-acceptance mechanism and the Boston mechanism, using two different treatments. In one treatment, the repeated treatment, groups of five subjects engage in a matching mechanism where three different types of objects are being allocated and do so for 20 rounds with random matching after each round. In other words, subjects are allowed to repeat playing with the mechanism 20 times and presumably are able to learn how best to behave. In a second treatment, the own-advice intergenerational treatment run with different subjects, 20 independent generations of subjects engage in the matching mechanism once and only once but pass on advice to their successors after each generation as to how to behave. In this treatment, the only source of learning is social learning via intergenerational advice. (Each generation has incentives to pass on payoff-maximizing advice since each subject in a generation gets a payoff equal to what she earns during her lifetime plus half of what her successor earns.)[3]

We find that, when the Gale–Shapley mechanism is used, the evolution of behavior is very different when we compare the time path of play across our treatments. For example, when the same subjects

---

is probably the paper closest to ours in that she also studies "peer-to-peer advice"; however, the advice in her treatments is given by experienced subjects who have repeatedly participated in the mechanism for 15 rounds.

[3] Finally, as a robustness check, we add another intergenerational treatment, the multiple-advice intergenerational treatment, in which we allow each subject to give two pieces of advice, one to a subject of her own type in the next generation and one to a subject of a randomly chosen other type. This is done to move the experiment closer to reality where people get a variety of opinions about what they should do from people with a variety of preferences. While receiving disparate advice may be confusing, subjects may also find it informative to learn more opinions and thereby better assess what is the best strategy for themselves.

repeatedly play in the Gale–Shapley mechanism (a mechanism where truth-telling is a dominant strategy), the fraction of subjects who report their truthful preferences increases monotonically over time so that in the last five rounds 77.14% of subjects report the truth compared to 64.57% in the first five rounds. Surprisingly, the opposite is true in our own-advice intergenerational Gale–Shapley treatment, where the fraction of subjects telling the truth falls from 72.00% in the first five rounds to 44.00% in the last five rounds.

When the Boston mechanism is used, there exists no statistically significant difference between our repeated and own-advice intergenerational treatments. The fraction of subjects reporting the truth in the first five rounds (generations) are 56.00% and 48.00% in the repeated and own-advice intergenerational treatments, respectively, while in the last five rounds (generations) those percentages are 62.00% and 72.00%, respectively. The fractions of truth-telling increase in both the treatments, and there is no statistically significant divergence in behavior across these treatments.

The lesson learned here is similar to that of Chapter 12, where advice was passed on between contemporaneous subjects via social networks (horizontally) rather than intergenerationally (vertically), and is that, when one tries to test the performance of a matching (or other) mechanism, one must be careful to test it in an environment similar to the one where the mechanism functions in the real world rather than the one envisioned by theory. After a mechanism is used in the real world, participants in the mechanism develop a sense of conventional play and that play gets transmitted across generations. The object of interest is the convention created, which may be very different from what subjects learn by themselves after enough experience. Our results, therefore, run counter to the idea that more experience with an incentive-compatible mechanism should lead to higher levels of truthful revelation. As we show here, when experience is gained via intergenerational advice, this may not be the case.[4]

---

[4] Our experiment is definitely not the first experiment to report that school matching mechanisms may not perform as desired. In fact, Chen and Sonmez (2006)

Finally, as you may notice, this is one of the few instances in this book where advice has deleterious consequences. In almost all of our previous chapters, advice guided behavior in a more "rational" direction. Here, it leads subjects to deviate from dominant strategies.

The question that remains, and which will attract a large amount of our attention in this chapter, is why are the results so different. Why is intergenerational social learning less efficient than reinforcement learning? This is the puzzle we explore here.

13.1   EXPERIMENTAL DESIGN

Because most of the elements of our experiment here are identical to those in the experiment discussed in Chapter 12, we will not repeat all of those details again but refer the reader to Chapter 12 to refresh their memory.[5, 6] For example, in our experiment here, we will again compare performance in the Boston 16 and Gale–Shapley mechanisms whose descriptions were offered in Chapter 12. In addition, in any experimental session, we recruit 20 subjects and when they arrive in the lab we randomly allocate them to groups of five and designate subjects as type 1, type 2, type 3, type 4, and type 5. Within each group there are five objects grouped into three types, which are called object A, object B, and object C. In total there are two units of object A, two units of object B, and one unit of object C.[7]

The preferences induced over objects are the same as those used in Chapter 12, where subjects would receive 24 ECU if they

demonstrate that subjects may fail to report truthfully even in textbook many-to-one matching models. When these conventional models are complicated to include such things as limiting the number of schools that can be listed, coarse school priorities, etc., the lack of truth-telling may be exacerbated.

[5] For a full set of instructions see Ding and Schotter (2019).

[6] All our experiments were conducted in the experimental laboratory of the Center for Experimental Social Science at New York University. Three-hundred and seventy-five students were recruited from the general undergraduate population of the university using the CESS recruitment software. The experiment was programmed using the z-tree programming software (Fischbacher, 2007). The typical experiment lasted about an hour, with average earnings of $24.08. Subjects were paid in an experimental currency called Experimental Currency Units (ECUs) and these units were converted into US dollars at a rate specified in the instructions.

[7] Some sessions have fewer subjects due to lack of attendance.

Table 13.1 *Student preferences.*

Type	1	2	3	4	5
First preferred	C	C	C	A	A
Second preferred	A	A	B	B	C
Third preferred	B	B	A	C	B

are allocated their first-best object, 16 ECU if they receive their second-best object, and 4 ECU if they receive their third-best object. Table 13.1 presents the full ordinal preference matrix of our subject types.

Again, as in Chapter 12, in addition to their induced preferences, each subject is endowed with a priority in the allocation of certain objects. In all treatments, it is common knowledge that types 1 and 2 are given priority for object A, while type 3 is given priority for object B, and types 4 and 5 are not given priority for any objects. As we know, these priorities come into effect when there is more than one subject vying for one existing object. In such cases, the subject with priority for that object is allocated it. When the number of subjects of equal priority applying for an object is greater than the number of objects available, the algorithm employs a lottery to break ties.[8]

Subjects are told their own types and matching payoffs for each object as well as a priority table, but they do not know the types or the object payoffs of any subjects other than themselves. They are then required to state their rankings over objects. Based on the information subjects provide, one of the matching algorithms (either the Boston or the Gale–Shapley mechanism) determines the allocation outcome. Each subject is matched to one and only one object.

13.1.1   Treatments

In our study, we have four treatments, which differ according to whether the subjects use the Boston or the Gale–Shapley deferred-acceptance mechanisms and by whether they are allowed to repeat

---

[8] In our experiment we use a single lottery instead of object-specific lotteries to break ties.

the experiment 20 times, with random matching between each round, or whether they can perform the experiment only once and then pass on advice to subjects who replace them in the mechanism.[9]

More precisely, for each mechanism we run two treatments, which we call the repeated and the own-advice intergenerational treatments. In the repeated treatment, subjects repeatedly engage in the matching mechanisms 20 times, with random matching of subjects after each round. Subjects retain their types in each round. At the end of the experiment, one of the 20 rounds is drawn for payment. In the own-advice intergenerational treatments, after subjects are allocated into groups of five and given a type, each group is randomly assigned a number from 1 to 4. Subjects in group 1 will play the matching game first. After they finish, they are replaced by subjects of their own types in group 2 (their successors), who then engage in an identical decision problem among themselves. Similarly, after the participation of group 2 subjects is over, they will be replaced by group 3, and group 3 will be replaced by group 4. Group 4 subjects will be replaced by group 5 subjects, but since we only recruit 20 subjects, their successors will be the first group in the next experimental session. Hence, the experiment extends beyond the session being run.

After a subject is done with her part in the experiment and knows the outcome of her own match, she is asked to give advice to a subject in the next generation. Each subject has a successor of her own type, so subjects of type 1 give advice to successors of type 1, and the same for types 2 to 5. The advice given is of two forms. First, a subject suggests a ranking of objects that her successor should state first, second, and third. In addition, she is allowed to write a free-form message to explain the rationale behind this suggestion. Hence, except for the first generation, each generation is presented with advice before they enter their preference rankings. The payoff of a subject is equal to the payoff she receives for her match plus

---

[9] We also administered a Holt–Laury risk aversion test (Holt and Laury, 2002) to our subjects but do not use its results for any of our analysis since it is not of use in explaining our results.

Table 13.2 *Experimental design.*

Treatment	Learning mode	Mechanism	No. of rounds (gen.)	No. of sessions	No. of subjects
1	Repeated	Boston	20	2	40
2	Intergen. (own-advice)	Boston	20	6	100
3	Repeated	G-S	20	2	35
4	Intergen. (own-advice)	G-S	20	8	100
Total				18	275

an amount equal to half of the payoff of her successor. This payoff structure incentivizes subjects to offer payoff-maximizing advice.

When all four groups in a session are done, each is paid for their participation, with the last group told that they will receive the second portion of their payoffs after the next session is run and we know the payoff of each subject's successor. When the 20th generation is done, since there are no successors, all subjects are told that there will not be another session run and each is given a payoff equal to half of the mean payoff of the 20th generation. Note that in this design we generate one time series of length 20 with each generation consisting of five subjects playing the matching game, so that in total there are 100 subjects engaging in each intergenerational treatment.

Table 13.2 describes our experimental design.

13.2   RESULTS

Let us start by presenting our main results in the repeated and own-advice intergenerational experiments, and then turn our attention to offering an explanation.

13.2.1   Truth-Telling and Efficiency

Matching mechanisms are typically designed to implement stable matches or, as described in Chapter 12, matches that, in the case of school matching, leave no student in a position of being allocated to a school for which there is another school she would prefer, has priority for, and which was allocated to another student without priority. Such stable matches are facilitated when students reveal their true preferences for schools. The Gale–Shapley mechanism elicits truthful revelation as a weakly dominant strategy and guarantees stable matches, but not efficient matches. In fact, there exists no mechanism that is simultaneously truthful revealing (or strategy proof) and leads to stable and efficient outcomes. One has to trade these features off.

The main result of our experiment is that there is a qualitative and quantitative difference in the way subjects behave in our intergenerational and repeated treatments when the Gale–Shapley mechanism is used, but not so when our subjects use the Boston mechanism. Over time, subjects in our intergenerational treatments deviate further and further from truth-telling while those in our repeated treatments do the opposite. This is the stylized fact that we will concentrate on in the remainder of this chapter and try to explain why this happens. Ironically, despite their failure to report truthful preferences, subjects in our own-advice intergenerational Gale–Shapley treatment capture a higher percentage of the first-best allocation payoffs in the last five generations than do subjects in any of the other treatments.[10]

One reaction to these results is to conclude that our truth-telling results are not of concern since efficiencies are highest in the own-advice intergenerational Gale–Shapley treatment where truthful revelation is the lowest. This conclusion is not totally well founded, however. First, strategy-proofness is an important property valued by mechanism designers because they believe it "levels the playing field" in the sense that it does not penalize less-educated parents for not strategizing or being as strategically sophisticated as their wealthier and better-educated competitors.[11]

---

[10] This is true because, while truth-telling bolsters stability, some lying is needed for efficiency.

[11] In public hearings, Boston school officials emphasized: "a strategy-proof algorithm 'levels the playing field' by diminishing the harm done to parents who do not strategize or do not strategize well. [...] [T]he need to strategize provides an advantage to families who have the time, resources, and knowledge to conduct the necessary research" (Pathak, 2017).

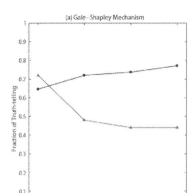 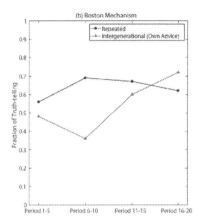

FIGURE 13.1 Truth-telling in Gale–Shapley and Boston mechanisms.

Second, as we will see, behavior in our intergenerational treatments is more variable than in our repeated treatments. As a result, despite the high efficiency observed in this experiment, in general these high efficiencies may not be reliable because of the heightened volatility of behavior.

Figure 13.1(a) shows the fraction of subjects reporting truthful preferences over the 20 rounds (generations) of the repeated and own-advice intergenerational Gale–Shapley treatments, while Figure 13.1(b) shows the same fractions for the Boston treatments. Here rounds (generations) are placed on the horizontal axis and the fraction of subjects submitting truthful preferences on the vertical axis. Rounds or generations are aggregated into four bins aggregating behavior in rounds (generations) 1–5, 6–10, 11–15, and 16–20.[12]

What is striking is how the fraction of subjects who report the truth in the own-advice intergenerational Gale–Shapley treatment

---

[12] Note that, while in our repeated game experiments we aggregate over groups of five subjects every five rounds, in our intergenerational experiments, since we only have one time series, we aggregate over five different generations each containing five subjects.

monotonically decreases from the first five to the last five generations, while it monotonically increases in the repeated Gale–Shapley treatment. More precisely, while the fraction of subjects reporting truthful preferences in the repeated Gale–Shapley treatment increases from 0.65 to 0.77 over the 20 rounds of the experiment, the fraction reporting truthful preferences in the own-advice intergenerational Gale–Shapley treatment decreases from 0.72 to 0.44. The difference between the fraction of subjects who report truthfully across the last five rounds and generations of the repeated and own-advice intergenerational Gale–Shapley mechanisms is significant (the p-value reported by a Pearson's chi-square test is 0.000).

No such difference exists when we compare behavior in the 20-round repeated and 20-generation own-advice intergenerational Boston treatments. While truth-telling increases over the 20 rounds (generations) from 0.56 to 0.62 in the repeated Boston treatment and from 0.48 to 0.72 in the own-advice intergenerational Boston treatment, there is no difference between the fraction of subjects who report truthfully across the last five rounds and generations of these treatments (the p-value reported by a Pearson's chi-square test is 0.329).

To evaluate the efficiency of mechanisms, we calculate the fraction of the available surplus (i.e., the first-best payoff sum) that is captured by subjects in each market. Figure 13.2(a) describes the efficiency captured by our Gale–Shapley treatments over time, while Figure 13.2(b) presents the efficiency for the Boston treatments. One immediately obvious feature of Figure 13.2(a) is that, over time, the efficiency of our own-advice intergenerational Gale–Shapley mechanism approaches 96.67%, which is significantly higher than the 86.67% efficiency attained by the repeated Gale–Shapley mechanism and the 86.67% and 87.40% captured in the own-advice intergenerational and repeated Boston treatments (the p-values reported by Wilcoxon rank-sum tests are 0.028, 0.040, and 0.046, respectively). In contrast, when the Boston mechanism is used, there is no significant difference between the repeated and own-advice intergenerational

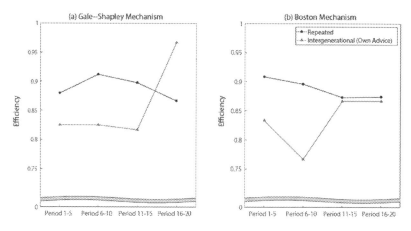

FIGURE 13.2 Efficiency in Gale–Shapley and Boston mechanisms.

treatments during the last five rounds (the p-value reported by a Wilcoxon rank sum test is 0.854).[13]

13.2.2 Volatility

Another stylized fact exhibited by our data is that behavior is more volatile in our intergenerational as opposed to our repeated treatments. Such volatility prevents behavior from converging to a stable convention of behavior which may involve truth-telling. To characterize volatility, we use the term "run", which is defined as a sequence of identical choice in a series of strategies. For example, denote strategies as follows: $1 = \{1-2-3\}$, $2 = \{1-3-2\}$, $3 = \{2-1-3\}$,

---

[13] While it may seem paradoxical that efficiencies can be higher when using the Gale–Shapley mechanism when subjects do not truthfully reveal, it has a simple explanation. Recall the preferences of subjects over objects or schools shown in Table 13.1. The first-best outcome is for type 5 and type 1 (or 2) to receive their first-best objects and for types 2 (or 1), 3, and 4 to receive their second-best objects. This is a Pareto-efficient and stable outcome. Note, however, if each subject truthfully reveals his preference, the first-best allocation may not be guaranteed because schools need to use a lottery to break indifference; there is some chance that types 3 or 4 may obtain their first-best object and then type 5 will be left with his third-best object. When types 3 and 4 do not tell their truthful preferences, such a tie-breaking lottery is not needed and the first-best outcome is then guaranteed. This is actually what happens more often during our intergenerational treatments where we get higher efficiencies. Finally, note that this example is not an artifact of the preferences we use in the experiment, since the problem of the tie-breaking procedure we point out is general (Erdil and Ergin, 2008).

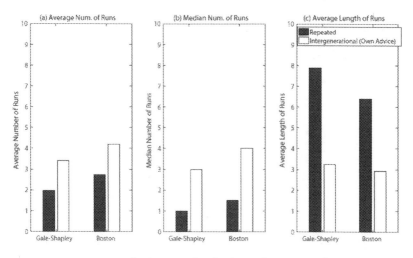

FIGURE 13.3 Volatility in Gale–Shapley and Boston mechanisms.

$4 = \{2-3-1\}$, $5 = \{3-1-2\}$, and $6 = \{3-2-1\}$. The numbers in the brackets are the subject's first, second and third choices. So strategy $1 = \{1-2-3\}$ is a truth-telling strategy, since a subject submits her first-best object first, her second-best object second, and her third-best object last. Strategy $3 = \{2-1-3\}$ is a strategy in which a subject places her second-best object first, then her first-best object, and finally her third-best object. A sequence of strategy choices $\{1, 1, 1, 2, 3, 3, 3, 4, 4, 4\}$ contains four runs of lengths 3, 1, 3, and 3, respectively, with an average run length of 2.5, while a sequence of strategy choices $\{1, 1, 1, 1, 1, 1, 1, 3, 3, 3\}$ contains only two runs of average length 5. We define behavior as less volatile if it contains fewer runs (or runs of longer duration) over the last 10-round (generation) history of the experiment. Given this definition, we can see the first sequence shown above is more volatile than the second.

Figure 13.3 presents, for each treatment, the average and median number of runs as well as the average run length of runs over the last 10 rounds (generations) of the experiment.[14] As we can see, no matter which matching mechanism is used, behavior appears to be more volatile in the own-advice intergenerational as opposed to the

[14] These averages are taken over all subjects of any type in a given round or generation.

repeated treatments. For example, when the Gale–Shapley treatment is used, there are fewer runs of strategies (and hence fewer changes in behavior) in the last 10 rounds of the repeated treatment (1.97 on average) than there are in the last 10 generations of the own-advice intergenerational treatment (3.4), with each run being of longer duration (7.89 rounds versus 3.23 generations). Similar results hold for the Boston mechanism, where there are, on average, 2.73 runs over the last 10 rounds of the repeated Boston mechanism treatment compared to 4.2 runs when we look at our own-advice intergenerational Boston treatment, with average lengths of 6.40 and 2.92, respectively. As a result, we are less likely to see convergence to one particular strategy (like truth-telling) in the own-advice intergenerational treatments than in the repeated treatments, as we conjectured.

13.2.3 Explaining Our Results: Social versus Experiential Learning

From our description above, it would appear that what needs to be explained is why truth-telling behavior diverges between the repeated and own-advice intergenerational Gale–Shapley treatments but not for the Boston treatments. In addition, the greater volatility in the intergenerational treatments needs to be explained. In this section we provide one explanation for our truth-telling results, which relies on a distinction between experiential and social learning.

We attribute this difference to the different types of learning that take place in our repeated and intergenerational treatments. As we will explain in more detail later, in the repeated treatments, learning, if it takes place, is experiential, while in the intergenerational treatments it is social. More precisely, in a repeated game treatment, even if there is random matching after each round, a subject might be expected to learn experientially and gather experience over time. This can be done by experimenting with different preference-reporting strategies and altering one's behavior given the reinforcement provided by the feedback of the mechanism. Such learning may take many forms and might be captured by a reinforcement (Erev and

Roth, 1998) or experience-weighted attraction type of model (Camerer and Ho, 1999).

In the intergenerational treatments, learning is primarily social, with each subject engaging in the experiment only once and making her choice on the basis of her understanding of the instructions and on the advice she receives. Given this lack of experience, behavior can be expected to be more volatile in our intergenerational treatments for three reasons: (1) there can be a natural randomness to behavior; (2) a current subject may receive a bad payoff and, as a result, suggest to her successor that she should deviate; or (3) a newly arrived subject consciously refuses to follow the advice she receives. Hence, for these reasons, we expect more stable behavior in the repeated treatments than in the intergenerational ones, and in the last 10 rounds (generations) it is more likely to observe a broader variety of behavior in the intergenerational treatments.

As is true in most experiments, we do not expect subjects to reach the equilibrium of the game they are playing in the first round of play. Rather, they learn it as the game is repeated. When the game they are playing has a dominant-strategy (truth-telling) equilibrium, we expect that, over time, our subjects would converge on such an equilibrium. In fact, if our subjects learn using a reinforcement learning rule, as we will assume later, then, as Beggs (2005) demonstrates, they should in fact converge to an all-truthful equilibrium. This is our expectation for the repeated Gale–Shapley treatment. However, when the matching game is played as an intergenerational game, we no longer expect such convergent behavior, since each subject plays the game only once and is forced to make a decision on the basis of her interpretation of the instructions and the advice she receives. In such an environment, the result of Beggs (2005) is no longer relevant and we should not expect the same type of convergence to truth-telling even when all subjects have dominant strategies. This is true because the lack of experience with the game and the stochasticity of advice and choice will, as we have seen, introduce a large volatility in behavior, which will disrupt convergence. As a result, the greater volatility in behavior in the own-advice intergenerational Gale–Shapley treatment goes a long way in explaining the divergence we observe across these treatments.

While our discussion above explains why we experience a divergence in behavior between our repeated and own-advice intergenerational Gale–Shapley treatments, it does not explain why we fail to observe this divergence when the Boston mechanism is used, since there the fractions of subjects reporting truthfully in the last five rounds (generations) of the repeated and own-advice intergenerational treatments are not significantly different. The answer here is simple. In our experiment all mechanisms are performed by providing the subjects with limited information. While they know their own preferences and priority, they are given very scant information about the constellation of preferences they face. As such, they are not given enough information to construct the (full information) equilibrium and hence, unlike the Gale–Shapley treatments, where truth-telling is dominant, it is not clear in the Boston treatments what strategy is beneficial. As a result, there is no particular advantage to playing the game repeatedly when the Boston mechanism is used. Despite the increased volatility of behavior in our own-advice intergenerational Boston treatment, the truth-telling behavior of our subjects across the two Boston mechanism treatments end up, over the last five rounds (generations), to be insignificantly different.

13.3   STRUCTURAL ESTIMATION AND SIMULATION

To support our explanation, we will present two learning models, one for the repeated treatment (where, as mentioned before, reinforcement learning is relevant) and one for the own-advice intergenerational treatment (where social learning is relevant), and estimate their parameters using maximum likelihood. Using these parameter estimates, we then simulate the behavior in each of our treatments and investigate whether the stylized facts generated by our experiment are replicated in our simulation. To economize on space, we refer the reader to Ding and Schotter (2019) for the results of our simulations.

Before we look at the results of our estimation exercise, let us pause to discuss the data that our experiment generates. In the repeated treatments we have a total of 75 subjects who function in groups of five over a 20-period horizon. There are eight groups of five subjects in the repeated Boston treatment and seven groups of five in the repeated Gale–Shapley treatment, generating a total of 800 and 700 observations, respectively. In the own-advice intergenerational treatments, we have 200 subjects (100 using each mechanism) who each engage in the experiment for one period and who collectively generate one 20-generation time series for the Boston and the Gale–Shapley mechanisms. Hence, our intergenerational results are based on one and only one time series each. Note, however, that the advice-giving, advice-following, and choice behavior that we observe in each intergenerational treatment is determined by 100 subjects making decisions in virtual isolation of each other (except for advice). To examine how robust our intergenerational time series results are, we use our behavioral data to estimate two structural learning models, one for the repeated and one for the own-advice intergenerational treatments, and use the parameter estimates to simulate what behavior would look like if we generate 10,000 time series for our 20-period experiment based on the estimated behavior generated in our structural estimation. We find that our experimental results are in line with our simulations but differ on some quantitative dimensions. We present only a sketch of our procedures in the discussion below. Those interested in more details should consult Ding and Schotter (2019).

We start with our repeated treatments, where we use a simple, off-the-shelf reinforcement learning model. Say the strategy space of subject i consists of m discrete choices. After reading the instructions of our experiment, subject i has an initial propensity to play her j-th pure strategy given by some non-negative attraction number $A_i^j(0)$. If she plays her k-th pure strategy at time t and receives a payoff $\pi_i(s_i^k, s_{-i})$, at time $t + 1$ her propensity to play strategy j is updated by setting:

$$A_i^j(t) = \begin{cases} \phi A_i^j(t-1) + R_i^j & \text{if } j = k, \\ \phi A_i^j(t-1) & \text{otherwise,} \end{cases} \qquad (13.1)$$

where $R_i^j = \pi_i(s_i^j, s_{-i}) - \min_{l,s_{-i}} \pi_i(s_i^l, s_{-i})$. Note that we normalize the reinforcement function by subtracting the minimal payoff.[15] The parameter ϕ is a decay rate which depreciates previous attractions. Choices are made using the exponential (logit) form to determine the probability of observing s_i^k at time t:

$$P_i^k(t) = \frac{e^{\lambda \cdot A_i^k(t-1)}}{\sum_{j=1}^m e^{\lambda \cdot A_i^j(t-1)}}, \qquad (13.2)$$

where the parameter λ measures sensitivity of subjects to attractions.

Estimating a comparable model for our own-advice intergenerational treatments is different because, rather than having one subject update her initial attractions over a 20-period horizon, we have subjects arriving sequentially, reading the instructions, receiving advice from their immediate predecessors, and then choosing. Hence, in the own-advice intergenerational model, subjects make their choices of strategies based on their initial attractions to strategies and the advice they receive.

To formalize this, let us say in the own-advice intergenerational game there are two processes: the decision-making process and the advice-giving process. First, consider the decision-making process. Assume subject i in generation t, after reading the instructions, is initially attracted to strategy s_i^j with a non-negative measure $A_i^j(0)$. If her predecessor suggests she choose strategy $a_i(t-1)$, her attraction to play s_i^j will be updated as follows:

$$A_i^j(t) = \begin{cases} A_i^j(0) + \omega & \text{if } a_i(t-1) = s_i^j, \\ A_i^j(0) & \text{otherwise.} \end{cases} \qquad (13.3)$$

In other words, since subjects in our intergenerational experiments have no experience, their initial attraction to a strategy is incremented

---

[15] Similar normalization is done by Erev and Roth (1998) and Camerer and Ho (1999).

only if that strategy is suggested to them by their predecessors.[16] The probability of subject i to choose strategy k in generation t is therefore

$$P_i\big(s_i(t) = s_i^k | A_i(0), \lambda_s, \omega\big) = \frac{e^{\lambda_s \cdot A_i^k(t)}}{\sum_{j=1}^m e^{\lambda_s \cdot A_i^j(t)}}. \tag{13.4}$$

After she plays strategy s_i^k and receives a payoff π_i, she then gives advice to her successor. The advice she offers will be governed by a logit function whose arguments are the attractions of the various strategies available to the subject after her experience in the game. Let $V_i^j(t)$ be the updated attraction of subject i in generation t for strategy j, which is defined after she observes her payoff during her participation in the mechanism. Then $V_i^j(t)$ is determined as follows:

$$V_i^j(t) = \begin{cases} \beta\big(A_i^j(0) + \omega\big) + R_i^j & \text{if } a_i(t-1) = s_i^j \text{ and } s_i = s_i^j, \\ \beta\big(A_i^j(0) + \omega\big) & \text{if } a_i(t-1) = s_i^j \text{ and } s_i \neq s_i^j, \\ \beta A_i^j(0) + R_i^j & \text{if } a_i(t-1) \neq s_i^j \text{ and } s_i = s_i^j, \\ \beta A_i^j(0) & \text{otherwise,} \end{cases}$$

$$\tag{13.5}$$

where $R_i^j = \pi_i(s_i^j, s_{-i}) - \min_{l, s_{-i}} \pi_i(s_i^l, s_{-i})$, which is the normalized actual payoff as defined in the reinforcement learning model, and β is the decay rate with $A_i^j(t)$.

This attraction reinforcement rule is simple. If a subject was told to use strategy j and followed that advice, her attraction to strategy j is $\beta\big(A_i^j(0) + \omega\big) + R_i^j$. The parameter ω reflects the fact that her predecessor felt that strategy j was worth using, while R_i^j reflects her personal experience with strategy j. Just like the reinforcement learning model, we let subject i depreciate her previous attraction with a decay rate β after she experiences the game. If she was told to use strategy j but did not follow that advice, her attraction to strategy j is only $\beta\big(A_i^j(0) + \omega\big)$, since she had no personal experience with

---

[16] Note that the advice is offered after the predecessor observes the outcome of his interaction with the mechanism and our subjects know that the advice giver also received advice from his predecessor. Hence, the informational content of the advice is certainly non-zero.

strategy j.[17] If strategy j was not recommended but used nevertheless, it is reinforced by the normalized payoff received by using it. Finally, if strategy j was neither recommended nor used, it is not reinforced at all.

The probability of giving advice s_i^k in generation t is then determined by

$$P_i(a_i(t) = s_i^k | A_i(0), \lambda_a, \beta, \omega) = \frac{e^{\lambda_a \cdot V_i^k(t)}}{\sum_{j=1}^m e^{\lambda_a \cdot V_i^j(t)}}. \qquad (13.6)$$

We allow different sensitivities with respect to attractions, that is, λ_s and λ_a.

For each mechanism, we pool all the repeated treatment and own-advice intergenerational treatment data together and jointly estimate the parameters $\Theta = \{A^j(0)_{|j=1,...,4|}, \phi, \lambda, \lambda_s, \lambda_a, \omega, \beta\}$ using a maximum-likelihood estimation procedure. We normalize the initial attraction to strategy 3–1–2/3–2–1 to 0 since they were almost never used by our subjects.

The estimation results as well as 95% confidence intervals are presented in Table 13.3. Several things are of note in Table 13.3. First, remember that a subject's initial attraction is her attraction to a strategy after reading the instructions but before playing the game. It is basically her intuitive response to what she thinks would be the best thing to do. In a repeated treatment, this initial attraction will be updated as a subject gets experience. In the own-advice intergenerational treatment, it gets updated as a result of receiving one piece of advice. It is interesting that the initial attractions seem different across the Boston and the Gale–Shapley mechanisms. This implies that subjects, after reading the instructions, noticed a difference in these two mechanisms. However, because of the parameters in the

---

[17] Note that unlike the experience-weighted attraction model of Camerer and Ho (1999), we do not reinforce strategy j by the counterfactual payoff player i would have had if he had chosen strategy j, since in this setting it is impossible for our subject to figure out what that payoff would have been. Still strategy j is given an extra weight, since it was recommended.

Table 13.3 *Structural estimation.*

	Gale–Shapley	Boston
$A^1(0)$	71.37	39.69
	(35.74, 168.94)	(21.65, 79.55)
$A^2(0)$	0.00	0.00
	(0.00, 0.00)	(0.00, 0.00)
$A^3(0)$	59.89	35.16
	(28.61, 144.85)	(19.25, 71.18)
$A^4(0)$	29.51	15.54
	(13.17, 68.42)	(0.00, 37.87)
ϕ	0.88	0.76
	(0.76, 0.98)	(0.64, 0.87)
λ	0.05	0.09
	(0.03, 0.09)	(0.05, 0.13)
λ_s	0.04	0.07
	(0.02, 0.10)	(0.03, 0.13)
λ_a	0.18	0.13
	(0.12, 0.26)	(0.08, 0.19)
ω	42.17	19.16
	(16.95, 117.73)	(8.48, 46.28)
β	0.10	0.39
	(0.02, 0.28)	(0.13, 0.94)
Observation	35(R) + 100(I)	40(R) + 100(I)
Log likelihood	−470.17	−638.06

logit choice function, the initial choice probabilities do not differ substantially (see the "Before advice" columns in Table 13.4).

Second, while the initial choice probabilities do not appear to differ across mechanisms, our estimated ω parameter indicates that advice is a powerful influence on choice.[18] As can be seen in "After advice" columns of Table 13.4, the probability that a subject

[18] We calculate the initial probability using only the estimated values of λ_s and $A(0)$, that is,

$$P(s^k) = \frac{\exp(\lambda_s A^k(0))}{\sum_{j=1}^{m} \exp(\lambda_s A^j(0))}.$$

Table 13.4 *Impact of own advice.*

	Gale–Shapley		Boston	
	Before advice	After advice	Before advice	After advice
1–2–3	0.5347	0.8754	0.4771	0.7622
1–3–2	0.0250	0.1354	0.0353	0.1139
2–1–3	0.3266	0.7477	0.3545	0.6586
2–3–1	0.0887	0.3728	0.0979	0.2760
3–1–2/3–2–1	0.0250	0.1354	0.0353	0.1139

chooses any one of her six strategies is greatly affected by whether she was advised to do so. For example, look at the truthful strategy 1–2–3. While after reading the instructions our model predicts that subjects choose this strategy with a probability of 47.71% in the own-advice intergenerational Boston treatment and 53.47% in the own-advice intergenerational Gale–Shapley treatment, these probabilities rise to 76.22% and 87.54%, respectively, after being advised to do so. A similar rise occurs when subjects are advised to use their strategic strategy 2–1–3. Finally, it is curious to note that advice even increases the probability that a subject uses an irrational strategy, i.e., ones like 3–2–1 or 3–1–2, that are easily dominated. For example, while before advice a subject would be inclined to use strategy 3–1–2 (and 3–2–1) with only a 2.50% probability in the own-advice intergenerational Gale–Shapley treatment, this probability rises to 13.54% if the subject is advised to do so. Advice is powerful.

If strategy s^j is suggested by the immediate predecessor, A^j is updated as the following:

$$A^j = A^j(0) + \omega \cdot I(s^j, s),$$

where $I(s^j, s)$ is the indicator function whether s^j is advised. The probability of using each strategy is then calculated by

$$P(s^k) = \frac{\exp(\lambda_s A^k)}{\sum_{j=1}^{m} \exp(\lambda_s A^j)}.$$

Third, our estimation results show that, in both mechanisms, subjects depreciate their previous attractions significantly more in the own-advice intergenerational treatments than in the repeated treatments. When the Gale–Shapley mechanism is used, the depreciation rate β in the social learning environment is 0.10 while the depreciation rate ϕ in the reinforcement learning environment is 0.88. When the Boston mechanism is used, a similar difference can also be found: the depreciation rates in the own-advice intergenerational and repeated treatments are 0.39 and 0.76, respectively. This implies that, when subjects give advice, they rely more on their own personal experience, which may lead to greater volatility.

Finally, there does not seem to be any important difference in the precision with which subjects choose their strategies as indicated by the estimates λ_s and λ across our repeated and own-advice intergenerational treatments.

The own-advice intergenerational results reported on above are based on the behavior of 100 subjects spread over 20 generations. However, they provide us with only one time series of intergenerational behavior. While economists are used to doing statistical analysis on the basis of a single time series – take, for example, the unemployment, interest rate, or inflation time series we have in our national statistics – it would be nice to reassure ourselves that what we observed in our experiment was not an outlier. To investigate this concern, we use our structural estimates and simulate 10,000 time series to see if we can replicate the stylized behavior exhibited in the lab. The results of this simulation are presented in Ding and Schotter (2019).

13.4   ADVICE GIVING AND RECEIVING

In an intergenerational treatment, subjects are somewhat informationally starved, since the only thing they can rely on in making their decisions is their interpretation of the mechanism as manifested in their initial attractions, and the advice they receive from their immediate predecessors. Given that advice plays such an important

Table 13.5 *Fraction of subjects or whom advice = action.*

	Own-advice	Own-advice	
	Gale–Shapley	Boston	p-value
All	0.8300	0.7400	0.1214
Type 1	0.9000	0.7500	0.2119
Type 2	0.9000	0.7000	0.1138
Type 3	0.8000	0.8500	0.6773
Type 4	0.9500	0.8500	0.2918
Type 5	0.6000	0.5500	0.7491

role in the behavior of our subjects (see Table 13.4), it might make sense to dig a little more deeply into what factors determine both the advice-giving and advice-following behavior of our subjects.[19]

13.4.1 Advice Giving

Our first result is that most subjects tell their successors to do what they themselves did. In fact, 83.00% of subjects in the own-advice intergenerational Gale–Shapley treatment and 74.00% of subjects in the own-advice intergenerational Boston treatment suggest the same strategies they used. A breakdown of this advice-giving behavior by type as well as the p-values reported by a set of Pearson's chi-square tests are presented in Table 13.5.

Table 13.5 demonstrates two points. One is the obvious fact that people tend to pass on advice which is equal to the action they themselves took. While this tendency might lead to social inertia or herding, i.e., people all doing the same thing and advising their successors to do so as well, there is a high enough likelihood that this advice is not followed to provide the volatility we observed before. Second, except for type 3 subjects, subjects in the own-advice intergenerational Gale–Shapley treatment are more likely to pass on

[19] A strong impact of advice is also found in all other papers using an intergenerational game design, such as Schotter and Sopher (2003, 2006, 2007) and Chaudhuri et al. (2009).

Table 13.6 *When a subject suggests a different strategy than what she did.*[a]

Variables	Coeff. (std err.)
Type 1	−0.2574 (0.6004)
Type 2	−0.5779 (0.5914)
Type 3	0.1985 (0.6119)
Type 4	−1.0338 (0.6833)
Third-best	1.6000*** (0.5264)
Truthful	−0.6928*(0.3847)
Gale–Shapley	−1.0435*** (0.3712)
Constant	−0.1519 (0.5092)

[a] Asterisks: * = significant at 10%, *** = significant at 1%.

advice equal to the action they took, although the difference between these two treatments is not significant.

This tendency to advise what you did raises the question as to when subjects violate this rule and suggest a strategy different from the one they themselves used. To investigate this question, we ran a regression where the dependent variable is an indicator variable, with 1 indicating a subject suggests a strategy different from the one she chose and 0 indicating the opposite, and the independent variables include indicators for whether a subject told the truth in her matching game, whether a subject was matched with her third-best object, a set of type dummy variables, and a mechanism dummy variable (0 indicating the Boston mechanism and 1 indicating the Gale–Shapley mechanism). The default situation is a type 5 subject who used the Boston mechanism, did not tell the truth when submitting her preference ranking, and was matched to her first- or second-best object.

Our results are presented in Table 13.6. Several aspects of this regression are of note. First, it is interesting that no type variable is significant, meaning that whether a subject suggests a strategy different from the one she used is not a function of her type. Second, it is not a surprise that a subject who ended up being matched to her third-best object would be more likely to suggest a change in strategy to her successor. However, there seems to be a built-in inertia with respect to the use of the truth-telling strategy in that subjects who use it are less likely to tell their successors to deviate from it. Finally, there seems to be less suggested strategy changes when the Gale–Shapley mechanism is used.

13.4.2 Advice Following

In the advice-giving, advice-following game, it takes two to tango. Advice offered but not followed can lead to deviations from the herd and disrupt social behavior. However, such deviations may be beneficial if others are herding on inefficient or unprofitable outcomes. To investigate advice following, we run a regression to examine what factors persuade subjects to follow advice. The dependent variable is an indicator variable denoting whether a subject follows advice from her predecessor or not. The independent variables include an indicator of whether her predecessor suggested truth-telling, type-variable dummies, and an indicator for which mechanism was used. The default situation is a type 5 subject who uses the Boston mechanism and her predecessor suggested not telling the truth.

The regression result is presented in Table 13.7. It appears that suggesting a subject report truthfully has a strong influence on a subject's willingness to follow advice. Note, however, that this influence is independent of which mechanism is being used, since the mechanism coefficient is not significant.

13.4.3 Verbal Advice

To provide some texture to our discussion of advice, we will present a brief discussion of what exactly our subjects told each other over generations and what strategies they recommended. While we will not engage in a full coding of the advice offered across generations, we will offer some insights by presenting the history of advice and actions for type 1 subjects.

Table 13.7 *When a subject follows advice.*[a]

Variables	Coeff. (std err.)
Type 1	−0.1302 (0.5380)
Type 2	0.1767 (0.5195)
Type 3	−0.1971 (0.5263)
Type 4	0.4800 (0.5600)
Truthful advice	0.9199** (0.3696)
Gale–Shapley	0.4606 (0.3445)
Constant	0.3337 (0.4039)

[a] * = significant at 10%, ** = significant at 5%, *** = significant at 1%.

Table 13.8 presents the advice offered over generations for type 1 subjects (unrestricted advice) as well as the strategies they chose, whether they followed the advice received, and the actual strategy they recommended (restricted advice) during the own-advice intergenerational Gale–Shapley treatment.

There are several things to note here. First, as we suggested before, rather than converging to one strategy, the behavior of our type 1 subjects is volatile, with periodic episodes of truth-telling followed by episodes of dissembling. For example, while from generation 6 to 11 all subjects chose to be truthful (strategy 1) and also told their successors to do so, this truthful behavior abruptly ends in generation 12 where over the next eight generations subjects submit their second-best object first (strategy 3) in five of the next eight rounds. Further, note that subjects many times repeated the exact same phrases offered to them as justification for the advice they offer to their successors.

In summary, behavior in the intergenerational treatments appears to be episodic, with periods over which each generation acts in an identical manner and tells their successors to do so, yet this behavior is inevitably disrupted by some renegade subject who starts a new thread of advice and action. Such patterns of social learning yield the volatility results reported on above.

Table 13.8 *Type 1: strategy, suggested advice, and verbal advice.*[a]

Generation	Follow advice?	Strategy chosen	Suggested strategy	Verbal advice
1	—	3	3	In my opinion choose priority first
2	0	1	3	Choose priority first so that you can definitely get the 16!
3	1	3	3	By choosing this order, you guarantee that you will get the 16 ECU
4	1	3	3	This guarantees getting 16 ECU
5	0	1	2	As given, C has the highest payoff
6	0	1	1	Make sure C is your first choice. You are guaranteed max payout because there is no priority for decision C
7	1	1	1	C is max payoff and no priority
8	1	1	1	C has the maximum payoff, and there's no priority for that object
9	1	1	1	C has more ecu and no priority
10	1	1	1	C has more ECU and no priority, whereas if you put A as your second choice, you'll have more of a chance to get at least 16 ECU because you have priority for A
11	1	1	1	I chose C, A, and B. I was matched to A since I had priority for A. You should also choose the same options as me, because that increases your chances of earning 24 ECU and at least a minimum of 24 ECU good luck :)
12	0	3	3	Go with A, since our type gives us priority as well. Then C, then B if you're feeling adventurous go with C!
13	1	3	3	I would go with A, C, B as the best option because it gives more priority to us. But if you choose C though it could might maybe ha-ha payoff. But it is a gamble

Table 13.8 *(Continued)*

Generation	Follow advice?	Strategy chosen	Suggested strategy	Verbal advice
14	0	1	1	I would go with C, A, B, because there is a chance you might get C and you really don't have much to worry about by listing A as your second choice, since you have priority and there are two object A's. I did C,A,B, and I got A so it wasn't much of a gamble really. At least for me. You might get luckier than me and end up with C so I'd do that, but I like risk
15	1	1	1	I would choose C, A, B. Put C first because it has the highest payoff. You may get it if you're lucky. You'll most likely get A, since you're type 1 and you have priority and there are two object As
16	0	3	3	Choose A first followed by C and B. Everyone will choose C first therefore if you choose A as your first priority you will definitely get it. Your chances are high. Getting 16 is a sure chance whereas if you choose C first you may get 24 by lottery or you may end up getting 4 or 16
17	1	3	3	I chose A first, because type 1 automatically would get the 16 points as it has the priority. If you chose C as your first choice, you would have a lottery, and could end up with 24 or 4 points. A is a guarantee of 16 points, while C is a chance
18	1	3	3	I chose A first because I had priority for that and so I had more chances of receiving that instead of B. Choose C second because that nobody has priority over. I ended up getting a payoff of 16

Table 13.8 *(Continued)*

Generation	Follow advice?	Strategy chosen	Suggested strategy	Verbal advice
19	0	1	1	I chose C first. I got a payoff of 24. Choose A second you will most likely get a payoff of 16 or 24
20	1	1	1	I picked C first, A second, and B last. I got A and 16 ECU. The person before me also picked the same order and got 24. You will probably get 16 or 24 ECU

[a]Truthful preference ranking: C–A–B. Strategy (advice) definition: 1, C–A–B; 2, C–B–A; 3, A–C–B; 4, A–B–C; 5, B–C–A; 6, B–A–C.

13.5   CONCLUSION

This chapter has spilt a little cold water on our previous enthusiasm for advice. While in our previous chapters advice appeared to be rationality-enhancing, in this chapter the darker side of advice, reared its ugly head. The problem appeared to be that bad advice, once entrenched in intergenerational advice takes on a life of its own and gets passed down from generation to generation. This is what we saw in our matching experiment here, where deviations from truth-telling grew over time. As mentioned before, from a policy point of view, these results are interesting, since they imply that economic mechanisms, once in place, may have a life of their own that is not the one envisioned by mechanism designers. If this is true, then those who administer the mechanism, such as school administrators, may need to repeatedly intervene in the process to straighten out misguided behavior that has become conventional as a result of intergenerational advice. It's comparable, perhaps, to computer programmers who have to be vigilant to prevent viruses from being introduced into their programs.

The fact that the failure of subjects to submit their rankings truthfully actually enhanced efficiency should not necessarily be taken as a benefit. As mentioned before, stability is a feature of matches that is far more important politically than efficiency. One reason for this is that people may be able to easily see a match that is not stable for them, because they may see a child sitting in a school they would have preferred and which would have preferred their child (or for which their child had priority), but seeing inefficient matches is difficult since it may involve a sequence of altered matches. So we concentrate, as does the matching literature, more on stability than efficiency.

One question that arises is why this happens here (in the school matching mechanisms) and not in the previous problems that our subjects faced in previous chapters. While we can only conjecture as to an answer, one explanation has to do with complexity. In problems like the battle of the sexes discussed in Chapter 4, the strategic tensions are clear. Are we going to coordinate on the equilibrium that is good for you or for me? If I get the short end of the stick, then eventually my ancestors may rebel and try to turn things around. The problem is self-evident even if the solution is more complicated.

In a school matching problem or an auction, the problem faced is more complicated, as is knowing when you have come upon a good rule of thumb to solve it. Subjects are groping in the dark for something intelligent to do, and it is hard to know when you have found it. In such settings, bad advice can flourish because its consequences are hard to evaluate. As we mentioned, in the school matching problem, if you receive your second- or third-best outcome (out of 10, let's say), you may consider that a fine outcome. In such settings, decision makers grope in the dark for an intelligent way to behave and are more receptive to suggestions, even bad ones.

These bad outcomes are exacerbated by the fact that our subjects in the intergenerational game gain very little experience with the mechanisms. They engage in it once and leave. Hence, unlike the situation where they repeat the school matching many times (note they would have to have many, many children to become expert in it), they are likely to be influenced by the choices and advice of those who have gone through the match, since they have no experience with it. Just like subjects in our social learning experiment in Chapter 10, a kind of information cascade may occur in our school matching setting where subjects feel they need to rely more on the advice of their predecessor rather than trust their own instincts.

REFERENCES

Beggs, A. (2005). On the convergence of reinforcement learning. *Journal of Economic Theory*, 122(1), 1–36.

Bo, I. and Hakimov, R. (2020). Iterative versus standard deferred acceptance: Experimental evidence. *Economic Journal*, 130(626), 356–392.

Braun, S., Dwenger, N., Kubler, D. and Westkamp, A. (2014). Implementing quotas in university admissions: An experimental analysis. *Games and Economic Behavior*, 85(3), 232–251.

Camerer, C. and Ho, T. H. (1999). Experience-weighted attraction learning in normal form games. *Econometrica*, 67(4), 827–874.

Chaudhuri, A., Schotter, A. and Sopher, B. (2009). Talking ourselves to efficiency: Coordination in inter-generational minimum effort games with private, almost common and common knowledge of advice. *Economic Journal*, 119(534), 91–122.

Chen, Y. and Sonmez, T. (2006). School choice: An experimental study. *Journal of Economic Theory*, 127(1), 202–231.

Ding, T. and Schotter, A. (2019). Learning and mechanism design: An experimental test of school matching mechanisms with intergenerational advice. *Economic Journal*, 129(623), 2779–2804.

Erdil, A. and Ergin, H. (2008). What's the matter with tie-breaking? Improving efficiency in school choice. *American Economic Review*, 98(3), 669–689.

Erev, I. and Roth, A. E. (1998). Predicting how people play games: Reinforcement learning in experimental games with unique, mixed strategy equilibria. *American Economic Review*, 88(4), 848–881.

Fischbacher, U. (2007). z-Tree: Zurich toolbox for ready-made economic experiments. *Experimental Economics*, 10(2), 171–178.

Guillen, P. and Hing, A. (2014). Lying through their teeth: Third party advice and truth telling in a strategy proof mechanism. *European Economic Review*, 70(3), 178–185.

Hassidim, A., Romm, A. and Shorrer, R. (2017). Redesigning the Israeli Psychology Master's Match. *American Economic Review*, 107(5), 205–209.

Holt, C. A. and Laury, S. K. (2002). Risk aversion and incentive effects. *American Economic Review*, 92(5), 1644–1655.

Pathak, P. A. (2017). What really matters in designing school choice mechanisms. *Advances in Economics and Econometrics*, 1(12), 176–214.

Rees-Jones, A. (2018). Suboptimal behavior in strategy-proof mechanisms: Evidence from the residency match. *Games and Economic Behavior*, 108(3), 317–330.

Schotter, A. and Sopher, B. (2003). Social learning and coordination conventions in intergenerational games: An experimental study. *Journal of Political Economy*, 111(3), 498–529.

Schotter, A. and Sopher, B. (2006). Trust and trustworthiness in games: An experimental study of intergenerational advice. *Experimental Economics*, 9(2), 123–145.

Schotter, A. and Sopher, B. (2007). Advice and behavior in intergenerational ultimatum games: An experimental approach. *Games and Economic Behavior*, 58(2), 365–393.

Zhu, M. (2015). Experience transmission: Truth-telling adoption in matching. *Working Paper*, Université de Lyon.

14 Conclusions

It's time to take stock. After 13 chapters we have covered a lot of ground. Our basic aim has been to open the door to contemplating how decision making changes in the presence of advice, and how the conventions we share today are affected by the social learning we and those before us have done in the past.

Our claim is simple. In the real world, people seek advice before making decisions, and if such advice alters their decisions, it should be included in our models and experiments. It also should be included in our policy deliberations, since if consumers and investors are making their decisions based on advice (on the Web or else-where), then interventions into our advice-giving infrastructure may be important.[1]

We have learned that some of our behavior is conventional, and we engage in it because we are socialized by the advice passed on to us by previous generations and our expectations that others have also been so socialized. In terms of experimental methods, we have seen that including advice in our experimental designs can provide a wealth of information into the thought processes of our experimental subjects. As such, I would strongly urge experimentalists to try to find a place in their designs for advice.

In our discussion, we have answered some basic questions about the role of advice in the evolution of conventions of behavior. To summarize what we have learned let us list these questions one at a time and outline where we stand in answering them. The extent to

---

[1] While fake news parades as information, and hence not advice, its impact does suggest that people are very easily influenced by what they see on the Web. This suggests that society take a careful look at the persuasive nature of advice and information on social media.

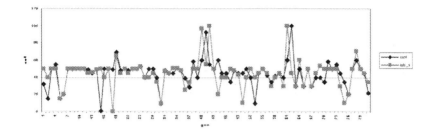

FIGURE 14.1 Amount sent and advised to be sent: advice and history treatment.

which we are not able to offer iron-clad responses to these questions is the extent to which we urge others to try to pick up where we have left off.

Question 1: Do people listen to advice?

Just as in the old adage about leading a horse to water but not being able to make him drink, we have found that you can offer a decision maker advice but you cannot make her either listen to or follow it. Still, our general result is that advice is listened to and influences the decisions that people make. By this, we mean that either people follow advice exactly or the advice they receive affects their choice by serving as a cognitive anchor or reference point from which they adjust their choice. If the advice is public and common knowledge, then people will, in addition, need to best reply to how they think others will react to the commonly known advice.

For example, in Figure 14.1, which describes offer behavior in our ultimatum game experiment of Chapter 5 in the treatment where subjects had access to advice from their immediate predecessor and the past history of the game, we can see a close relationship between the advice offered and the amount sent by senders.

With generations on the horizontal axis and amount advised and actually sent on the vertical, Figure 14.1 demonstrates how closely subjects follow advice. As we see, the amount sent is highly correlated with the amount advised to be sent (with some obvious exceptions).

The fact that people follow advice is understandable because the world is complex and we do not know either the optimal, morally correct, or conventional thing to do in many situations. Hence, in such informationally scarce environments, we tend to follow advice when it is offered. As with tipping waiters in foreign countries, we just want to be told what is conventional.

In Chapter 9, which focuses on learning in a one-person decision task with a meddlesome boss, we again see that subjects are more likely to follow advice than to use the data available to them to estimate the optimal action and choose it (adjusting their choice to include the cost of disagreeing with their meddlesome boss when they have one). Chapter 10, where our subjects could follow that action taken by their predecessor or the advice offered to them, we see that subjects tend to make choices consistent with the advice they receive 74.1% of the time in the advice-only treatment, but only 44.2% of the time do people follow their predecessor's action in the action-only treatment where no advice is available.

In all of these cases, the reason for advice following seems obvious. In complicated settings, even when a decision maker has all the information at her disposal to calculate an optimal action, the cognitive costs involved may be so great (or perceived to be so great) as to lead lazy decision makers, which many of us are, to opt out of thinking and simply do what they are told.

While Figure 14.1 and the examples mentioned above are examples where advice tends to be followed, we also have many instances where it serves as a reference point from which people choose an action. For example, in the trust game of Chapter 6, senders are advised to send relatively low amounts to receivers but tend to send more money than recommended. Still, the amount they send is lower than the amounts sent in the treatment where no advice exists, meaning that, while subjects did not follow advice exactly, it did influence their behavior and led them to send less than those who did not receive advice. So the result is that advice lowers the amount sent but does so by defining a low reference point from which subjects adjust upward.

The same thing happened in Chapter 8 in the two-thirds guessing game where public advice which was deemed meaningful by the subjects was used as an anchor to define the level-zero behavior for our level-k analysis. Put differently, since the advice was public, subjects could assume that no one would choose above it and hence it served as a focal point to which our subjects started best-responding.

In other cases when advice was ignored, subjects learned to regret it. In the minimum-effort game of Chapter 7, subjects many times rejected advice and chose higher efforts than advised, at least when advice was private. These subjects later appeared to regret not following their predecessors' advice since, when it became their turn to offer advice to their offspring, they offered the same advice that they received from their laboratory parents but rejected. This is a typical pattern in life. Young people reject the advice of their parents only to learn their mistakes during their lifetimes and, after realizing their parents were correct, advise their children to do the same thing they were advised to do and rejected, only to see their children reject their advice as well. The folly of youth does not seem to be eliminated in a setting where new decision makers are born every period.[2]

The punch line here is that advice affects choice either because it is followed or because its presence alters the choice that a decision maker would otherwise make without it.

Question 2: Does advice lead to more stable conventions?

The answer here is yes, but with some exceptions. In the battle of the sexes game of Chapter 4, our subjects were far more successful in coordinating their behavior in those treatments with advice than without it. In addition, in our ultimatum-game experiment of Chapter 5, we saw some significant evidence that when advice is present people exhibit more conventional behavior. We measured how closely behavior was to what we called a strong convention across our different treatments and showed that conventions were "stronger" when advice was present.

---

[2] Of course, this sentence was written from the perspective of a parent/grandparent. Twenty-somethings may have a different view.

Despite these results, we have also seen instances where advice is destabilizing. For example, in our school matching experiment of Chapter 13, behavior became much more volatile when advice was offered. In fact, advice led our subjects away from submitting their truthful preferences despite the fact that it was a dominant strategy. While some of this behavior may be attributed to the fact that in our intergenerational setup subjects engage in the match only once and hence do not gain experience, that fact is especially true of school matching in the real world, since if parents only have one child, they have to rely on advice and not their own previous experience before they submit their school rankings.

In addition, the type of advice available to our subjects may have an impact on the stability of the conventions they create. For example, as our discussion in Chapters 7 and 8 suggests, conventions may be hard to establish and maintain when adhering to them is risky (see the minimum-effort game in Chapter 7). In such cases, adherence can only be achieved if the advice received from previous generations is common knowledge but making it common knowledge, as we have seen, is many times difficult. Second, once established, as our discussion in Chapter 4 on the battle of the sexes game suggests, they may break apart or disappear despite the fact that, overall, advice is a stabilizing force in this experiment.

One reason for this destabilizing influence is that if even one generation offers advice that suggests deviation from the established convention, that may be enough to disrupt well-established patterns of behavior for future generations. Also, if social agents only have access to the advice of their immediate predecessor, they have no idea whether that predecessor is a deviant or a wise person. Hence, following advice can be risky.

Finally, whether advice is stabilizing or not may depend on the complexity of the situation we place our subjects in and the nature of the feedback they receive. For example, the ultimatum and battle of the sexes games are fairly transparent. The trade-offs that exist in these problems are obvious. The matching experiments of Chapters 13 and 14, using either the Gale–Shapley or the Boston mechanism, are different. Here the situation is far more complex, and finding out what is your best strategy (even when it is a dominant strategy) is not easy. In the Boston mechanism, in fact, it is very hard. Furthermore, it is hard to determine if you did the right thing once you received feedback, since it is difficult to know what your payoff would have been had you acted differently. This lack of transparency leaves people vulnerable to the influence of advice and less likely to settle down to one type of behavior.

Question 3: Does advice make people more rational?

When answering this question, we are going to assume that "more rational" means more constituent with the predictions of economic theory based on selfish preferences. In other words, does advice make people look more like the decision makers depicted in our textbooks?

The answer to this question has important ramifications for the way we do economic theory and conduct our experiments. More precisely, economic theory does not have any role for advice. If decision makers are rational, computationally sophisticated, and fully informed, then what role could an advisor play? Anything an advisor could do, the decision maker could do herself. As we mentioned in Chapter 2, economic theory considers advice only in strategic situations where the advisor has preferences that are not aligned with the decision maker. Here the theory solves for the equilibrium of the resulting Bayesian game, but from our perspective it is hard to call that situation one of advice giving and receiving. It is just a communication game with misaligned preferences. Such situations are fascinating, but not what we consider to be advice.

In chapter after chapter in this book, we have seen that the advice offered to subjects tended to move them in a direction closer to the predictions of economic theory with selfish preferences. For example, we have seen higher rates of coordination (equilibrium) achieved in our intergenerational battle of the sexes game of Chapter 4, lower (more selfish) offers made in the ultimatum game in Chapter 5 with advice (i.e., offers closer to the subgame-perfect equilibrium), trusters advised to send less in the trust game of Chapter 6 (again as predicted by subgame perfection), and improved social learning in both our meddlesome-boss experiment of Chapter 9 and our social learning experiment of Chapter 10.

All of these results suggest that advice moves decision makers in the direction of the predictions of economic theory. Of course, that is not always the case. In our already mentioned school matching experiments in Chapter 13, and in some unpublished auction experiments by McClellan and Schotter (2021), it is seen that the conventions created by intergenerational advice can lead decision makers astray and perpetuate behavior that violates weak dominance.

We have offered some explanations for why advice encourages rationality. The most compelling one might be that advice encourages decision makers to rethink their instinctive choices and reconsider their conclusions. It is as if advice replicates experience by allowing the decision maker to contemplate the consequences of her proposed actions without actually receiving feedback (see Weber (2003) for a similar result about learning with no feedback).

Question 4: Does advice offer insights into human nature?

Our results also offer insights into human nature. In recent years there has been a large body of literature (see, e.g., Henrich et al., 2001) indicating that people, rather than being selfish, have fairness, reciprocal, or other-regarding preferences. However, these results are based on choice data, meaning that we have to infer a subject's preferences or motives from their actions. But, as we mentioned in our introductory chapter, allowing intergenerational advice permits an investigator to look inside the head of our decision makers and see the logic of their actions.

Early on in this literature Binmore et al. (1985) tried to identify whether subjects playing an ultimatum game were "gamesmen" or "fairsmen" (i.e., cared about fairness or their own selfish payoffs) by devising a pair of ultimatum games that allowed subjects to reverse roles and see if they behaved differently depending on the role they played. This clever design cast some doubt on the "fairsmen" hypothesis, but again used choices to infer preferences. With advice, we can hear a subject's logic directly from the horse's mouth and, since such advice is incentivized, it is certainly more reliable than post-experiment interviews or even, perhaps, choices.

What our advice data suggests is that fairness functions as a constraint for some people and a preference for others. (See Ribeiro (2021) for a formal study of this difference.) Some people reveal a distinct preference for doing as well for themselves as they possibly can and view fairness as a burden that we humans have to bear, while others seem to understand the equity issues involved in acting selfishly and actually have a preference for fairness. As discussed in Chapter 5, however, few subjects unabashedly express fairness sentiments. In fact, in all the advice statements made by our subjects, there were only three that actually mentioned the word "fairness". From what we can glean from these statements, people care about themselves first and foremost but are willing to trade off their well-being for some sense of fairness. However, the burden of being fair appears more like a constraint than a preference. Bicchieri's (2016) discussion of social and descriptive norms also suggests that some of our behavior is determined by the constraints imposed on us by the expectations of others and not our personal preferences.

The advice statements of our subjects make one simple point, which is that people have mixed emotions when they play the games we ask them to play in the lab. They want the money but are annoyed by inequality. Yet, from these statements, we must recognize that people cannot easily be categorized into caring about fairness or being selfish. They trade them off against each other in a complex way, so when we observe their actions, it is hard to identify their motivations in a clear way.

Question 5: Do subjects prefer advice over other types of information?

When our subjects have a choice of the type of information they would rather have before making their decisions, they many times reveal a preference for advice. For example, in our social learning experiments of Chapter 10, in one treatment, subjects are able to see both the advice offered by their predecessor and the action they took when it was their turn to choose. Hence, these subjects could decide to either follow advice or imitate the actions of their predecessors. When advice and actions are contradictory, in that they each suggest different decisions, we saw subjects tended to opt for advice, indicating a preference for it.

This result is contradicted, however, when in Chapter 11 we set up a market for advice and information and find that subjects tended to bid more for data as an input into their decision making rather than advice. This was a surprise, given our previous results.

One explanation might be that in that experiment subjects were offered advice from specific types of advisors whose descriptions they knew. Hence, their preference for data rather than advice might be a preference for objective data over the opinion of someone with a background the decision makers deemed suspect. This introduces the idea that it is not only advice that is important but the identity of the advice giver, a subject that is dealt with to some extent in the psychology literature but not in economics. The fact that decision makers have preferences over types of information is many times ignored in models, where decision makers are only offered one type of information.

Question 6: Is social learning as effective as experiential learning?

There are many ways to learn in the social world. We, as humans, are educated in the "school of hard knocks". We explore the world and get rewarded or punished. Behavior that gets rewarded gets repeated and that which gets punished is chosen less often. While this may be a good model for decisions we make often, the fact is that we have relatively little experience with the most important decisions we make in our lives. For example, you get married once (or typically not more than four times), buy a house maybe two or three times, and car maybe five times, etc. These are the big decisions in your life, and because you engage in them so infrequently, you are not able to learn easily from experience. As a substitute, you ask for advice, and through that advice engage in social learning.

This type of learning, as described before, is very different from experiential learning. Modes of behavior are passed on from generation to generation without any of them being tested extensively by any one agent. Hence the advice we receive is what we have called "naive" advice in Chapter 1, and social learning advances through a process of generations of naive decision makers passing on advice from limited experience. It's almost like the blind leading the blind and the question is where does such myopic behavior lead and to what does it converge, if anything? Can inefficient behavior get "locked in" as it does in a "two-armed bandit" problem and perpetuate itself? Fortunately, because each time the problem is faced a new social agent makes the decision, it is perhaps less likely that such inefficient behavior will be locked in before some new agent deviates and generates new information. To that extent social learning is beneficial. However, for the same reason, it might be harder to maintain an efficient convention of behavior once it is established, since there are ample opportunities to break the chain of convention transmission and adherence as new generational agents arrive and either ignore the advice of their predecessors or refuse to pass it on to their successors.

Since much of what we have done is game-theoretic, the question is, does social learning with naive advice converge to some type of Nash equilibrium in the stage game that is repeated over generations or does it veer far away? We have seen examples of both. In our battle of the sexes game in Chapter 4, we saw social learning leading to better coordination and higher welfare while, in our school matching experiments in Chapter 13, we saw the opposite – social learning leading people to choose dominated actions.[3] However, we have also seen that, while social learning with advice may not be perfect, the ability of our subjects to learn from history is, perhaps, even worse.

Where next?

So where to go next? First, one needs to come to a decision as to whether advice is really worth studying. In other words, for what decisions do people seek advice? Are they the small things in life, like which is the best brand of cola to drink, or the big things, like what college to go to, whether to have a child at age 22 or wait until 30, or whom to marry? Advice seems relevant mostly for big or important decisions that we do infrequently. If we seek advice for the big stuff in life, then it may be worth thinking about.

If you are convinced that advice is worth studying, then there is a whole host of things one can do. For example, if advice is rationality-enhancing, it could have significant implications for the theory of decision making. However, since we have seen that in some situations advice moves people in the direction of the predictions of economic theory, while in others it does not, a systematic investigation of these different circumstances seems called for. When can we expect advice to have a rationality-increasing impact? Could many of the biases and mistakes that have been reported previously by behavioral economists and psychologists be eliminated if decision makers were allowed to seek advice? Since data on behavioral biases many times comes from laboratory experiments run without advice, and since advice alters behavior, our results suggest that past researchers may be missing something important, especially if, in the real world, people tend to solicit advice before making decisions. It could be that advice accentuates biases or it might tamp them down. That is something that might be profitable to investigate.

---

[3] A similar result is obtained by McClellan and Schotter (2021) on auctions, where bidding behavior diverges from the Nash equilibrium in an intergenerational-game setting.

The same might be true of other types of behavior that have been recorded as anomalous. If the proof of these anomalies rests with experiments run without advice, it might be worthwhile verifying their existence when people are allowed to seek it.

Second, we found that advice has different impacts depending on the context within which it is used. For some types of situations, advice is rationality-increasing, while in others it seems to lead people astray. In some situations people learn better when advice is present, while in others they don't. What is needed is a map outlining the different implications of advice for behavior across these different environments. This would require many more experiments than we were able to run here but might be a fruitful avenue of investigation.

Third, it may be interesting to investigate who people listen to as advisors. We hinted at this in Chapter 11, where we set up a market for advice and asked if there was a consensus on the part of decisions makers as to whose advice is most reliable. In that experiment, the subjects were a fairly homogeneous set of students whose age and experience were narrowly defined. It might be of interest to investigate more broadly who are perceived as being the most reliable types of people to receive advice from. If no consensus exists (which is most likely), then it would be of interest to investigate whether there is a way to match people with the types of others they are more inclined to listen to. For example, teenagers are likely to spurn the advice of their parents and listen to their peers, many times with devastating results. Are there other advisers that they might listen to? Finding the right match between adviser and advisee might be a way to increase the welfare of society.

The next step on our agenda is to take this research out of the lab and into the field or, at least, into survey research. My feeling is that advice is so important that it helps explain why the rich get rich and the poor stay poor. Maybe the rich simply get better advice about important life decisions.

The idea is simple. Bad advice for many of life's important decisions, if followed, can doom someone to a life of missed opportunities. Smart kids advised either not to attend college or to apply to colleges beneath them can dramatically affect what such kids attain in life. Decisions to choose myopically and not postpone gratification for a worthwhile human capital investment can also have poor life consequences. What one needs to do is investigate whether the quality of advice people receive is systematically related to socio-economic variables like income and education, and also whether advice systematically differs across ethnic, racial, and religious groups. In the old days (read any Edith Wharton novel) upper-class WASPs looked down on certain types of occupations as being beneath them. They were advised not to enter them despite many of these fields being lucrative. Such advice can pave the way for downward economic mobility in the long run, as was the case for a number of upper-class WASPs.

In addition, advice is only as good as the knowledge or aspirations of the advice giver. One can see this in college applications. Take two students with identical (high-school quality-adjusted) grades and SAT scores graduating from two very different high schools in terms of income per student and geographic locations, and look at the advice offered by their college advisors. I would be willing to bet that the schools suggested for these students to apply to would be very different, and if college quality has any impact on life outcomes, the consequences of this advice can be substantial.

Advice can have a major influence on the important life decisions that people make, decisions that will affect the quality of their life. Investigating this is the next step on my agenda, an agenda, as I mentioned in the Preface, that I never thought I had.

REFERENCES

Bicchieri, C. (2016). *Norms in the Wild: How to Diagnose, Measure, and Change Social Norms.* Oxford, UK: Oxford University Press.

Binmore, K., Shaked, A. and Sutton, J. (1985). Fairness or gamesmanship in bargaining: An experimental study. *American Economic Review*, 75(1), 1178–1180.

Henrich, J., Boyd, R., Bowles, S., Camerer, C., Fehr, E., Gintis, H. and McElreath, R. (2001). In search of Homo economicus: Behavioral experiments in 15 small-scale societies. *American Economic Review*, 91(2), 73–78.

McClellan, A. and Schotter, A. (2021). Social learning and the winner's curse. *Mimeo*, New York University.

Ribeiro, M. (2021). Choice and welfare under social constraints. *Mimeo*, New York University.

Weber, R. A. (2003). Learning with no feedback in a competitive guessing game. *Games and Economic Behavior*, 44(1), 134–144.

Index

Printed in the United States
by Baker & Taylor Publisher Services